Hollywood's Tennessee

Hollywood's Tennessee

The Williams Films and Postwar America

R. Barton Palmer and William Robert Bray

University of Texas Press ⤙⤚ Austin

Excerpts from letters by Tennessee Williams from *Selected Letters: Volume I, 1920–1945,* copyright © 2000, and *Selected Letters, Volume II, 1946–1957,* copyright © 2002, by The University of the South, are reprinted by permission of New Directions Publishing Corp. World rights, excluding British Commonwealth.

Excerpts from letters by Tennessee Williams are from *Selected Letters, Volume I, 1920–1945,* copyright © 2000 by The University of the South. Reprinted by permission of Georges Borchardt, Inc., on behalf of the Tennessee Williams Estate. United Kingdom and British Commonwealth rights.

Excerpts from *The Gentleman Caller* and *Letters to Joseph Losey; Audrey Wood; Irving Rapper; Elia Kazan; Jack Warner, Feldman, and Wald* by Tennessee Williams, copyright © 2007 by The University of the South, are reprinted by permission of Georges Borchardt, Inc., on behalf of the Tennessee Williams Estate.

The authors are indebted to the Harry Ransom Humanities Research Center, The University of Texas at Austin, for permission to quote from numerous letters in its collection and to the Margaret Herrick Library in Los Angeles for permission to quote from its archival materials.

Requests for permission to reproduce material from this work should be sent to:
Permissions
University of Texas Press
P.O. Box 7819
Austin, TX 78713-7819
www.utexas.edu/utpress/about/bpermission.html

⊗ The paper used in this book meets the minimum requirements of ANSI/NISO z39.48-1992 (R1997) (Permanence of Paper).

LIBRARY OF CONGRESS CATALOGING-IN-PUBLICATION DATA

Palmer, R. Barton, 1946–
    Hollywood's Tennessee : the Williams films and postwar America / R. Barton Palmer and William Robert Bray. — 1st ed.
        p.   cm.
    Includes bibliographical references (p.) and index.
    ISBN 978-0-292-71921-7 (alk. paper)
    1. Williams, Tennessee, 1911–1983—Film and video adaptations.   2. American drama—Film and video adaptations.   3. Southern States—In motion pictures.   4. Film adaptations.
I. Bray, William Robert, 1951– .   II. Title.
    PS3545.I5365Z7995   2009
    812'.54—dc22
                                                                2008042066

Contents

Preface

THE MAIN FOCUS of this book is not Tennessee Williams the dramatist, poet, essayist, and fiction writer—that figure so well known to literary history.[1] Beyond rehearsing some familiar facts about Williams for the reader's benefit, we have little information or comment to add about his dramatic career, his personal life, his undisputed place within the pantheon of great American writers, and his connections, multifarious and intriguing, with the traditions of twentieth-century dramatic literature. Instead, our concern here is only with the fifteen Hollywood films made from various Williams properties (all commercially produced plays except for one novella) during roughly two decades of the early postwar era, from 1950 to 1968. Our aim is not to offer a comprehensive treatment of these adaptations, whose production histories are in many cases immensely complex, because such a volume would be impractically large. Considerable information on the Williams films is contained in two earlier books, which continue to be valuable sources, and there has been no reason to repeat it here.[2] Also for reasons of space, the Williams films produced since the 1970s, a steadily increasing body of texts, figure here only in an appendix intended as a reference for the interested reader. These later films testify to the still-growing popularity of a playwright who, at the time of his death, had seen his star fall for almost two decades. The later adaptations will soon merit a book-length treatment of their own. Space limitations also preclude our treating much of the interesting, but critically irrelevant, material we have discovered in our research, such as back-lot gossip, amusing anecdotes, and surprising trivia. The fifteen classic Williams films, because of the rich circumstances of their production, are thickly veined with such material, as a recently published study of *A Streetcar Named Desire* has indicated.[3]

Produced during the period of Williams's greatest popularity (even notoriety) and critical acclaim, these classic Williams films naturally demonstrate what interest and value audiences at the time discovered in them. Therefore, these films constitute important evidence for assessing the impact of Williams on American culture. But they hold an additional significance. What has been not hitherto been well recognized is that Williams exerted a considerable influence on the forms and history of American commercial filmmaking. It is this story that we are most eager to tell. And so in this book we do not focus mostly, or even often, on Williams's authorship as such.

A comparison of the films with their dramatic originals inevitably figures prominently in our discussion at times. However, we are not concerned with exhaustively noting the many inevitable differences with a view toward assessing how relatively faithful the films can be said to be. Like many contemporary students of literature-to-film adaptation, we find blinkered considerations of fidelity to the original not only problematic, but often irrelevant. It is, we believe, an especially pointless exercise to fault a text for its supposed deviations when adaptation occurs precisely to recast that source in some substantially different form. We are more interested in exploring what lies behind that difference. Thus we unapologetically promote a consideration of the adaptation as a cultural artifact of inherent interest and value. Undeniably, this book is traditional in the sense that it treats a body of adaptations whose source texts bear a common authorship, thereby defining and privileging a literary rather than a cinematic series. But we discuss this body of author-related work not for its inherent worthiness (which it undoubtedly possesses), but rather to trace how the texts of Tennessee Williams served the commercial cinema of the 1950s and 1960s, suiting its often desperate hunger for particular kinds of source materials.

As the title suggests, *Hollywood's Tennessee: The Williams Films and Postwar America* seeks to chronicle, describe, and explain the connections between Tennessee Williams and the film culture of the initial decades of the postwar era. Asking questions about these connections inevitably leads us to consider the evolving nature of film production and reception in a period of rapid social change that plunged Hollywood into steep economic decline. Our main point is that the amazing success Williams found in Hollywood at the time did not flow from some transhistorical excellence his works might be said to possess. We are hardly moved to argue that the Williams oeuvre lacks such excellence. But we do find obfuscating the familiar assumption that because a given text has been canonized as a masterpiece it will inevitably find its way to the commercial screen, naturally achieving success with filmgoers, even though they might be seeking an aesthetic experience qualitatively different from that enjoyed by novel readers and theatre audiences.[4] Instead, we undertake here to contextualize the industry's eagerness to adapt Williams, as well as (and perhaps more importantly) the influence these films exerted on Hollywood institutions and practice.

Williams, we will argue, was a figure suited admirably to that period of transition in which Hollywood found itself situated almost immediately after the war. Within American culture, his was beyond question a new, unique voice, but though he challenged and, in the process, modified long-established protocols of the Broadway theatre (especially regarding the dramatization of erotic life), he also addressed time-honored subjects upon whose appeal the film industry had long depended. These included the ravaging effects of time on human destiny, the irregular passages of romantic life, the moral and psychological contradictions of sexual desire, the unavoidable discontents of family relations, and—in a more specifically national vein—the exotic, attractively perverse nature of southern culture. Williams, we show, provided ideal source materials for a cinematic age eager for the new, yet reluctant to let go of the tried and true.

Like American culture itself, this postwar audience was very much caught up in rapid social change, as many older filmgoers began to abandon the habit of going to the movies, or would soon do so. The ever-decreasing group venturing out regularly to theatres was beginning to consist in large part of those who had been old enough (but not too old) to be transformed by their experience of World War II. Though these Americans were as yet unaffected by the radical revisionisms of the sexual revolution and the decline of traditional "family values," they were still uneasy with inherited pieties that purported to explain life's texture and meaning, having witnessed the dislocations brought on by national mobilization and then, global victory achieved, by a hurried return to normalcy. Along with Arthur Miller and William Inge, among others, Williams brought new subject matter and innovative forms of dramaturgy to postwar Broadway, ushering in what became during the '50s the commercial stage's "golden era of dramatic writing." Transformed by Hollywood to fit the industry's own peculiar requirements, Williams's works found there a second (and seemingly inextinguishable) life as well as a much larger and more diverse audience, offering filmgoers an attractive, even compelling form of newness and difference.

Until recently in academic work on film adaptation, neoromantic assumptions about the preeminent value of the source text have precluded any exploration of the symbiotic relationship between the literary and cinematic arts or the multifarious and ever-shifting connections between the commercial institutions responsible for their production. The often unspoken assumption that the purpose of an adaptation is to further the reach of the original has discouraged a thorough analysis of the complex negotiations (financial, commercial, legal, formal, generic, cultural, etc.) that bring adaptations into being and deeply affect their reception. Traditional aesthetic considerations about originality routinely foreclosed discussion of the place of adaptations within the history of the cinema, including how the industry found itself transformed in the process of accommodating forms and themes from another medium. Writing the new kind of institutional history we propose requires the identification and exploration of contextual issues that have little or anything to do with the source as such. From this point of view, comparing the source and its screen adaptation can draw attention to the specific negotiations involved in the process of transformation. On the one hand, such an approach (taking what Dudley J. Andrew calls a "sociological turn") helps us recognize how "particular literary fashions have at times exercised enormous power over the cinema."[5] On the other, when brought to bear on a body of films with a common authorial source, this kind of sociological analysis casts light on important but hitherto underemphasized or ignored aspects of the authorial oeuvre—namely, its peculiar sources of appeal, even, paradoxically enough, as the author is displaced from focus.

Hollywood's Tennessee: The Williams Films and Postwar America is the first full-length study to address such questions by examining the screening of a substantial and honored oeuvre. Our discussion engages with the material facts of production history, and this concentration permits us to offer accurate assessments of the contributions of the playwright, directors, and screenwriters, which have been established through a thoroughgoing survey of archival material, including much hitherto unexamined correspondence. Especially important has been the wealth of information found in the Production Code Administration files, access to which was not available to earlier researchers. *Hollywood's Tennessee* treats the films "in themselves," as cultural productions whose value and importance are not to be measured by the artistic capital of their source texts. Identified with the emerging field of cultural studies, such a protocol, as Robert Stam relates, accords the adaptation the same potential for independent cultural significance as its source: "From a cultural studies perspective, adaptation forms part of a flattened out and newly egalitarian spectrum of cultural production. Within a comprehensively textualized world of images and simulations, an adaptation becomes just another text, forming part of a broad discursive continuum."[6]

In this book, we approach the importance of the Williams films to Hollywood from three distinct but connected perspectives: as products of complexly negotiated transformations from stage to screen; as "packages" of filmed entertainment marketed with various appeals (including those afforded by genre and stars) to national and worldwide audiences; and as constructions of contemporary reality that spoke, and perhaps still do, to shared fantasies of desire, deliverance, and disaster. An important proviso: *Hollywood's Tennessee* does not pretend to offer a cultural history of postwar America. We do not mine this admittedly critical and revelatory body of films for evidence of historical change, but the Williams films, as we show, have in fact frequently figured in cultural histories of the era. Our focus is always on the films and their connection to the film industry, although in exploring this connection, we occasionally comment on larger cultural trends, particularly the initially gradual, then quickly accelerating liberalization in sexual attitudes from the middle fifties to the early sixties. This development, it goes without saying, deeply affected the Hollywood film industry as well as American society more generally.

In assessing the importance of the Williams films for an understanding of both the playwright and also the Hollywood cinema of the postwar era that quickly became so enamored of his works, we have found, not surprisingly, that some are more important than others. The bulk of the book is devoted to exploring the production history and cinematic importance of the seven major adaptations that hit the nation's screens in little more than a decade: *The Glass Menagerie* (1950), *A Streetcar Named Desire* (1951), *The Rose Tattoo* (1955), *Baby Doll* (1956), *Cat on a Hot Tin Roof* (1958), *Suddenly, Last Summer* (1959), and *Sweet Bird of Youth* (1962). Almost all of Williams's properties are in some sense "southern," and we also discuss three additional Williams films, all admittedly minor releases, that figure in the series of postwar southern releases: *The Fugitive Kind* (1959), *This Property Is Condemned* (1966), and *The Last of the Mobile Hot-Shots* (1969).

As the 1960s began, Hollywood production completed its transition from what historians have called a "cinema of sentiment" (films whose dramatic interests were of paramount importance) to a "cinema of sensation," in which a film's ability to offer striking affect, often of various kinds, was stressed. Though Williams's 1950s films, *Menagerie* excepted, belong to this emerging cinema of sensation, by the early 1960s the industry was moving beyond his dramatic evocations of the erotic and the sexual life more generally toward an increasingly graphic presentation of the human body and of sexual connection. Williams's properties proved generally old-fashioned in these rapidly evolving circumstances, as demonstrated by the failure of *The Roman Spring of Mrs. Stone* and *Summer and Smoke* (both 1961) to connect with audiences. The increasing popularity of international art films exhibited in the United States, however, showed Hollywood one way to produce entertainment that was both sensational and intellectually appealing. Two Williams adaptations, *The Night of the Iguana* (1964) and *Boom!* (1968), were accommodated, with sharply contrasting degrees of success, to American forms of the art film.

Chapter 1 offers a brief overview of Williams's career on Broadway, some comment on his enthusiasm for film and connections to Hollywood, and a historical survey of the American cinema in the early postwar period that identifies those particular conditions then prevailing in the industry that made Williams's sensational and challenging properties attractive. Only a few years previously, much of what he wrote would have been dismissed as unfilmable. In their subject matter, Williams's plays are characterized by a notable break from the nostalgic, poignant, but unprovocative domestic drama of *The Glass Menagerie* to the themes and characters that first take shape in the radically different *Streetcar*, which treats of sexual malfeasance, the connection between desire and violence, and the complexities of contemporary gender politics. Like prewar Hollywood production, postwar American filmmaking remained in large part a cinema of genres, and *Menagerie* was treated by the industry as a "woman's picture." Chapter 2 traces the production history of this film, emphasizing the extent to which what we might call the pressures of genre affected the adaptation process. The next three chapters, devoted respectively to *Streetcar*, *Tattoo*, and *Baby Doll*, focus on the challenges these properties, by their thematizing of sexuality, posed to the Production Code Administration and its unofficial ally in the field of film censorship, the Catholic Church's Legion of Decency. These chapters trace what is essentially a dialectical process, as the code and the Williams plays were accommodated to one another, a process that resulted in the "bending" of the code and its eventual abandonment in 1968. Chapter 6 explores the way in which three other notable Williams properties—*Cat*, *Sweet Bird*, and *Suddenly, Last Summer*—were accommodated to one of 1950s Hollywood's most important genres, the family melodrama, which provided an ideal showcase for the playwright's examination of developmental crises and familial dysfunction. In large measure the transference of notable literary works of the Southern Renaissance to the screen, the postwar Hollywood southern film especially featured the works of Tennessee Williams, whose influence, we will show in Chapter 7, was decisive on this genre's most successful production, *The Long, Hot Summer* (1958), only ostensibly an adaptation of several William Faulkner texts.

Our concluding chapter discusses how Williams's properties (some too old-fashioned, others overly avant-garde) became increasingly irrelevant in the 1960s, an era that saw Hollywood lose its traditional audience and begin to woo younger and hipper viewers, who were less likely to be pleased by what the playwright had to offer. As in *Hollywood's Tennessee* more generally, we attempt here to illuminate the complex forms of symbiosis that, as the classic studio period began to wane, linked literary and cinematic modes of production. Our hope is to shed light on the Hollywood that was transformed by the Williams texts it recycled and on the playwright whose image and cultural significance were decisively transformed in the process.

Acknowledgments

No book of this scope could be written without the selfless help of many friends and colleagues; we have been conspicuously blessed in this regard. Archival sources proved crucial to the project, and we benefited from, as Tennessee would have it, "the kindness of strangers," from one end of the country to another, and even, for some important material, across the Atlantic to the United Kingdom. We owe a huge debt of gratitude in particular to Mark Cave and Siva Blake from the Todd Collection of the Historic New Orleans Collection; to Barbara Hall and her energetic colleagues at the Margaret Herrick Library in Los Angeles; Jane Klain from the Museum of Television and Radio (Manhattan); Sandra Joy Lee and her helpful colleagues at the USC/Warner Brothers library; Timothy Murray from the University of Delaware Special Collections Library; Leith Johnson from the Wesleyan University Cinema Archives; Thomas Keith, Peggy Fox, and Dennis Palmore at New Directions Publishers; Nancy M. Tischler, coeditor of *The Selected Letters of Tennessee Williams*; Richard Workman of the Harry Ransom Humanities Research Center (University of Texas at Austin); Caroline Cisneros of the American Film Institute and the Charles K. Feldman Collection (Los Angeles); the staffs at the Billy Rose Theatre Library and the Columbia University Library; and especially Kate Johnson from the Georges Borchardt Agency. We are also grateful to the staff of the British Film Institute for providing needed access to (at the time) uncatalogued correspondence from the Joseph Losey archive, which contains, among other treasures, a little-known trove of letters from the director to Williams.

Helen Madden put her considerable skills as a librarian at our disposal out of love for Tennessee and his works. We owe her a huge debt for the extensive bibliographical references she provided us with, and we are grateful to Jonathan C. Williams for preparing the bibliography. We are also very grateful to Greta Tasedan for preparing the index.

Jim Burr of the University Press of Texas waited patiently for a manuscript that took much longer to prepare than anticipated. We appreciate his tolerance and always sound advice. Special thanks to other Texas staff: Kip Keller for his close reading of the manuscript while it was in copyediting, and Lynne Chapman for helping prepare the final manuscript. Annette Saddik and Murray Pomerance provided us with very useful comments. We accept, of course, full responsibility for any remaining shortcomings.

Barton Palmer is grateful, as always, to the Calhoun Lemon family for its generous support of his research. The College of Art, Architecture and Humanities at Clemson University also provided needed sabbatical support and travel funds. Robert Bray could not have completed his share of the research and writing without released time and financial support from the Department of English at Middle Tennessee State University and the Harry Ransom Humanities Research Center at the University of Texas.

Carla Palmer and Elizabeth Bray tolerated, mostly with good humor, their husbands' five-year preoccupation with dusty letters and decades-old films, trusting that we would discover therein an interesting story to tell. We hope that they will not be disappointed.

Hollywood's Tennessee

CHAPTER ONE

Williams, Broadway, and Hollywood

Challenging the Existing Theatre

While the Broadway theatre has witnessed the emergence and flourishing of dozens of playwrights since the 1930s, none has achieved more enduring popular appeal and critical acclaim than Tennessee Williams. Although Williams did not enjoy the production of four plays in a single annus mirabilis (as did Clifford Odets), he did see fifteen of his plays produced on Broadway between 1945 and 1961, far more than any of his notable contemporaries, including Arthur Miller, William Inge, and Edward Albee. Perhaps even more remarkable is that seven of these plays (as well as his novella, *The Roman Spring of Mrs. Stone*) were adapted for the screen during this time, a record unsurpassed by any other writer of the immediate postwar era—dramatist or novelist. Odets, Somerset Maugham, Neil Simon, and many others may have captivated play-going audiences for a few years, but Williams, by producing a varied and extensive oeuvre, remained the leading figure of the Broadway theatre throughout its remarkable and unexpected renaissance during the first fifteen years of the postwar era.

The film versions of his plays and fiction mostly met with a similar popularity and critical acclaim, and all added substantially to the notorious reputation he had gained through his stage productions. The screen presence of his works quickly made him a central figure not only in New York and Hollywood, but internationally as well. By 1961, in fact, the shy and retiring (though ambitious) Williams had become a household name in America and abroad, arguably more recognized than any

American writer of the century, including Ernest Hemingway, perhaps the most relentlessly self-promoting author whom our national culture has ever produced.

Tennessee Williams, however, was no Neil Simon or Somerset Maugham. He was by no means a purveyor of sophisticated entertainment, titillating audiences with witty, craftily designed comedies of manners that easily pleased, rarely challenged, and never disturbed. As with the work of O'Neill, Miller, and Inge, Williams's plays explored, in innovative and dramatically effective fashion, the drama of the self, probing the dark corners and difficulties of desire and exploring the ties of love and family that bind (and entrap) troubled characters. His vision of the human condition, coupled with the poetic form with which it was enacted, quickly achieved recognition for their unique beauty and depth. In the space of only a few years, he won four Drama Critics' Circle Awards, two Pulitzers, and a Tony, being quickly elected to the National Institute of Arts and Letters. To be sure, Williams experienced his share of commercial failures and negative reviews, yet his critical success was unrivaled by any other playwright during Broadway's most fecund artistic period.

The work that Williams later produced did not earn him either the acclaim or the box-office receipts and movie-rights returns he had enjoyed during the "golden period" of his early career. From 1962 until his death in 1983, Williams managed to have a string of plays produced, sometimes on Broadway but also, as the New York theatre changed and his work was less easily accommodated to the more popular venues, in off-Broadway theatres. As testimony that he was still thought a quite bankable author by those in the film industry, eight more Hollywood versions of his plays hit the domestic and international screen in the last two decades of his life, making him one of the most adapted authors of all time. Thus, Williams joined the elite company of such beloved writers of enduring appeal as William Shakespeare and Jane Austen. In this later part of his career, Williams also devoted a considerable portion of his inimitable creative energy to other literary forms. He wrote another novel (*Moise and the World of Reason*, 1975), oversaw the assemblage of collections of his considerable body of poetry and short stories, and penned the autobiographical *Memoirs*, which achieved a worldwide *succès de scandale* for its sensationalized revelations about the playwright's private life, especially his homosexuality.

Williams's output was enormous, matched by few authors of any age, but the true range of his writing was not revealed, at least to the public, until after his death. It then became clear that he had left behind a huge volume of works, including poems, plays, and stories, that had never seen publication.[1] Despite the considerable accomplishments of this mature period, Williams's work after *The Night of the Iguana* (1961) has often been regarded as inferior to what he produced as a young writer. His later plays were neither as popular nor as well received by journalistic critics. This was, perhaps, because they demonstrated the playwright's growing interest in art theatre and avant-garde practice, as well as his progression from the "poetic realism" of his earlier period. As critic Annette Saddik remarks, "Throughout the 1960s Williams was becoming increasingly suspicious of realism's desire to naturalize the relationship between stage presentation and the outside world."[2] In fact, in these late plays he habitually rejected virtually any artistic concession to realism, and this departure made them less appealing to theatergoers who had grown accustomed to the more accessible early productions.

However, these later plays have attracted the interest and admiration of academic critics in the two decades following the playwright's death. Many have enjoyed successful new productions that have prompted more favorable evaluations of Williams's accomplishments. Most contemporary students of Williams, in fact, would agree with Saddik about the undeserved neglect and, sometimes, disdain with which his new plays were greeted in the 1970s and 1980s: "His later reputation . . . tells us more about the critical biases in the popular and academic press in this country than about Williams's work per se."[3] In any case, the evaluation of Williams's oeuvre very much remains a task in progress. Any final judgments must await not only the production of newly discovered plays, a task that has been proceeding with energy and much success since the 1990s, but also the publication of the various texts in other genres Williams completed before his death. This project promises to take many more years because of both various codicils involving the literary estate and the sheer volume of material involved. Yet the debate over the relative value of Williams's later writings, and the somewhat unknown worth of what was left unpublished at his death, have not affected the very high regard his other achievements continue to enjoy today, not only with playgoers and movie spectators (as new stage productions and films continue to appear with some regularity), but also within literary circles, where his influence on the American theatre is exceeded only perhaps by that of Eugene O'Neill.

Liberating the Stage

Williams was certainly driven by the artist's compulsion to create art for its own sake. But he also felt a strong desire for critical approval, a well-deserved popularity, and financial success. As is true for most artists, Williams's struggle for (and with) recognition and eventual fame was long and difficult. Although the playwright won some early literary awards and achieved modest popular success with the St. Louis Mummers during the 1930s, his first major production, *Battle of Angels* (1940), never made it to Broadway. The directors of the Theatre Guild, who had sponsored the production, imprudently chose Boston for the play's tryout instead of a more liberal New Haven or Philadelphia.[4] Conservative Bostonians were completely unprepared for a play that melded the sacred and the profane. In the manner of European drama, *Battle of Angels* invoked the power of Christian myth (à la John Milton), even as it provided a heavy dose of southern-gothic wit and bawdiness—a recipe too spicy for many New Englanders. Voicing a typical judgment, the critic for the *Boston Globe* opined, "The play gives the audience the sensation of having been dunked in mire."[5]

After the Boston debacle, Williams remained determined to prove himself.[6] He focused his energy on various stage and screen treatments of the life he had led as a young adult with his family in St. Louis, a story that, after achieving several widely divergent incarnations, was destined, as *The Glass Menagerie*, to become his first commercial success. Although he longed to see his name on a Broadway marquee, Williams's iconoclastic view of the then-current theatre fare made him feel very much the distraught outsider. Mailing his agent Audrey Wood *The Gentleman Caller* (as the initial version of *The Glass Menagerie* was called) for her to evaluate, he wrote that this would be the last play that he would write for "the *now* existing theatre."[7]

The young playwright's judgment, however, is somewhat inaccurate, for Williams perhaps slights the innovative, though neither radical nor audacious, nature of *The Glass Menagerie*. For example, Tom's unconventional (for its time) framing the play in the present and then reappearing as a character from the past surely caused some early confusion among audiences accustomed to missing-fourth-wall realism. If his largely autobiographical first Broadway production recalls the family-centered drama of then-celebrated playwrights like Lillian Hellman, *The Glass Menagerie* eschews the stagy melodramatics of plays such as her *The Little Foxes* (1939), with its clear-cut, climactic moment of recognition that assigns the characters simple moral labels. In *The Glass Menagerie*, by way of contrast, Laura's realization that hopes and dreams are likely to evaporate quickly hardly resolves the play's several dramatic tensions either simply or completely. *Menagerie* consists entirely of Tom's memories of life with his mother and sister. And in the present frame from which he narrates the past, Tom exhibits precisely the same unbreakable attachments of love and dependency that earlier compromised his struggle for independence. In the expressionist manner, Williams's world established on stage is thoroughly subjectivized (even as it is ironized) by the framing narration, which emphasizes Tom's nostalgia for a past that must be understood as corresponding to both his guilt and his longing.

Williams's first commercial success rejects the predictable formulae of what passed in the postwar era for serious drama. In fact, as later works would demonstrate in more striking detail and depth, Williams's expressionistic innovations, which he called his "new, plastic theatre," helped liberate the American stage from restrictive traditions of realism, established genre, and notions of structural and thematic correctness. No doubt, Williams's theatre, its serious themes complemented by complex, even contradictory emotional appeals, helped transform audiences' appetite for the customary light fare found on Broadway—the musicals, domestic comedies, and well-made topical plays that had dominated the scene until the advent of Williams, Arthur Miller, and William Inge. Of course, this postwar renaissance of the American art theatre had been prepared by O'Neill, who demonstrated, decades before Williams arrived on the scene, that intellectual seriousness and Broadway productions need not be mutually exclusive.

But beyond O'Neill's pioneering efforts in the 1920s, and despite, in the next decade, the partial reorientation of the American stage under the leadership of the Group Theatre toward social realism and political engagement, Broadway, during World War II, found itself committed only to customary forms of dramatic entertainment. The range of offerings was quite limited. Diversion of an amusing and heartwarming kind was offered by comedies such *Harvey* (1944) and musicals such as *Oklahoma!* (1943). Plays with an ostensibly serious theme tended to be military pageants, such as Moss Hart's *Winged Victory: The Air Force Play* (1943), or melodramatic antifascist tracts, such as Hellman's *Watch on the Rhine* (1941). Williams summed up his feelings about those current Broadway offerings in a letter to his mother around 1941, complaining that "serious, poetic plays" "have not had a fighting chance this season," and observing that "drum-beating, flag-waving, and pure musical comedy entertainment are the chosen fare. The dice will be loaded against us till after the war—but of course popular stuff dies quickly and the future accepts more readily what the present rejects."[8]

This prediction certainly proved accurate when Williams's luck dramatically changed in December 1944. At the pre-Broadway opening of *The Glass Menagerie* in Chicago, while much of the country was gripped by the decisive battles being waged in western Europe, audiences and critics began taking note of this exceptional talent who, Prometheus-like, was intent on breathing life into a moribund theatre. *Menagerie* quickly moved to Broadway and opened on March 31 to twenty-four curtain calls. Before it finished its run of 563 performances, the play had won the New York Drama Critics' Circle Award as well as the Donaldson and Sidney Howard Memorial awards. No doubt, America had found a new voice on the stage. Distinctly southern, it displayed the poet's unswerving determination to pry open the secrets of the heart, betraying, as C. W. E. Bigsby has remarked, "the romantic's fascination with extreme situations, with the imagination's power to challenge facticity, with the capacity of language to reshape experience, and the self's ability to people the world with visions of itself."[9]

A Romantic's Fascination with Extremes

This energetic romantic visionary quickly achieved a rare real-world feat. Williams found himself with back-to-back spectacular successes when *A Streetcar Named Desire* premiered on December 3, 1947, going on after spectacular notices to enjoy an amazing run of 855 performances. *Streetcar* was the first play to win the Pulitzer, New York Drama Critics' Circle, and Donaldson awards. The play was also notable for launching the stage career of Marlon Brando and for establishing Williams's long and mutually profitable stage and screen collaboration with Elia Kazan, arguably the most talented stage director of the century and a central figure in postwar Hollywood filmmaking as well. With *Streetcar*, Williams showed his commitment to a drama that probed the discontents of sexual desire, not the least of which was a violence that the American stage had never before witnessed. Not only did *Streetcar* break with Broadway tradition, it also demonstrated that Williams, after the poignant, even genteel domestic tragedy of *Menagerie*, had found the subject matter and themes that would define the remainder of his career.

Still a relative newcomer to Broadway, Williams had written, and seen produced, two plays that would almost immediately become classics of world drama. It was perhaps inevitable that his third commercial production would prove something of a letdown. *Summer and Smoke*, Williams's allegory of the flesh and the spirit, opened on October 6, 1948, to tepid reviews. Almost all critics compared the play with *The Glass Menagerie* and *Streetcar*, and the consensus was that *Summer and Smoke* lacked the punch of the playwright's previous efforts. *Variety* called it a "pale, disappointing facsimile of his previous 'Streetcar' and 'Glass Menagerie.'"[10] In late 1948, Williams traveled to Italy and published his first collection of short stories, *One Arm*. The playwright soon found himself enamored of Italy—a love affair that would last his whole life. He became particularly fond of Sicily, which was the ancestral home of his longtime lover Frank Merlo. The next year he began to outline what would become his first novel, *The Roman Spring of Mrs. Stone*. Italy began to feel like a second home for Williams as he cultivated friendships with Anna Magnani, Luchino Visconti, and Franco Zeffirelli as well as other major players in the Italian film industry. His experiences there prompted Williams to craft what was, in some respects, a vehicle for Magnani.

The popular actress, however, did not accept the playwright's gift of a leading role written expressly for her.[11] When *The Rose Tattoo* opened in Chicago at the end of 1950, Maureen Stapleton (a first-rate performer but by no means a sex goddess) played Serafina. Williams's first full-length "serious comedy" moved to the Martin Beck Theater on February 3 of the following year and opened to generally positive reviews, despite its celebration of Dionysian bawdiness. Some critics found the sexual references gratuitous and the playwright's intentions prurient. George Jean Nathan, for example, christened *The Rose Tattoo* Williams's "latest peepshow."[12] Others, however, praised Williams's inventiveness and his turn toward a comic embrace of the primitive. In 1951, Brooks Atkinson wrote that Williams was "at the top of his form,"[13] and Walter Kerr summed up his meteoric rise to prominence by declaring that "Tennessee Williams is the finest playwright now working in the American theatre."[14] *The Rose Tattoo* won a Tony and has gained stature over time because of superb revivals and Magnani's inimitable incarnation of Serafina in Daniel Mann's famous film version, for which she won an Academy Award.

Confident of his grasp on popularity, Williams was ready in 1952 to launch his boldest experiment to date—*Camino Real*. As with all of his works, this play evolved from several earlier versions, including the one-act *Ten Blocks on the Camino Real,* which he wrote in 1946. To direct the play, Williams returned to the collaborator for whom he held the greatest respect—Elia Kazan. Williams felt that only Kazan would appreciate the play's lyricism and find the dramatic means to transfer the poetry success-fully to the stage. Williams called this play his "Mexican poetic fantasy," and certainly the "poetic fantasy" was not a form of drama that the American stage—and perhaps no stage—had ever seen before. Walter Kerr, usually a strong advocate for Williams's more unorthodox efforts, called it "the worst play yet written by the best playwright of his generation."[15]

Reinvigorating the Plantation Myth

With two successes and one failure of almost equally astounding propor-tions, Williams had by early 1955 come to regard Broadway as the most fickle of mistresses, realizing that his commercial popularity (and hence career) could end at any time. As he prepared his revisions for *Cat on a Hot Tin Roof,* he told a reviewer, "If this new one doesn't make the grade, I'll have to go back to writing plays for art and little theatre groups."[16] Fortu-nately for Williams, *Cat* succeeded beyond his most optimistic expecta-tions. It opened at the Morosco Theatre in March 1955 and became one of Williams's most critically acclaimed and commercially successful plays, winning the Pulitzer and the Drama Critics' Circle Award and running for almost 700 performances. It certainly did not hurt the play's busi-ness that *Cat,* in typical Williams fashion, generated considerable con-troversy along the way because of its treatment of homosexual desire and the intimacies of married life. Even more than *Streetcar, Cat* explores the discontents of desire—and its polymorphous perversity as well. This may not have been new territory for Broadway to explore. Plays with a homo-sexual theme (albeit generally muted) had certainly hitherto been pro-duced and favorably received (a notable example is Lillian Hellman's *The Children's Hour,* which opened in 1934). No previous production, how-ever, had dealt at such length and in such depth with sexual questions, contesting not only notions of, as contemporary cultural critics would say, heteronormality, but also the view that women were as much the *subjects* as the *objects* of physical desire. Broadway's leading critic, Brooks Atkinson, judged that after the success of *Cat,* Williams had proved that "he is not only a man of poetic sensibilities, he is a master dramatist with a terrifying knowledge of the secrets of the mind."[17]

In just ten years, Williams had won most of the cherished Broadway and literary awards (some more than once) and had proved, with three major film adaptations of his work, that his characters and themes enjoyed a wide popularity. He had challenged American theatre audiences to explore previously forbidden psychological territory and to confront sexual themes that no playwright before him had dared investigate. He had liberated the sensibilities of the play-going public with his inimitable combination of lyricism and sensual (and for its time) even lurid language. Williams, who had helped change public taste and Broadway productions (at least in part), would now turn toward more mature and realistic portrayals of human relationships and desires. Williams had attained a powerful position in the commercial theatre, for, in those days, as Arthur Miller said, "the playwright was king of the hill, not the star actor or director."[18]

The postwar renaissance had made Broadway a leading institution of American culture, thanks to the energies and talents of authors eager to remake the literary scene into which they had been born. As Arthur Miller said, "I could not imagine a theatre worth my time that did not want to change the world, any more than a creative scientist could wish to prove the validity of everything that is already known. I knew only one other writer with the same approach, even if he surrounded his work with a far different aura. This was Tennessee Williams."[19]

Exploring a Poetics of Violence

In the fall of 1956, as *Cat* was completing its twenty-month run, Williams published his first collection of poems, *In the Winter of Cities*, and remained in New York City reworking *Battle of Angels*, making extensive changes even as he provided the play with a new and more appropriate title, *Orpheus Descending*. He hoped that Anna Magnani and Marlon Brando would agree to star as the leads Lady Torrance and Val Xavier, but, occupied with other projects, they both declined (although Brando and Magnani would later appear in the film version, *The Fugitive Kind*). *Orpheus* premiered at the Martin Beck Theatre on March 21, 1957, to mostly negative reviews. It closed after two months and probably would have done so sooner had Williams's considerable reputation not boosted ticket sales.

This failure was not easily endured, and quickly precipitated a psychological crisis. Williams recounts: "*Orpheus* brought all my problems to a head. I knew I must find help or crack up, so I went to an analyst and poured out all my troubles."[20] The short run and the bad reviews coincided with the death of Williams's father and also with his growing estrangement from longtime lover Frank Merlo. To add to these difficulties, he was becoming increasingly dependent on drugs and alcohol to soothe his considerable anxieties and bouts of depression. Desperate for help, Williams began psychotherapy in 1957 with Dr. Lawrence Kubie, a Manhattan Freudian analyst. He advised Williams to take a sabbatical from writing and to separate from Merlo. Believing, like most therapists of the time, that homosexuality was a developmental failure that could (and should) be cured, Kubie hoped these measures would result in Williams's conversion to "normality." The advice did not strike the playwright as a workable plan: "I wouldn't break up with Frank, of course, so I broke up with Kubie. Besides, if I got rid of my demons, I'd lose my angels."[21] His experience with psychotherapy, however, helped provide material for one of his most compelling and suspenseful plays, *Suddenly, Last Summer.*

Here William's art once again served as a thin veil for his own experience. For the dialogue and plot, he drew on not only his therapy sessions with Kubie, but also the lobotomy his sister Rose underwent in 1943. Though he had treated bisexuality, drunkenness, frankly acknowledged lust, and rape in his previous plays, even Williams must have wondered how audiences would react to a play that featured a young woman threatened with lobotomy, a talented poet who arranges for his mother and cousin to procure young men to satisfy his insatiable sexual appetite, and a bizarre reversal in which the exploited youths kill and eat the man who had hired them for sex. The play premiered at the York Theatre off-Broadway on January 7, 1958, under the title *Garden District* (it was paired with a superb one-act, *Something Unspoken*). Writing for the *New Yorker*, Wolcott Gibbs found *Suddenly, Last Summer* "an impressive and genuinely shocking play."[22] Walter Kerr, appalled by the play's "pure horror," nevertheless found it a "compelling . . . serious and accomplished work to be seen."[23] Williams apparently felt more comfortable having his most controversial play to date staged in the off-Broadway venue because of the increasing critical and financial pressures for producing a "major hit." He also believed it was impossible to continue living up to his growing reputation as America's greatest dramatist. As he told Mike Wallace in a 1958 interview, "nobody is as good as publicity makes them appear, and if he's reasonably objective with himself he knows that that's true and it gives him an awfully shaky feeling. And this increases with each production—the reputation grows as he becomes more conscious of the discrepancy between the reputation and the actual self."[24]

However, Williams was sufficiently cheered by the success he found with *Suddenly* to make another attempt at a full-scale Broadway production. He teamed up once again with Kazan for *Sweet Bird of Youth*, which enjoyed a successful run at the Martin Beck of 383 performances. Most critics praised the play, but there were some dissenting influential voices. Robert Brustein found it "disturbingly bad"[25]; Harold Clurman wrote that "it interested me more as a phenomenon than as a play";[26] and Brooks Atkinson was repelled because he thought the play "ranges wide through the lower depths, touching on political violence, as well as diseases of the mind and body."[27] In its theme, *Sweet Bird* explored what had become familiar Williams territory: its main character is an aspiring actor at the end of his youth who, employed as a gigolo by a fading Hollywood star, returns to the small town of his birth to claim the affection of the girl he had left behind. These plans quickly go awry when he learns that on a previous visit he infected Heavenly with a venereal disease that required a mutilating hysterectomy; at the play's end, Chance undergoes a mutilation of his own—castration.

Connecting the Domestic and the Spiritual

While *Sweet Bird* was still in rehearsals, Williams began work on something strikingly different. His domestic comedy, *Period of Adjustment*, was a response to complaints that he wrote only about the distressing aspects of experience. About this play, Williams said: "I am through with what have been called my 'black plays.' From now on, I want to be concerned with the kinder aspects of life . . . with more concentration on the quieter elements of existence."[28] Although the play deals with a potentially serious subject—dysfunctional marriage—the plot seems more Neil Simon than Tennessee Williams. It is a bedroom farce that closely resembles *Plaza Suite* and *Barefoot in the Park* (among other Simon hits that apparently followed Williams's lead) and only barely accords with the playwright's declaration that "these non-black plays won't be all white."[29]

Williams had begun work on what was to prove his last major critical and commercial success, *The Night of the Iguana*, during his first visit to Mexico, in 1940. Produced on Broadway in late 1961 at the Royale (after a lengthy series of road tryouts), it is perhaps his most ambitious drama. In the manner of *Camino Real*, *Iguana* traces the unpredictable, illuminating encounters among a bizarre gallery of characters (notably Shannon, an Episcopal priest undone by sexual excess, and the virginal Hannah, an older woman traveling with her poet grandfather). Critical notices were mixed, but the play won Williams his fourth Drama Critics' Circle Award.

As *Iguana* drew to a close after 316 performances, *Time* magazine put Williams on its cover and devoted a long article to evaluating his career.[30] Drama critic Ted Kalem praised Williams as a "consummate master of the theatre," noting that his only "rival," Arthur Miller, "has been silent on Broadway for more than six years." While Kalem praises Williams's artistic abilities, his article also emphasizes the sensational, notorious themes of his plays, echoing perhaps the then-current public judgment that Williams was a dramatist intent on shock and provocation. Kalem's brief, distorting summaries of the plays read mostly like entries from a textbook on aberrant behavior: "He is the nightmare merchant of Broadway, writer of *Orpheus Descending* (murder by blowtorch), *A Streetcar Named Desire* (rape, nymphomania, homosexuality), *Summer and Smoke* (frigidity), *Cat on a Hot Tin Roof* (impotence, alcoholism, homosexuality), *Sweet Bird of Youth* (drug addiction, castration, syphilis), *Suddenly, Last Summer* (homosexuality, cannibalism), and *The Night of the Iguana* (masturbation, underwear fetishism, coprophagy)." And yet Kalem found that this "nightmare merchant" was also "the greatest U.S. playwright since Eugene O'Neill and barring the aged Sean O'Casey, the greatest living playwright anywhere."

The Nightmare Merchant Rejects Realism

During the remaining two decades of his life, Williams succeeded in having multiple revivals as well as six new plays produced on Broadway (*The Milk Train Doesn't Stop Here Anymore*, *The Seven Descents of Myrtle*, *Slapstick Tragedy*, *Outcry*, *Vieux Carré*, and *Clothes for a Summer Hotel*). Others enjoyed significant off-Broadway productions or had their main runs in major cities such as San Francisco, Chicago, Miami, and Atlanta. Williams never stopped working and never lost interest in having his plays staged, but, as he had predicted, his drama clearly underwent changes that saw him move beyond the poetic realism that characterized not only many of his early plays (including all the commercial successes), but also the best received and most popular productions of his notable contemporaries Arthur Miller (*All My Sons*, *Death of a Salesman*, *A View from the Bridge*) and William Inge (*Picnic*, *Bus Stop*, and *Come Back, Little Sheba*). Audiences and critics alike were totally unprepared for Broadway's nightmare merchant to become an art dramatist in the mold of Jean Anouilh, Harold Pinter, or Edward Albee.

Voltaire wrote, with a double sense of cynicism and self-satisfaction, that "fame is a heavy burden," and no one could have shared the sentiment more than Tennessee Williams. For roughly seventeen years, from 1945 to 1962, no American playwright at home or abroad was more lionized. During his last two decades, however, no American author was more vilified, perhaps because he more or less publicly turned his back on the kind of work with which he had hitherto pleased Broadway audiences. Though *Iguana* had completed its successful run only a year before, Williams's critical obituaries began to be written as early as 1963, the year *Milk Train* was produced on Broadway. The theme of Richard Gilman's devastating review, entitled "Mistuh Williams, He Dead," was obvious from the infamous title.[31] The playwright, in Gilman's view, was an incarnation of the overreaching protagonist of Conrad's *Heart of Darkness*, who expires in the horrifying world of violence and degradation he helped create. Later critics (especially academics) defended Williams against these scurrilous attacks. In a study of the reviews, John McCann concludes that "the castigation of Williams in this decade would reach a pitch of verbal abuse that rivaled the most scabrous criticism of the past thirty years as a whole."[32] Because of his early, stupendous success, Williams found himself in a no-win situation at this stage of his career. If he returned to familiar territory, his new play would be unfavorably compared with the classics of his "golden period." And yet if he took off in some boldly experimental direction, the critics would plead for another *Streetcar* or *Menagerie*. These critical denunciations took their toll on the playwright. As he told an interviewer in 1970, "Almost every time, at least in ten years—I had a play on Broadway, I swore I'd never write a Broadway play again. . . . But as you start to write again, and when you've written something that has potential, there are pressures. There are producers and there are agents. And you find yourself giving under those pressures and going back to Broadway, where you said you'd never go again."[33]

Reassessing Williams

The consensus among contemporary students is that the playwright's post-*Iguana* work never received a fair hearing from the professional critics.

Annette Saddik concludes that "in his later years, Williams was defeated before he ever began; reviewers tended to exhibit hostility toward experimental drama in general, and Williams never had a chance to be taken seriously in the first place by the critics."[34] In 1975, he won the National Arts Club gold medal for literature. But that same year Williams, sickened by caustic reviews, also expressed his disgust with the direction of American theatre: "I'm quite through with the kind of play that established my early and popular reputation. I am doing a different thing, which is altogether my own, not influenced at all by other playwrights at home or abroad, or by other schools of theatre."[35]

Yet if fame is a heavy burden, it is cyclical. Twenty years after his death, Williams's popularity with audiences and critics is approaching that of his glory years. In 1999, *Not About Nightingales*, one of his apprentice plays, opened to wildly enthusiastic reviews on Broadway and in London, garnering Williams more praise in a few months than he had received during the last ten years of his life. New productions of old and previously unpublished work were given a major showing at Hartford Stage in September 2003. A new film version of *The Roman Spring of Mrs. Stone* was broadcast on Showtime the same year. The Kennedy Center sponsored a Williams festival in 2004 that featured several revivals as well as the first public stagings of several one-acts. In 2003, a production of *Cat on a Hot Tin Roof* appeared on Broadway to great critical and popular approbation, and 2005 witnessed major revivals of *Streetcar* and *Menagerie*. Following and summarizing a popular trend, as is its wont, *USA Today* proclaimed in a front-page banner that "Tennessee Williams Is Hotter Than Ever."[36] The release of a collection of his most notable films on DVD in 2005 affirmed his still-developing status as a mammoth figure in American culture. His long-forgotten screenplay, *The Loss of a Teardrop Diamond*, was produced in 2008.

Throughout his long career, Tennessee Williams always tried to give his audiences more than just a show, even if, while following his inspiration more uncompromisingly as a mature artist, he was obliged to seek out friendly and accommodating stages a few blocks away from the bright lights of Broadway.[37] No doubt, audiences of the era were eager for an art that provided difficult satisfactions rather than the deceptive pleasures of wish fulfillment. In short, the vein of taste mined by Williams, Miller, Inge, and others was resolutely high cultural, accommodating tragic themes and modernist techniques, scorning traditional pieties, including what had hitherto been a more or less tacit ban on those "adult" subjects, such as homosexuality, drug addiction, sexual predation, and prostitution, that were so central to Williams's conception of dramatically arresting character. Catering to a minority, elite culture, the Broadway stage in the postwar era could, and did, readily adapt to the new vision offered by Williams and others. We should not forget that when Williams turned more resolutely to experimentalism and avant-garde themes, his plays continued to find commercial production, even if audiences and critics, at least for the most part, were baffled and displeased by the direction in which his mature artistic vision led him.

A Movie-Made Playwright

Williams would have become a central, controversial figure in American culture in the fifties and sixties had no movie ever been made from any of his plays or works of fiction. But if Hollywood had not been receptive to the playwright's earnest efforts to have his plays brought to the screen, he would never have become the most familiar (even notorious) literary figure in a country where playwrights, even world-famous ones like O'Neill, had never found real celebrity. Scornful of Hollywood because he believed, with some good reason, that it was a dream factory manufacturing ersatz art, Arthur Miller showed little interest in having his plays filmed, at least until he married a movie actress of some note (Marilyn Monroe) and determined to provide her with a tailor-made part. *The Misfits*, despite a famous director (John Huston) and able costars (Clark Gable, Eli Wallach, and Montgomery Clift), proved a spectacular miscalculation. No worthy Hollywood production was made in the fifties from either of Miller's two spectacular stage successes—*Death of a Salesman* and *The Crucible*—mainly because of the playwright's indifference. Williams, in contrast, sought from the very beginning the popular reputation and the considerable financial rewards that the filming of his plays would provide.

Tennessee Williams was twenty-seven when he first visited Hollywood, and it was only some eleven years later that he began to play a substantial role in the film industry centered there, when he helped director Irving Rapper and producer Jerry Wald adapt *The Glass Menagerie* for the screen. Approaching forty, Williams was almost ancient to be a novice in a business that counted youth among its most valuable commodities. Though he undoubtedly got a late start, the playwright had in some respects been preparing for a career in filmmaking all his life, especially after leaving rural Mississippi at age seven (1918) and moving to St. Louis, one of the country's most populous and bustling metropolitan areas. Despite the gloomy setting depicted in *The Glass Menagerie*, the Williams family established itself in an upscale urban neighborhood called University City, where film theatres were within easy walking distance or a short streetcar ride. In early childhood, Williams became a habitué of the local picture palaces, like the famous Tivoli, which were then doing a thriving business.[38] His experiences with a medium still very much a sensational cultural novelty exerted a powerful fascination. Growing up in what film historian Robert Sklar has termed a "movie-made America," where "movies were the most popular and influential medium of culture," Williams developed a lifelong interest in, and an enthusiasm for, films and filmmaking.[39]

Young Tom Williams's obsession with the cinema was by no means exceptional; it was certainly shared by many of his generation and time. The 1920s and 1930s saw Hollywood secure its hold on a broadly middle-class audience of all ages. The films of the era offered entertainment of different kinds, some of which were viewed by the more conservative and religious within American society as immoral because of their sexually suggestive or violent themes. But in 1930, by the time Williams had graduated from high school, the studios were in the process of adopting a production code that was intended to ensure the wholesomeness of their product and its consistent support of consensus values. In 1934, the Production Code Administration (PCA) office was founded, and under the strict stewardship of Joseph Breen, all Hollywood productions began to be carefully vetted. Only those deemed to be in conformity with the code were granted the certificate necessary for nationwide release to theatres. Issuing from the studios in increasing numbers as producers sought to satisfy a huge popular demand, the Hollywood films of Williams's youth offered idealized worlds of glamour, adventure, and romance where the problems of life found unambiguous and crowd-pleasing solutions. Such fantasy was intoxicating and addictive, especially for an unhappy young man with an exceptional imagination. At home, there were a mother and father who constantly battled; at school, he enjoyed little relief from the teasing to which the shy and physically unaccomplished are subjected. Not surprisingly, Williams found that the make-believe world conjured up on the screen offered a ready refuge from the daily anxieties and depressing episodes of his St. Louis childhood.

A Cinematic Imagination

Especially after the conversion to sound at the end of the 1920s, the spectacular forms of Hollywood performance art also appealed to his developing artistic sensibilities. The complementary processes involved in moviemaking, especially the coordination of musical, lighting, and camera effects, fascinated Williams, who, much more than other playwrights of the era, was to devote great attention to conceiving his plays as multilayered productions that put heavy demands on art designers, lighting experts, and sound engineers. With its uninterrupted formal flow and its shots linked by narrative, graphic, and aural devices, the classic Hollywood film also deeply influenced his conception of theatricality. Williams usually wrote fluid scenes and rarely seemed comfortable with the conventional division of stage plays into discrete acts.[40] In an important statement of his dramatic principles, he argued for the necessity of a "sculptural drama" that emulates cinematic mise-en-scène, with the playwright, like a film director, designing elaborate tableaux as if for the camera. Williams wrote *The Glass Menagerie* and many of his apprentice works, such as *Stairs to the Roof*, with both stage and screen production in mind, and he even tailored some of his short stories for ready film adaptation. For *Menagerie*, Williams designed a "screen device" on which images would be projected; such a technique (described at length in the notes he penned for the original version of the play) shows how in his mind the boundary between the artistic forms of theatre and film occasionally became productively blurred.

One book published posthumously—*Stopped Rocking and Other Screenplays*—contains four never-produced film projects, and Williams's unpublished work includes a considerable number of other screenplays. In the production notes for major plays such as *Sweet Bird of Youth*, *A Streetcar Named Desire*, *Cat on a Hot Tin Roof*, *The Night of the Iguana*, and *Camino Real*, he discusses scenic and staging effects designed to liberate, as filming might, the dramatic structure from the physical confines of a three-dimensional platform. It is hardly surprising, then, that scholars have often remarked on the cinematic structure of his theatre. George Brandt, for example, notes that Williams's deployment of fluid scenes and his "careful orchestration of sound—music as well as effects" are more closely aligned "to a cinematic vision of reality than to the [stage] expressionism of the post–World War I period."[41]

Contemporary critics may be enthusiastic about the cinematic elements in Williams's dramatic art, but the influence of Hollywood tinsel on young Tom was viewed by his own family with a disapproval bordering on alarm. In *The Glass Menagerie*, Amanda Wingfield turns to her son and says, "Tom, you go to the movies entirely too much." Amanda is never reluctant to offer her opinion about how Tom, somewhat given to aimlessness and self-indulgence, should spend his time, and neither was Williams's mother, Edwina, upon whom the character is closely modeled. According to Dakin, Tennessee's younger brother, Edwina thought that her older son's interest in the movies bordered on unhealthy obsession. Like Amanda, Edwina did in fact wonder whether her son was actually spending so much time in movie houses, and if so, whether those many hours in darkened auditoria had led him to even worse forms of moral dissolution.

Worrying about the supposed deleterious effects of frequent movie viewing on the young had, by the end of the 1920s, become something of a national obsession, to which not only religious leaders, but also the intelligentsia were moved to pay considerable attention. Outraged in the 1920s by "what the films are doing to young America," sociologist Edward Alsworth Ross warned that "more of the young people who were town children sixteen years ago or less are sex-wise, sex-excited, and sex-absorbed than of any generation of which we have knowledge."[42] Edwina Williams was by no means alone in demanding that her son take less interest in the movies, and Tom was by no means alone in ignoring her admonitions.

A Sort of Life in Pictures

If Williams, like many aspiring writers, actually entertained thoughts about moving west to seek a career in the "pictures," he did not act on them, at least for many years. His virtual obsession, first in junior high, then thorough high school and while in college, was to write—whether poetry, stories, or plays—and he enjoyed limited success in all three genres at a relatively young age. After attending the University of Missouri and Washington University, Williams graduated from the University of Iowa in 1938 and soon moved to New Orleans. It was at this time that, anticipating the beginning of his professional writing career (and needing to alter his name and birthday to suit the requirements of a writing contest), he started signing his name as "Tennessee Williams." After about six weeks of French Quarter life, drinking in the ambiance and meeting people whom he would eventually rework into many of his characters, he set out with friend Jim Parrott for Los Angeles. But the golden coast was not what he had expected. Once there, Williams ended up spending a few days alone at the downtown YMCA. The scene was desolate, decaying, and lonely—far from the romantic vision he had formed of California culture. He soon joined up again with Parrott, but the miserable first impression he had formed of Los Angeles and Hollywood would stay with him for life. Tennessee wrote his mother: "I have *not* decided to stay in Hollywood—how you got that impression I don't know. My original impression of the place still holds good—it is about the last place on earth that I would want to live. . . . it is full of sham and corruption and the atmosphere of the place is generally putrid."[43] That same year, however, Williams found work at a shoe store in Culver City just one block from MGM studios, where he would later work as a screenwriter.[44] After spending several desultory months on the West Coast, he briefly returned to St. Louis, and then lived the next several, unsettled years in New York City, Provincetown, Key West, New Orleans, and other cities in the states. In the meantime, he pursued his writing career, slowly building a reputation and becoming a client of well-known agent Audrey Wood.

Hollywood Calls

No one was more surprised than Williams himself when Hollywood suddenly beckoned in the spring of 1943. Wood sent him a telegram that changed his life: "Come at once to New York. Have arranged writing deal pictures which necessitates your leaving New York in time arrive California around fifteenth of May."[45] Williams was less than enthusiastic about this opportunity, even though it meant steady employment. In fact, adopting something of a conventional pose for the serious writer, he complained he had been "sold to Hollywood."[46] But he did not refuse the offer, and that summer began working for MGM at the standard rate of $250 a week. The playwright-turned-screenwriter considered this munificent salary "dishonest," and as it turned out, he spent most of his energy working on his own material rather than on assigned projects. Williams had agreed to the standard seven-year arrangement, which contained a six-month option. If his performance was judged satisfactory, renewal was automatic; otherwise, the studio could drop him without further obligation.[47] His first assignment, a quite typical one, was to rewrite a script for a Lana Turner vehicle that another writer had penned. Williams confessed his frustration with the project to Audrey Wood: "It would be useless for me to describe the script I have to work with, a scenario prepared by Lenore Coffee. It contains every cliché situation you've ever seen in a Grade B picture. They want me to give it a 'freshness and vitality' but at the same time keep it 'a Lana Turner sort of thing.' I feel like an obstetrician required to successfully deliver a mastodon from a beaver."[48]

For six months, and with increasing futility, Williams worked on the Turner script and other projects (including a treatment for a film about Billy the Kid), but during this time he also began devoting full attention to his rough treatment of *The Gentleman Caller*, which would, of course, become *The Glass Menagerie*. This same year (1943), his beloved sister Rose Williams underwent a prefrontal lobotomy, and chances are that the distraught playwright, in drafting *The Gentleman Caller*, sought catharsis by fully concentrating on his most autobiographical play. Had Williams been given full license to write his own material from the beginning, however, he might well have produced work that would have pleased studio executives. Many writers hired by Hollywood, even famous and gifted ones such as Scott Fitzgerald and William Faulkner, were discouraged or even forbidden from working on original material. At that time it was more common for properties thought promising, generally published works, to be purchased by the studio, often after competitive bidding. Producers then determined on a proper approach to this "presold" material, and their judgment about how to proceed would usually be based on short treatments prepared by contract writers. Once the project had reached this stage, it could be handed over to still another writer (or writers) for development, who worked under the always-watchful eye of the producer. Screenwriting credit for the film was determined by negotiations that were sometimes complex and even acrimonious; the Screen Writers Guild, formed in 1933, carefully oversaw the process.

Unlike playwriting, working on scripts for the commercial cinema was a collaborative activity over which no one writer exercised complete or, often, even substantial control. It was an occupation that might prove attractive to energetic hacks who had developed some facility for reinventing the formulae spelled out in screenwriting manuals or who could be depended on to write a scene or two of snappy dialogue, but it could hold little appeal for a romantic individualist like Williams, who believed that writing was, at its best, the most sincere and honest form of self-expression, the communication of hard-won inner truths.

No Spiritual Zombie

The advent of talking pictures required more elaborate forms of drama and dialogue, and so many of America's most talented writers, Nathanael West, Clifford Odets, and Ernest Hemingway among them, were lured by promises of steady, easy money to the coast, even though they regarded the movies as a negligible, debased medium. Williams agreed with such distinguished colleagues that much of what the commercial film industry produced was insipid, pseudo-art, ruined by an overcommitment to conventions and clichés. But he felt a genuine enthusiasm for the better Hollywood productions and for film as an artistic form. Working in the industry was an eye-opening disappointment. Williams found that the hired piecework of scriptwriting deprived writers of individuality, discretion, and responsibility. He complained to Audrey Wood in 1943 that a palpable malaise infected the studio writing corps: "I sensed it first in the writers I met out here. All spiritual Zombies it seemed to me."[49] Williams quickly determined that what Hortense Powdermaker has aptly termed "the dream factory" hardly provided the intellectual environment conducive to his own writing projects. He explained to his friend Donald Windham that "the atmosphere makes you lazy. I only work in spasms, not continually like I do other places."[50]

Having produced little that his employers could use, Williams was terminated after six months, when MGM exercised its nonrenewal option. Before he left Hollywood, Williams gave MGM a chance to purchase *The Gentleman Caller*. A diffuse, overly complex drama substantially different from the play that would soon be extracted from it, this property was promptly rejected, at least in part for being yet another story about southern women. This was a subgenre not only exemplified by Hollywood's most famous production, *Gone with the Wind*, but also by other more intimate and smaller-scale films, such as Frank Borzage's dark melodrama *Moonrise* (1948). Studio executives thought that this kind of narrative had already exhausted whatever limited popularity it might attain. They would regret this judgment. Once *The Gentleman Caller* became the Pulitzer Prize–winning *The Glass Menagerie*, there was a bidding contest for the screen-adaptation rights to this attractive property, which a now eager MGM lost to Warner Bros. The studio's initial position was that since Williams had been under contract while writing the story, the material was theirs, but this view was quickly shown to have no legal standing.

That *The Glass Menagerie* would be adapted for the screen pleased Williams immensely, and he was very concerned that the film be a popular success. Williams understood the power that film adaptations could give his plays, in effect providing them with productions that, frozen in time, never closed, and, by their very nature, reached a much broader audience. Williams was interested in helping transfer his work to the screen. In various ways, he often labored long and hard at these different adaptation projects, despite the fact that he did not always do all the screenwriting himself. Though he understood that changes, often quite substantive, would need to be made in order to adapt his material for a broader audience, Williams hoped a film would emerge in each case that would honor the original work.

Williams and Censorship

The playwright, of course, was well aware that in the late 1940s, Hollywood offered less freedom of expression than Broadway. There were signs that American audiences were becoming more accepting of "mature material," as we shall discuss in more detail below, but filmgoers were still quite conservative in their tastes, at least by early twenty-first-century standards. Even on the commercial stage, as we have seen, Williams's first play had been considered provocative and even risqué. His experiences in Boston with *Battle of Angels* would be repeated several times over in Hollywood during the 1950s, with Joseph Breen and his colleagues at the Production Code Administration often outraged by, and antipathetic to, his stories and themes. In the postwar era, the PCA began to show signs of weakness in the face of insistent social change, but the censors still narrowly circumscribed how approved films might treat sexual matters, even as they consistently condemned particular themes (such as rape, homosexuality, incest, and "promiscuity") central to Williams's exploration of the inner lives of the socially marginalized and the psychologically maladjusted.

To make matters even more difficult for Williams and others who wished to go beyond conventional Hollywood formulae, a second, informal body of censors stood ready to enforce moral standards sometimes even harsher than those of the PCA. The Legion of Decency, a Catholic lay organization that charged itself with protecting the morals of the nation's largest Christian denomination, wielded considerable power in the late 1940s and throughout the 1950s. The prospect of a "condemned" rating from the legion meant that Catholics, at least those that honored their pledge to abide by legion judgments, were prohibited from attending a film, and the disfavor of the organization might be enforced by theatre picketing and boycotts. The prospect of such economic difficulties and adverse publicity could reduce exhibitors and studio executives alike to fear and trembling. If more informally than the PCA, the legion had considerable ability, Williams was chagrined to discover, to effect changes in material and motifs that its reviewing staff found offensive and immoral.

It would be a mistake, however, to understand the code as embodying principles of story construction that were essentially at odds with mainstream industry practice; the studios, we must remember, created the PCA, whose function, at least in part, was to level the playing field for producers. The code's rules and regulations, in fact, accorded with central conventions of the Hollywood narrative that had been carefully enshrined in screenwriting manuals long before the PCA was established. An outdated aesthetic, confirmed by past success and enforced by an overly conservative and moralistic PCA, prevented Hollywood from making contact with the generation that had come of age in wartime America. Or at least this is what many young directors and producers of the period believed, Elia Kazan prominent among them. Robert Rossen spoke for this group when he said: "We have a new audience, an audience that has grown up out of the war and been in contact with greater realities."[51] The audience may have been new (if only in part), but by the time Williams started work on the screenplay for *The Glass Menagerie*, in 1949, Hollywood had yet to modify its approach significantly. For more than half a century the industry had enjoyed much success with stories featuring sympathetic characters who, their troubles resolved, are brought to a happy ending that emphasizes success rather than failure. It was still the case that in the typical Hollywood films of the era, righteous men triumph or find themselves vindicated, discover romance with the beautiful girls of their dreams, and are rewarded with wealth and social position.

Poetic Champion of the Outcast and Disconsolate

Williams, by contrast, was fast becoming the poetic champion of the outcast and disconsolate, of those who fail to achieve financial security and a glamorous spouse, of loners confused or undone, not transfigured, by the vagaries of desire. For Williams, abandoning the Broadway tradition of the serious play (with its high-minded or politically engaged comment on the American scene) meant dramatizing the psychosexual inner lives of the emotionally traumatized and socially marginalized, those either dispossessed of happiness or indisposed to grasp it. His main characters have been bypassed by the great American dream of public acclaim and bourgeois prosperity, often because of some sexual crime, indiscretion, or disability that alienates them from more respectable others. The drama that entangles them is always personal, seldom overtly political (after the apprentice plays of the 1930s at least), a function of complexly intimate relations with family or with fellow travelers met by chance on the road to self-confrontation.

The power and intensity of Williams's early Broadway plays revealed the well-made theme dramas of the time to be, by comparison, mistakenly committed to the visually uninteresting portrayal of irrelevant public selves. Not surprisingly, Williams's plays required spectacular forms of stagecraft because missing-fourth-wall sets often did not suit either his more fluid conceptions of time and space or his artful coordination of special effects (lighting and music) with dramatic action. Williams's characters, so possessed of inner lives, could be fully realized only by the kind of archly naturalistic acting that was capable of representing conflicted, multilayered selves: the so-called Method that had recently come into vogue with the founding of the Actors Studio.

Williams's drama appealed to a sophisticated, well-educated audience of playgoers much affected by the growing fashion for psychotherapy and the widespread endorsement of Freudian theory as an explanation of the human condition. They applauded Williams for putting sex on the theatrical agenda and sympathized with the guilt-ridden vulnerability of his protagonists. Responding to a contradictory historical moment that featured an intensifying Cold War but the proclamation of the "end of ideology," these playgoers did not resent the nearly complete absence of social or political engagement (at least in any overt or direct sense) in Williams's plays, or the pessimistic bleakness of his vision, focused on the problems of the individual. Because Williams was committed to thematizing sex and psychological discontent in new, more central ways, his plays seemed startlingly realistic and appeared, despite their stylized dialogue (and often obtrusive intellectual schemata), to move beyond the restricting decorum of the previous theatrical age. The poetry of Williams's transforming vision seemed to connect with life as it was most deeply and authentically lived.

Compromising with Hollywood

In contrast, the Hollywood film industry by the late forties had established itself solidly in another, rather distant area of cultural production: providing, for general audiences, clean, wholesome entertainment. Given the predilections of the industry (reinforced by many years of profitability), Williams's more complex vision of the human condition simply could not be transferred wholesale to the screen, as the playwright soon realized.

In 1954, after considerable experience with the triumphs and discontents of Hollywood filmmaking, Williams observed to Audrey Wood: "Films are more lasting than play productions and I'm afraid that my plays will be remembered mostly by films made of them, and for that reason it is terribly important to me that I should get as much artist's control as possible in all film contracts."[52] As an insider at one of the industry's largest studios, Williams learned early how the myriad decisions about production were made; he also discovered who within management hierarchy was authorized to make them. He was then better able to navigate the economic and political channels that determined the fate of each picture, acquiring (through careful contract negotiations) and then exercising (through astute intervention during production) "as much artist's control as possible."

Williams's extensive correspondence with agents and lawyers, producers and studio executives, as well with as various officials at the Production Code Administration, reveals his growing sophistication in (and consequent ambivalence about) dealing with the many factors that affected the production of each picture. No doubt, however, he was never able to share wholeheartedly the views of studio professionals about the kinds of dramatic structure and themes that the mass-public film audience would accept and enjoy. Main Street USA, where the nation's film theatres were located, was not Broadway, even though Williams, never much of a realist in such matters, always expected it to be.

Because a form of artistic re-creation over which he exercised little control was involved, Williams was profoundly ambivalent about the artistic value of the screen versions of his works and the popularity that they did, or did not, achieve. Because his reported or published comments are sometimes contradictory, it is difficult to determine exactly how the playwright felt about any film based on his work, if indeed he was ever of one mind. When asked whether an adaptation should be faithful, Williams took issue with the conventional wisdom: "No, I do not. I think they should create something entirely new in a cinematic form, you see. But they don't somehow get organized that way. They're afraid to. I don't know why they are. But they stick too close to the stage play and a stage play is not always effective on the screen, you know."[53]

Williams was often incensed at how the Hollywood versions of his plays substantially altered their conclusions, in his view, for the worse. Sometimes these alterations were to satisfy the demands of the PCA for a poetically just finale, in which either the virtuous might emerge victorious or, when they did not, a proper emphasis could be put on what code officials termed "compensatory moral value." Sometimes alterations would need to be made to satisfy the interests of producers or directors in a conventionally happy ending, such as "boy gets girl." Williams once told an interviewer that people should by all means go see his movies, but that they should leave before the final five minutes. He had a point. The studios considerably altered the endings of virtually all his films, often compromising, even reversing, the thrust of the dramatic action and character development. In 1960, Williams vented his frustrations about working within a Hollywood system in which writers did not enjoy the power they did on Broadway: "It [the film] passes through so many other hands, minds, tastes, and must cater to so many restricting attitudes not favorable to an art form that, I hate to say this, but I think that autocracy, or to put it more gently, autonomy, is the first essential of purity in making a work of art. All of the dramatic arts are essentially collaborative, but in writing for the stage you're fairly sure that your writing will always be your writing. But in the film, you're much less certain of this."[54]

During his Broadway career, Williams, of course, sometimes had to accommodate the views of others, especially director Elia Kazan, and revise his original play script accordingly. But he did not have to trust his works to the tender mercies and different sensibilities of other writers, and the plays remained "his" in ways that the film versions could never be. Williams is officially listed as the screenwriter for only seven of his Hollywood films, and in five of these productions the writing was a shared (but not usually a collaborative) task: *The Glass Menagerie* (with Peter Berneis), *A Streetcar Named Desire* (with adaptation by Oscar Saul), *Baby Doll*, *Suddenly, Last Summer* (with Gore Vidal), *The Rose Tattoo* (with adaptation by Hal Kanter), *The Fugitive Kind* (with Meade Roberts), and *Boom!* It is not insignificant that the two films for which Williams received full screenwriting credit (*Baby Doll* and *Boom!*) were made with directors (Elia Kazan and Joseph Losey, respectively) who took a very active role in the shaping of the final film script. All the productions based on his original properties certainly bear his collaborative fingerprints, as we will demonstrate in later chapters, but none of them allowed Williams that "autonomy," which is "the first essential of purity in making a work of art." Frustration with this forced collaboration led Williams in 1960 to complain to Arthur Gelb that he would never do another adaptation and that *The Fugitive Kind* would be his last movie.[55] He was mostly true to his word. There were eight major films produced after *The Fugitive Kind*, but Williams participated as screenwriter on only one of these projects, *Boom!* (1968), quickly forming an interesting partnership with an intellectually inclined director he greatly respected, Joseph Losey.

Something New and Different

Williams was understandably reluctant to view the adaptation process from the viewpoint of those who paid him huge sums for the screen rights and pressed him to participate in production. But why did producers seek out properties with themes that were so different from the usual Hollywood fare and would prove so difficult to screen? This question suggests a more general one. What were the needs and requirements of the institution that undertook the adaptations of Williams's works? The thesis of this book is that Williams's works played an important role within the unsettled and problematic evolution of the American cinema in the years immediately following the end of World War II, when Hollywood started to lose much of its audience and tried, with increasing desperation, to entice paying customers back with the promise of something attractively different on the screen. This "attractively different" something included what producers like Charles K. Feldman and Jack Warner thought, and quickly discovered, Williams could supply. Such a development was surprising. It might seem that postwar Hollywood, riding high on its success with established formulae and genres, would have had little use for Williams's two early successes, *The Glass Menagerie* and *A Streetcar Named Desire*. And indeed not a few in the business initially thought them too arty and too dependent on "adult" themes. But that would quickly change as Hollywood, enjoying its greatest success ever as World War II drew to a close, unexpectedly slipped into deep crisis.

The Postwar Boom Busted

During the 1940s, Hollywood filmmakers took care not to offend the more traditionally minded within their audience. Some Hollywood productions of the era, particularly the series now known as film noir, with its exposure of the dark underside of bourgeois respectability, voiced dissatisfactions with the existing order and catered perhaps to a segment of the audience already distancing itself from mass tastes.[56] For the most part, however, commercial films eagerly promoted an idealized and conservative vision of American values and society. The war films that began to dominate the nation's screens after 1942 drew pointed, often oversimplified contrasts between the benefits American democracy bestowed and the many evils perpetrated by European fascism and Japanese militarism. Such a strong endorsement of the national way of life was especially apparent for the duration of the war. Hollywood was allowed to continue to produce and exhibit films despite the fact that this was a business activity that used up "strategic materials" but did not contribute directly to weapons making.[57]

The reason was that the industry was called upon to support the aims of the government, which it then did energetically by making many morale-boosting and enlistment-encouraging films in close cooperation with the Office of War Information. As hostilities drew to a conclusion and U.S. military might was confirmed in its world dominance, the industry rode a boom in ticket sales. And so nothing of their experience during the war suggested to studio executives that there might be any problems with their time-honored strategy of appealing to a general, undifferentiated audience. Hollywood remained committed (at least for the most part) to purveying the same kind of glamorous fantasy that had entranced, and then disappointed, the young Tom Williams two decades earlier.

In 1946, the first year of peacetime exhibition, box-office receipts hit an all-time high ($325 million) as returning servicemen fueled a dating boom and consumer goods were not yet available in sufficient quantity to compete for the entertainment dollar.[58] Weekly attendance at film theatres, in fact, almost equaled the nation's population, at the time close to 140 million; this staggering figure indicates how important moviegoing had become for the many who must have attended religiously numerous times a week. Studio profits ran close to $120 million, nearly doubling the record figure of $60 million that had been earned just one year earlier. Gross revenues were an astounding $1.45 billion (also a record), and this box office success was largely fueled by a string of five films that each earned more than $5 million in domestic rentals, far exceeding expectations.

Each of these blockbusters was in some sense a genre exercise: *The*

Bells of St. Mary's (1945, religious melodrama), *Road to Utopia* (1945, musical fantasy, part of an ongoing "franchise"), *The Jolson Story* (1946, musical biography), *Duel in the Sun* (1946, western), and *The Best Years of Our Lives* (1946, a war melodrama). These last two films did hint at new directions for the industry. Though it emphasized three romantic (re)couplings, *Best Years* offered an unaccustomedly realistic engagement with current social and political issues, showing that viewers were eager for more than a heartwarming depiction of intimate relations. The romance (if we may call it that) between Gregory Peck and Jennifer Jones in *Duel in the Sun* was far from conventional; the striking finale shows the star-crossed lovers gunning each other down with near-orgasmic fury, and consequently, it provoked PCA ire and conservative protest. The sensational success of the film, which was quite risqué even with the cuts demanded by Breen, certainly predicted a shift in audience tastes toward a less Victorian treatment of sexual attraction. Otherwise, the five blockbusters were thoroughly conventional in theme and structure. An impartial analysis of the exhibition scene in 1946 would surely have supported the view that Hollywood should expect continuing success with "business as usual," especially if its approach were updated just a bit.

Because it had played such an important role in the war effort, Hollywood had established its closest working relationship with the government (though this was compromised to some degree by the death of industry-friendly Franklin Roosevelt in the spring of 1945). More importantly, fueled by wartime success, Hollywood had moved beyond Depression-era worries about profitability and audience shrinkage. It was hardly surprising that studio executives were optimistic about the future. America had become a global power, and with the reopening of vital foreign markets, the industry had every reason to hope for helpful support of its international operations. Domestically, despite labor problems and shortages (particularly in urban housing), the national economy managed to maintain momentum as wartime production was shifted to satisfying consumer demand, inaugurating a decade and a half of unprecedented growth that expanded the middle class and provided most Americans with a lifestyle that was rich beyond the wildest dreams of their parents.

Ill-Equipped for the World of Tomorrow

The film industry, it surprisingly turned out, was not to share in the country's good fortune. As Thomas Schatz declares, "Hollywood proved to be singularly ill equipped for 'the world of tomorrow,'" suffering instead both "an economic tailspin and a sustained fall from social grace."[59] The most newsworthy crisis was ideological: the investigation of purported communist influence in the industry by the House Un-American Activities Committee, which led not only to a bitter confrontation between right- and left-wing members of the film community, but also to the jailing of ten "unfriendly" witnesses and a blacklist that endured for years, ruining many careers. More destructive in the long run, however, was the fact that production costs, fueled by rising wages, rose steadily in the postwar era, while earnings, instead of matching the increase, fell substantially. By 1950, studio profits were down to about $31 million, only about 25 percent of what they had been in 1946, while those of exhibitors had slipped about 60 percent, to $111 million. The problem of profitability can be seen most easily in box-office gross earnings, which did decline, but only by a bit more than 20 percent, from $1.692 to $1.376 billion. A substantial difficulty was that the income from foreign markets did not meet expectations: American films were denied access to Iron Curtain countries; revenues were frozen or protectionist policies prevailed in many nations; and Britain, the most profitable overseas venue for the Hollywood product, suffered severe and long-lasting financial decline.

Profitability was hurt by problems closer to home as well. In an era that witnessed assertive union movements and recruitment, with organized labor achieving a position of unassailable power, commercial filmmaking suffered from the destructive competition between the International Alliance of Theatrical and Stage Employees (IATSE) and the Conference of Studio Unions. The eventual victory of IATSE led to substantially higher wages for skilled film workers—but this was a mixed blessing for those whose pay packets grew fatter because union employment in the industry fell precipitously, by more than 35 percent from 1946 to 1949, as financial crises forced the studios to cut production and eliminate many contract workers.

Such developments by themselves would have posed a serious enough threat to the industry. Even more disastrous, however, was the fact that Hollywood, through large-scale social changes it could not have anticipated and could hardly adjust to quickly, began to lose much of its traditional main market: the middle-class urbanites who lived close to downtown and neighborhood theatres. A severe inner-city housing shortage hit the country in the immediate postwar years, and the unexpected solution to this problem was quickly found in relatively cheap suburban developments. The building boom beyond city limits was largely fueled by the government loan programs mandated in the G.I. Bill of Rights. This new housing was far from movie theatres and frequently off public-transportation routes, making a trip back into town for the movies inconvenient and expensive.

A Runaway Audience

To make matters worse, a substitute for moviegoing that was home-centered and free of charge soon appeared in the form of television, whose broadcast service coverage and popularity expanded rapidly. By the end of the 1950s, most families in the country owned a set to which they tuned in many hours a week. With the establishment of a consumer economy devoted to the production of "durables" and the emergence of entertainment alternatives from boating to bowling, Hollywood's traditional customers increasingly chose to spend their discretionary income on washing machines, vacation travel, and do-it-yourself projects. Thousands of theatres around the country closed their doors forever, since it appeared that Americans after forty years had finally wearied of their fascination with the motion pictures. By 1963, when the decline flattened out, America had actually lost nearly half the houses that had been operating in the banner year of 1946.

There was a further, though less surprising, blow that the five major studios (Paramount, Warners, RKO, MGM, and Twentieth-Century Fox) had to endure. For three decades, an essential element of the majors' success had been vertical integration, in which production, distribution, and first-run theatrical exhibition were organized under one corporate umbrella. Such economic muscle allowed them to corner screen time and hence rental returns through coercive practices: blind bidding (the securing of exhibition contracts before a trade show of the film) and block booking (the offering of desired films for exhibition only when included in a group of less desirable ones). After decades of legal wrangling over the legality of such business arrangements, the U.S. Supreme Court ruled in 1947, in a case involving Paramount, that blind bidding, block booking, and even vertical integration itself were all illegal.

The Move to the Package-Unit System

In what precipitated a radical reorganization of the business, the major studios were all subsequently forced to sign consent decrees that led to their divestiture of theatrical holdings. Without a secure market for their product, the studios could no longer function as "factories" turning out hundreds of films annually by assembly-line methods. A gradual switch was made to one-off production (the so-called package-unit system), involving, as film historian Janet Staiger puts it, "a short-term film-by-film arrangement" designed to serve a market no longer controlled by group rentals. As she relates, producers now were required "to differentiate the product on the basis of its innovations, its story, its stars, and its director."[60] In particular, the competition from television encouraged the industry to outclass the fuzzy black-and-white images and tinny audio then available on the tube. Filmmakers also set out to provide the kinds of serious, gritty dramas that programmers of the new medium could not broadcast because they were answerable to sponsors, tightly controlled by Federal Communications Commission (FCC) protocols, and forced to operate on very limited production budgets.

The pressing need for innovation and differentiation led filmmakers to emphasize two dissimilar products. More traditional, in both story and their dependence on glamorous spectacle, were the blockbuster Technicolor films in one of the new wide-screen formats. These were filled with stars and featured elaborate, expensive production values (especially the proverbial "cast of thousands"), and they did not neglect the big-screen appeal of the scantily clad human body. The decade's run of biblical and historical epics, including *The Ten Commandments* (1956), *Quo Vadis* (1951), and *Demetrius and the Gladiators* (1954), treated religious subjects and fully exploited the titillation possibilities of period costumes. The "other" of the blockbuster was the small-budget black-and-white film, whose appeal was hardly what is now termed "eye candy," but rather an affecting, dramatic, stylish engagement with serious, arty, perhaps even adult themes.

An amazing, trend-setting success in the immediate postwar era was achieved by film noir and the social-problem drama, closely connected and sometimes indistinguishable genres that featured not only the thematization of discontents with American society but also the complex intersection of opposed stylistic regimes: expressionism and documentary realism, a mixture to be found in the Broadway theatre of the period as well. Arthur Miller's *All My Sons*, for example, was readily assimilated to the noir series when adapted for the screen in 1948, and the flashback narrative of *The Glass Menagerie* had been a staple of the noir tradition since Billy Wilder's *Double Indemnity* in 1944. The advent of film noir and the social-problem film was certainly unexpected. As if in anticipation of the economic and legal troubles soon to descend upon the industry, "American movie screens suddenly darkened," as Thomas Schatz puts it, yet this was a good omen, for it meant the opening of commercial exhibition to products other than those offering simple wish fulfillment.[61]

Such a maturation of audience tastes coincided with the coming of a new generation of directors to Hollywood, and the darkened screens that resulted could be explained, Schatz opines, as a kind of psychic release from "five years of enforced optimism and prosocial posturing."[62] But who were Hollywood's actual customers? Some proponents of the well-established forms of Hollywood entertainment in the late 1940s, most prominently reviewer Manny Farber, complained that Hollywood had moved away from the "old flowing naturalistic film" to embrace "mannerist works" that betrayed the accepted function of the corner theatre, that "simple mansion of leisure-time art."[63] Hollywood, so the conclusion ran, had chased away its traditional paying customers by catering to the arty set. Gilbert Seldes, in contrast, concluded that the film industry had continued to disappoint its more educated and discerning patrons through the marketing of lowest-common-denominator narratives; the current trend in further "juvenilization" was only making matters worse.[64] Empirical research into audience composition of the period, summarized by Leo A. Handel's famous book, *Hollywood Looks at Its Audience* (1950), points toward the opposite conclusion. Among other trends, Handel found that in the postwar era, people higher up the socio-economic scale tended to attend the cinema more than those lower down and that the regularity of movie attendance increased with the level of education.[65] These findings suggest (though they are not exhaustive enough to prove) that postwar movie attendance declined more among the less well-off and those of limited education. If true, this goes a long way toward explaining the increasing popularity of various forms of the small film during the era, which intellectuals, including influential film critics such as Bosley Crowther, found particularly appealing.

The Small Adult Film

In any case, the small films of the postwar years were often showcases not only for topical themes, but also for excellent acting, literate scripts, and interesting forms of visual stylization. It is hardly an accident that Elia

Kazan's second Hollywood feature, *Boomerang!* (1947), was a noirish re-creation of a sensational crime committed in suburban Connecticut; the murderer, though revealed to the spectator, is never brought to justice, thus denying the narrative the most conventional form of closure. *Boomerang!* melds visual styles, developing effective contrasts between its real location exteriors (shot in Stamford, where the crime had occurred) and claustrophobic studio interiors, carefully dressed and lit in the noir chiaroscuro style to suggest entrapment and enigma. For Bosley Crowther, the result was a "drama of rare clarity and punch" that "eschewed the stale patterns and photography of conventional cops-and-courtroom films."[66]

Many of the acclaimed films of the period were similar small pictures, notably Academy Award winners *On the Waterfront* (1954) and *Marty* (1955). Also filmed in black-and-white and featuring literate scripts, topical subject matter, and unconventional endings were the winners for best picture in 1950 (*All About Eve*) and 1953 (*From Here to Eternity*). Otherwise, spectacular productions garnered industry accolades in the era: musicals (*An American in Paris* in 1951, *Gigi* in 1958), a star-packed travelogue (*Around the World in 80 Days* in 1956), an outsized showbiz melodrama (*The Greatest Show on Earth* in 1952), the big-budget remake of a sentimental Christian epic (*Ben-Hur* in 1959), and a thematically unconventional but epic-sized war adventure (*The Bridge on the River Kwai* in 1957).

The two film types most characteristic of 1950s production were innovative in different ways: the blockbusters offered seldom-before-seen forms of visual spectacle, while the small films attracted audiences by their departure from Hollywood conventions. The small films tended to be more realistic, less connected to genre, less dependent on bankable stars, relatively uninvested in the confirmation of conventional pieties, and more open to theatricality in every sense. Unlike the new forms of spectacle quickly popularized by the blockbuster, such unconventionality required more effort from the spectator. The small adult films of the fifties were more difficult to understand than the standard studio product of previous decades. They elicited complex, often contradictory and provocative forms of emotion. Not surprisingly, the small films also stretched the boundaries of theme, challenging the Victorian aesthetic and moral principles of the production code and frequently forcing industry censors into lengthy and difficult negotiations about what would be permitted and what would have to be excluded.

If, by the middle 1950s, television had largely assumed Hollywood's former function as the provider of audiovisual entertainment for a mass public of all ages and tastes, then the film industry was surely wise to colonize a new area of production, one whose popularity with an important segment of the film-going public had been well established by the exhibition of European art films, especially those of the Italian neorealist tradition, such as Roberto Rossellini's *Open City* (1945) and then Vittorio de Sica's *The Bicycle Thief*, which was recognized by the Motion Picture Academy as best foreign picture in 1949. Though film exhibition in general suffered greatly from the end of the 1940s through the end of the 1960s, theatres that specialized in screening art films, mostly from Europe, became much more numerous and profitable at this time, yet another indication that there was indeed a loyal audience of educated adults who would pay to see a "film," even if they despised Hollywood "movies" as the mindless products of a hopelessly compromised culture industry.

Art Films and the "Sensational"

Because European films were not produced under the watchful eye of the PCA, they often transgressed the official standards the industry had established, especially with regard to the representation of sexual themes. Joseph Breen was inclined to view all European art films as smut, and he was at least half right. By the end of the 1950s, the term "art film" had become, if only in part, a euphemism for soft-core pornography. Normally, all films, including imports, needed PCA approval in order to secure exhibition contracts. The importers of *The Bicycle Thief* were refused a certificate because Breen objected to two scenes that they refused to excise: one in which a young boy pauses by the side of a wall, apparently to relieve himself; and another in which a thief is pursued into a bordello whose inhabitants, though fully clothed and otherwise decent, are obviously assembled to engage in the world's oldest profession. Though the film had been recognized internationally as an artistic triumph (and championed by the American liberal establishment), the PCA stuck by its decision. Even the Legion of Decency did not go along with the PCA, declining to issue the film a "C" (for condemned) rating. The lesson for film producers was obvious. There was a market for films that were "artistic" and violated or at least tested hitherto generally accepted limitations on the representation of sexual themes. The PCA had lost a good deal of clout in its defense of what now began to seem unnecessarily old-fashioned or prudish standards. Exhibitors could do well even with controversial films that lacked PCA approval, but only if these could be justified as either artistic or sensational.

Conditions within the industry, in other words, were right for the production of American films modeled on European prototypes, small productions that would be intellectually satisfying, artistic, and perhaps even titillating. This was a trend to which Williams's groundbreaking plays could make an important contribution if they were adapted in the proper fashion. Purchasing the film rights to *The Glass Menagerie*, independent producer Charles K. Feldman, in cooperation with producer Jerry Wald at Warner Bros., intended to do just that, preserving the distinctive, innovative quality of Williams's poetic yet drab domestic drama, but making it into a film that the general public, with tastes quite distinct from those of Broadway audiences, would enjoy and appreciate. If later Williams texts were to become part of Hollywood's successful strategy of making small adult pictures in the 1950s, providing shock and sensation in carefully calibrated doses, *Menagerie* was easily assimilated to an already existing and much more conservative series: the woman's picture, or melodrama.

CHAPTER TWO

The Glass Menagerie: A Different Kind of Woman's Picture

The Suds of Soap Opera

In the late 1940s, after achieving unprecedented success on the Broadway stage, Tennessee Williams was beginning a second career: adapting his own properties for the screen. At the same time, the Hollywood studios were promoting and developing, as Mary Ann Doane has described them, "films that [were] in some sense the 'possession' of women, [whose] terms of address [were] dictated by the anticipated presence of the female spectator."[1] The rise to prominence at this time of what the industry called "the woman's picture" (or sometimes, more derogatively, the "weepie") was conditioned by a number of factors. Most importantly, perhaps, was a group of female stars with strong box-office appeal. It was therefore natural that Hollywood sought out vehicles for the exhibition of these attractive personae. Jane Wyman, who was to star in *The Glass Menagerie*, was one prominent example, having won an Academy Award the year before for her tour de force performance in the title role of *Johnny Belinda* (1948) as a deaf mute who triumphs over her handicap and the abuse she unjustly suffers from others.

The decade had also witnessed the increasing popularity of the woman's novel, that is, books written by a woman, featuring a female protagonist, and anticipating a female reader. These bestsellers revealed the existence of a readership eager for an imaginative experience suited to their sensibilities. Much the same can be said of Broadway, which featured the continuing rise to prominence of female playwright Lillian Hellman. Her several commercial and critical successes, including *The Children's*

Hour (1934), *The Little Foxes* (1939), and *Watch on the Rhine* (1942), all featured female main characters, something of a departure from customary Broadway practice. With its close ties to the commercial stage and popular literature, Hollywood quickly attempted to capitalize on adaptations of these books and plays (or to produce scripts modeled on them). Both the producer (Jerry Wald) and the director (Irving Rapper) who were assigned by Jack Warner to the *Menagerie* project had achieved their greatest success with the adapted woman's picture, to which, so the studio hoped, this new property would make an important and financially remunerative contribution. As he began the difficult process of transferring Williams's spectacular stage success to the screen, Wald drew on his recent experience with two critically acclaimed women's pictures that were also prestige adaptations: *Mildred Pierce* (1945, directed by Michael Curtiz and based on a bestseller by James M. Cain), which garnered five Academy Award nominations and one win; and *Johnny Belinda* (directed by Jean Negulesco and adapted from the play by Elmer Harris), which fared even better, earning nine nominations and one win. Rapper had also been greatly praised for his work in the genre, having directed several notable productions, including *The Corn Is Green* (1945, based on the famed play by Emlyn Williams), also a woman's picture of sorts, which received two Academy Award nominations, as well as the very popular *The Voice of the Turtle* (1948, adapted from the stage version by playwright John Van Druten).

In the classic Hollywood film generally, romantic fulfillment (the "constitution of the couple," as academic theory terms it) customarily provides the plot with the requisite sense of an ending by reaffirming conventional wisdom about personal destiny. The woman's picture of the forties and fifties was less concerned with the discovery of true love and the projection of untroubled marital happiness, and more interested in a contradictory movement that, while allowing the woman a certain independence (a "room of her own," so to speak), also forced her to accept a conventional place within the social order. In purchasing the screen rights to *The Glass Menagerie*, the executives at Warner Bros. knew that they were not only acquiring a property that, because of its successful stage run, was "presold" and hence likely to please filmgoers. Knowing full well that the play was by no means a conventional romance, they also calculated that with Irving Rapper and Jerry Wald in charge of the project, Williams's play could be transformed into a woman's picture featuring a bittersweet romance.

The film, it was hoped, would please audiences familiar with the form, who would also be intrigued by the unconventional complexity of Williams's characters and the pathos they inspire thanks to his poetic dialogue; the playwright's artful design of a plot that seems to resolve everything, yet solves nothing, even with a more conventionally happy ending (as negotiated by the filmmakers, in place of his bleaker original conclusion). Here was a property with very familiar contours that, bearing the cachet of prestigious awards and a successful Broadway run, offered something different to lure back the much-desired adult audiences. The publicity campaign designed by the studio reflects these two somewhat contradictory appeals. On the one hand, the various poster designs call attention to the film's quality and pedigree. These bear the legend: "The year's most real, most-to-be-honored Warner Bros. Picture . . . from the Tennessee Williams play that won the Critics Prize for 'Best of the Year.'" On the other hand, a more obvious pitch was made to those interested in a conventional woman's picture. In much larger letters beside a shot of Jim (Kirk Douglas) caressing Laura's face, prospective viewers are rather deceptively told: "This is the story of a Gentleman caller and a young girl who suddenly found what she thought was love . . . the trouble was . . . she believed him!"[2]

Williams's play was suited to adaptation as a woman's picture precisely because of the extensive rewriting that had readied it for stage production. As was characteristic of his method of working, Williams considerably altered his original conception. This reshaping produced a riveting yet low-key drama that focuses on a young woman's difficult path to maturity, in this case Laura's growing away from dependence on her mother and brother. Here, too, an unassertive young girl finds (after shame and disappointment) a self-possession that belies destructive mythologies of success. Did the changes made to the play's original form reflect in some way the lessons about Hollywood dramaturgy and generic conventions Williams surely absorbed both during his brief employment at MGM and as an eager filmgoer during several decades of viewing the commercial product? This is an intriguing though probably unanswerable question, even if there is some evidence that the playwright was aware of the customary themes and structures of the woman's picture and planned, at least at an early stage in shaping the material, to have his drama conform to them.

In any event, the similarities between the Williams property and the woman's picture did not go unnoticed by those involved in the adaptation project. Having explored the trials and triumphs of a similar character the year before in *Johnny Belinda*, producer Jerry Wald was eager to repeat that success with the same star and a similar property, this time working with a director who was the acknowledged master of the genre. The connection between the two projects was very much on his mind. Wald declared to coproducer Charles K. Feldman during the later stages of preproduction, "In readying the final script, it is my deep conviction that we should indicate more of Laura with camera shots. I don't think she needs more to say, because as in BELINDA, the story is about her. The clashes between Tom and Amanda are over Laura. The concern of the mother is for Laura."[3] The playwright might not have agreed with the film's producer. Wald's reductive reading of the play arguably unbalances a carefully constructed focus not only on Laura's struggle to grow up, but also on Tom's ambivalent urge for disconnection and on Amanda's profound disappointment with her children. But the playwright could hardly have disputed that the "problem" with Laura's quest for happiness is at the center of the family's difficulties. The plain fact is that *The Glass Menagerie* was eminently suited to being adapted as a woman's picture.

"A Most Awful Travesty"

And yet Williams, as he reworked the first version of the play, likely did not do so with eventual film adaptation uppermost in mind, even though *The Glass Menagerie* had been originally written as a screenplay. However, the kind of intimate drama Williams made out of his experiences as a young adult coping with difficult family circumstances would play well not only on the stage but also on the screen. But that was because, with its emphasis on dialogue and interior scenes, the Hollywood film of the era could readily adapt stage properties that today might be considered hopelessly set-bound. More importantly, the dramatic confrontations of family life were a staple of both Broadway and Hollywood, and this familiarity eased the passage of such works from stage to screen. Among other productions of this kind, William Wyler's successful mounting of Lillian Hellman's *The Little Foxes* (1941) provided Wald and Rapper with a convenient model if they needed one. In any event, Williams's fascination with female characters often had deep autobiographical roots (as was the case with *The Glass Menagerie*) and reflected as well his obsession with the marginalized and oppressed and with those seeking some accommodation with the destructive vagaries of sexual desire.

As his dramatic oeuvre demonstrates, Williams discovered that these struggles could in some ways be more readily represented in the trials of women, the imagining of whom suited his talents and sensitivities. In *The Glass Menagerie*, characteristically, ties of love and dependence bind Laura more tightly than Tom to their mother. Her emotional weakness precludes any desire to leave the confines of the family home and find her way in the world. Like his father, who has (with no apparent regrets) deserted the family before the action of the play begins, Tom eventually finds it possible to abandon his mother and sister. Being women of the time, they are imagined as remaining behind, with an as yet merely generic "gentleman caller" the only hope for Laura's eventual deliverance.

Though the woman's picture does not eschew representing the contradictory, entrapping roles that society assigns to women, the stock in trade of the genre was a strong sense of uplift produced by the triumph of the protagonist over difficult circumstances and personal inadequacies. At the end of the play, Laura and Amanda must accept the bitter though sometimes salvational truth that comes from profound disappointment. Shy and awkward, Laura fails to make a success at business school. She is then let down by the gentleman caller, whose apparent interest, though it builds her self-confidence, is revealed as irrevocably ephemeral. Although Laura is thereby delivered from both her mother's destructive illusions about romance and her own protective but imprisoning world of make-believe, Wald, Rapper, and Peter Berneis, the screenwriter, it soon became apparent, disagreed strongly about how Laura was to be imagined triumphing over her fears and her mother's overprotectiveness. Was there some way that Laura could both succeed and fail, losing Jim and yet, having gained confidence from that abortive relationship, expect that there would someday come a gentleman caller who would remain? Williams, albeit reluctantly, concurred in principle with this transformation in the play's tone, but he would resist vigorously the particular plans for Laura's passage to maturity that his erstwhile collaborators had in mind.

The play's transference to the screen, as a result, was hardly smooth and trouble-free. Despite his quite evident awareness that properties such as his would require substantial changes before being made into Hollywood films, Williams was convinced that *The Glass Menagerie*, having pleased Broadway audiences and critics alike, could and *should* be adapted fairly faithfully. Producer Charles K. Feldman, after all, had enthused that the play was a "masterpiece" as originally written and had arranged to purchase the property for the then considerable amount of $150,000, plus a share of the net profits. Williams might also have hoped that the changing artistic atmosphere in postwar Hollywood would be more accepting of his play's claims to greater realism as well as its disavowal of comforting clichés. In this period, as historians Leonard J. Leff and Jerold L. Simmons suggest, "Stanley Kramer, Elia Kazan, and others wanted to move the American screen toward a new maturity. They advocated a more honest, less cautious cinema, one built on a simple, unaffected realism and aimed at providing the audience with food for thought."[4] Interestingly, Jerry Wald, in discussing his production of *Flamingo Road* (released in 1949) with director Michael Curtiz, advocated "a blast of realism, which we hope will make people sit up in their complacency."[5] But *Flamingo Road*, Robert Wilder's racy, even sordid chronicle of southern politics (much like Robert Penn Warren's *All the King's Men*, which found its way to the screen the same year), offered a much more accustomed kind of realism (that is, "blasting" with sensationalism) than Williams's intimate drama, with its sensitive but uncompromising portrayal of the drab discontents of ordinary family life. In any case, Rapper and Wald, after years of experience in the industry, had formed a somewhat different conception of what would please filmgoers than Williams, who, like most authors, was understandably most interested in bringing his play as intact as possible to a wider audience. Ironically, in large measure, the judgment of the producer and the director was confirmed by what experienced industry critics had to say about the completed film.

The collaboration between the playwright and the filmmakers was marked by a turbulence that nearly came to a disastrous conclusion when Williams, while the film was in the early stages of release, expressed his dissatisfaction in too public a fashion, providing a juicy story for showbiz journalists and making it necessary for the studio to engineer an elaborate public relations campaign to save the film's prospects for box-office success. By turns unconcerned about the progress made on the script and desperately fearful that the resulting production would dishonor both him and his play, Williams was a somewhat unreliable participant in the adaptation process. But he was eager to have the film succeed and willing for the most part to craft or approve necessary changes.

Williams could scarcely hide his disappointment with the result, judging it very harshly at the time as "the most awful travesty of the play I've ever seen."[6] His view matched that of influential *New York Times* critic Bosley Crowther, who suggested that Rapper's film "comes perilously close to sheer buffoonery in some of the most fragile scenes," with the result that there is a "painful diffusion of the play's obvious poignancy." The "fatal weakness" of the film, Crowther maintained, was the script's misguided conception of Amanda, who becomes a "farcically exaggerated shrew," an effect exacerbated by Gertrude Lawrence's rather inept performance.[7] Other critics, in contrast, found much to praise. *Newsweek*, for example, observed that "exceptional acting and the direction of Irving Rapper have succeeded in giving the Jerry Wald–Charles K. Feldman production a soundness that is not very often achieved in film rewrites of such delicate stage material."[8]

An examination of the production history confirms this judgment of "soundness." Whether thought a failure or success on other grounds (particularly the acting of the principals), the film was meticulously made from a script Williams either approved or wrote himself. If *The Glass Menagerie* proved less successful at the box office than all concerned had hoped, this was likely in large part because much of what (from a Hollywood point of view) was original and striking about Williams's moving drama had been retained, not callously discarded.

The St. Louis Play

Williams had been tinkering for several years with fictional treatments of his life at home as a young man (what he sometimes called his "St. Louis play") when in 1943 a family crisis prompted him to devote his full attention to finishing both screen and stage treatments of what would become *The Glass Menagerie*. As mentioned earlier, shortly before Williams arrived in Hollywood to begin his short career at MGM, his sister Rose, who is the "Laura" of his play, underwent a prefrontal lobotomy in an attempt to ameliorate her worsening schizophrenia. As his letters and journals suggest, Williams quickly became absorbed in the painful story of his sister's slow decline, neglecting his official duties at the studio in order to complete a project he hoped would exorcise painful memories and, more positively, further his reputation. Unsure whether to shape the material for stage or screen production, he famously submitted a film treatment to the executives at MGM, who quickly declined the offer, as we noted in the previous chapter.[9] What Williams showed them was likely identical, or at least very similar, to a surviving nineteen-page typescript entitled "Provisional Film Story Treatment of *The Gentleman Caller*." This synopsis is remarkable for its dissimilarities to both the finished play and eventual film adaptation, as a brief summary below will make clear.

Opening shots of the Mississippi Delta provide the setting for young Tom's narrative of the family past, particularly the courtship of his mother and father. In a long flashback, gentleman callers "come in droves" on Sunday afternoons to his mother's home in Blue Mountain, Mississippi, in the years before America's entry into World War I, hoping to gain the young beauty's affection. Amanda is particularly intrigued by Tom Wingfield, who, according to local gossip, "drinks" and "has a *fast* reputation." Tom becomes a pariah in the eyes of his family when he falls down and breaks a whiskey bottle in his pocket during an altercation with one of Amanda's other admirers. Amanda decides to marry him anyway, and the couple elopes to Memphis, where they set up housekeeping in the Peabody Hotel. There she eventually gives birth to her daughter, Laura, and becomes pregnant again (with Tom Jr.) just before her husband enlists in the army and is shipped off to France. Wingfield returns home a war hero but, shell-shocked, becomes an idler as the family moves back to Blue Mountain. No one knows where he gets the money to buy a new car until it is revealed that he is operating a still and selling moonshine. The still explodes, however, and Wingfield's "Negro" helper is killed in the blast. The Wingfields find themselves pursued by bloodhounds, which traumatizes the sensitive Laura. After Tom is arrested, the family leaves Blue Mountain in disgrace.

The second part of the story is set in St. Louis, where the Wingfields are living in a "little three-room apartment." Laura, still troubled, has become mute, but is cured one day when her father plays a recording of "Dardanella" on a Victrola he has brought home to comfort her. Amanda berates Wingfield for spending too much on the record player, and he leaves, never to return. Deserted and forced to work, Amanda gets a job cooking in a high school cafeteria to support her children, who grow up under her very watchful eyes. At this point, the story narrows its focus to the introverted Laura, who is obsessed with her record player and collection of glass animals. To supplement his mother's meager income, young Tom has resigned himself to working at a local warehouse. In the conclusion, as Williams puts it, "the dominant theme . . . is the introduction of a gentleman caller, building up to it and the climactic night of his arrival." The sequence of events in this third section is more or less what the Broadway play script dramatizes. Tellingly, however, the original conclusion does not emphasize Tom's devastating desertion of his mother and sister, but rather Amanda's resolve to carry on. She is said in the end to be "making dauntless plans for the future," determined to find Laura a gentleman caller.

The synopsis ends with this note: "For film version ending, see following page." There Williams indicates that "this would deviate from the stage version or rather carry it further to a lighter and more cheerful conclusion." Williams offers two possibilities, both of which are more or less conventional happy endings. In the first, Amanda and Laura return to idyllic Blue Mountain, where the daughter comforts her aging mother. The other is more interesting, especially in light of the pressure Williams eventually felt from Wald, Rapper, and Berneis to provide Laura with a second gentleman caller at the film's end. In this version, Laura is in fact besieged by a host of gentlemen callers in the same way that Amanda was as a young girl. To give the plot even more closure, Williams suggests that "perhaps even—at the very end—the first Tom Wingfield or the second returns from his travels." He stresses the happiness of this proposed dénouement, observing that "at any rate—Amanda has finally found serenity and rest. What she searched for in the faces of gentleman callers."[10]

That this script differs so radically from the stage play (and hence from the screen version) would not surprise Williams scholars. The playwright's personal papers reveal that all his works, major and minor, went through many developmental drafts, sometimes changing almost unrecognizably in the process. The important point is this: the early synopsis reveals that Williams understood that the stage version of his "St. Louis play" would likely require significant alterations when transferred to the screen. But he would be less willing to compromise after he wisely excised the overly melodramatic and implausible events (such as the exploding still and subsequent bloodhound pursuit); thus the resulting intimate, more compressed drama achieved an unexpected commercial and critical success.

Filming a Fragile Property

The Glass Menagerie, produced by the mercurial Eddie Dowling, opened in Chicago the day after Christmas 1944; reviews of the play were almost uniformly positive, but ticket sales were weak, suggesting that the young playwright had produced a work of quality that simply outdistanced audience taste in the midwestern metropolis. Going against professional wisdom, Dowling kept the production alive, and it gradually gained momentum; his confidence was rewarded when the play moved to New York City the following March, there to enjoy a run of 563 performances, finally closing August 3, 1946. It had been one of the American commercial theater's most successful first runs, and not surprisingly, the Hollywood studios, including MGM, began showing interest in securing the film rights while the play was still in production. Already in March 1945, just before the move to New York, Williams's agent Audrey Wood responded to such an inquiry from MGM's Sidney Fleisher, informing him that negotiations would have to wait until the Broadway run came to an end. According to Wood, an article in the *Herald Tribune* had suggested that Williams and his agent were entertaining bids for the property: "After the publication of this nearly every movie company called because they were concerned that the picture rights were being disposed of."[11] Some years later, independent producer Charles K. Feldman, who emerged as the successful purchaser of those rights, would tell Williams that initial interest in the property had been slight: "I thought *Menagerie* a great, great play. Most studio heads, however, never thought *Menagerie* could be made into a popular and successful picture and as you know there was very little bidding."[12] But the evidence, including Feldman's own correspondence, suggests otherwise.

Warner Bros., it turns out, was eager to partner with Feldman on the proposed production (a common arrangement at the time, since the major studios, enduring hard times, sought to share the risk on this kind of project). In May 1948, Jerry Wald wrote Warner's Steve Trilling an urgent interoffice memo, exhorting him to take whatever measures were necessary to finalize the deal. Wald had learned that Samuel Goldwyn was trying desperately to move on the project. MGM, it was rumored, wanted to feature Teresa Wright and Dana Andrews as Laura and Jim, repeating their spectacular romantic pairing in one of Goldwyn's biggest critical and popular successes, William Wyler's *The Best Years of Our Lives* (1946). Wald exhorted Trilling: "I can't urge you strongly enough to do everything you can to get this property for us. It will make an important, artistic, and tremendous box-office film for us."[13]

Once Feldman and Warner Bros. finalized the financial arrangements, an attempt, only partly successful, was made to secure big-name talent for the leads from among contract personnel and available "independents." Jane Wyman's participation was quickly confirmed, but casting Amanda proved more difficult. In January 1949, Jack Warner wrote Feldman to suggest Tallulah Bankhead, but the studio head later soured

Jim O'Connor (Kirk Douglas) enthralls Laura Wingfield (Jane Wyman) in a scene from The Glass Menagerie. *Photo courtesy of The Historic New Orleans Collection.*

on the prospect, reportedly because of the actress's severe drinking problem. Later that year, Wald discussed other choices with Feldman for what promised to be in some ways a juicy but also quite problematic role. Though she is obsessed with dreams of her glamorous youth, Amanda is aging and worn out, living vicariously through her children. Tellingly, Laurette Taylor, obviously suffering the ravaging effects of severe alcoholism, had achieved a great success in the Broadway production, and she died soon after the play finished its initial run. Though her last notable screen appearance, which was in a supporting role, had been nearly fifteen years earlier in Alexander Korda's spectacular biopic *Rembrandt* (1936), stage actress Gertrude Lawrence, perhaps faute de mieux, got the part. Hers would not have been a familiar name to many moviegoing regulars, even though the producers were willing to hold up production in order to secure her participation and even engaged a voice coach to help perfect her southern accent. With Jane Wyman and Kirk Douglas as the only firmly established names in the cast, Wald's production would be at a distinct disadvantage in this regard. Warner Bros. would have to sell the story more than the performers.[14]

A Tale of Two Writers

The producers were also disappointed, at least initially, with the arrangements that were made for producing the screenplay. His disastrous experience at MGM had left a sour taste, and Williams, though requested, refused to do the work himself, in part because it would have likely necessitated his decamping to the coast. The relatively inexperienced Peter Berneis (this was his first major assignment) was hired to undertake the project.[15] Williams approved the young man's initial efforts (probably developed in a relatively short treatment), but Rapper and the producers were eager for more input from the playwright. Rapper even flew to Rome to see Williams and hold an extended conference with him on a number of key points. For example, the playwright was brought to understand that the narrative should be opened up beyond the confines of the Wingfield apartment. Consequently, he not only agreed to the inclusion of scenes set in other locations, notably the warehouse episode, but even helped write the dialogue. Influenced by the current fashion for shooting not only in plausibly authentic settings but even in the precise places where the action is supposed to occur, the filmmakers agreed to travel to St. Louis, where they might stage, with Jane Wyman, Laura's trips to the city's art museum, the famed Jewel Box exhibition hall, and other noteworthy locales, such as a commercial building where she attends the typing class. All these changes were agreed to in Rome, and a detailed memorandum was written up for distribution to all parties.[16] Notably absent from the conference, however, was Peter Berneis.

Berneis and Williams, in fact, were never encouraged to cooperate by the producers. As a result, they worked on the project in parallel and occasionally at cross-purposes. After the Rome conference, Williams remained somewhat remote from the process until a fuller version of Berneis's script was sent for his review and comment, rather late in preproduction. Distressed, the playwright raised serious objections in a long letter to Wald and Feldman. The script now seemed "a good deal less agreeable," Williams wrote, and in fact contained "grave and important faults" that could be eliminated only if all concerned remained faithful to the play as originally conceived:

> The *basic* qualities of the play *must* be kept if it is going to come off successfully on the screen. The qualities that made it a successful play were primarily its true and fresh observation, its dignity, its poetry and pathos, for it had no great dramatic situations as a play

nor has it any as a screen-play, and the plot was slight and simple as it still is and must remain. Now I feel that a great deal of the truth, dignity, poetry and pathos of this play has gone out of the window.

Williams, perhaps somewhat patronizingly, proclaimed his commitment to having his play transferred to what he recognized was a more popular art form, affirming that he was genuinely interested in having a successful yet faithful film made of his award-winning drama:

> I think you all know that I have no reputation for being "arty" or "highbrow," and that, on the contrary, I am known to be an exponent of sound and popular theatre which gets across to a large public, and nothing that I object to or suggest is going to hazard the popular acceptance of the screen-offering, but, on the contrary, is especially intended to preserve and increase that appeal.[17]

His argument is that the film can succeed only if it follows the play closely.[18] The story, he declares, already has demonstrated its popular appeal. Such a view, however, pays scant attention to technical differences between the two art forms. The theatre, to make the obvious point, is more suited to an intimate, static drama whose plot is "slight and simple," as Williams concedes. And one might question the statement that any Broadway play "gets across to a large public" in the same sense that Hollywood films of the era needed to in order to achieve financial success. The two "publics," especially in the late 1940s, were distinct and hardly comparable in their tastes. In any event, Williams's comments ignore his more practical perception, made at an earlier stage in the evolution of the material, that a film version would require a different kind of ending. Now faced with an otherwise unacceptable alternative, however, the playwright would eventually provide one that was not too different in effect from those proposed in his initial synopsis years before.

Not without good reason, Williams particularly faulted "all the sequences involving 'the other young man,' the one who teaches art to children and who provides 'the happy ending.' I object to him, first of all, because he is such a Sunday school sissy of a character with no reality or interest. . . . He is a most palpable device." What Berneis intended was that, having failed to attract Jim, Laura would end the film firmly attached to a second gentleman caller who, his character merely sketched in the closing sequence, would indeed seem a tacked-on happy ending.

Such a false and illogical conclusion, the playwright suggests, would produce an "effect of bathos and sentimentality." The power of the original, in Williams's view, lay precisely in its rejection of the conventional wisdom about human happiness enshrined in that particular form of Hollywood romance proposed by Berneis.

Women's pictures conventionally conclude with the heroine failing to couple, at least in the usual sense, with the man she loves. Such a failure, as we have argued, is the paradoxical sign of her success in achieving a certain independence from expected, assigned gender roles. Though likely not conscious he was doing so, Williams was reflecting the core theme of the Hollywood genre when he wrote the producers: "The heartening message in the character of Laura is to those thousands of girls who do *not* find the dream-boy who sets everything magically right in the final sequence." Despite its not being a clichéd romantic truth, the lesson Laura learns could, as Williams recognized, be more aptly tailored to the expectations of a film audience if the original shaping of the material was left mostly intact: "This heartening message can be underscored and played up in the screen version without violating the essential meaning and truth of the play." By this time in his career, Williams had learned that the best way to avoid the problems that an unsympathetic screenwriter might create would be through direct involvement in the project. He declared to Wald and Feldman that he was "happy to undertake these revisions, provided I have the assurance from you, the producers, that it is equally your will to make this a really true and dignified picture."[19]

The producers eagerly accepted his offer of assistance, persuading Williams to make the trek to Hollywood in order to complete the job. Before he departed for the coast, however, Williams wrote back to say that he had arrived at a solution to the problem of the film's ending:

> I think it is all right to suggest the possibility of "someone else coming." And that "someone else," remaining as insubstantial as an approaching shadow in the alley which appears in conjunction with the narrative line "the long delayed but always expected something that we live for"—it strikes me as constituting a sufficiently hopeful possibility for the future, symbolically and even literally, which is about as much as the essential character of the story will admit without violation. As you say we will undoubtedly find a solution in California, but it would add to my peace of mind if you could assure

me now that there has been no reversion of opinion in favor of the old type of ending.[20]

Williams was obviously worried that Berneis's views would carry the day.

A Sense of an Ending?

In the original, Laura and Amanda are equally dismayed that, in the daughter's oft-quoted words, "the long delayed but always expected something that we live for" is little more than a deceptive mirage, an unreasonable hope that the drabness, injustice, and helplessness of a difficult existence might be magically transformed by a male suitor. In the new ending penned by Williams once he arrived in California, however, Laura speaks the same line, not with resignation and hard-won knowingness, but with optimism and hope. Already, in Berneis's cinematic reshaping, Laura had been taken out of the house to the aptly named Paradise Ballroom across the way, where for the first time in her life she danced with a handsome young man, discovering that her lameness need not keep her from companionship and pleasure. The confident and ebullient Jim had shown her that fears could be overcome, that the self-imposed limits of an enclosed existence might be transcended. Life's possibilities are thus suddenly thrown open to Laura, and, in Williams's revision of the scene, she now expects that "long-delayed" but as yet unidentified gentleman caller who, unlike Jim, might indeed cherish her.

Had the film ended as the playwright now designed, Laura's romantic deliverance would have been appropriately hazy, remaining, as it were, in the subjunctive, as a possibility that now, more optimistically, is not foreclosed. The final image would have been the dream that Laura can now rightly entertain and claim as her own, a dream that is supported by the hopes of the now-distant Tom, whose memories and thoughts of the family, as the reversion to the frame story at this point recalls, constitute this subjective narrative. The film would also have been more "heartening" because, after Williams's changes, Tom's closeness to his sister and their reciprocal affection would have been emphasized, once again in a significant alteration of tone from the original stage version.

As Williams was to tell Rapper after the film wrapped, however, he was not truly engaged in this process of rewriting: "My own difficulty is that in my heart the ending as it exists in the play was the artistically inevitable ending."[21] In any event, Williams felt his new conclusion provided sufficient uplift, but Wald and Rapper did not agree. Without informing Williams, they arranged for Peter Berneis to make the second gentleman caller less a vague, imagined figure, as the screenwriter had in fact previously advocated. As preproduction plans were being finalized, Wald wrote Feldman: "In the new version of the script, which I'm enclosing, we have tagged on the ending for Laura and Tom that was written by Peter Berneis. Williams knows nothing about this. His ending is used in *addition* to the scene between Laura and Tom. . . . My over-all feeling is that this last version is a tremendous improvement over the other scripts. The role of Tom has been built up considerably, Laura's role has much more sympathy piled on it, and the addition of the new scene with the Gentleman Caller is well worth all the effort that you went to in getting Williams out here."[22] The most salient studio change from the original script involved a shot with an indeterminate male figure walking up the alleyway toward Laura—obviously the new Gentleman Caller, one delivering more promises and permanence than that afforded by Jim O'Connor. In the theatre, script changes must pass muster with the playwright. As Williams was to discover with his first film project, however, the writer was not king in Hollywood, in spite of the special treatment he had received earlier in the project, when Rapper flew to Rome just to hold script consultations with him. Writers (including award-winning authors of original properties) were in the final analysis employees, subordinate to the producers, who made final judgments about scripts and were not required, or even expected, to consult about proposed additions or deletions.

In a statement reflecting the conventions of Hollywood melodrama in general and those of the woman's picture in particular, Berneis declared that the film should make manifest how "a bitter experience can prepare a soul for a new life." Thus, he envisioned a fundamental change for Laura, not simply an emergent optimism about and openness to new experience. In his view, the narrative should deliver Laura fully to happiness: "If we don't show that Laura changes after the unicorn is broken, if we don't have a basis in her for an eventual open heart and open mind to receive a man, then we might as well stick to Williams's original tragedy."

Perhaps somewhat intimidated by the famous playwright (who by this time had written two successful, critically acclaimed Broadway dramas), Berneis hastily opined that Williams's own personal experience with his troubled sister had made him "prejudiced" against the screenwriter's supposedly useful ideas. Williams, Berneis wrote, "will not accept that Laura can break out of her shell as I think I motivated it fully in my ending."[23] With his talk of "motivation," a concept drawn directly from industry manuals, the screenwriter showed his commitment to tried-and-true formulae, a far cry from the notion of "artistic inevitability" invoked by Williams. In fact, a similar, rather simpleminded paint-by-numbers approach is evident in many of the screenwriter's comments about the film script. In regard to the scene of Laura in the museum, for example, he wonders "what it contributes besides showing that Laura has a feeling for beauty." As if that were not in fact everything.

Berneis's original intention, it appears, was to go beyond the successful "failure" formula of the woman's picture, the double movement of the plot that endorses the heroine's isolation and yet celebrates her mature integration into society. He told Feldman that *The Glass Menagerie* should end with Laura married to her new beau, not just imagined as closer to her brother. The young screenwriter was not one to mince words: "I think it is wrong to team up two cripples in the end. It may be poetic but it does not make use of what to me is inherent in the play, namely, Laura's breaking through her shell at the time the unicorn is broken." His view was that the filmmakers could either "satisfy Williams at all costs" or find the "*best* solution," meaning his own, of course, to the various problems the script presented, especially the ending. But the compromise ending would stand as Wald and Feldman had agreed. If Williams did not see his vision for the film make it to the screen intact, neither did Berneis. Hollywood filmmaking of the period, after all, was an eminently collaborative art or, perhaps more particularly in this case, a complex tapestry of contradictory or even competitive creative contributions.

Strenuous Objection

Williams would make one more urgent plea for changes after the picture was finished and just beginning its release. At this stage, reediting (and of course significant deletion) was still possible, even if reshoots were likely not. In a letter to Jack Warner, Jerry Wald, and Charles Feldman, the playwright praised them for "this picture, which you have made with great care."[24] His kind words for the cast were similarly effusive, perhaps suspiciously so (it was, after all, too late for perceived inadequacies of this kind to be addressed): "I can't remember a picture in which four important actors give such uniformly fine performances and each so perfectly suited to the part." Just a few changes, Williams goes on to say, would significantly improve the film and, an added bonus, shorten it by about ten minutes. He made sure that the filmmakers had no doubts about his opinion: "The things that I object to most strenuously and very strenuously indeed, are certain changes that were made in the script after I left Hollywood and which came to me as a complete and very distressing surprise when I first heard them from the screen."

As Williams pointed out, Amanda's distorted memory of a glorious debut, during which she received "twenty-three proposals in a single evening," is now dramatized rather than simply reported, in a scene that accomplishes little more than affording Gertrude Lawrence a chance to shed her drabness and enjoy some glamorized screen time. Williams thought the sudden change of dramatic tone unsettling; it was "like a bit of an MGM musical suddenly thrown into the middle of the picture." Berneis had also, in Williams's view, overwritten Tom's "drunk scene," which had been added to the original stage play only when director Eddie Dowling insisted upon a humorous interlude that would also motivate the effusive confession of sentiment and frustrations from an otherwise rather taciturn Tom. But to Williams the further emphasis Berneis gave the scene does "untold damage to the dignity of the picture as a whole, the bathos and corny philosophizing are so incongruous to the spirit of the film as a whole." A similarly untoward shift of tone, he thought, marks Laura's final scene with Tom, in which, as she follows him into the alley, there is an "exchange of some more lines from the cornball department."

But, predictably, it was the more substantial presence of the second gentleman caller that most troubled the playwright. Williams had imagined him as disembodied, as, at most, "the sound of approaching footsteps." Making this wish-fulfillment figure more substantial, he thought, destroyed that "quality of poetic mystery and beauty which the picture badly needs in its final moments. Now we not only see him very plainly, his whole figure, but he is also provided with a full name, *Richard Henderson*. This little touch is going to stand out like a sore thumb." If this sequence were not reedited, including the removal of all shots of the figure appearing in the alley, it would, Williams predicted, "gravely affect your critical reception . . . among that relatively small, but terribly important, segment of the film public to which such things make a difference."

As soon as he received the letter, Jack Warner telegraphed Williams to say that he was "in complete sympathy with everything you said." The studio head had attended a Hollywood preview that same day: "Reaction to picture by everyone present was wonderful. Individual scenes thru-out entire production were applauded many many times. Irrespective of reception picture received tonight am making substantially all cuts you requested." Warner also pledged to "fight with Breen office" to preserve Tom's final monologue as written, and he was confident that the play-wright would agree the "complete integrity of [the] play has been pre-served."[25] The somewhat overzealous head of the PCA had thought that Tom's evident affection for Laura suggested "incest" and that the broth-er's closing expression of love and closeness should be eliminated or toned down. Warners was able to lobby Joseph Breen successfully for no such changes, but this lead-footed suggestion of impropriety had incensed the incredulous playwright.[26]

Rapper and the film's producers agreed to make most of the changes Williams suggested (particularly in the "drunk scene"). As Charles Feld-man telegrammed Audrey Wood, just a few days after receiving Wil-liams's letter: "Will you please tell Ten we have made practically all changes including diffusion of retrospect scenes, eliminations Ten desires in Kennedy drunk sequence, insertion of sister narration at finish, etc."[27] The key word here is "practically." On the matter of the ending, which was of course the most important point to the playwright, the filmmak-ers (and studio head) remained unmoved. They knew they had made a picture with an important difference, but they were unwilling to make less than inevitable Laura's prospects for appropriate accommodation within the social order.

"Life Isn't a Bust Just Because You've Got a Bum Gam"

When the film was released, the main trade publications were not slow to recognize its departure from accepted norms. These reactions are worth an extended look. The reviewer for the *Hollywood Reporter* called *The Glass Menagerie* "unusual and off-beat celluloid entertainment." Here was a story dramatized with "utmost honesty," and therefore requiring "more of the onlooker than the usual motion picture."[28] In its usual Run-yonesque style, *Variety* offered a similar opinion: "Co-producers Jerry Wald and Charles K. Feldman saw to it that current market demands for something different would be fulfilled by off casting four top thesps in the main roles. . . . Possibly the most remarkable factor in this artsy but commercial entry is the subtle restraint employed to register Laura's awakening under the Gentleman Caller's bumpkin cajolery to the fact that life isn't a bust just because you've got a bum gam."[29] One wonders what Williams, if he read this notice, thought about such a summary, whose accuracy, in a certain vulgarian sense, cannot be challenged.

Reflecting the cautious attitudes of theatre owners toward the unaccustomed, *Motion Picture Daily*'s William Weaver was a bit more uncertain than his counterparts at the *Herald* and *Variety* about whether the Williams-Rapper film would do good business. In a sense, his judgment was confirmed when the film did not live up to the high expectations producers Wald and Feldman held out for it; perhaps the "difference" of *The Glass Menagerie* did not prove attractive or appealing enough for a broad audience. Of course, Williams's "quiet play," as he called it, lacks the sex and violence, the raw emotions that certainly boosted the popularity of the film version of *Streetcar*. Weaver has this to say:

> Audiences pre-conditioned by specialized promotion to experience the un-ordinary may be relied upon to emerge from the theatre praising the fine performances and superb direction they have witnessed, but the casual dropper-in, shopping for a story in the form to which he is accustomed, stands a fairly good chance of winding up wondering whether the last reel or two may not have been omitted by a careless projectionist. Unless advance preparation is assiduously applied, this unorthodox ending, artistically sound though it be, could prove an exhibition hazard of substantial proportions. On the other hand, it could turn out to be the mainspring of word-of-mouth publicity counting for much in the box office fortunes of an attraction no one can charge with hugging the line of least resistance.[30]

Challenging the Conventions

As this trade reviewer implies, Williams's unique, "unordinary" material was leading to something new within the film industry. What exactly is different about this film? Weaver offers a short and very provocative list: "The Williams presentation of his characters and their problems are [*sic*] a departure from screen norms on several counts. He approaches a drab situation, scans it interestedly and in great detail but altogether detachedly, and leaves it substantially unchanged. He finds humor as well as pathos in the situation, giving somewhat more attention to the former than to the latter, and he neither glorifies nor condemns any of the participants in the proceedings witnessed." Weaver opined that the production, with its refusal of a conventional ending, "may strike many as an unfinished symphony."

Certainly, as Weaver points out, *The Glass Menagerie* goes against well-established conventions of Hollywood filmmaking, the accepted dos and don'ts that by 1950 had come to define what scholars now term "the classic studio text." Like the European art film, which was just starting to achieve a substantial presence on the American exhibition scene, the Williams-Rapper production is character- rather than plot-centered. Throughout, it resists the temptation to glamorize, one of the most potent lures Hollywood filmmaking used to attract customers. With Laura, for example, we see no sudden transformation from wallflower to pinup girl as she prepares for her next gentleman caller. Perhaps more importantly, the film does not tell the viewer whom to "root" for or against. It neither condemns nor idealizes any of the characters, all of whom have their particular virtues and faults. Avoiding customary Hollywood melodrama, the film makes no attempt to arouse only those simple but intense emotions whose purging would provide what many expected from their celluloid entertainment every week. Such viewers indeed might think that a careless projectionist had omitted the final reel. As Williams suggested, however, he was interested in pathos, not bathos.

Though the adaptation process had turned it into more a woman's picture than the playwright wanted, Rapper's film respects the play's careful avoidance of excessive and insubstantial sentimentality, offering nothing like the much-mocked final scene of his *Now, Voyager*, in which Bette Davis and Paul Henreid, debarring themselves from further sexual consummation, seal their bargain of eternal, now celibate love with a sensuous exchange of lighted cigarettes. The playwright's modernism had infused a drab situation, never animated by exciting incident, with a poetry that reveals the depth of love and discontent that unites the characters, and that modernism, while altered in some fashion for a more general audience and accommodated to a quite different Hollywood aesthetic, had been substantially preserved. Interestingly, the reviewer for *Variety* correctly concluded that what he euphemistically terms "current market conditions" did make for something different, and that this is what Williams and the filmmakers had delivered. Another way of expressing this truth about the film would be to say that, as we have seen in some detail, neither Peter Berneis, the professional screenwriter, nor Tennessee Williams, the prize-winning playwright, prevailed completely in their struggle over the story's structure and meaning. It cannot be doubted, however, that the film belongs more to the playwright than to the young man who criticized his more successful counterpart for operating "in extremes, blacks and whites."[31] Berneis is right, of course, but we might better term Williams's style an expressionism that infuses the drama with a poetic (never forensic) realism. Such an artistic sensibility, it seems, was barely comprehensible to those concerned less with representing the deeper, universal truths of experience through a stylized heightening, and more with formal (one might say superficial) questions of motivation and plausibility, which were the ABCs of a different storytelling tradition.

The Temperamental Derelict Has His Say

Warners probably erred in inviting Williams to a private screening of *The Glass Menagerie* while the film was being previewed in selected theatres; only his lover, Frank Merlo, and his friend Marlon Brando, hardly representative of the regular film-going audience, accompanied him. As a result (or so he would later inform Jack Warner, Feldman, and Wald after two more viewings, one in a local theatre), "in the cold light of a private screening, my reactions were unavoidably more critical than those that you had expressed to me in your wires."[32] But this concession is offered in the very letter that otherwise pleads for substantial changes in the final-release cut, only some of which were made, as we have seen. In any case, before Williams changed his mind somewhat, he was not reticent about expressing his considerable disappointment and dismay rather publicly while in New York, a city anxious to record and publicize every musing of Broadway's latest enfant terrible. Word of Williams's discontentment quickly got back to the film's producers on the West Coast, prompting an angry telegram from Jack Warner to Mort Blumenstock, the Warners' representative in New York: "Am surprised at Tennessee. He should be thankful that anybody would have brought this property to the screen and made as an important picture out of it as has been done. In long version went over as good as any picture we have made. These temperamental derelicts who get rich on the efforts of others after they create something should offer prayers of thanks instead of finding fault with producers, studios, directors, cameramen. Am not interested in any form shape or manner with his being indignant."[33]

In an attempt to avoid negative publicity that might kill the picture, Charles Feldman wrote Audrey Wood a succession of frantic letters, since the crisis was continuing despite the playwright's avowal to the producers that he was substantially pleased with the final result. Toward the end of May 1950, when the revised film was in national release, Feldman urged Wood somehow to silence Williams: "I can't impress upon you too much the wisdom of cautioning Tennessee not to make any adverse comments to anyone."[34] But this was closing the barn door after the horse had already trotted out. Williams's disappointment with the film had come to the notice of influential gossip columnist Dorothy Kilgallen (with whom he later became fast friends), and Kilgallen rushed the sensational item into print.

The filmmakers decided that only a strong statement from Williams endorsing the film could save them from financial disaster. Feldman pleaded with Audrey Wood: "You must get him to write something very complimentary about the picture which we can use."[35] A statement was prepared for Williams to sign that was to be distributed to the *New York Times*, the *Chicago Tribune*, and other major dailies. It read: "Of course the stage and motion picture are distinct media. As the author of 'The Glass Menagerie' I wholeheartedly feel that with the added scope the screen gives the material it surpasses the play. The characters are precisely as I wrote them. Can any author ask more?"[36] Warner Bros. arranged for a newsreel team to film a happy Williams landing in Los Angeles after a flight from LaGuardia. Of course, it was in reality more a penitential journey, since Williams was obediently showing the world that he was at the beck and call of the studio.

Though he made this required personal appearance, Williams refused to sign the prepared studio statement, writing his own instead after arriving at the Hotel Bel-Air:

> Of course the stage and the screen are two different media and it is always a mistake to try to transfer a story directly from one to the other without some adaptation. This mistake was not made in "The Glass Menagerie." The greater latitude of the screen has been effectively put to use. In the picture there is less darkness and more light, more humor and less tragedy, but I feel that the essential spirit of the original, whatever it had of human warmth and understanding, has not been lost in transition. It is one of those rare films that depict the world we really live in as inhabited by the people we really are, and it also contains four of the greatest star performances ever assembled in a single film.[37]

Interestingly, the playwright had much more to say about *The Glass Menagerie* than the newspaper equivalent of a "sound bite" required of him by the filmmakers. In his own inimitable style, Williams accomplished both these assigned tasks, but he went further, giving voice to a much more plausible view of Rapper's adaptation. He acknowledged that the screen version differs from the play, since there is now "less darkness and more light," and argued that despite this change of tone, the "essential spirit of the original" was preserved. The film, he observed, retained whatever the play had offered of "human warmth and understanding." Even more, Rapper's production was one of those "rare films" that accurately represent "the world we really live in as inhabited by the people we really are." Designed for public consumption and calculated to maintain his growing reputation as the purveyor of a different kind of drama, this statement must be viewed with some skepticism, especially in view of the playwright's more consistently derogatory comments about the film over the years. We should not forget, however, that the reviewer for the *Hollywood Reporter*, an astute observer of the industry scene, had praised the film's "utmost honesty." In a generous mood, even if under studio pressure, the playwright had done much the same.

CHAPTER THREE

Bending the Code I

A Streetcar Named Desire

A Wholesome Screen

In the course of the 1920s, Hollywood solidified its national and international position as an important cultural institution through the production of elaborate, emotionally affecting feature-length narratives. To capture the attention of the American and world publics, these films attempted, perhaps above all else, to tell the stories of modern life, even at times in period pieces and costume dramas. The studios released for the entertainment of millions across the country and around the world a continuing flow of drama whose discontents also played out in the "private" lives of those inhabiting the film colony, who were put on constant display by the press and by studio publicity departments.[1] When, in 1922, Hollywood's profitable business relationship with its eager consumers was threatened by scandal, both on- and offscreen, the major film producers empowered Will Hays, a very Waspish, Republican former postmaster general, to manage the industry's public relations. By the end of the twenties, Hays had been charged in particular with ensuring (or, perhaps better, restoring) the conventional morality of the films that Hollywood released. He would remain in his role as the first president of the Motion Picture Association of America until 1945.

As agitation for reform from religious groups grew ever more intense, the studios agreed to abide by the Production Code, written not by industry insiders but by Father Daniel J. Lord, a noted Catholic scholar and academic.[2] Hays failed, at least in the eyes of many, to enforce the code properly, and increasing pressure from Catholic clergy and laity led to the establishment of the Production Code Administration. The responsibility to act as the industry's moral guardian then fell to journalist Joseph Breen, a conservative Catholic who steadfastly oversaw the operation of the Production Code Administration from 1934 to 1954. If the code, put into force only by the genteel suasion of Hays, had not served to reform Hollywood, then an office created by the studios themselves and staffed by a tough-minded director with the power (albeit limited because he was an industry employee) to have offending material removed or rewritten might do the trick—or at least Hollywood's outraged opponents thought so.

The PCA worked (though informally) in conjunction with the Legion of Decency, a Catholic lay organization that had been formed during the 1930s as part of the National Catholic Office for Motion Pictures to pressure the film industry to create and maintain what the legion hoped would be a wholesome screen. The legion's purpose was not to ensure that Hollywood films were morally acceptable as such. Instead, it was to safeguard the spiritual welfare of the Catholic laity. Despite their different aims, these two institutions, one outside and the other inside the film industry, managed to work together, despite occasional conflict and disagreement. Their joint purpose, according to liberal critics, was to prevent social reality from ever playing out on the nation's screens.

For roughly three and a half decades (1930–1968), the PCA and the Legion of Decency, often seen as monolithic institutions of social conservatism, were forces to be reckoned with in American film culture. Whatever its official stance, the PCA, as Leonard J. Leff has demonstrated, showed itself to be committed to more complicated, even contradictory aims. A good deal of sexually and politically controversial material was permitted in the films overseen by Breen, who, according to Leff's interesting formulation, operated as "the agent of ambivalence." In this role, Breen helped "producers translate the 'dangerous' into the ambiguous and, on occasion, even into the subversive."[3] Under Breen's ambivalent stewardship (he was, after all, an employee of the film industry), the advent of more adult-oriented filmmaking in the 1950s meant, among other developments, that the screen adaptations fashioned from the works of Tennessee Williams would offer filmgoers much more than comfortable illusions. This was a development that was somewhat resisted, but also enabled by Breen, who "never quite bridged the chasm that opened up between the 1930 Production Code and the postwar American moral code."[4] Tennessee Williams, we might say, made the chasm that much wider, forcing Breen into a series of compromises. As film historian James M. Skinner has remarked, "of all the playwrights to raise censorial ire at this time, none did so more frequently and vexatiously than Tennessee Williams."[5] Yet it is even more significant, perhaps, that no screen version of a Williams work was ever killed by PCA displeasure.

A Different Aesthetic

Williams's texts promoted a form of realism that, by probing deeply into the spiritual and moral experiences of his characters, has often, and with much justice, been termed "poetic." But by refusing to honor conventional taboos, the playwright's realism was also provocative in ways that filmmakers thought might be appealing to Hollywood's erstwhile customers, who seemed less and less interested in going to the movies. Perhaps a new kind of film might lure them back to theatres. Though displaying an obvious indebtedness to long-standing traditions of theatrical realism (especially of the Chekhovian variety), the typical Williams play, in the apt formulation of David Savran, is "adamantly plural, strewn with multivalent symbols, and reluctant to provide the interpreter with a master perspective or code."[6] To be sure, such modernist elements (or perhaps even postmodernist, as some have argued) were modified by the adaptation process, but they were hardly eliminated from the Hollywood versions, which were, as a result, substantially different from the ordinary studio release. What attracted progressive and innovative filmmakers of the postwar era to these Williams texts, however, was not only their evident literariness; it was also that, in their stage runs, they had succeeded, as Savran puts it, in "undermining conventionalized presentations of sexuality and gender," helping reenergize a commercial theatre hitherto becalmed in intellectual and formal doldrums.

If such cultural reframing proved shocking for the Broadway theatre, which had long catered to an educated, culturally liberal northeastern clientele, it was even more so for the Hollywood cinema, which had become by careful design Middle American and conservative in its representations and themes. This was an artistic tradition that directors such as Elia Kazan, John Huston, Joseph L. Mankiewicz, Daniel Mann, Joseph Losey, Richard Brooks, and Sidney Lumet, among the very best that postwar Hollywood produced, were committed to transforming—with the help of Tennessee Williams, among other leading contemporary novelists and playwrights. By the end of the 1960s, this distinguished directorial company had all directed films based on Williams's Broadway productions. His plays were desirable properties precisely because they were problematic in the sense of inviting conflict with the established formal and intellectual traditions of commercial filmmaking, especially as these had been enshrined in the Production Code.

If the adaptation process, perhaps inevitably, modified what Williams had written for the stage, the code itself was reshaped by the encounter, bending to accommodate an innovative form of dramatic presentation. Hollywood would never be the same after the release of *A Streetcar Named Desire*. Breen's assistant Geoffrey Shurlock said of this film that "for the first time we were confronted with a picture that was obviously not family entertainment. . . . *Streetcar* broke the barrier . . . Tennessee Williams was something new to movies. . . . The stage got a shock from Tennessee Williams. We got twice the shock. Now we know that a good deal of what we decide in censoring movies is not morality but taste. It began with *Streetcar*."[7]

A brief synopsis is in order to frame the following crucial scene from the film version. Blanche DuBois is an affected, aging southern belle who is the victim of her family's dissolution, which results in the loss of their plantation home and property. Her questionable sexual conduct has cost her a teaching position and forced her to leave Mississippi, so she seeks shelter and comfort in New Orleans with her sister Stella and her husband Stanley Kowalski. At the Kowalski apartment she meets Mitch, Stanley's poker buddy, with whom she finds affinity and hopes to develop a romance. Their relationship reaches a crisis when Mitch learns of Blanche's scandalous sexual past from her suspicious and jealous brother-in-law. Mitch accuses her of only pretending to be a proper young woman, one worthy of respectful courtship. Angry at having been deceived, he forces Blanche out of the shadows she seeks and into the harsh glare of a naked bulb so that he can take a good look at her. Blanche, ever the coquette, confesses to preferring "magic" to realism but complies, and Mitch sees at once that she is no blushing maiden. Unmasked, Blanche herself then surprisingly becomes the source of deeper and more disturbing revelations, providing Mitch with a sketch of her sordid personal history. Mitch admits that he will never again consider her virtuous enough to share as his wife a household with his mother. At the same time, Blanche's unladylike candor arouses him. Hitherto somewhat timid, Mitch is suddenly inspired to force himself on

A sweating Stanley Kowalski (Marlon Brando) as the object of Blanche DuBois's (Vivien Leigh) gaze in A Streetcar Named Desire. *Photo courtesy of The Historic New Orleans Collection.*

her. Now, so it seems to him, Blanche is fair game for a brusque seduction, her reticence about lovemaking no longer to be believed or acceded to. But she angrily pushes the clumsy would-be rake away and chases him out of the apartment, refuting his view that she has forfeited any right to refuse him.

The scene is unconventional in its penetrating examination of the sexual life and its discontents, but also classically Aristotelian in its balanced, affecting development of a dynamically effective encounter that is first verbal and then provocatively physical. Here Williams both reproduces, even as he deconstructs, the sexist gender politics of the postwar era, especially the notion of the "double standard" and its cruel typing of women as either respectable or "easy." But his realism is also poetic, much more than a naturalistic mirror held up to contemporary American society. In this scene, Williams gives expression to the play's central theme: the complex conflict between a not-so-innocent innocence, on the one hand, and, on the other, a self-righteous brutishness, bordering on misogyny and given emotional force by disappointment and humiliation.

Dramatically speaking, Blanche's encounter with Mitch (a structural and thematic reverberation of her one with Stanley, when he rapes her) exemplifies the interest that Williams shows, here and elsewhere in his more realistic plays, in shining a penetrating light on his characters, who are thereby forced to yield up inner truths: in this case, not only the transgressive, irresistible power of sexual appetite that Blanche admits to, but also her refusal to abandon the maidenly, schoolmarmish pose that Mitch has just exposed as a lie.

A Cinematic Modernism

And yet, as David Savran suggests, Williams's anguished outsiders like Blanche never fully reveal themselves, for they are also "decentered and dispossessed, stumbling through a dramatic structure that is similarly decentered and unstable."[8] Acting out Williams's rejection of stability and fixity, Blanche approaches but avoids self-understanding (the so-called recognition of classical dramatic structure), descending by play's end into an insanity, likely irrevocable, that is nothing less than a fully dissociative break, or inability to distinguish reality from the fantasies she spins to protect herself from unpleasant facts. To put this another way, Blanche is never "determined" by the plot, never rides a trajectory of development from introduction through crisis to a resolution that confirms for us (and, more importantly, for her) "who she is," as studio screenwriting manuals advised, reflecting the popular conventions of the well-made play and its dependence on unified, consistent characters. Committed to a modernist view of personality as contradictory, ever shifting, and finally unknowable, Williams has Blanche evade the choice between magic (pretense, the understandable urge toward refinement and respectability) and realism (the reformative acknowledgment that she is more like Stanley—and Stella—than she can bring herself to admit, as attracted as they are by, and as driven to experience, what Stanley, in a poetic moment, terms the "colored lights" of sexual indulgence).

Throughout the early decades of Hollywood's operation, its characters, by way of contrast, had reflected, as film historians David Bordwell, Janet Staiger, and Kristin Thompson have shown, the literary traditions of an earlier era:

Models for structuring a film came, not from drama and fiction in general, but specifically from the late nineteenth-century norms of these forms—norms which lingered on in popular stories, plays, and novels of this century. The cinema tended to avoid the more innovative, contemporary forms of drama and fiction. Strindberg, Ibsen, and Shaw, or Hardy, Conrad, and James figure very little in the formation of the classical cinema, either as narrative models or as direct sources for scenarios.[9]

But by the early 1950s, that aesthetic was losing its appeal for an audience that was increasingly sophisticated and well educated. At least this was one lesson that Hollywood drew from the unremitting box office crisis that gripped it beginning in 1947. Faced with a precipitous decline in weekly attendance throughout the 1950s, filmmakers sought out new materials and developed different models of what film art might be, exploiting the modernist literature and drama it had hitherto largely either ignored or transformed beyond recognition. *Streetcar* and other Williams plays forced Hollywood to accommodate a radically different kind of literary property. But as in any time of profound cultural change, the film industry's traditional aesthetic (and the PCA, its moral guardian) did not give ground without a struggle, at least until popular taste had shifted decisively toward a liberalization of moral attitudes.

Father Harold C. Gardiner, an influential American Catholic literary critic of the postwar era and an ardent supporter of both the PCA and the legion, argued that the most important thematic requirement of literature (and by extension, visual fiction) is not only that sin must be recognized for what it is, but also that it "may never be so described as to become a proximate temptation to sin for a normally well-balanced reader."[10] The wholesome screen promoted by the legion called for the kind of moralistic aesthetic that Father Gardiner found in the "great Western literary tradition" that he traces back to Aristotle's *Poetics*. Art, he suggests, must find the "general idealized truth lurking . . . beneath and behind the concrete actions and situations," for this will constitute the "'oughtness' that is implicit in the act of imitation which is the essence of artistic creation."[11]

Like Williams's other works, however, *A Streetcar Named Desire* resists any reduction to some sort of "general idealized truth," including (and especially) the recognition of sin for what it is. The plot, though it unravels and concludes in some sense, produces no felt sense of "oughtness," indeed produces no felt sense of sin as such. *Streetcar*, as Williams himself strongly averred, does not lack for moral themes. But the playwright is not interested here in the triumph of virtue over vice, but rather in limning truths of the human condition, especially, but not only, how misunderstanding leads us to inflict pain because of our inability to see ourselves and others clearly.

Correct Standards of Life and the Question of Truth

Joseph Breen and his assistants reviewed the development of scripts and, subsequently, the rough cuts of films in production, engaging in a continuing dialogue with producers, directors, and writers about what needed to be either eliminated or added. Following this model, even though it was not officially part of the organization's function, the Legion of Decency also pursued contacts, often secret, with filmmakers, who were eager to avoid box-office damaging "C" or "B" ratings. Along with his colleagues, Breen advised moviemakers of the changes that needed to be made to bring films into conformity with the letter and spirit of the code, whose major provisions all enjoyed the support of Martin Quigley, the advisor to Father Lord. A prominent lay Catholic like Breen, Quigley was editor of the *Motion Picture Herald*, an important trade paper, as well as a key figure in the legion. Because the self-appointed and official task of the legion was to rate films rather than shape their production, Quigley and the various clergy who directed its operations were forced to confront issues that Breen could ignore or at least finesse.

Primary among these was the question of literary value. Although it could have adopted a simple thumbs-up or thumbs-down approach, rating films as either "A" (unobjectionable) or "C" (objectionable), the legion chose to include a third category. Some films, though not many, were also classified as "B" ("morally objectionable in part"). Most of the films so rated were literary adaptations. The ambiguous "B" category caused the legion no little difficulty. What were conscientious Catholics to do? Were such films to be avoided entirely? If not, what kind of occasion of sin did they present?

Distinguishing clearly between exploitation and film art is a crucial though perhaps ultimately insoluble problem because it rests on the crafting of workable definitions for such elusive and contested concepts as obscenity. After decades of evolving case law, archconservative Supreme Court justice John Marshall Harlan (the second Justice Harlan) wrote in 1971 that "the obscenity problem is almost intractable, and that its ultimate solution must be found in a renaissance of societal values."[12] It was such a "renaissance" that pundits like Quigley had begun advocating two decades earlier, hoping for some kind of gently encouraged retreat from the increasingly liberal sexual morality of modernism. In the continuing negotiation of difficulties encountered by filmmakers with the PCA, Quigley exercised great power behind the scenes, often acting as a liaison between the PCA, the various officials of the legion, and influential and concerned American bishops on the one hand; and anxious film producers on the other. Because the concerted Catholic pressure on the film industry received a good deal of criticism from liberal pundits and public intellectuals, Quigley undertook to write a popular defense of both the global reshaping of the Hollywood product and also the moral classification to which films, even after undergoing such intense scrutiny, were then subjected.

Quigley's *Decency in Motion Pictures* offers a reasoned and sophisticated argument supporting the need to promote "decency in public entertainment" through the "recognition of objective moral standards."[13] As an example of modern moral relativism and the misguided support of a forensic form of realism, Quigley quotes with evident distaste *New York Times* reviewer Brooks Atkinson, who proposes that the "function of art is not to promote a code or standards or to establish social ideals but to tell the truth about all the people who inhabit the world."[14] In contrast to the popular neo-Freudian notion that mental health depended on facing squarely the facts of life, an educational function to which literature and the cinema could certainly contribute, Quigley argues that "the function of art is to ennoble. Art is as much a servant and tool of civilization as science." We must acknowledge, he thinks, that "mankind is not lacking in knowledge of human frailties; its lack is only in capacity to avoid the exceedingly well-known frailties."[15]

Art, including the motion picture, does not therefore take as its purview the broadening of experience or the exposure of truths with which we might not be familiar. Its function instead is to point out the moral road down which we should travel, identifying without titillation the discontents of sinful behavior while persuasively advocating virtue. With its rejection of the modern enthusiasm for various forms of realism ("to tell everything about everybody," as Quigley somewhat snidely puts it), *Decency in Motion Pictures* promoted a moralistic view of motion-picture arts for the film reviewers employed by the legion, for whom the book was required reading.[16] It provided a simple, direct statement of a traditionalist aesthetic whose realism was limited to such representations as could be said to ennoble and whose general principles conservative Protestants and Jews as well as Catholics could readily endorse.

Father Gardiner sums up the philosophical basis of this aesthetic: "Certainly the Catholic position entertains the utmost respect for the power of truth . . . but that respect is not so naïve as to believe that here and now, in these circumstances, when the truth should already have won and its delayed victory imperils the common good, error must be left uncontrolled." Quoting Catholic theologian Yves Simon, Gardiner reminds the reader that "liberalism is an *optimistic naturalism*" because it stands unsteadily on what he considered the erroneous prior assumption that "the truth will always vanquish error if allowed to compete on an equal footing." Not all men, concludes Gardiner, are "equal in taste, inclination to virtue, powers of self-control."[17] Human beings therefore need "the pedagogy of coercion and restraint." Father Lord, Joseph Breen, and Martin Quigley quite evidently agreed. It was the business of the PCA, with the cooperation of the Legion of Decency, to furnish moviegoers with appropriate instruction and control.[18]

What is seldom recognized about the PCA and the legion is that their operations can scarcely be called "censorship" in the classic sense. Censorship involves the governmental proscribing of individual texts or styles; that is, the state-authorized removal from use or display of forbidden items and the admonition to artists *not to create* in a certain manner, as, for example, the banning during the Soviet era in Russia of key modernist texts such as James Joyce's *Ulysses* and the prohibition against composing in what were considered "formalist" styles. In the 1930s, alarmed by developments within the publishing business, American Catholic bishops set up what might perhaps be best described as a censorship advocacy group, one that used extralegal (but not illegal) pressure to gain its ends. The National Office (later Organization) for Decent Literature (NODL) attempted to have proscribed materials removed from sale, especially pulp magazines and comic books, but also those modernist novels considered morally dangerous, including works by such acclaimed authors as Ernest Hemingway, Edmund Wilson, and William Faulkner. It is hardly surprising that NODL attracted the condemnation of the American Civil Liberties Union (ACLU) and in short order found itself opposed by an organization named the National Book Committee, which, in its manifesto, *The Freedom to Read: Perspective and Program*, makes the case that "on philosophic grounds . . . censorship is unsound, impractical, and undesirable."[19] The publishing industry, convinced indeed that censorship was "undesirable," correctly saw NODL as a formidable opponent of their view of what liberties the press should enjoy.

Yet things were different in Hollywood, as one might expect in the case of an organization sponsored by the very industry whose activities it was charged with overseeing. Producers might be advised that a given property presented serious problems, but Breen and his staff were always prepared to take a subsequent look at reworked scripts of problematic material. The code itself implicitly reflected a commitment to the continual flow of textual production by offering a complex mixture of proscriptions (themes, plot structures, representations that would not be countenanced) and prescriptions (mostly very general, and not unambiguous, narrative formulas that filmmakers were required to follow closely). The code, in other words, promoted an aesthetic, one that was in no sense narrowly "Catholic" or opposed to the cinema as an art form, as is often commonly and erroneously thought. Its underlying assumption (later to be endorsed by Pope Pius XII in his influential 1957 encyclical *Miranda Prorsus* [On Entertainment Media]) was that the motion picture "builds character, develops right ideals, inculcates correct principles, and all this in attractive story form." This was a series of positive propositions about the cinema with which Aristotle himself might well have agreed.[20]

Streetcar on a New Set of Rails

The story of *Streetcar*'s film production has often been told as a heroic, if perhaps ultimately failed, attempt to transfer Williams's groundbreaking drama to the screen untransformed, but there is much more to this most complex of production histories, as we hope to indicate here.[21] In the traditional narrative of the film's making, there are several heroes: Williams himself, who persevered in securing the purchase of the screen rights to the play; independent producer Charles Feldman, who had faith in the commercial value of the property when others in Hollywood did not; and director Elia Kazan, who fought vigorously to have the core elements of the Pulitzer Prize–winning drama preserved in the screen version—only to fall victim, if only in part, to the legion and the spinelessly accommodating executives at Warner Bros. once his back was turned.

Arguably, *Streetcar* was as substantially unfaithful to the playwright's final Broadway text as some critics have complained. Such a judgment, however, hardly does justice to the remarkable, groundbreaking film that was made by Kazan, screenwriter Oscar Saul, and the cast as well as the other creative people involved in the production. *Streetcar* was hardly derailed but was rather directed along another, parallel track, continuing its important journey through American culture, this time for a mass audience that otherwise might never have been exposed to Williams's affecting and penetrating vision of modern life. From this point of view, an essential part of the play's journey is an account of the readings it received from Hollywood's producers and censors. These alternatives were mostly rejected for the final film version. However, they identify key elements in the struggle over meaning at the core of the adaptation process. To put it simply, the "something different" of *Streetcar* emerged relatively intact from the complex negotiations involved in its transference to the screen.

Although *Streetcar* won the Pulitzer Prize and achieved a success on Broadway such as few plays before and since have done, Hollywood filmmakers initially showed little interest in purchasing the screen rights. An exception was Paramount's William Wyler, a member of the Hollywood old guard famous for his adaptation of difficult literary and dramatic properties (including Lillian Hellman's *The Little Foxes* [1941] and Henry James's *Washington Square* [*The Heiress*, 1949]). *Streetcar*'s suitability for commercial production was explored for Wyler and the studio executives by Russell Holman, who called it "one of the best plays of the current decade . . . the finest and most mature work of America's foremost young playwright." More to the point, Holman also concluded that *Streetcar* "has the ingredients for a great motion picture of international appeal and it undoubtedly will be bought for pictures at a big price." He acknowledges that there are "important censorship problems," but thinks they can be "licked."[22] Both problems are connected to Blanche, whom Holman assumes is the play's main character (a view shared by screenwriter Oscar Saul and Elia Kazan).

First, the heroine's "emotional turning point," which is not dramatized but remembered, would have to be changed. In the play, it comes at a point some years distant in the past when the young Blanche discovers her homosexual husband in flagrante delicto and confronts him angrily and cruelly.[23] Ashamed, he kills himself in response, and Blanche is devastated by remorse, which provides a psychological explanation of sorts for her subsequent sexual misbehavior, or what many at the time termed her "nymphomania." If the husband were not indeed presented as a homosexual, the logic of the play, Holman admits, would still require some explanation of how Blanche became "a lady with a stained moral past," since, he appears to assume, her unconventional (at least for the pre–Erica Jong era) sexual appetite must be shown as pathological in some sense. He suggests, in order to avoid any reference to what the code called "sex perversion," that Blanche might still happen upon her husband in a compromising position, but this time with a woman. Resulting feelings of jealousy, inadequacy, and rage might then reasonably account for Blanche's subsequent proclivities.

The second problem, of course, was the rape, which, if retained, would make PCA approval unlikely, since the code explicitly proscribed any depiction of sexual assault. Interestingly, Holman also thought that the rape "louses up the character of Stanley, who should be in pictures a more sympathetic person than he is in the play." Making Stanley more sympathetic would ameliorate one problem that the play presented to a prospective screen adaptor, that it was "too tragic and down for the taste of screen audiences."[24] Holman wanted to add a scene at the end of the play in which Blanche, who faints before Stanley can rape her, is taken away to the hospital, there to suffer a mental breakdown. Stanley then tells Blanche's sister, Stella, that this is all for the best, effecting a reconciliation of sorts. The film would close with his comment to Stella that "people like her can't take care of themselves in the world today, and they can't take care of the world. That's up to people like you and me, and that new kid of ours. We've got a job to do for him, ourselves and the world."[25]

A protocol that guided PCA practice (though not enshrined in the code itself) was that if a story emphasized sinfulness or character failure, it should offer "compensating moral value," a gesture of some kind toward reformation or virtuous behavior, which might redeem a film from ethical bleakness: a finale generally unacceptable to both the code ("correct standards of life" must be shown) and industry practice, which required happy, upbeat endings. Following a similar kind of logic, Holman proposes something along the lines of "compensating emotional value," a mitigation of the "tragic and down" tone of the play. Blanche's emotional self-destruction would be balanced by the new father's optimism about the way in which his nuclear family might change the world in which Blanche "fails" to make a place. Blanche's problem, as Holman sees it, is more sociological than psychological, having little to do with "that streetcar named desire" that is the play's main theme. For him, the plantation myth Williams evokes (a once glorious and aristocratic South facing the unpleasant realities of the contemporary industrial world) is more central.[26] Blanche represents "a dying segment of American life confused in facing the rigors of modern existence by dreams of its past soft glories." This somewhat single-minded reading of Blanche ignores that way in which she finds herself trapped between a purportedly genteel familial past and a present that must acknowledge the less palatable truth, what she calls the "epic fornications" of the DuBois family (misdeeds among which we must surely include her own). As mentioned earlier, the family's cumulative wantonness has destroyed them all, bringing on the loss of the property and thus reducing Blanche to penury (and, at least in conventional terms, moral bankruptcy).[27] In Williams's rewriting of the plantation myth, the conventional aristocratic vices of lust and prodigality replace the "Lost Cause" as the source of the South's economic and spiritual decline. In so doing, the playwright gives voice to an important element in Hollywood's postwar representation of southern culture.

Holman's vision of the film to be made by Paramount would have given us, on the one hand, a Stanley who, saved by fate from taking out his anger on Blanche, becomes the improbable spokesman for cultural advancement and a bright, reformist American future; and, on the other hand, a Blanche who cannot face "the rigors of modern existence" because she is unable to acknowledge that the privileged world of her childhood has passed from the scene. Thematically, such a film would have ideally suited Hollywood's pronounced ideological preference for progressivism, its valuing of living demotic modernity over the dead aristocratic past. It would have been a far cry from what the playwright explained to Elia Kazan was the essence of his creation, a play that, instead of depicting our world as "we would wish it to be," (or, as Blanche says, "what ought to be") was marked by "authenticity or its fidelity to life."[28] Williams, so he says, did not have in mind reproducing our experience of others. Instead, he intended to show his characters "as we never *see* them in life but as they *are*." Such a perspective, the playwright argues, means that conventional moral judgment, with its investment in assigning blame and praise, is irrelevant: "It was not that one person was bad or good, one right or wrong but that all judged falsely concerning each other."[29] Only the "detached eye of art," as Williams terms it, makes possible such truthfulness, for the playwright has assumed, in his memorable phrase, the guise of a "ghost [who] sat over the affairs of men and made a true record of them."[30]

For this reason, Williams declares that "a play of this kind does not present a theme or score a point."[31] It follows instead a modernist aesthetic (a fidelity not to the surface, but to the underlying realities of life)

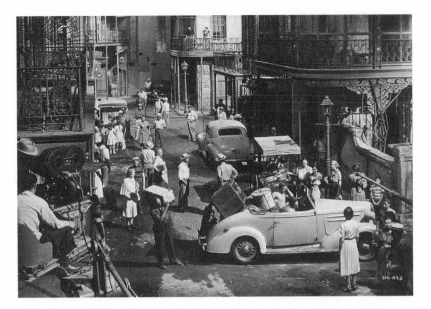

Stanley (Marlon Brando) sits in the convertible on the set of A Streetcar Named Desire. *Photo courtesy of The Historic New Orleans Collection.*

that could not contrast more strongly with that of Hollywood in the age of the PCA. The stories that the industry had made a fortune purveying always had both a pronounced moral rhetoric (distinguishing between sympathetic and unsympathetic characters) and also a "point" (a reaffirmation of conventional values in some sense). Such formal and thematic aims are evident in the sketch of the screen version that Russell Holman provided to William Wyler and the executives at Paramount.

Selling *Streetcar* to Hollywood: A Closer Look

Successful artists require forceful advocates, and Tennessee Williams was fortunate to have as his literary agent a strong-minded woman who held great faith in his abilities. Audrey Wood had held his hand through the numerous difficulties during the filming of *Menagerie*. But she was initially reluctant to reciprocate the playwright's considerable enthusiasm for a Hollywood version of *Streetcar*, fearing that the play's sexual themes would ensure that the property would be universally viewed as a risky project because of anticipated PCA opposition. Williams was less patient about initiating negotiations. Sensing that the opportune moment for moving ahead was slipping away, he tried to shop the property to producer Irene Selznick, writing in January 1949: "Are there any picture deals at all imminent or likely for *Streetcar*? I hope too much money is not being demanded: if I could get, say, an assured income (after taxes) of three or four hundred a month out of it I would be very happy and I think some deal could be made on that basis."[32] This kind of back-channel bargaining infuriated Wood. Throughout their relationship, she continually cautioned Williams against trying to work his own deals, reminding him that *he* was the playwright and *she* the one with proven experience in deal making. In any event, Selznick remained open to coproducing the project as long as her father's studio, MGM, would be involved. Wood, apparently eager to avoid some of the difficulties that had plagued the adaptation of *Menagerie*, wanted to shop the film rights of *Streetcar* only after securing a cast and director.[33]

Meanwhile, Paramount's inquiries to the PCA about the suitability of the play had yielded results that were by no means discouraging. The studio was told that three problem areas would have to be addressed satisfactorily for approval to be forthcoming: the reference to Blanche's husband as a "sex pervert," her unconventional sexual behavior, and the rape scene.[34] When Selznick in turn consulted the PCA (albeit informally), she was reminded by its director that "everything possible in a play is not possible in a film," because "the larger the audience, the lower the moral resistance to suggestion."[35] Eventually in 1949, Charles K. Feldman, who had produced *Menagerie* and developed a good working relationship with the playwright, purchased *Streetcar* for the considerable sum of $350,000. Williams was to be paid an additional $50,000 for assisting Oscar Saul with the screenplay. When Feldman, with the playwright's help, was able to sign on Elia Kazan as director for $175,000, Williams secured another formidable ally. Without Kazan's artistic talents and his tireless advocacy for the project, especially with a rather intractable Breen, the film version of *Streetcar* would undoubtedly have been substantially different from the groundbreaking production that it became.

The partnership between playwright and director was, of course, preceded by their collaboration on the stage play. Williams had found in Kazan a director sensitive to his psychologically complex characters. The director's notebooks, which offer extremely detailed character insights that have rarely been eclipsed by any critical analysis, demonstrate the thoroughness and depth of his preparation. For him, Blanche was less mentally disturbed and more (following the insight of Russell Holman) trapped in the wrong place and time. As he recorded in the notebooks, "The more I work on Blanche, the less insane she seems. She is caught in a fatal inner contradiction, but in another society, she would work. In Stanley's society, NO!" Stanley, in turn, is no simpleminded brute. In fact, he does not underestimate the threat that her arrival in New Orleans poses to him: "One of the important things for Stanley is that Blanche *would wreck his home*. Blanche is dangerous. She is destructive." Kazan remained faithful to Williams's view that "Blanche must finally have the understanding and compassion of the audience," while Stanley should not be developed as a "black-dyed villain."[36]

With a fine creative team under contract, Williams showed little concern about the PCA, believing that the picture could receive a seal without extensive cuts because recent Hollywood history had shown that even the code's most stringent prescriptions were sometimes ignored. As he wrote to Audrey Wood, "There is no real need to worry about censorship as rape has been handled in 'Johnny Belinda' and the slight alteration of a few lines ought to take care of the other angle."[37] If he thought that the "other angle" was Blanche's "immoral" behavior, Williams did not prove to be wrong, surprisingly enough. Kazan had prior occasion to study the code carefully. Even his social-problem film *Gentleman's Agreement* (1947), with its pious treatment of liberal politics and its general avoidance of subjects that were controversial (at least from the viewpoint of the PCA), had made Breen uneasy (and the legion distraught) because the main character's love interest is a divorced woman.[38] Tellingly, Kazan and producer Darryl F. Zanuck refused to compromise, and that aspect of Laura Z. Hobson's tale of suburban ethnic and class politics was transferred faithfully to the screen. Kazan knew that *Streetcar*, its notoriety already established by a lengthy and controversial Broadway run, might face hardened opposition from Breen and his aides unless substantial concessions were made. He considered for a time refusing either to submit the script to the PCA or to seek its final approval of the film in order to get a seal. Kazan eventually agreed that bypassing the PCA was impractical because it would affect box office too severely. It seems doubtful that Feldman, independent but by no means a maverick, would have taken on the project had Kazan not compromised on this point. Certainly Warner Bros. would otherwise have balked at both investing needed production funds and also handling distribution.

As plans for the film progressed, Kazan was also concerned about the preparation of the script. Believing that Williams would take charge of the writing, the director had concurred with the hiring of a competent professional (Oscar Saul) who, nonetheless, had no experience at all with adapting a major literary property. "I think Saul is perfect," Kazan wrote Williams, "the premise being that you'll in effect and finally really do the screen play."[39] Satisfied at first with what the professional screenwriter had produced, Williams was initially reluctant to do any work on the adaptation in spite of the financial arrangements that had been made. He wrote to Kazan in December 1949, stating, "I hope you will approve of my so-far passive role in the collaboration. I don't really believe in collaborations as I don't think that creative work is done in that way. For that reason I am deliberately standing aside for the time being and letting Oscar go full-steam ahead with his own ideas."[40] If Kazan was disappointed by this decision, there is no record of it; perhaps he simply let events take their predictable course. In any case, it proved to be a wise decision.

Williams's confidence in Saul dissipated quickly when he saw his property accommodated to Hollywood conventions in a manner he simply could not countenance. Just a month after adopting a "passive" role, he complained to Kazan: "Oscar Saul has also completed his script. I read half of it last night and became disheartened and thrust it under the bed. I had so hoped that I would not have to work at all on this *Streetcar* script but it appears that I shall have to take a hand in it."[41] Sensing Williams's fears that the film version of *Streetcar* might prove a public embarrassment, Kazan told him of his own misgivings and sent along a laundry list of changes that needed to be made. Preoccupied with other projects, Williams felt overwhelmed by the immensity of the rewriting that now stared him in the face: "I am terrified by the amount of work you still want to be done on Streetcar. Why, honey, it looks like you want me to sit down and write the whole fucking thing over!!? The script is going to be the biggest patch-work quilt since the death of Aunt Dinah, and you might as well be reconciled to it. I am going to do my work on it in bits and pieces."[42] As it turned out, Williams did so much work on the script that he received principal credit for the screenplay, while Saul, in recognition of his more limited participation, was billed as doing the adaptation.

"What Taste Is and What Vulgarity Is"

As plans for the production moved ahead, the filmmakers initiated discussions with the PCA that would prove extensive and, at times, acrimonious. Since Kazan had decided, in his words, to "just shoot the play," all sides in the negotiations, including Williams and Charles Feldman, anticipated myriad obstacles in filming such objectionable content as unpunished rape and references to homosexuality, and they were, of course, correct about their apprehensions, as the director would later recall.[43] Feldman was worried enough to suggest on his own to Kazan (tellingly, not to Williams and Oscar Saul) a wholesale revision of the proposed script, then nearly completed. He hoped the changes he proposed would both avoid the problems previously identified in contacts with the PCA and leave intact the playwright's conception of the relationship between Blanche and Stanley.[44]

In Feldman's view, the story is about "the conflict between the realism of Stanley and the extreme sensitivity of Blanche." Though Stanley is not "a heavy," he is a man of definite views and so does not look with favor upon his wife's intruding, haughty sister. This antipathy manifests itself in Stanley's "constant effort to tear down Blanche," a psychological assault that climaxes (tragically, according to Feldman) in Stanley revealing Blanche's sordid personal history to his friend Mitch, thus breaking up their affair. Feldman's reading of the play is hardly unpersuasive. He observes with some justice that "it is fully within the realm of possibility that if these people had been allowed to go on without interference, the whole situation would have been resolved pleasantly and effectively for everyone concerned," given Mitch's need for a woman to displace his mother and Blanche's desire to have some man "play the cavalier" for her.

The force of Williams's drama derives precisely from the melodramatic possibility, quickly demonstrated to be a mirage, that Blanche's problems (her sense of social-economic dislocation, her erotic restlessness, her mythomania) might be happily resolved by marriage to Mitch, who would likewise be delivered from the psychological bondage of "Momism," a malady much discussed at the time.[45] In its foregrounding of both Tom's ambivalence toward his mother's smothering affection and also, somewhat contradictorily, Amanda's determination to "settle" Laura into marriage, *Menagerie* draws on, even as it effectively deconstructs, the same ideological energies, so powerfully present in postwar America, in which a cult of domesticity (centered on a strong paterfamilias figure) was developing. As Feldman commented about the projected film of *Streetcar*, echoing the social philosophy of many Americans, a solid romantic relationship would "strengthen Blanche's hold on sanity and, therefore, on real life," an element of conventional wisdom that (in the early 1950s at least) could have been uttered about Laura Wingfield as well.[46]

Williams, in fact, sees Blanche's pursuit of Mitch as motivated by her desire for normality and respectability, including the possibility of an emancipation from self-reliance and, presumably, the end of opportunities to indulge the malfeasance toward which she is powerfully drawn. Feldman's reading of the play leaves the rails only when he opines that "the chief actor in this tragedy . . . is Stella," whose error is said to be her misguided attempt to get Stanley and Blanche to live amicably together under one roof. Jealous and resentful, Stanley then attempts to revenge himself upon Blanche by "destroying her illusions, by insisting that she face the reality about herself." In Feldman's view, Blanche's hold on sanity has been "her belief in her background, in her aristocracy and in the feeling, in this particular case, that a millionaire from Texas wants her to go on a trip with him on his yacht." And so when "Stanley destroys these illusions he is destroying Blanche." This means that, dramatically speaking, the rape is no longer necessary and can in effect be eliminated (it would be threatened, but not carried out), for Blanche has "been subjecting herself to rape for years as a sort of penance or hairshirt for her treatment of her husband."

The Melodramatic Road Not Taken

Feldman's proposed changes would have had one major effect, one that was very much in line with studio-produced melodrama: containing the force and obscuring the significance of the erotic. Blanche would have been reduced to a weak-minded fantasist (in other words, according to the conventions of the era, a typical manless woman) who, interfering in her sister's domestic tranquility, gets what she deserves. In this way, the main point of Williams's treatment of the inner life would be forgotten as the story engaged instead in a series of clichés about domestic politics. His complex characters would have become stereotypes: the jealous and resentful husband, the well-intentioned but misguided wife, and the pain-in-the-neck relative who cannot be accommodated within the nuclear family's domestic order. Stanley's assault would no longer have been sexual (in the broader sense that the play makes of that term), and it would certainly not have been the fulfillment of the date he proclaims the two have had from the beginning. His sexual attention, in other words, is something that she wishes for but also is disgusted by because it brings to light the repressed truth of her own nature.

Instead, if Feldman had had his way, the rape would have become

Stanley's final attempt to establish "his masculine superiority over her," a punishment he retreats from inflicting once he realizes that Blanche is insane and that the submission he hopes for has been otherwise achieved. If a rapist, Stanley would become an unsympathetic character—in Feldman's terms, "a complete S[hit] H[ead]." Such a character portrayal did not suit the producer's melodramatic understanding of the property or the pronounced industry predilection for sympathetic main characters. One is reminded that Feldman had invested a good deal of money as well as his reputation in the project.

In Feldman's version, Stanley's sudden discovery of inner virtue (if that is what makes him cease and desist) "paves the way for Stella" to send her sister away because this is the only way that she can restore domestic tranquility. And so, just as in Russell Holman's proposed version, the possibility of a conventional happy ending emerges, albeit of a somewhat different kind from what the MGM executive had imagined. Feldman writes: "Out of this tragedy we should at least have the hope that Stanley, Stella and the family will go on, perhaps better and certainly wiser." In the Hollywood manner, Stella and Stanley would realize the error of their ways and thus reform, especially for the good of their newborn child, while Blanche, condemned by her violation of bourgeois sexual norms and Stanley's self-righteous interference, would suffer the (perhaps not unjust) fate of social and psychological marginalization.

Streetcar, in short, would become a drama that, above all else, confirmed the essential sanctity and social utility of the nuclear family, a point made with routine enthusiasm by Hollywood films of the period. The temporary breakup of Stanley's home at the end would not demonstrate the weakness of family values, but rather, because those who deviate from such values (that is, Stanley and Blanche) are chastised or expelled from the home, the conclusion would offer proof of their essential sanctity. With this strong endorsement of poetic justice, the story would have a finale very much in line with the code admonition that "correct standards of life" be made manifest on the screen.

Feldman's speculations, however, describe only yet another conventional path not taken. Neither Williams nor Kazan would have been willing to transform the playwright's sensational and penetrating examination of human experience into a melodramatic programmer. There is no trace of Feldman's influence in the final script, which was, in accordance with standard practice, submitted to the PCA—which on April 28, 1950, after a conference between the filmmakers (Feldman, as well as Finlay

McDermid and Walter MacEwen of Warner Bros.) and Breen officials (Geoff Shurlock and Jack Vizzard) issued a report very much in line with what had been communicated to Irene Selznick some months before.[47]

The PCA Has Its Say

Interestingly, no comment was made about the overall theme of the drama; instead, the PCA concerned itself only with details. Three problem areas were identified: the mention of "sex perversion" in regard to Allan Grey; the "inference of a type of nymphomania with regard to the character of Blanche herself"; and the rape scene. The explanation for her husband's suicide would have to "get away entirely from sex perversion," with the screenplay "affirmatively establishing some other reason." Blanche's "approaches to the various men referred to in the course of the story" (a rather delicate way of describing her *moyen de vivre*) would be reframed to suggest that she has been "searching for romance and security, and not for gross sex," a not unreasonable, though certainly a partial, interpretation of her restlessness, as the relationship she eventually pursues with Mitch indicates. However, the Breen functionaries and their studio counterparts certainly showed their lack of good literary judgment when they collectively opined that Blanche's continuing search for romantic (as opposed to sensual) fulfillment might be offered as a credible reason for her expulsion from the hotel in which she had taken residence after the loss of the family home.

Even less satisfactory was the solution arrived at for dealing with the rape. While "the big scene of the assault on Blanche by Stanley would be kept relatively intact," what followed would be radically changed, removing any ambiguity about Blanche's ultimate fate at her brother-in-law's hands. The poor woman would still sink into dementia, accusing Stanley of having raped her, but he would vigorously reject the charge and prove his innocence. Tellingly, as the group awkwardly conceded, "the device by which he proves himself is yet to be invented." One wonders what it might have been. The testimony of some eyewitness hidden in the Kowalski apartment? An exculpatory medical exam ordered by the accused? The improbable revelation that Stanley is impotent?

Even more laughable was the motive Blanche would be assigned for her false witness. Despite her impending psychotic breakdown, she would supposedly remain rational enough to plot against Stanley in order to get revenge on her sister, Stella, of whom she would prove jealous enough to destroy the poor woman's marriage. Two other alternatives, equally risible, were suggested at the meeting: Blanche would call Stanley "Allan" as they embrace, indicating that her desire is for her dead husband (but why, then, do the pair embrace?). She would subsequently go on to imagine the rape (because that is what she really wants, confirming the Freudian view of such fantasies?), and "this is known to the audience" (once again raising the problem of how this might be established—a revealing soliloquy perhaps?). The solution preferred by Shurlock and Vizzard was the one proposed by Feldman. Stanley would attempt the rape, but stop when he realizes that the poor woman has slipped into insanity. The implausible result: Stanley Kowalski, always the gentleman, never a rapist of completely defenseless women—hardly the intriguingly caddish yet strangely sympathetic character Williams had imagined.

The difficulties experienced by the unwieldy committee of filmmakers and censors in dealing with the question of Blanche's character and the "date" that she has had with Stanley "from the beginning" make clear the centrality of these two aspects of the play. Change either one, and *Streetcar* is reduced to unconvincing, second-rate melodrama. Feldman was astute enough to realize not only that Williams and Kazan would not go along with any of these suggested alterations (they had already, perhaps not very kindly, rejected his own), but also that, if they were made, the project would likely turn into an expensive fiasco.[48] After the meeting at the PCA offices, Feldman diplomatically suggested that the playwright and director be contacted by phone for their comments. Neither Kazan nor Williams was reticent to express an opinion, and they were hardly pleased by what had been suggested. As the PCA's Jack Vizzard reports: "The results were highly unsatisfactory from the point of view of nearly everyone concerned. Kazan and Williams were inclined to make speeches about the integrity of their art and their unwillingness to be connected with a production which would emasculate the 'validity' of their production. Mr. Williams actually signed off in a great huff, declaiming that he did not need the money that much, and Mr. Kazan had to continue the second telephone call with a little more sobriety and temperateness than the writer."[49] A quick call was made to Feldman, who, likely fearing the loss of the considerable investment he had made in the project, requested a second conference with Vizzard and Shurlock; at which, from the PCA's point of view, satisfactory assurances were given by the filmmakers about the Allan Grey and Blanche problems.

The Sticking Point

Only the rape, on which Kazan and Williams were not inclined in the least to compromise, remained a problem, despite further suggestions about how this scene might be rendered acceptable. Another meeting in late May 1950, this time at Warner Bros. with Joseph Breen in attendance, also ended in deadlock. Kazan threatened to quit the production, as did Williams, if the rape scene were cut or otherwise transformed. If this was a bluff, Breen could not afford to call it, especially since the director and playwright said they intended to publish an annotated script that would explain clearly to one and all why they had not been allowed to make the film. This threat was most likely the brainchild of the fiery and combative Kazan. The director concluded the discussion by demanding to know what *had* to be cut in order to earn a seal. Notes from the meeting record Kazan's frustration. He is said to have remarked: "I only want to do this script if it can be done honestly and I don't want to do another story or a different story. We think it has things which are pure and moral and are the very essence of the story and we have no intention of doing it [the cuts]. We will stop right here."[50]

Breen's office was already under sustained assault from liberal critics in American society, and he could not afford the negative publicity that would flow from a noted Hollywood director's very public and angry withdrawal from the filming of a Pulitzer Prize–winning Broadway play.[51] Breen eventually conceded that the rape could remain if "done by suggestion and delicacy," a vague directive that Kazan, after shooting, could claim he had fulfilled, though not perhaps in the precise manner that the PCA director would have preferred.[52] As he remembered later, Kazan also agreed that if the rape were to be included, "Stanley would be 'punished' and that punishment would be in terms of his loss of his wife's love. In other words, that there would be a strong indication that she would leave him."[53] As shooting progressed, Breen tried to get some specific commitment in writing about how the rape would be handled, but the director temporized, refusing to alter substantially what was already in the shooting script, as a later memo for the PCA files (likely penned by Vizzard) makes clear, following yet another contact with the filmmakers quite late in the production process: "With regard to the rape scene, we again reiterated our belief that, in its present form, this element of the script could not be approved. We urged upon Mr. Kazan the advisability of considering our solution [Stanley slaps Blanche but does not rape her], but he felt that he could not definitely accept this important story change, without consulting Mr. Williams, the author of the play."[54]

The PCA Gives In, More or Less

Williams and Kazan were intransigent, if passive-aggressively so, because they believed that they could successfully flout current standards of censorship, for which neither had any use or sympathy. But Breen saw their resistance as an assault on his office. As historians of the PCA have frequently pointed out, Breen at this time essentially found himself in a no-win situation. If he insisted on the elimination of the rape (or the reduction of the scene to something less violent and erotic), he would likely reinforce the view, held by many within the industry and in the culture at large, that the code promoted standards of representation that were either, at the least, outmoded and irrelevant—or, at the worst, hostile to accepted notions of what was acknowledged to be great art. But if Breen allowed the filmmakers to include material explicitly forbidden by the code, then he was also, even if implicitly, admitting that its standards were no longer worthy of being strictly enforced.

Recent precedent was of no help in this predicament. In the much-applauded *Johnny Belinda* (Jean Negulesco, 1948), the heroine is made pregnant by a rape, and she subsequently raises the child born of the assault. Despite the seemingly sensational material, however, this was very much the stuff of standard melodrama. In fact, the film is oddly old-fashioned, its implausible, tear-jerking narrative out of place in a postwar era otherwise characterized by a greater desire for realism. In its refusal to engage with sexuality as such, *Johnny Belinda* harks back more to the eminent Victorian D. W. Griffith than to the modernist D. H. Lawrence. The film hardly offers anything like the disturbing yet compelling mix of misogynistic violence and forbidden eroticism that gives Stanley's contentious relationship with Blanche its dramatic and cultural power.

Breen did not trust that Kazan and Williams would alter the script's version of the scene in accordance with the bargain he believed had been struck in May. So Breen had Jack Vizzard monitor the production closely. The rape scene was being shot in early October 1950, when Vizzard contacted Finlay McDermid at Warner Bros. by phone (a written record of their conversation was made for the files, a somewhat unusual step that probably indicated Breen's growing anxiety). Vizzard was told that Kazan was improvising a solution on the set (in other words, it had not been added to the script for Vizzard to pass judgment on). Skeptical, Vizzard reports that he told "Mr. McDermid that if Mr. Kazan's solution was one of those fence-straddling devices which would let the scene be interpreted either way—either as a rape, or not—it probably would not be satisfactory; and that if protection shots were going to be taken, one should be made which would prove *affirmatively*, by any device they wished to invent, that a rape did *not* take place."[55] An indication of the atmosphere of anxiety and distrust then prevailing at the PCA, Breen's "solution" emerged as an unreasonable, perhaps even ridiculous standard to which the filmmakers should be held. In effect, Breen was asking Kazan and Williams not only to modify, but also to reject explicitly in the film version the scene that, more than any other, had made the Broadway play a notorious national sensation. The filmmakers could hardly accede to these demands. And—an intriguing question—would Breen and the PCA really have profited from this "victory" if Williams and Kazan had caved in? Moreover, from a practical point of view, what convincing dramatic device could be invented to show that something does not take place?

One of the Very Few Really Moral Films

While Kazan kept the PCA watchdogs in the dark about his precise plans for the ending, Williams faced their opposition more directly, firing off a letter to Breen in order "to clarify the meaning and importance of that scene" and, in general, to defend his creation against the charges of immorality he saw as implicit in the PCA's hardening attitudes. Going on the offensive, Williams not only stated that *Streetcar* "is an extremely and peculiarly *moral* play, in the deepest and truest sense of the term." He also turned the tables on Breen, the industry's appointed spiritual guardian, by contending that it is "one of the *very few* really *moral* films that have come out of Hollywood," a scarcely veiled dismissal of the industry's supposed "wholesomeness," for which the PCA was officially responsible.[56]

Breen could scarcely miss the pointed insult. Blanche, Williams goes on to say, is no tramp, but "a person of intense loneliness, fallibility, and a longing which is mostly spiritual for warmth and protection." As far as the playwright was concerned, terms such as "nymphomaniac" misidentify and trivialize the complexity of her psychological struggle. Explaining his treatment of what he terms "sensuality" (what for Breen would be "gross sex"), the playwright proclaimed that he indeed knew well "what *taste* is and what *vulgarity* is" (his emphasis). Instead of representing cheap sensationalism, Williams concluded, "the rape of Blanche by Stanley is a pivotal, integral truth in the play . . . we are now fighting for what we think is the heart of the play, and when we have our backs against the wall—if we are forced into that position—*none* of us is going to throw in the towel!"[57]

Williams was hardly being disingenuous about his own accomplishments; he did firmly believe that both the stage and film versions of *Streetcar* reflected his deeply moral, albeit unconventional, view of human experience. Later in the decade when Kazan, perhaps not intending the epithet as a compliment, called him a "moralist," Williams responded: "I think you are probably right. Perhaps when my collected works are subjected to final analysis I will make Cotton Mather look like a motherfucker or beatnik."[58] Always more the showman than Williams, Kazan celebrated the film's sensationalism, but not at the expense of ignoring its literary qualities. While the final editing of the film was underway in early 1951, he wrote to Jack Warner:

> The thing that makes this piece great box office is that it has two things. 1/It is about the three F's. 2/It has class. No person who tries to keep in any kind of step can afford to miss it. Both are equally important. What made it a Pulitzer Prize winner—the poetry— must be kept in, untouched so that it will appeal to those who don't want to admit that they are interested in the moist seat department. (Everybody, of course, is!) . . . This is the only picture I ever made that I'm completely proud of.[59]

The Rape Stands

Jotting down notes for the censorship article that would be published in the *New York Times*, Kazan remarked informally, "Pictures with really *decent intentions*—they are the ones that suffer. The tit shows get away with it." In his view, *Streetcar* is "a poetic tragedy, based on realism—not a naturalistic ('sordid') drama!"[60] As Kazan told Jack Vizzard in their famous meeting of April 27, 1950, "This story and this script are completely moral. . . . It ran two years and family after family came to see it. Not a special audience and I think the motion picture ought to grow up."[61] In fulfillment of this demand that Hollywood reach maturity, Kazan staged the rape scene in such a way that only the youngest and

Elia Kazan directs Mitch (Karl Malden) on the set of A Streetcar Named Desire *as Blanche (Vivien Leigh) listens in. Photo courtesy of The Historic New Orleans Collection.*

most naive among its audience would not be absolutely clear about what Blanche suffers at the angry hands of her brother-in-law. The mental and physical wrestling match between the ill-sorted couple moves offscreen as the camera dollies in to a close-up of a broken mirror, providing a symbol whose import was difficult to miss. If there were any lingering doubts among more sophisticated viewers, the cut to a spewing fire hose in the next sequence metaphorically punctuated the point. So much for Breen's injunction to provide an "affirmative demonstration" that there is no rape. The solution crafted by Kazan and Williams could have been viewed by the PCA not only as an evasion, but also as an insult, perhaps even a provocation.

Whatever his feelings, Breen had little choice but to approve the scene without comment, begging Warner Bros. only to be discreet in their advertisements, presumably because he did not want to be shown up too obviously by the filmmakers. There remained only the problem of the ending. In the stage version, Stella is upset at what she suspects Stanley has done to Blanche while she was in the hospital giving birth to his child, but the presumption is that her anger is only temporary and that the erotic bond between the couple is as strong as ever—and perhaps grows even stronger with Blanche's departure. Kazan and Williams had agreed that the film, true at least in some sense to the principle of poetic justice enshrined in the code, should show that Stanley pays a price for his violence and betrayal. Following a cordial meeting with Breen in November, Williams crafted the solution, which Kazan used as written. After Blanche is taken away, Stella refuses Stanley's attempt to reconcile and return to the apartment; then, "as Stella is crying she whispers to the baby these words of promise and reassurance. 'We're not going back in there. Not this time. We're never going back. Never back, never back again.'"[62] This finale, more than the "rape" scene, lent itself to different interpretations (it is still possible to read Stella's rejection of Stanley as only temporary), but it did satisfy Breen and company. The PCA approval sheet (dated December 11, 1950) lists "rape" as part of the content of the picture, a laconic but telling acknowledgment of the extent to which Kazan and Williams had "bent" the Code. But the film that the PCA certificated as "acceptable" would be viewed in an entirely different light by the Legion of Decency.

"This Bastard Kazan"

The story of *Streetcar*'s second, and more notorious encounter, with moral critics is well known, probably because, as Leonard Leff points out, "tales of a moralistic and repressive code make the romantic artist (director or writer or actor) seem even more romantic" and, moreover, suit "those who shape Hollywood history as fictional narrative."[63] Anticipating some difficulty after a Catholic reviewer panned the film, but hardly the firestorm that ensued, Warner Bros. arranged for key legion officials to preview *Streetcar* under the watchful eye of Jack Vizzard, a former seminarian who, it was felt, could speak the language of the priests and their pious lay reviewers. While preview audiences of regular cinemagoers in California had overwhelmingly indicated their approval, legion officials reacted differently. Father Patrick Masterson and Monsignor Thomas Little, along with Mary Looram (head of the group's female reviewers), viewed with dismay the groundbreaking screen treatment of the inner life that had been crafted by Kazan and Williams—with something of a blessing from Joseph Breen. Martin Quigley, perhaps less shocked, quickly saw that the finished film would be troublesome, especially because of the rift it might open up between the legion and the PCA, organizations equally jealous of each other's prerogatives and power. It seemed likely that the film would receive a "C" rating, a development that spelled serious box-office trouble. But the problem with Williams's drama was not, as the PCA had surmised, its exploration of certain forbidden topics. It was instead, as Vizzard wrote to Breen, "its *overall gross emphasis on sin and carnality*" (his emphasis).[64]

Thinking he had lessened or perhaps even eliminated the play's exploration of forbidden themes, Breen must have been shocked to discover that, at least in the eyes of his counterparts at the legion, he and his associates had missed the forest for its trees. No doubt, the priests and their cadre of very sharp and sophisticated female raters can hardly be accused of insensitivity to the playwright's intentions. They proved to be better than PCA officials at reading Williams. *Streetcar* (if incidentally also treating what could be called sin) is centrally about "carnality," or the life of and in the body itself (what Williams preferred to term "sensuality").

Oriented by the code toward the identification and removal of specifically forbidden motifs, Breen and associates had focused on the trio of "sex perversion," promiscuity, and rape, but had ignored the "flesh," the desire that, in Williams's foundational metaphor, drives us toward death at the end of the line. As an indication of the vastness of the evident cultural divide between the playwright and this part of his audience, the legion officials and raters saw the film's exploration of sensuality as a too-pervasive engagement with the experience of the flesh. Carnality was not a forbidden subject as such (though none in the industry would have employed such a loaded theological term). In fact, at this time carnality was in some sense Hollywood's chief attraction, for films, so industry wisdom had it, would not succeed without prominently featuring attractive and charismatic actors, whose bodies were carefully (though tastefully, for the most part, under Breen's watchful eye) eroticized. In contrast, the film made by Williams and Kazan was in effect being charged with something like intellectual malfeasance: a thematizing of excessive sexual desire.

The violation here was thus not so much representational; that is, an unsanctioned display of naked or barely clothed bodies, but rather what seemed to legion officials a distortion of the properly subordinate role that the flesh as such (as opposed to its sublimation in the cultural concept of romance) was meant to play in human life. Tellingly, the relationship in the film that aroused the ire of the legion was not the brutal, unquestionably immoral, yet transient (mis)connection of Blanche and Stanley, but rather the deeply passionate (and ardently violent) marital coupling of Stanley and Stella. Surprised at the erotic force of the finished film, Jack Vizzard described to Breen the legion's deliberations about *Streetcar*, which had surreptitiously been reported to him by Mary Looram, who was not authorized to reveal them even to PCA officials:

> But Joe, a very strange thing has happened. In concentration on our two leading characters, with whom most of the problems lay, we completely missed what this bastard Kazan was doing with Stella . . . the lustful and carnal scoring they introduced into the final print underscores and highlights what were mere subtleties and suggestions in a way I never thought possible. The result is to throw into sharp relief in the finished film the purely lustful relationship between Stella and Stanley, that creates a totally different impression from the one we got when we saw it. This impression was further heightened . . . by the addition of a scene which I do not remember having seen when we reviewed the picture. It has to do with some lines of dialogue which reprise, in the body of the picture, the idea of the title, that desire is a streetcar on which you climb for a ride (to the Elysian fields). It puts the whole thesis of the picture in sharp focus, and makes it a story about sex—sex desire specifically—and this is the quintessence of the objection by the Legion.[65]

The Flesh, the Flesh

Such a global problem was not by its nature amenable in any meaningful sense to the remedies available at this late date (basically, rather short cuts that would not disrupt story continuity and require expensive, or perhaps impractical, reshoots). Through much behind-the-scenes maneuvering, Warner Bros., aided substantially by Vizzard (the PCA was a de facto ally of the studio in these circumstances) managed to get the legion to provide a series of suggested cuts that, if implemented, would guarantee a change of the film's rating to "B." Like Breen, the legion was also forced to bend its principles considerably. No more than the PCA could the legion afford the inevitable widespread publicity, much of it quite negative, that would attend its condemnation of a Pulitzer Prize–winning drama, thought by many at the time to be one of the finest that

American literature had produced. Such a condemnation would raise the question whether the legion was hopelessly out of step with a rapidly changing American culture.

Agreeing to a list of cuts in exchange for a change in rating (in other words, adopting for the nonce the modus operandi of the PCA) certainly did not serve legion officials well. The moral problem they had discovered in *Streetcar* was only minimally ameliorated. This was still a film that thematized carnality in disturbing ways, even without the four purportedly offending minutes. As Kazan would later *publicly* proclaim in the *New York Times*, this final transformation of the film made little sense. If, as he argued with considerable exasperation, the organization's aim was to "protect the morals of . . . Roman Catholics," then "when something is cut out of a picture on such grounds, it is only natural to assume that it is something of a special and daring character, somehow very different from what is permitted to remain." But since the banned footage was "just about indistinguishable from the body of the picture, which you are allowed to see," then a reasonable person might ask, "What difference does it make?"[66] He had a point.

A further difficulty was that once its demands and the resulting changes in the film were made public, the legion found itself mired in a public relations nightmare. Since the legion was officially committed only to rating films for the benefit of the nation's Catholic community and not to any kind of censorship, its backstreet negotiations with Warners, facilitated by Martin Quigley and the PCA's friend at the legion, Mary Looram, offered strong evidence that the organization had other designs on American film culture. Kazan would question "how the end result differed from direct censorship by the Legion."[67] Indeed. Interestingly, his view of the legion would be confirmed by his experience with the release of *Baby Doll* five years later, as we shall see.

At first, however, Kazan (who, when *Streetcar* wrapped, started shooting *Viva Zapata!*) and Williams were kept very much in the dark about the film's difficulties in gaining the minimum approval of the legion. They were not consulted about the agreed-upon deletions. The studio found itself in a very difficult situation—caught, as it were, between competing aesthetics and rival ideological agendas. If Warners were forced to concern itself with the objections of the legion (and by extension those of culturally conservative filmgoers), the reaction of intellectual elites, from whose ranks the more influential film critics were mostly drawn, could also not be ignored. As Vizzard reminded Breen:

Warners at this point are terribly anxious to avoid the impression that what they are going to offer to the public is anything less than the exact masterpiece of Mr. T. Williams. They are fearful, I think, of a drubbing at the hands of the arty set, should the idea seep forth that they had to compromise for a chopped up and . . . "emasculated" version of the play. This is only my best guess, but I'm reasonably sure of it. They have conned the critics so far into the belief that they have the play pretty much intact. They don't want it found out now that what the critics saw at the press previews is going to be in any way diminished.[68]

Thus the studio hardly publicized what it had in some haste done to the already edited and painstakingly vetted picture. Quite pointedly, the film's director (a card-carrying member, one supposes, of the "arty set") was not informed. Kazan discovered what was going on more or less by accident; he ran into editor Dave Weisbart in New York, and Weisbart, in response to Kazan's question about what the Hollywood-based technician was doing on the East Coast, told him that he had been brought to town in order to make the cuts required by the legion. Confronted with their perfidy, Warners executives explained, as Kazan recalled, that they were afraid that "theatres showing the picture would be picketed, might be threatened with boycotts of as long as a year's duration if they dared to show it, that priests would be stationed in the lobbies to take down the names of parishioners who attended."[69] Kazan was not even allowed to enter an uncut final version of his film in the Venice Film Festival competition. The legion stood firm in its determination to ensure that this version of *Streetcar* would not be exhibited even thousands of miles beyond U.S. borders, and for a very restricted audience, without incurring the imposition of a "C" rating for all subsequent screenings. Unwilling to buck the legion over a film that was doing very well with the critics and at the box office, Warners would hear no appeals from the distraught and frustrated director.

Kazan, however, did find some revenge in taking the legion to task in the pages of the country's most respected newspaper, where he praised the studio and Charles Feldman for having "shown courage in purchasing a fine and unusual play" and for being "extremely cooperative and exceptionally generous throughout the making of the picture."[70] He bitterly reported that Martin Quigley (unnamed, but readily identifiable as a "prominent Catholic layman"), while praising the film's artistic achievement, had sought, in suggesting to legion officials what cuts to request, to make clear "the primacy of the moral order" as expressed by a code that is "not the code of the great majority of the audience." Long after the dust had settled, however, Kazan reserved his greatest scorn for studio officials: "Warners just wanted a seal. They didn't give a damn about the beauty or the artistic value of the picture. To them it was just a piece of entertainment. It was business, not art . . . the whole business was rather an outrage."[71] Ever the businessman as well as the intellectual, however, Kazan understood that such controversy, while indicative of the difficulties that the artist encounters in a commercially oriented business, also offered filmmakers "excellent publicity" at no cost.[72]

Kazan would remember the box-office value of controversy when, again working with Williams, he helped confect, in the film eventually known as *Baby Doll* (1956), a dramatic property that, like *Streetcar*, was both arty and controversial, eventually to become, after being shaped by Kazan's calculated authorial, directorial, and marketing strategies, one of the most notorious films of the 1950s. Warners, he had realized, wanted *Streetcar* "dirty enough to pull people in," even as they were afraid to include material that "might keep anyone away."[73] Quite so, but this was actually a well-conceived formula for box-office success. As we will see, Kazan would disregard the dangers involved in giving offense when making *Baby Doll* "dirty enough." As Jack Warner and company probably warned him, the result was entirely predictable: nagging problems with exhibitors that substantially reduced gross earnings.

The Primacy of the Moral Order?

At the time of *Streetcar*'s release, however, Kazan was more interested in playing the role of the betrayed and offended artist. Not willing to surrender without exhausting all options, Kazan wrote to Martin Quigley in the hopes of obtaining some kind of redress—or, at the least, to vent his anger and outrage. He admitted that he felt "oppressed by the uncomfortable irony of the situation," namely, that he had to request the inclusion in his own film of "scenes and material which I consider essential." That the legion could wield such power was, Kazan thought, "extremely dangerous" in a society in which the protection of the First Amendment was highly valued. Pointing out that he, Quigley, and Williams each had their own set of "morals," Kazan wrote: "When you speak of the primacy of moral values, my only question is: WHOSE? And my only objection is to a situation in which, regardless of motive, the effect is the imposition of the values of one group of our population upon the rest of us. This limits one of our fundamental American rights: freedom of expression. This, to my way of thinking, is immoral."[74] Quigley's somewhat haughty reply states with admirable clarity a quite different sense of morality, one grounded not in the liberal conception that freedom is freedom from constraint, but rather in the traditional, conservative view that freedom flows from proper adherence to a code that transcends not only fashion and artistic sensibility—but also individuality: "You ask *whose* moral values I am talking about. . . . I refer to the long-prevailing standards of morality of the Western World, based on the Ten Commandments—nothing, you see, that I can boast of inventing or dreaming up. . . . The American Constitutional guarantee of freedom of expression is not a one-way street. I have the same right to say that the moral consideration has a right of precedence over the artistic consideration as you have to deny it."[75] The PCA and the Legion of Decency drew their strength from the belief that "the moral consideration has a right over the artistic consideration." If that principle was denied by Kazan, it was rejected even more strongly by Williams, whose adapted works furthered a trend that, before two decades were to pass, witnessed the passing from the American scene of the institutionalized reshaping of films that had begun in 1930.

By the end of the 1960s, the PCA, its founding code increasingly irrelevant in an America dominated more and more by a secular modernism, had become the Code and Rating Administration. This was a body whose charge was not to shape films (that is, by imposing moral principles), but to classify them (the ratings system was officially established November 1, 1968). The Legion of Decency, which was committed (as its title suggests) to cultural warfare on the behalf of threatened traditional religious values, had become the National Catholic Office on Motion Pictures (NCOMP), an agency dedicated more to celebrating the cultural value of the medium than to pointing out and eliminating the moral threat that "transgressive" films purportedly posed. In the twenty-first century, NCOMP is no more, its role having been taken over by the U.S. Catholic Conference Office (USCC) for Film and Broadcasting, which still rates films. But most people in this country, including, perhaps, a good number of Catholics, are unaware that the USCC publishes a weekly *TV and Movie Guide*, which classifies films as acceptable or offensive in a fashion that, at least in general, would likely meet with Joseph Breen's approval.

Those developments, however, lay in the future. *Streetcar* undoubtedly bent the code, but it in some ways hardened the resolve of PCA officials. Subsequent Williams properties would find, at least for a time, no easy road to approval, as the playwright and his collaborators would soon discover. If *The Glass Menagerie* served as Williams's initiation into the fraternity of filmmaking, the process of adapting *A Streetcar Named Desire* was more akin to a trial by fire. With *Menagerie*, Williams had maneuvered through the production process by (for the most part) choosing his battles wisely and compromising when faced with intractable demands; he did learn, however, not to repeat the mistake of throwing a public tantrum after viewing the finished film on the eve of its commercial release. In short, he gleaned valuable lessons that would serve him well in future film projects.

With *Streetcar*, the playwright found out that his idealistic notions of artistic control, largely even if not entirely accommodated during a theatrical production, would have to give way in part, as they had during the filming of *Menagerie*, to the collective opinion and will of studio executives, who were committed, almost reflexively, to long-established industry views about entertainment value. This project also brought Williams into heated and frustrating conflict with PCA officials and, more indirectly, with the raters and clerics of the Legion of Decency, who, holding to a different moral outlook, were inclined to care little about his growing reputation as one of the country's most celebrated playwrights. But Williams endured his difficulties with admirable patience. And this time the only tantrum in evidence was thrown by Elia Kazan, who publicly vented his outrage. Most importantly, perhaps, through his participation in both adaptations, Williams learned to distrust professional screenwriters and producers eager to offer advice because they were inclined to follow traditionalist narrative and dramatic models largely irrelevant to his own interest in various forms of modernism.

This Hollywood "education" might have given Williams reason to slow down and reflect upon the movie business, yet the outstanding critical and popular success achieved by *Streetcar* encouraged him to pursue other film projects. Eager to follow up a profitable release with others by the same author, Hollywood filmmakers, including Elia Kazan, sought to bring other Williams properties to the screen, and the playwright was a willing partner in these ventures. Among these, both *The Rose Tattoo* and *Baby Doll* met with considerable opposition from the PCA and the legion, but emerged relatively intact, demonstrating how Hollywood filmmaking in the 1950s had begun to "bend the code" as it eagerly sought to adapt not only daring forms of modern fiction (such as the novels of John Steinbeck and William Faulkner, as well as the middlebrow sensations published by the likes of John O'Hara and Grace Metalious), but also the increasingly sophisticated fare then issuing from a revitalized Broadway theatre under the unofficial leadership of Tennessee Williams.

CHAPTER FOUR

Bending the Code II
The Rose Tattoo

Erotic Realism and Pornography

By the 1950s, John D'Emilio and Estelle B. Freedman suggest, "the mores of the middle class had shifted profoundly," with the result that American "purity crusaders" now "acted from outside the mainstream."[1] It may well be true, as these two historians of America's changing attitude toward sexuality suggest, that "the Kinsey reports [the study of men released in 1948 and that of women in 1953] stimulated a nationwide examination of America's sexual habits and values," but the areas most obviously under contention were literary or, perhaps better, representational. Because of the American tradition of antiobscenity legislation, the public battlefield eventually became the Supreme Court, which, under the leadership of erstwhile conservative Earl Warren, issued a succession of rulings that "progressively contracted the domain of obscenity, in large part by affirming the appropriateness of sex as a matter for public consumption."[2] The most important of these decisions came in *Roth v. United States* (1957), in which the court held that only literary materials that could be found to lack "redeeming social importance" were legally obscene, thereby placing its "imprimatur on tendencies inherent in the logic of sexual liberalism."[3]

But the *Roth* test (as it came to be called after further judicial refinement) provided only a very vague and contentious standard with which to determine, as Tennessee Williams had put it, the difference between "taste" and "vulgarity." In 1959, psychologists Phyllis and Eberhard Kronhausen, a husband-and-wife research team, gave influential and persuasive voice to the increasingly popular neo-Freudian view about the frankness of expression then becoming, under the influence of literary modernism, a more prominent element on the cultural scene.[4] In their *Pornography and the Law: The Psychology of Erotic Realism and "Hard Core" Pornography* (a volume enthusiastically endorsed by sex theorist Theodor Reik), the Kronhausens did not support the growing availability of pornography, whose main purpose in their view was "to stimulate sexual response," but they did not condemn it either.[5] However, in literary works written in the style of "erotic realism," which is dominated by the "truthful description of the basic realities of life," they found much to praise.[6]

In an America that was becoming more and more invested in a therapeutic sensibility, it is not surprising that the Kronhausens supported erotic-realist literature not on the basis of First Amendment protections of freedom of expression, but because they thought that such representations could play a culturally ameliorative role. Because "the denial of man's basic corporeality can only lead to distortions of the body image" and hence to "mental states of depersonalization and irreality which mark the more severe emotional disturbances," erotic realism, in their view, "reflects a basically healthy and therapeutic attitude toward life."[7] Such art is designed to tell the truth about human experience, not provide titillation. For the Kronhausens, appalled by the dehumanizing influences of postindustrial consumerism and its "organization men," erotic-realist texts played an important, reformist role in reversing the "progressive eradication of individual differences" and enabling that search for identity which was, as they saw it, fast becoming a "matter of spiritual survival."[8]

A Different Side of Human Nature

These views exemplified an attitude toward sexual life that Tennessee Williams found very congenial, especially after a long, sensual sojourn in Italy with companion Frank Merlo during the winter of 1949 had shown him "a different side of human nature than any I had ever known." Here were people, he observed, who were "like Southerners without their inhibitions," "poetic" but lacking in "Protestant repressions."[9] Working furiously those months in Rome, Williams turned out two radically different texts: a brooding novella, eventually to be titled *The Roman Spring of Mrs. Stone*; and a comic play, *The Rose Tattoo*, which, depicting a coastal village in the American South populated mostly by Sicilian immigrants, offers as its major theme what is perhaps best described as "sexual healing," a therapeutic outcome that the Kronhausens—as well as cultural liberals more generally—would have applauded.

The Rose Tattoo abjures a tragic treatment of erotic attachment, celebrating instead through its humorous exploration of physicality and desire "the warmth and sweetness of the Italian people" that Williams encountered that winter, especially in the person of actress Anna Magnani, for whom the leading role was written (though she declined to participate in the stage production). Williams would say, "If this is a warmer and happier play than anything I've written, it is because of that experience."[10] Audiences apparently agreed, since *The Rose Tattoo* enjoyed a quite respectable run of more than three hundred performances. *Tattoo* received only mixed reviews from the critics, but Williams, his reputation growing, was duly compensated with the Tony Award.

In addition to its ribald elements, meant to both amuse and shock, *Tattoo* gently satirizes traditional Catholicism as part of its intellectualized, perhaps even programmatic examination of the experience of the body. In fact, the play's melding of the sacred and the profane elicited from the PCA objections similar to those that had been voiced more than a decade earlier by the puritanical audiences and reviewers who saw *Battle of Angels* during its abortive run in Boston. The censors hardly appreciated (perhaps did not even recognize fully) *Tattoo*'s highbrow engagement with perennial themes of the Western literary tradition, any more than Boston playgoers had connected with Williams's startlingly original blending of Christian and classical mythology.

The play examines the grieving and healing process of Serafina Delle Rose, an Italian immigrant living on the Mississippi Gulf Coast, who has been widowed by a man she literally worshipped. She retires from her job (as a garment maker for the local community), and her house, which contains her husband Rosario's ashes, becomes her hermitage. As members of the community try to cajole her out of her psychological disintegration, into her life comes a buffoonish suitor named Mangiacavallo, who tries, initially with no success, to woo her. Serafina sees Mangiacavallo as a radically imperfect facsimile of her husband, but by the play's end, their eventual union seems to be guaranteed. A subplot involving Serafina's daughter Rosa and Rosa's boyfriend, Jack, complements the difficult courtship between Mangiacavallo and Serafina, but the obstacles to the young couple's romance, like those of the older couple, eventually give way to their attraction for one another. In *The Rose Tattoo*, dramatic tension derives in part from a conflict in ideas (antisexual Christian doctrine versus a neo-pagan joy in the life of the body) as enacted in Serafina's movement from self-pitying celibacy to erotic renewal and tolerance, a reversal of the tragic trajectory that takes both Laura and Blanche from their unsuccessful encounters with "gentleman callers" to isolation, social marginalization, and perhaps even madness. Serafina's transformation is evident not only in her surrender to an ardent suitor, but also in the blessing she eventually bestows on her daughter Rosa's developing romance with the young sailor, Jack. Williams here offered playgoers a psychomachia enacted by rather flat characters (especially the excessively typical Rosa and Jack) who stand for different positions or ideas, in an antirealist manner reminiscent of European modernism. This was a somewhat surprising change from the poetic realism of *Menagerie* and *Streetcar*, plays structured around the dramatic encounter of carefully observed, psychologically and morally complex, rounded characters.

Despite this self-conscious "artiness" (most evident in the play's baroque proliferation of symbolic roses), what gives *Tattoo* dramatic force is that these dueling human (and historically opposed) impulses are unified at the level of the dramatic action, which is intriguingly multilayered. The angelically named Serafina is already rendered earthy as the action begins, suffering from the loss of her husband, Rosario, to whose body she was inordinately attached. And so when she surrenders after a struggle to the energetic physicality of Alvaro Mangiacavallo, Serafina regains in a sense her former attachment, though this victory is not without its ironies. For this simpleton possesses a beautiful body that uncannily resembles Rosario's. To please his prospective beloved, Mangiacavallo has his chest tattooed with a rose, thereby becoming even more a physical double of his predecessor; Rosario bore the same symbol, an image of his attachment to Serafina, upon whom a rose image had miraculously appeared, indicating the metaphysical appropriateness of their connection. And yet the two are not the same; Serafina brings herself to accept a man who does not appear to inspire the same devotion in her that Rosario had done, even dead. At the same time, a future with Mangiacavallo is clearly for Serafina the most positive alternative to suffering through life alone.

At play's end, her mystical rose is burning once again, a sign perhaps of spiritual and physical renewal (including the possibility that she may now be carrying Alvaro's child). Though his widow idealized and idolized the man while he lived, posthumous revelations of his faithlessness and criminality debunk Rosario's claims to moral and spiritual perfection, a comic bringing of high to low also evident in Rosario's displacement by Alvaro. Serafina's disillusionment with Rosario (including the discovery that his girlfriend, Estelle Hohengarten, had had herself tattooed with a rose as a sign of her devotion to him) eases her eventual, grudging acceptance of Mangiacavallo's devotion. Thus, somewhat heavy-handedly, the play's seemingly omnipresent symbol of the rose represents different aspects of the contradictory unity of sensuality and idealistic sublimation.

We might say that Serafina's idolatry of Rosario is deconstructed by her subsequent seduction by Mangiacavallo, a carnivalized and somewhat grotesque figure whose name means "eat a horse" (also a slyly humorous personal reference to Williams's lover, Frank Merlo, whom the author called "the Little Horse"). Yet both views of the erotic life are reminiscent of the ways in which romanticization and carnality are held in uneasy suspension. Such eroticism and worship of the flesh run counter to the official morality of the Catholic Church, whose teachings, though they have deeply marked this transplanted Sicilian community, prove unable to either contain or correct the natural energies of the body and the spirit. In essence, human nature triumphs over the religious structures that are here presented as somewhat foolish attempts to define and contain it. The parish priest, Father De Leo, adamantly opposes Serafina's persistence in preserving Rosario's ashes in an urn rather than burying them. In addition to being unsympathetic, Father De Leo is also ineffectual, defending the image of a stern God, yet misunderstanding the weaknesses and foibles of the people he serves.

A Breezy Paganism

If *Streetcar* offended the traditionally minded in the PCA and the legion because of its serious treatment of sexual transgressions, *Tattoo* aroused the censors' ire because of its breezy paganism, its irreverent, life-affirming refusal to take desire only *au grand sérieux* and therefore to punish its "excesses" in the manner that even *Streetcar* could be understood as doing. We should remember that Williams's original conception of the dramatic action in *Streetcar* (preserved in both the Broadway and Hollywood versions) emphasizes the devastating losses suffered by Blanche, Stanley, and Stella because of their sexual proclivities, excesses, or malfeasance. In its recommendations for revisions of the film script, the PCA required only that these losses be identified as the inevitable outcomes of wrongdoing, an interpretation that Williams, as we have seen, strenuously resisted. Interestingly, however, Williams even imagined Blanche's husband, shamed at the discovery of his true sexual nature, as passing something like a conventional judgment on his misbehavior, killing himself out of disgust and shame, a finale to his tragic story that the PCA would have thoroughly approved of had it been able to endorse the representation of a love whose name could not be spoken. In the film version, then, "Protestant repression," as Williams so aptly puts it, is evident in the self-destructive obsessions of Blanche, Stella, Stanley, and the remembered Allen Grey. Reflecting a Mediterranean sensibility, *Tattoo*, in contrast, presented Breen with a more subversive property, one in which it was more a question of blunting the radical nature of the play's sexual themes rather than fixing appropriate punishments for characters who could, without much difficulty, be interpreted as having violated conventional moral principles.[11]

Beaten, Unkempt, Depressing People

After its somewhat notorious, though not sensational, run on Broadway (critic Moira Walsh, for example, recalled that the stage version was "ultimately very offensive"), studio executives could see clearly that a Hollywood version of *Tattoo* might encounter some serious problems with the PCA.[12] But producer Hal B. Wallis was very interested in acquiring the film rights, especially after the critical and box-office success of *Streetcar* and other pictures of the early 1950s that pushed the limits of the code and seemed, for that very reason, to attract filmgoers; *Tattoo*, Wallis calculated, would do much the same. The play would also suit Wallis's long-standing interest in stories that had evident literary quality (a profitable area to work in during the early 1950s in Hollywood). Perhaps most importantly, the Williams play would offer a suitable role (in the part of Alvaro) for Burt Lancaster, then signed to do a number of pictures for the producer.

Wallis had just achieved substantial success, both popular and critical, with the film version of William Inge's Broadway sensation *Come Back, Little Sheba* (Daniel Mann, 1952), in which Lancaster had starred with Shirley Booth, and the producer was especially eager to secure the rights to another play that offered a strong female lead to serve as an appropriate foil to Lancaster's dynamic style. Serafina Delle Rose was such a role, making the film an ideal Lancaster vehicle with which to follow up the success of *Sheba* (which had included an Academy Award for Booth). A significant bonus was the play's connection to international superstar Anna Magnani, who was perhaps the most sensational actress of the era, rivaled only by Marilyn Monroe. Magnani had been solicited strongly for the Broadway production, but had declined because, among other reasons, she felt her English was not strong enough for continuous stage performance, even though she was immensely flattered when learning that Williams had written the role with her in mind. Wallis rightly thought that she could be secured for the film version because her acting could be done in short bursts, and retakes were always possible.

When Wallis saw the stage version during its Chicago tryouts, he went backstage personally to open immediate negotiations with Williams, evidently fearing that some other enterprising producer might secure the rights if he waited until the Broadway run and inevitable popular success. With such a strong show of interest, Wallis was able to persuade Williams to work informally on roughing out a screenplay and even writing some additional scenes. In the event, a final agreement was quickly forthcoming. Wallis would produce the film for Paramount, with Daniel Mann, who had directed the stage version, reprising his role. Williams was uncomfortable that Mann would be directing, writing Wood: "I did so hope that it could be offered to Gadge [Kazan] for whom it was written along with Magnani, and who told me that he would like to make a film of it . . . if he could fit it into his schedule." Williams was wary of, as he called him, "the intellectual Mr. Mann" and thought that "with a fine director, 'Tattoo' and Magnani would out-shine 'Streetcar.'"[13]

Williams would prepare the screenplay, with significant help from Hal Kanter, who received screen credit for the adaptation. Mann (b. 1912) was no novice and by no means an insignificant figure on Broadway or in Hollywood, where his maiden directorial effort, which was to bring *Sheba* to the screen in 1952, had met with considerable acclaim (he would go on to direct such other notable films as *I'll Cry Tomorrow* [1955], *Teahouse of the August Moon* [1956], *The Last Angry Man* [1959], and *Butterfield 8* [1960]). But Mann was no Kazan, and no one on the set was ever in any doubt about the man actually in charge of the production being Wallis, all of whose films bear his strong personal stamp. In addition to *Sheba*, Wallis had just produced (with Daniel Mann directing) one of the most noted woman's pictures of the early 1950s (though it was a box-office disappointment). *About Mrs. Leslie* (1954) features Shirley Booth as a landlady who reminiscences with poignant bittersweetness about her lifelong "backstreet" affair with a rich and powerful man.

Along with *Sheba* and *Mrs. Leslie*, *Tattoo* would constitute an impressive triptych of powerfully realistic dramas with strong female leads, each of whom, in the tradition of screen melodrama, suffers from a profound sexual discontent that results from an unbreakable attachment to an unattainable man (married, alcoholically disaffected, or dead and cremated). Aware that he was departing from tradition, Wallis encountered considerable opposition from studio executives when he determined to make films of this kind. He recalled that those at Paramount were "appalled by the idea of filming *Come Back, Little Sheba*" and "shocked at the thought of making a picture with beaten, unkempt, depressing people." *Tattoo* would offer more of the same; here also were no "glamorous men and women in melodramas of the seamy side of life," as had hitherto been industry practice.[14]

La Magnani

As shooting progressed it became obvious that Magnani would be no ordinary "widow lady," and this film would be no *Marty* (Delbert Mann, 1955), the famous "small film" of the era in which the romantic couple, in a complete rejection of industry wisdom, is played by performers (Ernest Borgnine, Betsy Blair) who are not especially appealing. And yet *Tattoo* is likewise no *From Here to Eternity*, whose notorious beach-rendezvous scene shocked and titillated audiences, with a scantily clad Lancaster and Deborah Kerr embracing on the shore as the surf washes over their entwined bodies. Truer to a kind of Americanized neorealist style, Mann's film avoids the glamorizing escapism of Zinnemann's more conventional melodrama, including such set-piece romantic scenes. And yet it is nonetheless sensational.[15]

The reason was Anna Magnani. A unique film personality, her appeal did not depend on fine clothes and flattering setups; in fact, it might have been ruined by such an approach. Dressed in a slip or bathrobe with her hair hanging in uncombed strings, Magnani spends much of *Tattoo* in a state of profound dishabille, as had Shirley Booth in *Sheba* (though to very different effect). Emerging to prominence late in life (she was already well past forty when she made *Tattoo*, and had been playing minor film roles since the 1930s), Magnani established an international reputation for her earthiness, energy, and obvious delight in her increasingly substantial body. These unconventional qualities were displayed in a series of virtuoso performances in some of the most renowned Italian

"You forgot the watch!" screams Serafina Delle Rose (Anna Magnani) to her daughter Rosa (Marissa Pavan) in The Rose Tattoo. *Photo courtesy of The Historic New Orleans Collection.*

neorealist films of the late 1940s and early 1950s, beginning with a small part in Roberto Rossellini's *Open City* (1945), in which her impassioned death scene quickly made her an international sensation.

Williams confessed to being "overwhelmed" by Magnani's ungrantable demands to secure her participation in the stage play, but rightly felt that "it would be very easy to get her to do the *picture*."[16] Wallis agreed; as he remembers it: "I told Tennessee it would have to be Magnani."[17] When the two went to her apartment in Rome to finalize the deal, the encounter was certainly memorable, as Wallis recounts: "She plied us with large quantities of Johnnie Walker Red Label, the only thing she liked to drink, apart from wine. The sum total of her outburst was that the play was 'beautiful' and 'wonderful,' she would die to play Serafina, and she would master the English language in one night if necessary. She was prone to monumental exaggeration."[18]

A Hal B. Wallis Production

Because the same creative team was involved in producing *Sheba, Mrs.*

Leslie, and *Tattoo* (Wallis, Mann, and James Wong Howe as cinematographer), this series is marked by a palpable thematic unity: a flat, deglamorized, and largely unsentimental approach to life's "ordinary" problems (in which regard, Viña Delmar's midcult novel about womanly suffering and self-denial strangely complements the more highbrow dramas of Inge and Williams). In 1958, Wallis would try to repeat the success of these three films with *Hot Spell*, based on yet another Broadway play (by Lonnie Coleman), in which Mann would direct Shirley Booth again, this time starring as the long-suffering wife of a middle-aged man (Anthony Quinn) eager to leave his family for a twenty-year-old mistress. Even though set in that steamy South that Williams had almost single-handedly made into a cinematic cliché, as we shall see in Chapter 7, *Hot Spell* failed to equal the artistic and financial success of both *Sheba* and *Tattoo*. Within the context of Wallis's extensive work in the woman's picture during the 1950s, *Tattoo* stands out for its casting of Magnani. The thematic daring of the other three productions—all of which focus on the discontents of desire and illicit sexual connections of one kind or another—is somewhat muted by the presence of the decidedly plain, though charming and talented, Shirley Booth.

Tattoo would also break new ground for Wallis in its pagan celebration of life, a quality certainly present in the stage version, which he would emphasize, if not in the highly expressionistic manner that the playwright desired. A clear sign of Wallis's approach to the adaptation was his decision that experienced comic writer Hal Kanter should help Williams devise the dialogue (Kanter did not work on any of the other films in this Wallis series). Williams may have thought of *Tattoo* as what he called a "slapstick tragedy" (the carnivalesque treatment of Serafina's plight not fully recuperating the deep pain of her experience with an unfaithful husband). Wallis, by contrast, evidently saw the story as more gently comic, and therefore in need of the lighter touch that an experienced humorist would bring to the project. Incidentally, the changes demanded by the PCA and eventually made by the filmmakers contributed strongly to a perceptible shift away from the semitragic tone of the stage production toward an even happier ending for Serafina, Alvaro, Rosa, and Jack.

In fact, as was the case with many of Williams's plays, there seemed to be a particular problem with the finale. In one proposed Broadway conclusion, Serafina and one of her neighbors morbidly gather up Rosario's scattered ashes, but Kazan argued that since up to this point, the play "seemed to be in praise of life, and its undying sensual base," the ending, in keeping with this tone, should be "COMIC (in the biggest sense of that word, optimistic and healthy and uncontrollable)."[19] Once Williams embraced Kazan's idea of balancing the tragic with the comic, however, he found it difficult to decide how the play should end, going through at least twenty alternatives. As already mentioned, Williams eventually decided on a fairly positive conclusion: Serafina discovers that the mystic rose on her breast, the image of her love for Rosario that disappeared with his death, has come to life again, suggesting that her future with Alvaro will be happy and fertile.

The film, however, emphasized even more strongly the comic aspects of life, undercutting the pathos of Serafina's prolonged mourning period. In a gesture with obvious, bawdy implications, Alvaro climbs the mast of a beached sailboat to proclaim his intentions to the shocked neighborhood. Both amused and embarrassed by her lover's antics (but obviously impressed by his physicality), Serafina makes Alvaro a present of Rosario's rose-colored shirt and turns on the player piano, whose celebratory honky-tonk she had hitherto found distressing. The film then ends with a scene, though it is brief, of their boisterous laughter and conversation, suggesting that her self-imposed isolation is at an end. As with all of his film adaptations, Williams was dissatisfied with this conclusion, which, in its original form, had too obviously reflected the adaptor's humorous touch. He had observed of the earlier version that "the ending must be rewritten," confessing to being "sorry that Kanter re-wrote the scene that I gave him. Bits like this can only be written by the original author."[20] And with Wallis's agreement, he penned the final rewrite, which, still comic, was not entirely to his taste.

Questions of Love and Gross Sex

It may have surprised the project team that the treatment initially submitted to the PCA met with even stronger disapproval than that of *Streetcar* had received. Wallis and company, perhaps, had considered only the ways in which *Tattoo* might be thought to violate specific code provisions. After all, this property had no dramatized rape, no reference to a homosexual husband, and no heroine with a desperate yen for rather young men. And yet, in a personal conference with Breen, Wallis discovered that he would be asked to surmount a rather formidable obstacle if *Tattoo* were to be brought to the screen. Breen advised him of "the basic unacceptability of the story," the most important reason being that it "seems absorbed from beginning to end with questions of love and gross sex," an undeniably accurate judgment that (could it be an accident?) closely echoed the legion's damning evaluation of *Streetcar*. Recalling that embarrassing and damaging earlier experience, Breen must have been wary about being hoodwinked a second time by a Williams property. Specific objections to the play's sexual themes included the fact that "Serafina's problem of 'fulfillment' is solved by a sex affair with Alvaro" and that "Rosa is clearly begging Jack for a sex affair before she gives the indication she wants to go off and marry him."[21]

Tattoo, however, also posed problems of a different kind. The PCA judged that "Serafina's primitive confusion between religion and superstition seems calculated to put religion in a rather ridiculous light," once again an accurate evaluation of the way in which *Tattoo* invokes, but refuses to take seriously, Catholic antisexualism, indirectly associating it with that faith's somewhat populist, even superstitious practices. In the spirit of comedy and that genre's fundamental opposition to authoritarianism of any kind, Williams prefers a gentle debunking of unsophisticated lay-Catholic culture to a serious intellectual engagement with the religion's underlying values, for whose undermining or overthrow he certainly did not intend to push. Perhaps in the eyes of PCA officials, however, that comic approach made his treatment of religion even more offensive because it could be viewed as dismissive.

Interesting evidence of the yawning cultural divide between Williams and PCA officials is to be found in a memo, "Notes on the Filming of *Rose Tattoo*," that the playwright penned as plans for the production went forward. The purpose of this document is unclear, but it seems likely to have been an attempt to forestall PCA objections to the submitted treatment by not only suggesting that comedy should be given more latitude in subject matter, but also by offering to remedy what, based on his experience with the adaptation of *Streetcar*, Williams thought the censors would identify as *Tattoo*'s main problem. Alvaro's coupling with Serafina was technically "fornication," and hence unacceptable in the absence of some punishment being visited on the "malefactors." Somewhat mysteriously, however, "Notes on the Filming of *Rose Tattoo*" was not mailed initially to the PCA office, but rather to Audrey Wood, who may have in fact commissioned its composition, perhaps in consultation either with Wallis (who was a sophisticated Hollywood old hand) or his assistants at Paramount.

It is hard to believe that Williams himself, very busy with a number of projects at the time, would have conceived of composing a lengthy memo that was not a response to already-expressed PCA objections. Whatever the circumstances of its origin, Wood forwarded the carefully written and somewhat lengthy document to Wallis's assistant Paul Nathan, who sent it on not to Breen, but to his junior assistant Jack Vizzard. Within the industry, the younger man was more culturally liberal and broadminded than his boss and was perhaps thought to be more sympathetic toward the project.[22] "Notes" arrived at the PCA offices only three days after Wallis's discouraging meeting with Breen. Facing substantial opposition, Wallis and company, it seems, had immediately played their trump card: having the noted author himself reply to Breen and his assistants, perhaps in the hope of gently intimidating them. It seems likely, therefore, that the filmmakers had prepared their defense in advance, expecting ongoing negotiations in which questions of artistic value, as well as conformity to the code, might profitably be raised.

Humanity Itself?

Williams's comments address both these issues. As an opening gambit, he advanced the premise that "in a heavy drama the censorship problem is much more serious than in a play that is primarily a comedy such as 'Tattoo.'"[23] Translation: This play is funny, and thus no *Streetcar*. But such a transparent plea to the censors to take it easy this time was certainly debatable, since comedies can play fast and loose with consensus values, especially sexual mores. And those in charge at both the PCA and the legion needed little reminding that this could be the case. Otto Preminger's light sex comedy *The Moon Is Blue* (1953) had recently given both organizations a good deal of trouble. Tellingly, Preminger's film was also based on a Broadway smash (by F. Hugh Herbert), and the playwright had to struggle mightily to have his play transferred to the screen. Preminger and Herbert were unwilling to make all the requested changes, and so released— quite successfully—the film uncertified. After this trying experience, the PCA and the legion were both suitably warned about the moral and, consequently, institutional dangers to be found in comedies.[24]

After begging mercy, the playwright pleaded the mainstream, unobjectionable nature of his play. Williams may have believed that "the basic values of 'Tattoo' are its warm humanity and its humor and its touching portrayal of a woman's devotion to her husband and daughter." And yet this summary is obviously inadequate. Breen would not be so easily persuaded that this sensational and shocking play was nothing more than a companion piece of sorts to John Van Druten's famous Broadway tearjerker *I Remember Mama*. Even more provocative, perhaps, was the playwright's summary judgment of the ease with which he thought that PCA approval should be forthcoming: "Unless humanity itself has begun to fall under the censor's ban, there should be no serious difficulty in making a film out of this play that will not in any way violate either the story of essential truth of the characters *or* the code." Williams's proposed solution was for Mangiacavallo to return to Serafina's house drunk, lunge toward her eager embrace, fall in a faint, and be unreceptive thereafter to her attempts to revive him. In other words, the spirit would be willing but the flesh weak. Williams also thought that there would be little rewriting necessary to make the relationship of Rosa and Jack conform to the code: "As neither's chastity is violated, there will be no serious censorship problem in that scene." Notoriously unwilling to compromise on aspects of *Streetcar*, Williams now presented himself to Breen as a cooperative partner in the necessary reshaping of the material, demonstrating that he recognized in advance what might cause offense. Williams undoubtedly approached the writing of the first part of "Notes" as a somewhat unpleasant chore. It was necessary (or so he must have been advised) to ease the passage of the play from stage to screen, but disagreeable because he felt forced to recast his drama in terms he felt Hollywood censors might approve (the bathetic phrase "touching portrayal" would not have come naturally to him).

Plastic-Poetic Elements?

The concluding section of the memo, however, overflows with his genuine enthusiasm for the project; here he maintains that "the great problem is an artistic one," not one of censorship. At this point, the playwright's intended audience seems to be Wallis and Mann rather than Jack Vizzard. Williams argues that *Streetcar* was more successfully adapted than *Menagerie* because the Kazan film was "more faithful to the artistic concept of the original," and thus in a profound sense its equal. With *Tattoo*, however, the change in medium ought to result in substantial improvement because "the stage imposed merciless limitations on what was really the most valuable new aspects of 'Tattoo,'" those "plastic-poetic elements," of which only "the barest glimpse . . . was provided in the

Broadway production." As Williams saw it, what was crucial to the play's intended effect (and what he regarded as his "plastic" elements) was what filmmakers call mise-en-scène: the visual and aural background that should provide meaning and depth to Serafina's resurrection, including such motifs as, in the playwright's colorful enumeration: "the wild play of the children, the Dionysian antics of the goat's escape and capture, the crazy Strega, the volatile life of the primitive neighborhood, the church, the chanted Mass, the organ music, the simple mysteries of the faith of a simple people, the surrounding earth, and sea, and sky, the great trucks thundering along the highway, the scarlet kite."

However, such an expressionistic concern with creating an affecting *stimmung*, or "tone," through the careful design of spectacle would find limited reflection in the finished film, which embodies the very different aesthetic of fifties Hollywood filmmaking of the serious variety. Mann "opens up" the drama to some extent, but more according to neorealist protocols. To be sure, James Wong Howe's black-and-white cinematography is rich in chiaroscuro effects and finely conceived detailing, but these stylizations are unobtrusive, designed to provide the story with authenticity. In the neorealist manner, the camera sometimes focuses as much on the community—particularly the chorus of village women, who serve mainly as comic relief—as it does on the principals. Wallis (with Mann evidently not objecting) was more interested in making a muted, realistic drama, in the vein of *Sheba* and other small black-and-white adult films of the period. Frequent long takes afford the actors (particularly Magnani) the opportunity to shape multilayered performances, usually glimpsed in medium long shots that place the characters firmly within a carefully observed milieu. Once again in the neorealist manner, this effect is substantially heightened by the exclusive use of real locations for exteriors and interiors (including, coincidentally, the house of Williams's next-door neighbor in Key West). Sets were dressed with a careful attention to authenticating detail. Mann does not customarily use either analytical editing or close-ups to shape performances, allowing the drama in which the characters are embroiled to emerge without stylistic enhancement or montage pyrotechnics, in a manner of which French theorists at the time, especially André Bazin, would have certainly approved.

Vizzard quickly forwarded Williams's long memo to Breen, but the PCA head was unimpressed with Williams's argument and his proposed solutions. To his mind, these fell "far short of the basic requirements for making *Tattoo* acceptable under the Code" because "the only point with which Mr. Williams feels it is necessary to deal is the sex affair between Serafina and Alvaro." Unlike the playwright, Breen had been schooled in Thomist notions of sinfulness as primarily a matter of intentionality (the mental assent to wrongdoing being determinative of, and consequently more serious than, the resulting act). Williams's suggested rewriting, therefore, would not work, "since it will be quite evident that Alvaro returns to Serafina's house with the obvious intention of indulging in a sex affair with her, and only fails because he falls asleep in a drunken stupor." Breen makes the same point about the relationship between Rose and Jack, remarking that, even though the chastity of both young people is preserved, "a scene of a young girl begging a boy to take her sexually, would be thoroughly unacceptable under the Code." The PCA head was especially dismissive about Williams's plea that his characters were true to life (in essence, "humanity itself") and that such authenticity precludes moral objections; he snapped: "We do not know what Mr. Williams means by such statements." Breen concluded that the property would continue to be unacceptable as long as "Mr. Williams's idea of the 'humanity' of his characters involves their absorption in questions of sex and lust, as it does in the stageplay."[25]

This argument appears to be a strong stand against a by-then conventional thematic emphasis of a modernist text, but the PCA was no longer in a position to prevent such "carnality" from reaching the screen, as Breen quite evidently realized. For he ended his memo with an invitation to negotiate further after a screenplay was written: "We shall be very happy to read a script prepared from this material, if you see fit to develop one." As he had done in other cases, Breen could have simply reiterated his view of the "basic unacceptability of the story," effectively discouraging further work on the production unless major changes were made. Wallis, it seems, was supposed to read the message between the lines: compromises are possible in this case. Changes would thus be requested, made, and endorsed, but probably, on the part of Breen and his colleagues, with the somewhat dispiriting knowledge that there was no way Rosa, Alvaro, Serafina, and Jack could be freed from "their absorption in questions of sex and lust."

Romance rather than Lust?

But before shooting could start, Breen's objections had in some sense to be accommodated, even if in an essentially cosmetic fashion. A year

Alvaro Mangiacavallo (Burt Lancaster) charms Serafina (Anna Magnani) with a box of chocolates in The Rose Tattoo. *Photo courtesy of The Historic New Orleans Collection.*

passed, and the PCA, having received a revised script, commented on the acceptability of the changes that had been made. One was easily effected: the replacement of the statue of the Madonna (to whom Serafina prays for assistance and guidance and with whom she becomes furious at one point) with "some personal memento of Serafina's dead husband."

But if this change diminished the presence of religion in the story, and hence the possibility of its seeming in some sense mocked, it ironically increased the sense of Serafina's preoccupation with the very carnality that Breen otherwise found objectionable. All jokes at the expense of religion were excised. As for the play's central scene, Breen advised that "the emphasis will not be put on [Alvaro's] desire to sleep with [Serafina], but upon romance rather than lust," a vague and difficult-to-evaluate reformulation that was, of course, entirely in line with mainstream Hollywood practice (and perfectly in keeping as well with the other pictures in the Wallis "drab melodrama" series). In fact, the general thrust of Breen's comments would have been to turn *Tattoo* more completely into a rather formulaic woman's picture: "Fundamentally this will be a story of a woman, Serafina, who is inordinately devoted to the memory of her dead husband, and who, as a result, exercises an unjust sway over her daughter's life."

Instead of centering on an ironic and mystical form of sexual healing, the proposed plot, according to this agreement between the producers and the censors, would turn on a time-honored melodramatic transformation: "The resolution of this problem will consist in Serafina growing up as a person, abandoning her fixation about her dead husband, releasing her daughter, and finally taking her proper place in the community."[26] The elements necessary for this character development are more or less present in Williams's original conception, of course, but the "growing up as a person" that Serafina does in the play and film depends entirely on the erotic renewal effected by Alvaro, who is essentially (and, of course, ironically) conceived of as a replacement for Rosario's body, thereby providing an interesting twist on the standard melodramatic theme of restoration.

There was no disguising that central element of the drama, however much Wallis and Breen might talk about the plot as if it were the stuff of a standard woman's picture. No matter that Alvaro should somehow drunkenly pass out so that the bedroom scene between him and Serafina could be avoided, as Breen advised. Perhaps sensing the intractability of the problem, Breen thought he might be deceived by Wallis and company even after both parties agreed to this explicit memorandum of understanding. And so he politely insisted on an important proviso: "May we suggest that, because of the difficult nature of the original material from which this basic story is to be derived, you might find it to your advantage to send along even the earliest draft treatments which you might prepare, on the way to developing a finished script."[27]

More negotiations followed, but by April 1954, Breen was more or less satisfied with the shape of the film, though he quibbled about minor "indiscretions" such as Alvaro discovering Rosa asleep on the couch.[28] Tellingly, that very funny scene, like most of the bawdiness of Williams's original conception, remained in the film despite the censor's disapproval. Breen was certainly dreaming when he advised the filmmakers that "the ending would be altered somewhat to emphasize the impression that Alvaro was going back to Serafina's house with marriage alone on his mind."[29] Wallis, Williams, and Mann may have humored Breen by agreeing to this demand, but, at least to judge from the finished film, they had no intention of keeping such a commitment.

Man Can Live by Bed Alone

Williams was less than pleased by the results of his collaboration with Hal Kanter. Concerned that the poetry was being stripped out of his work, he complained to Audrey Wood about the direction that the script was taking. Williams thought that the material was "admirably suited to the screen," but he was determined to retain "the lyrical values, the plastic values" that he described in his "Notes," lest the thrust of the material be destroyed.

In an unpublished piece entitled "A Playwright's Prayer," Williams elaborates on the complex relationship he had with his collaborators, striking a humble pose while at the same time holding his own ground.[30] In his petition, Williams asks his "Dear Father in Heaven" to "help me receive with interest and advice, whether solicited by myself or offered to me gratuitously, to read and consider all notes no matter who makes them." He also asks to be reminded "if I ever seem to forget it, that I am working with other creative artists whose dedication . . . may equal or exceed my own." In both the theatre and the cinema, of course, artistic collaboration is not only desirable; it is obligatory.[31]

Williams asked Wood to discuss this issue with Wallis and to arrive at a solution involving "a collaborator who will be willing to work *under my direction*, since I think it is reasonable to assume that I, who created the play and the characters in it, am best able to judge whether or not they are being re-created for the screen."[32] Kanter, he thought, "couldn't write 'I see the cat.'" The playwright worried: "Perhaps Wallis does not want 'Tattoo' but another film loosely related to it." In particular, he was concerned that *Tattoo* "would be another 'Menagerie' or worse, for the episodes in 'Tattoo' will be grotesque and Serafina a ridiculous slob *unless* it exists in the poetic atmosphere of the original." The only thing he seemed satisfied with was the manner in which "all censorable material" had been eliminated.

Shortly after Williams sent Mann a new ending to *Tattoo* from Rome (presumably the ship's mast scene that appears in the finished film), he learned that Kanter had been removed from working on the picture, then wrote Wood that "if I am allowed to replace Kanter's stuff with my own, I think we will be in good shape."[33] The writing chores would thenceforth be his alone, and the finished film certainly bears the strong impress of his talent and interests. Wallis recalled that collaborating with Williams on the script was indeed a "happy experience," free from the producer-writer conflicts that can fatally compromise a project.[34]

Though he was initially pleased with the film fashioned from his play, Williams quickly became more ambivalent about both the picture and the work of the director, even though he managed to create more of a sensation with the Hollywood than the Broadway version. Later in 1955, the playwright declared, "It was inaccurate and unkind, equally both, to suggest that I blamed *Rose Tattoo*'s relative lack of success [on Broadway] on its direction. Daniel Mann did a beautiful job on the stage version of *Tattoo* and a still more beautiful job on the film. Gadge would have demanded a stronger, tighter script from me: Danny was willing to take a chance on the script submitted."[35]

This last observation is right on target. Mann did not ask for the extensive changes that Kazan, had he directed the film, would surely have requested. The result is that the film belongs more to Williams than to Mann, Kanter, or Wallis. But this is surely very much to the good. The textures of play and film are amazingly similar, despite Williams's often fussy misgivings. Much of the original bawdy dialogue was retained, including such memorable double entendres as the heavy cargo that both Rosario and Alvaro are said to haul. Could it be anything besides king-sized bananas? And did Breen even get the joke?

Whatever their opinion of the film (*Tattoo* found an equal number of enthusiasts and detractors), critics agreed that the original story had not been much transformed by the adaptation process. Moira Walsh suggests that "a little restraint has been imposed on the playwright, who wrote his own scenario, with the result that the movie is much better than the play." The result is "probably the earthiest film ever to come out of Hollywood."[36] Derek Prouse finds that *Tattoo*, because of the freedom allowed the writer, is "too personal, inartistic, and facile" in its contention "that man can live by bed alone." What *Tattoo* is about, then, is not romance (the standard Hollywood theme that Breen argued the filmmakers should adopt) but rather a "surrender to the purely animal challenge, with no thought of any other compatibility"; Williams offers sensuality as "a panacea."[37] Philip T. Hartung allows that "Tennessee Williams cleaned up the play somewhat, but it is still . . . mainly a character portrait of a vain, superstitious woman who is obsessed with sex."[38]

This steamy (for the era) adult fare found itself that year in great favor with the viewing public. *Tattoo* proved to be, after *Streetcar*, one of the playwright's most substantial screen successes; and Wallis, despite his prominence in the industry, produced no better film in the decade. Anna Magnani's performance was hailed as one of the international screen's greatest, while Burt Lancaster, following up his well-received performance in *Sheba*, solidified his reputation as a talented actor (rather than just another pretty torso). He would go on to appear in a number of similarly "serious" roles, including tour de force character performances in two of the era's most acclaimed films, *Sweet Smell of Success* (1957) and *Judgment at Nuremberg* (1960). *Tattoo* would be well received by the members of the Academy of Motion Picture Arts and Sciences, nominated for best picture, music (Alex North), supporting actress (Marisa Pavan), and supporting actor (Ben Cooper), and receiving awards that year for best actress (Magnani), cinematography (James Wong Howe), and art direction (Hal Pereira).

The Smell of Rose Oil in His Hair

After reading the treatment submitted by Wallis, Joseph Breen had objected to *Tattoo*'s being absorbed with "questions of lust and gross sex." The PCA gave the production a green light only when Wallis assured him that the characters' obsession with carnality would be given a more traditional melodramatic turn, with Serafina transformed from a jealous, bitter, and sex-starved woman into a mother who, recognizing her need to "grow up," eventually becomes a proper parent to her adult daughter and assumes her proper place in the community. Breen, of course, must have been aware that such a reshaping would have ruined the value of Williams's play, which was appealing to Wallis and Paramount precisely because it was naughty and unconventional, not just another entry in the time-worn tradition of long-suffering-mother-centered melodramas (such as *Stella Dallas* [1937], *Imitation of Life* [1934, 1959], and *Madame X* [1929, 1937, 1965]).

Tattoo, instead, would follow the controversial path that *Streetcar* had recently blazed. As we have seen, Legion of Decency raters had been struck by *Streetcar*'s improper thematizing of *marital* sexuality, which, in the case of Stella and Stanley, was found to be less *caritas* and more *cupiditas*, the kind of lust rather than love that church doctrine held was an occasion for sin, even within the otherwise sacramental bonds of matrimony. At the time, the threat to rate the film a "C" was taken very seriously by Warner Bros., which risked alienating one of Hollywood's hottest directors in order to accede to legion demands, though they amounted to, as Kazan would point out, a tiny pointless finger in a dyke whose walls had already been irrevocably breached. If both the legion and the PCA were in any doubt that their opinion of Williams's characters and themes was out of date, the public and the critics provided the proof, since *Streetcar* won not only four Academy Awards, but raked in huge profits at the box office as well.

The legion had objected to a scene in *Streetcar* in which a man and his wife embraced with too much ardor and unguilty pleasure. Just a few years later, *Tattoo* would offer much more daring and more obviously carnal caresses. At the beginning of the film, Rosario is napping before the midnight smuggling run whose unexpected tragic conclusion will soon make Serafina a widow. She comes into the bedroom, where he is glimpsed posed horizontally in the foreground of the frame, naked from the waist up and wrapped in shadows that do not reveal his face but allow the rose tattoo to be seen glowing on his chest. Serafina sits down beside this sleeping form, softly strokes the muscles of his arm and chest, nuzzles his neck and back, and, with obvious delight and barely concealed ardor, smells the rose oil in his hair.

This striking tableau adumbrates the future state of Serafina's unsatisfied, mournful longing. Rosario never sits up to face her but rather remains recumbent and entirely available to her hands and eyes. The only dialogue in the scene is Serafina's ungranted plea that he not go away that night. Rosario briefly and prophetically responds that this will indeed be his last trip. More importantly, this scene also makes palpable and affecting the depth of her desire for her husband, who, in the tradition of pornographic representation, is artfully depersonalized. Reduced to near muteness, his fragmented body posed aesthetically, Rosario becomes flesh itself, the lovely *thing* for which Serafina aches. Here is no embrace of a couple whose mutual lust has been fed by violence and bitter words, but the very image of *cupiditas*: the purely carnal urge to possess and enjoy through worshipful objectification. Never moving (and avoiding close-ups), the camera clinically analyzes Serafina's psychological state from a respectful distance as Magnani gives a deeply convincing performance as a woman in barely restrained heat for a male body. Hollywood cinema had never before produced anything like this. In fact, such depictions of empowered female desire and a thoroughly objectified male body remain rare even in the post-PCA era.

No Protest from the Legion

It was a sign of the rapidly changing times that the PCA said not a word about this scene and that the legion passed *Tattoo* with only the barest of demurrals and a "B" rating, signifying that the film was objectionable only in part. Just what part, we might well ask, would that be? In any event, the "B" perhaps meant that *Tattoo* found itself at the very limit of what conservative, but not necessarily philistine, reviewers would have found acceptable at the time. After all, the relationship between Alvaro and Serafina is not adulterous, and her desire for Rosario and then Alvaro is legitimated (at least after a fashion) by marriage, actual or implied. Both relationships could be understood as "romances," though that interpretation is something of a stretch. Perhaps more importantly, the film does not condone Rosario's unfaithfulness with Estelle, in this respect aligning itself much more closely and unambiguously with traditional moral strictures than does *Streetcar*. With the playwright's close participation, *Tattoo* could readily be given something closely approaching the conventional happy Hollywood ending, with the constitution of two heterosexual couples (Rosa's attachment to Jack is even less steamy than her mother's to Alvaro) and the promise therefore of all family and erotic problems neatly resolved or, at least, contained within the bonds of matrimony.

And yet, as with *Streetcar*, the subject of desire is figured in a fashion so innovatively excessive as to obfuscate quite effectively the film's otherwise deep engagement with consensus social values. *Tattoo* was indeed at the time "the earthiest film ever to come out of Hollywood." The legion, however, was not moved to condemn it as such. The "B" rating, we might say, nicely indexed a profound ambivalence that the filmmakers carefully and cannily nurtured. Williams and his collaborators were not so much strongly challenged as accommodated. And in the wake of the popular and critical success of *Streetcar*, they likely foresaw that this would be the case.

CHAPTER FIVE

Bending the Code III

Baby Doll

Formulating a Scandalous Success

The legion would not be so timid (or, perhaps better, indecisive) in its reaction, just a year later, to another Williams property brought to the screen: *Baby Doll*. The conservative Catholic community rallied to protest its exhibition, and no other Williams movie achieved such notoriety. *Baby Doll* proved exceptional in other ways as well. Though based on two one-act Williams plays, with additional material penned by the playwright, *Baby Doll* is fundamentally different from the three films discussed thus far. *Baby Doll* belongs more to Elia Kazan, its director, producer, and principal screenwriter, than to the author of its ostensible theatrical sources. Hollywood's *Menagerie*, *Streetcar*, and *Tattoo* are screen versions of works written expressly for the stage. Despite often substantial modifications, these properties were presented relatively intact for the larger audience the film industry could command.

Baby Doll, by contrast, was from the outset a collaborative confection. Only after its spectacular cinematic exhibition had garnered enormous cultural cachet and repute did Williams author a theatrical version based closely on the film, eventually to be officially titled *Tiger Tail* (though this play is more widely known as *Baby Doll*). Ordinarily, source text and adaptation share in a single identity; that is, they are versions of the same thing. Moreover, the process of adaptation does not normally involve rendering the source either disposable or in some sense obsolete; yet *Baby Doll* did just that. In this exceptional case, Kazan, with the cooperation

*Baby Doll Meighan (Carroll Baker) prepares Silva Vacarro (Eli Wallach)
for a nap in her famous crib from a scene in* Baby Doll. *Photo courtesy of
The Historic New Orleans Collection.*

of Williams, worked a radical kind of transformative magic. Why was
such magic necessary?

Earlier we outlined the reasons why Hollywood in the postwar era
generally found attractive the various properties of Tennessee Williams.
Always eager to acquire presold materials, industry producers in the 1950s
believed that one way to recapture moviegoers' interest was to offer them
the kind of serious adult drama, tested for popularity on the commercial
stage, that television (for commercial and legal reasons) could not provide. *Baby Doll* was not in any traditional sense a presold property, but
its author was. Because Williams had not yet written another full-length
play with the sensational punch of *Streetcar*, Kazan asked to review several one-act plays that would be used to form the spine of a film script,
one that might recapture the magic of their initial screen collaboration.
Williams obliged by sending him six one-acts written in the forties: *This
Property Is Condemned*, *The Last of My Solid Gold Watches*, *Hello from Bertha*, *The Case of the Crushed Petunias*, *The Unsatisfactory Supper*, and *27
Wagons Full of Cotton*. The script was based eventually on the last two of

these somewhat untested short dramas. Neither had enjoyed a substantial Broadway production and run. Neither, in fact, had achieved any real success to speak of.

Cotton, presumably, was chosen as the base text for the film project because it offered something similar to the tension-fraught, subversive, and tantalizingly disturbing erotic triangles that had contributed so much to making *Streetcar* and *Tattoo* screen successes. In the case of *Baby Doll*, the triangle needed "spicing up," as we may infer from the reworking it seems to have received from Kazan, who apparently drew on one of Broadway's most spectacular and scandalous successes of an earlier decade, Erskine Caldwell's *Tobacco Road*, for the film's most memorable element: the struggle over "conjugal rights" between Baby Doll Meighan and husband Archie Lee.

The adaptation of *Streetcar* and *Tattoo* had involved blunting the eroticism of the stage versions to make them acceptable to industry censors, religious tastemakers, and viewers while not vitiating their appealing sensationalism. In contrast, if *Baby Doll* were to achieve the same kind of success, a more sensational eroticism would have to be somehow added to the source material. Because it had not been presold in the ordinary sense, the project would not have been seen by many in the industry as very promising. Or, we should say, that would have been the case if the Williams name by itself had not become, by the early fifties, eminently "bankable" as the playwright's reputation for being an author whose texts were as sensational as they were artistic became international. Put simply, by the time Kazan was ready to begin filming *Baby Doll*, Warner Bros. executives had showed strong interest in this unusual project from the outset, even though they had no clearer idea than did Williams and Kazan of what it might finally turn out to be.

A Newtown Productions Release

In any event, the financial risk for the studio promised to be minimal. Kazan was envisioning a small film rather than a mainstream "A" feature with a sizable budget. Such a plan would work only if the rights to the Williams property were relatively inexpensive, yet another reason to use the one-acts rather than a Broadway-tested success. Hoping to avoid the limitations on his creative freedom that a large investment from the studio would impose, Kazan determined that he would not only direct, but also produce the film for his new company (Newtown Productions), with additional financing and distribution provided by the studio. *Baby Doll* would be the first in a series of independent releases from Newtown that would receive additional investment from and be distributed by Warner Bros. These turned out to be *A Face in the Crowd* (1957), *Wild River* (1960), and *Splendor in the Grass* (1961). Kazan would be able to retain the right to determine each film's final cut, and since Newtown was not a signatory to the PCA agreement, he would not be dictated to by the Breen office—or the Legion of Decency. In the event, he was not. But this "victory" over what he considered the dark forces of censorship turned out to be more than a little Pyrrhic.

As Kazan remembered, the project was very much his idea from the beginning: "When I proposed this film to Tennessee Williams, he wasn't interested. I went ahead anyway [presumably with adapting and modifying the material], put a script together, and sent him what I'd done; he gave me an unenthusiastic 'go ahead.'"[1] Kazan probably thought that an independent production in the tradition of the international art cinema would appeal to Williams. Like many intellectuals of the era, Williams favored Italian neorealism, a tradition that Kazan would follow in shaping the project.

Williams, however, showed little interest in writing the script. Besides Kazan's prodding, the playwright had only one other primary motivation—his deteriorating financial situation. With his film payments from *Streetcar* terminated and his government bonds not yet matured, Williams suddenly found himself in financial straits. In December 1953, he wrote to Kazan, "I'm working hard on the film script. It isn't easy as I had to stop work on a play to pick it up, but I do need the money real bad and this seems about the only way I can count on gathering any."[2] But later, as the project moved ahead, he wrote Kazan: "HELP! HELP! SEND ME A WRITER!" Uncharacteristically, Williams offered to "sacrifice the screen-writing credit" on the film if he were to be "given full credit for the authorship of the one-act plays it's based on."[3]

His interest, however, waxed as often as it waned. Only two months later, Williams informed Actors Studio guru Cheryl Crawford that he was working on the script with Paul Bigelow, a close friend. "The film," he wrote, "is going great."[4] But this positive mood was apparently short-lived, as Williams wrote another friend, Oliver Evans, later the same month, telling him that Bigelow had been sent to Key West by Audrey Wood "to apply the thumb screws: to get me to work on the Kazan movie-script which I loathed doing but which is now done."[5]

What Williams didn't realize, however, was that the script was far from being "done" and that he would not be the one to put it into final form. From 1952 until shooting was completed in 1956, dozens of letters exchanged between Williams and Kazan reveal that the director was the prime motivator behind the project—and the one who should really be credited with putting the material into its final, shootable form. With Williams often traveling in Europe, Kazan took charge of preproduction chores back home. Jack Warner also assumed an active role, urging Kazan several times in the early 1950s to cajole Williams into producing a script. In January 1952, he wrote to Kazan, "Leaving it in your hands, Gadg, to see that script is pushed forward post haste."[6] Kazan replied: "I am trying to get Williams to sit down one of these months and really complete his job on the script."[7] Warner knew well that "without a good script we are all stymied."[8] Williams's frequent letters to Kazan make it clear that the playwright returned to the film script only when goaded to do so by his collaborator.

Interestingly, the correspondence also brings to light the frequent, sometimes acrimonious disagreements over the script's tone and content. Although the myriad changes preclude a total listing of rejected material, jettisoned scripts contain scenes with Ruby Lightfoot (who would later appear in the play based upon the screenplay, *Tiger Tail*), a lengthy frog-gigging scene (Williams pleaded a lack of technical expertise in this area of rustic culture), and Kazan's characteristically scandalous (for the era) idea to have Baby Doll kiss an African American man. Rejected for the film, this motif oddly makes a reappearance in the sleazy advertising for its 1967 drive-in rerelease (more below), which deceptively led prospective viewers to anticipate some kind of encounter between Baby Doll and a "big black buck."

Particularly troublesome was Williams's characteristic difficulty in coming up with a satisfactory ending. An exasperated Kazan pleaded with the playwright: "What is the end of the actions we have started? What is the conclusion? What happens to Baby Doll tomorrow? Does she stay with Archie Lee? It seems to me the audience has a right to know . . . otherwise the whole picture becomes a gigantic cock tease. Which isn't bad. But that is all it is."[9] There were dozens of proposed endings, including: Baby Doll and Vacarro in a final roadhouse scene, with Aunt Rose being whisked away by a tornado; a frantic sequence in which Archie Lee kills Vacarro and is sent to a filthy jail with a black cell mate; and Archie Lee shooting and killing a black man complacently sitting in the Pierce Arrow auto. Many of these proposed endings were rather tragic or, at least, more serious (the tone that Kazan argued for) than the comic (in)conclusion that Williams persuaded Kazan, after much debate, to settle on.

Over the several years of *Baby Doll*'s script development, Williams sent in snippets from various places around the world, sometimes on hotel stationery, cardboard shirt backs, and bar stubs. Kazan would then provide rewritten continuities to Williams, who would often quibble with the direction the film was taking. As Kazan reminisced, Williams would "mail me a page or two on the stationery of whatever hotel he was at, with the instruction: 'Insert somewhere.' In places, these scraps helped; often they did not."[10] Kazan was eager to have Williams assist more substantially with preparing a script still very much in progress, but that proved impossible to arrange. While location shooting was proceeding in Benoit, Mississippi, the director-producer lured the playwright south with the promise of an available swimming pool, where he might enjoy his preferred form of daily exercise. However, Williams departed almost as quickly as he had come, leaving the director, the actors, and the crew to their own devices, though from a distance he still helped out with occasional problems. The film, we might say, was very much Kazan's baby. *Baby Doll* was unconventional not only in the process that brought it into existence, but also, and more importantly, in its handling of Williams's most characteristic dramatic structure: an unusual sexual triangle.

A Billboard Almost as Big as the Statue of Liberty

In his role as producer, Kazan took charge of marketing, which he understood would be crucial to the success of the project. He designed and supervised one of the most noteworthy and controversial campaigns the industry had ever witnessed. The producer could boast, and did, that the creative duo who had produced the sensational *Streetcar* had again teamed up in something of a sequel. But he otherwise created his own buzz. This did not prove too difficult, since he had made sure that the film offered more than its share of what at the time was viewed as a transgressive eroticism. The advertising campaign, however, raised these stakes considerably. Kazan adroitly exploited to maximum effect the notorious reputation that Williams by this point in his career was enjoying.

In *Baby Doll*, unlike the Williams properties that had preceded it to the screen, there is no question of "romance," a significant revision of the time-honored Hollywood formula. Under the slight cover of comedy, *Baby Doll* strongly challenges conventional mores and sensibilities, even as it also deliberately affects the stylistic regime of the international art film (mostly through a de-emphasis on plot, the deployment of unsympathetic characters, and an avoidance of glamorization). In its artistic approach and production values, *Baby Doll* bears little resemblance to the screen versions of *Menagerie*, *Streetcar*, and *Tattoo*; it is much less a "Hollywood" production. But this different direction was not the quality that Kazan would promote when selling the film to the American public.

His engagement with the international art cinema did not escape critical notice. Kazan reports that some people at the time remarked on the film's Europeanness, the way that it seemed very much "an artistic cousin to the films of [Marcel] Pagnol."[11] And that is a very apt comparison. As novelist and film director, Pagnol limned with humor and insight the lives of the country people of Provence, emphasizing their venality and petty though deadly feuds, especially in the justly famous *Manon des Sources* (1953), in which he directed the adaptation of his own novel. Unlike the glossier and yet more serious remake directed by Claude Berri in 1986 (a two-part production, including the "prequel" *Jean de Florette*), the original *Manon* is a low-key, realist production, an uproarious portrait of rural grotesques who are very similar to the white-trash characters who figure so memorably in Kazan's film. Interestingly, like *Baby Doll*, *Manon* deals with revenge taken for a wrong that has disastrous economic and personal consequences.

The viewing public was in general unimpressed by *Baby Doll*'s self-conscious artiness. Most who saw the film, and even those who only heard about it, never looked beyond its sensationalism, which Kazan, ever the showman, was more inclined to emphasize. The legion, at the height of its power in the decade (and encouraged by one of the most powerful prelates of the twentieth century, Francis Cardinal Spellman of New York) would fully mobilize in an attempt, partially successful, to thwart Kazan and have *Baby Doll* removed from theatres. In contrast, the exhibition three years earlier in New York of *Manon des Sources* had merely aroused intellectual interest, not the public controversy that soon swirled around *Baby Doll*.

Interestingly, the casus belli was not textual as such, but rather the marketing campaign whose centerpiece was the display (over astounded and mesmerized Times Square crowds) of a huge sign, hand-painted to Kazan's specifications, depicting star Carroll Baker, the young "baby doll" of the film's title, scantily clad and seductively recumbent in a child's crib. There she sucks her thumb teasingly, meeting the gaze of prospective viewers. Intending to attract holiday crowds, Kazan scheduled the film for a mid-December opening, with the outsized billboard going up just as Christmas shoppers crowded into midtown Manhattan. Hollywood marketing, hardly timid about crass erotic display (and thus subject to something like a code of censorship of its own), had never before seen anything like this image.

The film's pressbook enthused to potential exhibitors that:

> This is showmanship . . . Biggest painted sign in the world! It's 15,600 square feet (one-third of an acre)—the picture of 'Baby Doll' is almost as big as the Statue of Liberty—and it's seen by a million visitors to Broadway every day. A splurge so big and unusual the New York newspapers, national news and photo syndicates, news-reels, TV and radio all covered it![12]

In all their vulgarity and crassness, Kazan's comments about the sign to the production executives at Warner Bros. are even more revealing, especially of his desire to pump up the film's box office:

> This is the greatest idea since the days of Barnum. That half-sleeping, day-dreaming, thumb-sucking, long-legged chick . . . with only Warner Bros (small type, of course), Tennessee Williams and yours truly's names on the sign, and a big arrow pointing down to the Victoria Theatre will be the talk not only of Broadway, but of the show world, of café society, of the literati, of the lowbrows, and of everybody else. I really don't see how anyone could avoid going to the picture if we put that sign up there. What's wrong with show business is that its balls have been cut off and it is no longer show business. No one showboats anymore. . . . Trust my instinct. I'm known as the Greek Barnum and I care like a son of a bitch.[13]

Kazan, of course, wasn't the only, or even the first, Barnum wannabe who had made a big splash in film exhibition during the postwar era. Not every Hollywood producer was a castrato according to his definition. In fact, there was an obvious model for *Baby Doll*'s billboard advertising. After the first release of *The Outlaw* in 1943 was seen as more offensive than provocative by wartime filmgoers, Howard Hughes designed in 1946 what has been termed "one of the most vulgar advertising campaigns in motion picture history" for the second, and wildly popular, postwar exhibition of his much-maligned "breast epic."[14] Posters and billboards, featuring a thinly bloused Jane Russell, her twin assets prominently displayed, ran infamous slug lines: "Would you like to tussle with Russell?" and "What are the two greatest reasons for Jane Russell's rise to stardom?" An even better showman, Kazan improved significantly on Hughes's concept. The image on his billboard was so crassly eloquent it needed no clever slug lines to make it memorable. With its hard-to-miss hints of what Breen would have called "sex perversion," the striking tableau of a becribbed, thumb-sucking Carroll Baker sent out a message that spoke loud and clear to those in the know.

As they had done with *The Outlaw*, social conservatives judged Kazan's film on the basis of its advertising. The irony is that *Baby Doll* delivered less on its soft-core promise than did Hughes's sleazy film, which no doubt managed to satisfy in some sense what critics at the time termed the "pectoral curiosity" of paying customers. There is no sex as such in *Baby Doll*, no disturbing violence, no "adult" language, no nudity, no explicit discussion of forbidden subjects. The film's naughtiness consists entirely, to use today's ratings terminology, in its oblique evocation of "sexual situations." The marketing campaign promised something much more daring, even transgressive. What mattered more at the time was perception rather than reality. In addition to bringing in many eager viewers, the Times Square sign, like the subsequent newspaper spreads and posters that used the same image, was such an obvious provocation that the church, and its lay defenders, could not and did not ignore it, especially during the Christmas season.

Kazan feigned surprise and shock at the uproar that immediately greeted the initial release of *Baby Doll*. He states in his autobiography that "it took Cardinal Spellman to make it famous," but that is hardly true, because the billboard had created a huge public sensation, precisely as he had calculated it would, long before the prelate denounced the film from the pulpit in St. Patrick's Cathedral.[15] It would be more accurate to say that Spellman played perfectly the role that Kazan, his expectations for huge profits based on the film becoming a succès de scandale, had mapped out for him.

Kazan's role in the project has hitherto been the object of something like a deliberate campaign of obfuscation, in which the director himself played a principal role.[16] Disingenuously, he declared to his biographer Richard Schickel: "There's nothing in the movie except sweetness and humor." Schickel notes that this comment ignores the film's carefully exploited Lolita theme, perhaps its most surprising feature from the point of view of Williams's other work. The extraordinary erotic force of the triangular relationship among the lecherous Archie Lee, his still-virginal child bride Baby Doll, and her would-be seducer Silva Vacarro, so Schickel suggests, was not uppermost in Kazan's mind as he scripted, produced, and marketed the film: "I believe him when he says that the not-particularly-hidden subtext of *Baby Doll* did not consciously occur to him when he was making the movie. His calculations on a project often revolved around plot and characters, with its larger implications only vaguely rattling around in his mind."[17] Kazan was the most talented and influential director of postwar Broadway (and an immense presence on the Hollywood scene as well). And he became such a central figure in mid-twentieth-century performing art in large part because he worked with great care on all his projects. The heavily detailed notebooks he kept as he worked through every stage and film project, now archived in the Kazan collection at Wesleyan University, speak eloquently to this point. Contrary to Schickel's presumption, Kazan could not possibly have been only "vaguely" aware of the "larger implications" of *Baby Doll*. His reading of the film is spelled out clearly in the Times Square billboard.

Kazan was very eager for the financial and popular success that another hit along the lines of *Streetcar* might provide. He was, in his own words, a "Greek Barnum." But how could anyone who lived through the period forget, among his other Barnumesque moves, that a few years after *Baby Doll*, Kazan attempted to spike interest in his adaptation of William Inge's *Splendor in the Grass* by proclaiming that he intended to feature full-length rear-view shots of a completely nude Natalie Wood? No doubt, Kazan decided from the outset to make a sexually provocative film based on Williams materials. The project went through at least eight different titles, most of which, like *The Whip Hand* and *Mississippi Woman*, were deliberately suggestive, reflecting varying erotic agendas. What was uppermost in Kazan's mind was repeating the success of *Streetcar*. We recall that he once wrote to Jack Warner that *Streetcar* was a surefire bet because it was about the "3 F's" and also had "class." *Baby Doll* was likewise a film marked by these two signal qualities of the era's international art cinema, the only "growth area" in U.S. film exhibition during the 1950s.

Times change, however, and it is interesting to note that Kazan's approach to rereleasing the film in 1967 was substantially different. More

The drive-in advertisement for the double feature Shanty Tramp *and* Baby Doll, *with the curious billing of "The big, black buck." Photo courtesy of Margaret Herrick Library, Center for Motion Picture Study, Academy of Motion Picture Arts and Sciences, Beverly Hills, California.*

than a decade after *Baby Doll* had shocked the nation as a well-publicized "A" feature penned by one of America's leading writers, Kazan, making a deal with Cinemation, booked it to run in drive-in theatres as the top half of a double bill with *Shanty Tramp* (Joseph G. Prieto, 1967), a low-budget, laughably inept exploitation film that traces the sexual and violent exploits of its eponymous heroine: a southern girl from the wrong side of the tracks who spends most of the film implausibly bare-breasted as she becomes embroiled in a series of sleazy escapades. Kazan must have thought that the "shanty tramp" and Baby Doll Meighan could be seen as characters equally shaped by a "white trash aesthetic" that would prove attractive, so he hoped, to the late-sixties drive-in crowd. This was a viewership most notably cultivated during the era by the likes of Roger Corman, a director who notoriously specialized in low-budget exploitation fare and is not often mentioned in the same breath as the honored auteur Elia Kazan.[18] A further sign of changing cultural times was the fact that *Baby Doll* in 1967 received an "R" rating, but NCOMP, successor to the legion, launched no protest against its exhibition, which unsurprisingly was barely noticed by the cultural establishment.

In 1956, however, Kazan's intentions were more complicated. He aimed not only to attract audiences with the film's frank sexuality, but, eager to advance his reputation as one of Hollywood's younger generation of self-conscious auteurs, also to impress the critics with its artistry and poetry. Unfortunately, he underestimated the extent of the furor he was to arouse. The writer-producer-director certainly never anticipated providing the Legion of Decency with what many in the organization saw as its finest hour, and in the process disastrously compromising *Baby Doll*'s performance at the box office. Seduced by the naughtiness of Carroll Baker's thumb sucking, the film's unforgettable icon, viewers and reviewers alike found it difficult to appreciate *Baby Doll* as a minor masterpiece of comic social observation in the tradition of Marcel Pagnol and, more generally, the Italian neorealists, especially Roberto Rossellini.

A White-Trash Aesthetic

It was the film's southern themes, rather than its European stylizations, that shaped the initial critical reception. Reviewing *Baby Doll* after its New York premiere, and at the onset of the various controversies that were to engulf the film during its initial run, Bosley Crowther suggested that what Kazan and Williams had confected bore a clear affinity to a notorious text from the recent past that had largely defined the fictional image of the rural South in mid-century America. Crowther declared that the "ghost" of *A Streetcar Named Desire* had gotten "bogged down in the mud of Erskine Caldwell's famous 'Tobacco Road,'" with "the sort of personal conflict that occurred in Mr. Williams' former play taking place in an environment in which Jeeter Lester [Caldwell's morally dubious patriarch] would feel quite at home."[19] In Crowther's summary of Williams's career, the high-toned tragedy of *Streetcar* had made way for a "sardonic" drama whose characters are "pure white trash" in that fictional and dramatic vein of which Caldwell, still in 1956 enjoying a substantial (and scandalous) reputation, was the acknowledged master.

Though his politically engaged novel had mostly attracted the interest of the intelligentsia, the stage version of *Tobacco Road* (the adaptation done by showman Jack Kirkland) had enjoyed during the 1930s one of the American commercial theatre's longest runs (more than seven and a half years). In their amazingly popular Broadway reincarnation, Caldwell's grotesque characters, reduced to risible "cracker" stereotypes from their more sociologically observed novelistic models, securely passed into a mainstream American culture that, less than two decades later in the early 1950s, still retained a vivid memory of them.[20] Crowther was certainly not the only observer of the Broadway and Hollywood scene in 1956 to notice the Caldwellian strain in *Baby Doll*.[21]

Crowther, it must be said, did not intend his observation about this literary relationship as a compliment to Williams. Caldwell's amazing popular success in the 1930s had been matched by a considerable reputation soon acquired in literary circles. Caldwell was viewed as an insightful and socially conscious chronicler of the lives of the southern rural proletariat. His novel *God's Little Acre* (1933) had sold more copies by 1950 than *Gone with the Wind*, becoming the most popular, even if not the most respected or admired, representation of southern life on the American scene. The enthusiasm of critics for Caldwell's fiction had drastically declined by the middle 1950s, even though his novels still sold quite well in cheap paperback editions. James E. Devlin observed in 1984 that while "today . . . Caldwell is largely forgotten. . . . his mass audience followed him well into the 1950s but it too declined, though never to a point where he has not had a half dozen or more titles in print."[22]

Crowther admits that Williams "has written his trashy, vicious people so that they are clinically interesting," a judgment that could also be fairly passed on Caldwell's achievement in penning *Tobacco Road*. Devlin expresses essentially the same view in a more academic vein, finding that Caldwell's talent lay in "combining the objective narrative stance of naturalism with the intimate depiction of emotion and irrationality that characterizes the modern antihero" (Devlin iii). Like Williams, in fact, Caldwell enjoyed the Zolaesque talent of making not so respectable characters vital, intellectually interesting, and emotionally intriguing— even if also disturbing and more than a little offensive. These are the fictional and thematic qualities that dominate in *Baby Doll*, providing a strong contrast with *Menagerie*, *Streetcar*, and *Tattoo*.

Denizens of a Worn-Out Land

Like *Tobacco Road*, however, *Baby Doll* offers more than the dubious pleasures of slumming, even though neither author disregards the considerable appeal of sleaziness. Both Caldwell and Williams (though less directly) engage with the problem of a twentieth-century South mired in agricultural depression. Jack Kirkland's stage version of *Tobacco Road* emphasized, in crowd-pleasing fashion, not only the fact of a "worn-out land" but also "the fate of those who rely on it."[23] Similarly, Kazan stages the action of *Baby Doll* in the crumbling ruins of a large country house, providing a potent symbol for a South that he and Williams, dismantling the plantation myth even more thoroughly than they had done in *Streetcar*, also see as impoverished and decaying. Here is a region where limited economic resources lead first to a poisonous rivalry between competing cotton-gin owners and, eventually, to both arson and the threat of a murderous violence barely averted.

This is very much Caldwell country. In *Tobacco Road*, Jeeter Lester and his family teeter on the brink of financial disaster because he cannot afford the seed and fertilizer necessary to plant this year's crop. These bitter economic realities condition the manipulative and exploitative sexual behavior in which the novel's characters find themselves thoroughly enmeshed. A naturalist with a feeling for the provocative, Caldwell quickly became famous for his violation of literary taboos, anticipating the reputation Williams would dispose of in the 1950s and 1960s. Just one year after *Tobacco Road* (1932) appeared, Caldwell's *God's Little Acre* attracted the attention of that institutional relic of the Comstock era, the New York Society for the Suppression of Vice, which attempted to derail the book's publication. Viking Press, however, emerged victorious in a landmark court decision, providing the novelist and his works with a well-earned notoriety that did nothing but further his popularity and critical reputation.

It is hardly surprising, therefore, that Crowther perceives a general resemblance between *Tobacco Road* and *Baby Doll*, certainly the two most famous and scandalous works in that vein of southern renaissance writing that Sylvia Jenkins Cook identifies as the "poor white tradition." In her view, Caldwell, unlike Faulkner (who often romanticizes the Scots-Irish yeoman farmer), thinks of his poor whites as "grotesques" dominated by "idiocy, violence, religious hysteria, and promiscuity." His characters do not in the least belong to anything like "a very wholesome advancing proletariat."[24] Much the same was said of the characters in *Baby Doll*. Arthur Knight, for example, remarks that the film is "one of the most unhealthy and amoral pictures ever made in this country," presumably because the characters are presented "frankly for what they are: simple, lustful, and crude." But if Williams and Kazan, in the Caldwellian manner, decline to romanticize their characters, they also refuse to assume "any moral position toward them." According to Knight, "each lives out his shabby life completely by his own lights, convinced of his own rightness, able to excuse or justify the most outrageous conduct."[25]

The connection between *Tobacco Road* and *Baby Doll*, however, is likely more than a matter of shared traditions and literary models. *Tobacco Road*, it seems, offered the two screenwriters a device central to the transformation of the dramatic raw materials. In *Cotton*, Jake Meighan, an unscrupulous cotton-gin owner, secretly burns down the gin operated by his neighbor and business rival, Silva Vacarro.[26] Jake proceeds to gin the cotton of the unfortunate Vacarro (who has little other choice), but Vacarro meanwhile occupies himself with frightening the plump and youthful Flora Meighan, Jake's wife, into confessing that Jake is the arsonist. Intimidated by his whip, Flora does his bidding, but he then rapes her. Jake agrees to let Flora entertain Vacarro every time he brings his cotton for ginning.

The central modification in this plot made by Williams and Kazan is in the relationship between the Meighans, now called Archie Lee and Baby Doll. The connection between husband and wife is dramatically energized by the young woman's withholding of conjugal rights, an unusual motif that does not figure otherwise in the Williams oeuvre. Archie Lee, we learn, obtained permission from Baby Doll's father to marry the young woman only on the condition that he supply her with a fully furnished home by her twentieth birthday. The bargain has a built-in guarantee: Baby Doll will not consummate their marriage until and unless Archie Lee complies with the condition set by her father. As the film opens, the Meighans have been "married" for two years, and Baby Doll is on the verge of turning twenty—but Archie Lee is in such desperate need for cash that the furniture from his ramshackle home has just been repossessed by the finance company. Desperate to possess the beautiful young girl (who is sizzlingly attractive, not overweight like Flora, her dramatic model), Archie Lee resorts to burning down Silva's gin in order to gain the man's business and thus the funds necessary to buy back the furniture necessary to obtain his wife's sexual favors. Seeking revenge through the motif of the "good neighbor policy—tit for tat," Vacarro attempts to seduce Baby Doll, and moreover, to have her sign a note that implicates Archie Lee in the arson. At film's end, Archie Lee has still not succeeded in keeping to his bargain (and bringing his sexual frustration to an end), while Baby Doll and her erstwhile lover may (or may not) find a future together based on their mutual attraction.

Cotton's Flora Meighan is no inexperienced child bride, but a willing victim who finds the attentions of her more sophisticated Sicilian neighbor flattering and exciting, despite his sadistic treatment. Baby Doll is a more complex and sympathetic character, trapped in a loveless arranged marriage to a vulgar older man. Though Baby Doll and Vacarro's relations have nothing initially to do with either lust or love, Vacarro leads her into a sexual awakening whose several dimensions become the film's most interesting element. It seems that in reshaping Flora for the film, Kazan adapted for his purposes one of *Tobacco Road*'s most interesting subplots. At age twelve, Jeeter's daughter Pearl has been given to his neighbor Lov in exchange for some cheap goods (a few quilts and a gallon of oil) and the small cash payment of seven dollars. Pearl, however, stubbornly refuses Lov his "rights" as a husband, despite the man's alternating attempts to persuade the young girl with kindness and intimidate her with physical force (such as the occasional painful kick and a humiliating dousing with cold water). In *Tobacco Road*, this ill-starred relationship triangulates in a different direction from that confected by Kazan for *Baby Doll*, since the sexually frustrated Lov is rather easily, and comically, seduced by Pearl's older sister, the harelipped Ellie May.

In this grotesque and pathetic episode from *Tobacco Road*, Kazan perhaps found the perfect material for giving greater dramatic force to the relationship between Archie Lee and Baby Doll. He did significantly transform the model. Pearl is motivated by an inchoate sense of outrage in her refusal of Lov; like the rest of the Lesters, she finds herself trapped by poverty and moral bankruptcy, further proof of Caldwell's socially engaged point about the desperate plight of these impoverished Georgia farmers. In her insistence on getting what is properly hers, Baby Doll is driven first by an irrepressible desire for respectability, and, later, by a deepening sense of her own worth. In addition to Vacarro's prodding, it is a growing awareness of her situation that leads her to sign the statement bearing witness to Archie Lee's crime. Baby Doll's developing skill at self-fashioning, in fact, becomes the film's central theme. Caldwell's blackly humorous approach to the grotesqueries of white-trash culture finds an accurate reflection in the billboard image of a seductively childish Baby Doll. But in fact, this unusual heroine possesses a depth and strength that are not even hinted at in the film's official, trashy represen-

*Archie Lee Meighan (Karl Malden) fondles his wife, Baby Doll
(Carroll Baker), as Silva (Eli Wallach) looks on in a porch scene from*
Baby Doll. *Photo courtesy of The Historic New Orleans Collection.*

tation of itself. Baby Doll, despite her name, shows herself to be no easily
exploited and pathetic gamine.

The borrowed Caldwellian motif also lends Williams's plot a more
pleasingly ironic structure. Now motivated by his desire for the money
needed to satisfy Baby Doll, Archie Lee's arson appropriately prompts
Vacarro to help Baby Doll see her situation in a radically different light,
which is, in large part, to recognize the deep inadequacy of her relationship with Archie Lee. The consequence is that Baby Doll is initiated into
the erotic, but not in the self-serving and exploitative fashion Archie Lee
had anticipated. There is more to life, Baby Doll learns from Vacarro,
than the furniture needed to make her ramshackle house more livable.
She thus becomes a woman of more varied and unpredictable possibilities. In large part because of Kazan's skillfully conceived changes, Baby
Doll became yet another Williams heroine restored or brought to life by
a reformative encounter with Eros.

A Unique Moral Perversity

From the beginning, the project that was to become *Baby Doll* had deep southern roots. Kazan wanted to explore the region, where he had not traveled extensively, in order to prepare for their collaboration. Like most northeastern urbanites, Kazan was inclined to view the South as an exotic wonderland, but he quickly became engaged by the more complex social reality he discovered there. He would later say that he was charmed by the Mississippi locals, but "abominate[d] what their tradition is with the blacks."[27] This qualified admiration for rural southern culture is amply reflected in *Baby Doll*, which, in a move unusual for the era, conjures into existence a chorus of black townspeople who become bemused observers of the strange goings-on among the seemingly deranged crackers at the Meighan house.[28]

Before *Streetcar*, Kazan had made two films that featured southern locales and themes. *Pinky* (1949), a studio-bound melodrama, explores the region's racial politics, especially the phenomenon of passing, while *Panic in the Streets* (1950), a documentary-style noir thriller shot largely on the streets and docksides of New Orleans, dramatizes a threatened outbreak of the bubonic plague. In a sense specializing in films with regional themes, Kazan would go on to direct two more southern features in the years after *Baby Doll*, both of which likewise reflect his developing "realist" interests in the area's society and politics: *A Face in the Crowd* (1953) and *Wild River* (1960) feature complex and intriguing versions of white-trash stereotypes.

Beginning with his work on *Pinky* and the stage production of *Streetcar*, Kazan had come to see the South as a treasure trove of familial and social pathologies waiting to be displayed on stage and screen. With its popular image established as a regional garden of Freudian delights featuring incest, miscegenation, phallocentrism, feminine repression, and daddy worship, the South offered a rich vein to be mined, one that suited his developing interest in highbrow yet sensational properties. By the 1950s, as Philip Lopate reports, "the South became a code, liberating the film maker to explore everything on the edges of taboo. It was as though anthropologists had found a tribe where the unrepressed continued to thrive."[29] As the project that would become *Baby Doll* gained momentum, Williams suggested to Kazan that "there should be something grotesque and gothic about the whole thing, the half comic, half disgusting absurdity of human relations and behavior and existence." Kazan, Williams ordered, was to "get in all the squawk-squawks and the Mississippi shit and languor." Kazan apparently took Williams's comment literally and did his best to comply. In the continuities he penned, the chicken "Old Fussy" would provide appropriate sound effects, while the stereotypically supine African Americans would offer the "languor." As Kazan recorded in his project notebook, the numerous dogs that roamed the estate and "shit all over the place" would supply the final ingredient.[30] As far as regional stereotypes in the southern-gothic mode, Kazan and Williams covered all the bases, an aspect of the latter's work we discuss in more detail in Chapter 7.

As preproduction for the film proceeded, Williams's interest in the project was piqued by the casting. Marilyn Monroe read for the part of Baby Doll, but Williams and Kazan decided on newcomer Carroll Baker. Williams had first conceived of Baby Doll as an overweight woman: he thought the part should be played by a "sexy piglet." However, Kazan sensed Baker's potential early on, when she was just beginning her career as an actress and was not yet a member of the Actors Studio. As Kazan recalls, "Williams's heroine in *Twenty-Seven Wagonloads* [sic] *of Cotton* is a big, fat girl, so I said to him one day: 'There's this girl who has many of the inner qualities of your heroine, but she's not fat—would you like to see her?' So I did an improvisation with Carroll Baker and Karl Malden. The minute Williams saw Carroll Baker, he wanted to put her in the film."[31] For the two male leads, Kazan argued for actors he knew from his Actors Studio work. Williams wanted Marlon Brando to play Vacarro, but he was not available. Instead, Eli Wallach (who had been very successful as Mangiacavallo in the Broadway *Tattoo*) was picked to play yet another sexy Sicilian, while Karl Malden (reprising in some sense his role as Blanche's duped lover in *Streetcar*) landed the part of Archie Lee.

A Low and Sordid Tone

Because the film script featured a unique "romantic" triangle, Williams and Kazan harbored few doubts about the reaction of the PCA to the project. After reviewing an early treatment that was much different from the final script in August 1952, Joseph Breen complained to Jack Warner about being asked to make a decision based on "a very rough draft," but he was still deeply disturbed by what he termed "the low and sordid tone of the story as a whole," whose main themes were "crime, sex, murder and revenge." Not that these elements were absent from many Hollywood films of the period, but what distinguished this new Williams project, in Breen's view, was that "there is very little relief as the story now stands from what might be called reasonably normal or healthy people, or those representing decency and sanity." It is difficult to contest the accuracy of Breen's reading. Williams and Kazan were deliberately flouting the time-honored concept of providing compensating moral value to balance the material that was questionable in code terms. Breen was later heartened that the filmmakers promised to introduce a character from *The Last of My Solid Gold Watches* named Charlie, "who would act as commentator and narrator" because he "could also be used as the voice for morality vis-à-vis the sins and mistakes of the principals." In any case, Charlie's part was jettisoned in the course of the script's confection.

To judge from Breen's detailed comments, this early treatment apparently featured a serious, even tragic working-out of the adulterous triangle, with Archie Lee and Vacarro killing each other in a bloody finale. More importantly, perhaps, Vacarro's calculating seduction of Baby Doll could not be permitted, especially if it figured as a "weapon of retribution" against the arsonist Archie Lee. Defining exactly what "retribution" the script should offer constituted a major snag in its development, leading to dozens of letters exchanged between Williams and Kazan on how best to produce an ending that would satisfy the PCA. At the time, Breen envisioned a satisfactory resolution of difficulties, expressing his belief that the production, with careful revision, might express the truth that "there is a certain inexorable progression to evil." Ironically, this is a prediction that comes true in the film—though rather lightheartedly and certainly not in the moralizing sense that Breen would have preferred.[32] Williams and Kazan were instructed to make sure that Archie Lee was punished and Baby Doll freed from his pernicious influence.

Not long after this initial PCA evaluation, the screenwriters determined that a largely comic treatment of the material would be essential to the project's success. In December 1953, Williams wrote to Audrey Wood about the "major problem" of "reconciling, artistically, the hilarious comedy which is the keynote of the film, and the very heavy 'punishment for sins' ending of it demanded by the censors, but maybe that can be cheated a little the way we did the 'moral ending' in *Streetcar*."[33] But Kazan kept arguing for a more heavy-going resolution of the triangle. As the project moved closer to shooting, in 1955, Williams admonished his collaborator to keep in mind that "I feel my own original conception of the film-story as a grotesque folk-comedy of the modern South, with some serious over-tones, carefully kept within the atmospheric frame of the story, is still the only right one. The course which you indicate for the ending is far too heavy, at least for a work that is to have any sort of artistic unity."[34] By steering the script away from Kazan's preference for serious poetic justice and insisting on a comic, almost campy tone, Williams helped achieve what Kazan would later praise as the film's "ambiguity."

Nearly three years after submitting a preliminary script, Kazan and Williams sent a more finished version to the PCA for review. In October 1955, Breen met with Kazan to discuss what he saw as serious problems that had not yet been rectified. The theme of "justified adultery" could not be allowed, but, Breen reports, "Mr. Kazan stated categorically that he would make it quite clear that there was no adulterous affair." As it turned out, Kazan would finesse this objection as deceptively as he had the rape scene in *Streetcar*. The telling visual joke of the fire hose in the earlier film finds interesting parallels in *Baby Doll* with Carroll Baker's position next to the crib as Wallach falls asleep, as well as with her hardly subtle mouthing of a Coke bottle and her protracted affair with an ice cream cone—acting moves that delighted the cognoscenti.

As far as Kazan was concerned, Breen's second main objection was more problematic. He could not simply hint at, or express visually, what the PCA called "the element of Archie's sex frustration," which was, in terms of the interplay among the characters, the principal motor of the plot. Some months after this meeting with Breen (his role as director having passed to Geoffrey Shurlock), Kazan made his intentions clear to Jack Warner, who copied the memo to PCA officials, apparently hoping that the director's pleas might sway them:

> I will do everything the Shurlock office wants, except one thing. I cannot do that, if I did I'd have to throw away the whole picture. . . . this film is about one thing and only one thing. It's about a middle-aged man who is held at arm's length by his young wife. . . . Tell the boys that the hero of this film, for me, is Archie Lee. He is a pathetic misguided, confused, desperate man. Sin and violence and so forth come out of fear and desperation. Archie Lee should be pathetic. And will be. And amusingly so! I cannot reduce the element of Archie Lee's sex frustration.[35]

As he had with *Streetcar*, Kazan reminded the studio head that if the motion picture industry wanted to offer a viable alternative to television, then producers should "put on the screen *only* what they cannot and never will see on their tv screens at home."

In the end, Kazan got his way. Not, apparently, because he persuaded PCA officials of the current exhibition needs of an industry fighting for its financial life, but because, as with *Streetcar*, he waited until the film was actually in production before submitting anything like a final script. After receiving the above memo from Kazan, Shurlock and his assistants, including Jack Vizzard, conferred about the project with Steve Trilling and Finlay McDermid of Warner Bros. Shurlock wrote in a memo for the files: "We went over in detail the most objectionable of the scenes and lines of dialogue that have to do with the unacceptably pointed sex frustration of Archie. Later in the day Mr. Trilling stated that Mr. Kazan had agreed to change a number of these items but not all. I urged Mr. Trilling to get from Mr. Kazan a final script, with all the changes that he was prepared to make at this time."[36] But no final script was ever delivered for approval. When the rough cut of the film was reviewed by that office in July 1956, Jack Vizzard somewhat surprisingly reported that "the basic story seems to us acceptable under the Code. The principal concern which was expressed in our correspondence, about the sex frustration of Meehan [*sic*], was, in our opinion, satisfactorily handled so as not to be a code violation. The same is to be said with regards the discussion of the marital arrangement between Meehan and Baby Doll. The sex affair which was so vividly indicated at script level is, in keeping with Mr. Kazan's assurances, absent from the picture."[37]

A Conscienceless, Venal Attitude?

Vizzard's reading of the film is difficult to explain: the only sense in which the "sex affair" could be said to be absent from the picture is that it is not directly dramatized. Vizzard did confess to some lingering worries about the so-called swing scene, in which Vacarro teasingly makes love to Baby Doll while hardly touching her. Vizzard informed Kazan that this scene was "extremely offensive and "to the point of suggesting that the girl is having physical reactions which are orgiastic [*sic*]."[38] Ironically, the scene in which Eli Wallach lasciviously rides and flails the rocking horse met with no objection by the Breen office, even though it is as licentious as it is comic. Vizzard was also concerned about the afternoon nap that the Sicilian takes in Baby Doll's crib after their initial encounter. Did the couple enact their adulterous intentions in these cramped quarters? As the censor later reported, "Kazan argued that this would be physically absurd, since there was no room for gymnastics of any sort." To his chagrin, Vizzard later learned that the "word around town" was that Baby Doll had given Silva what "the more worldly term a blow job."[39] This is why, Vizzard was informed, Kazan instructed Baker to play seductively with her Coke bottle.[40]

Breen might have balked at approving the final cut, but he was no longer in charge, and the less experienced and more liberal Jack Vizzard gave Kazan the seal he wanted. His certification of the film would cause the young censor, a former seminarian and a devout Catholic, no little embarrassment. As the controversy over the film deepened, Vizzard would have to explain to Los Angeles bishop Timothy Manning why he had passed the film; the bishop was not impressed with Vizzard's reasoning and even wondered at the depth of his Catholic training. Manning himself was feeling pressure from legion officials, especially Martin Quigley, who were outraged at the PCA decision, regarding it as yet another indication that the code was no longer being enforced as it should.

Baby Doll was condemned by the Legion in November, substantially in advance of Kazan's planned Christmas-week opening. The quick decision reflected in part the producer-director's refusal to meet informally with legion officials—Warner Bros. had, as a courtesy, sent along a review print with the caveat that Kazan would brook no alterations. The reviewers were simply appalled by what they saw on the screen. *Baby Doll*, in the organization's judgment, was not only "morally repellent," but also "grievously offensive to Christian and traditional standards of morality and decency." No cuts were recommended, as they had been unofficially in the case of *Streetcar*. This time the unanimous legion view was "that neither deletions nor additions could salvage a basically bad theme," which once again was carnality in its most worldly and objectionable form (not tied in the least to "real" marriage and a committed relationship, as had been the case with *Streetcar* and *Tattoo*).[41] Kazan's unpardonable crime this time was apparently that he was not taking sex seriously enough.

Monsignor Little, the legion head, interpreted Kazan's intransigence as a challenge to public morality that, if not appropriately taken up, would result in a flood of films with similar themes. Industry insider Quigley, who was also outraged by the film, thought that only a firm statement by a nationally known Catholic figure would stir bishops in every diocese to unite against the film. Knowing that such an event would attract media attention, Quigley prevailed upon the American church's most powerful and best-known prelate to take a firm public stand. On December 16, with the film's billboard attracting New York City's curious only a few blocks away, Spellman delivered a thundering sermon at St. Patrick's Cathedral against *Baby Doll*, its makers, and an industry that, he proclaimed, was fast becoming too tolerant of a "corruptive, [*sic*] moral influence."[42] Catholics were warned, upon pain of mortal sin, to avoid the Kazan production.

Such strident and public attempts at censorship were not viewed favorably by many in liberal New York City. An editorial in the *New York Post* fumed: "The terror to which the Legion of Decency has intermittently reduced Hollywood bears some authentic, if minimal resemblance to the suppression against which Hungarians have rebelled [this was the period of the revolt in 1956 against Soviet domination]. They have had enough of cultural commissars and every other kind of ideological bully."[43] Kazan's view was that Spellman hardly possessed the moral authority to pass such judgments, for he was "a power broker who played the market, consorted with politicians, promoters, and real estate speculators, a wheeler-dealer priest, a drinker, a bully."[44] Williams, he recalled, was both offended and surprised at the furor. He reports the playwright as complaining: "I cannot believe that an ancient and august branch of the Christian faith is not larger in heart and mind than those who set themselves up as censors."[45]

Ideological bully or not, Spellman firmly believed that it was "astonishing and deplorable" that the PCA had certificated a picture so offensive to public decency; perhaps it was an indication that this hitherto robust institution had "fallen into decay and collapse."[46] If the PCA could no longer be depended upon to safeguard the moral sensibilities of the nation's moviegoing Catholics, then it was up to the legion, and the ecclesiastical leaders who provided its ultimate authority, to assume that role. Some prominent voices were raised against the Catholic campaign. Most notably, James Pike, dean of the Cathedral of St. John the Divine (an Episcopal institution), opined that Christians should make up their own minds. He saw no sin in his own attendance, thinking that the copious, bared flesh and scanty costumes in Cecil B. DeMille's *The Ten Commandments* (1956), a biblical epic whose appearance had been cheered by the legion, constituted a more serious temptation to malfeasance. Many Americans, it turned out, were indeed offended (or bored or bemused) by what they saw on the screen. Predictably, the film received very poor reviews in Catholic journals and newspapers, but it did not fare so well with the mainstream press either, including highbrow critics like Arthur Knight and Bosley Crowther. Unimpressed by its blackly humorous tone and unsympathetic characters, the reviewer for the *New Republic* derisively christened the film "The Crass Menagerie." This was perhaps a sign that Kazan may have pushed Williams's characters and themes too far in the direction of Erskine Caldwell and Marcel Pagnol.

The Legion Triumphant

In the weeks following Spellman's sermon, the nation's bishops worked to present a united front against the film, and eleven prominent clerics eventually issued a joint statement affirming their opposition. The legion was not content simply to warn off prospective Catholic patrons; great pressure was brought against exhibitors as well. Bishop Scully of the Ecclesiastical Committee imposed a six-month interdict on a theatre in his Albany diocese that dared book *Baby Doll* toward the end of the holiday season; Catholics were forbidden to patronize the establishment during the period of the ban. Legion pickets from the Knights of Columbus and the Catholic War Veterans marched in front of theatres across the country that did not respect the ban. Joseph P. Kennedy, father of the future president, refused to exhibit the film in his extensive theatre circuit, calling upon, and pressuring, business associates to follow suit. About four thousand theatres nationwide did eventually show *Baby Doll*, but this was only about half as many as could have been expected, without the widespread protests and a "C" rating, to do so.

Even in these difficult circumstances, the film did average business, earning $2.3 million at the box office, which placed it thirty-seventh on the 1957 charts. However, this was hardly the kind of financial success that filmmakers had come to expect from a Williams property.[47] Unsurprisingly, the film did best in larger metropolitan areas: New York, Philadelphia, Kansas City, Los Angeles, and Detroit. Academy Award nominations followed for Baker, Williams (best adapted screenplay), Mildred Dunnock (for her supporting role as Aunt Rose Comfort), and Boris Kaufman (for his artfully low-key black-and-white cinematography). In the end, however, audiences were not generally enthusiastic about a film that was much too European in its rejection of time-honored Hollywood conventions; most problematic, perhaps, was the lack of sympathetic characters for which to root.

If a sensation, *Baby Doll* was hardly either a critical or box-office smash. There seem to have been two reasons for this. First, its plot and themes, while interesting and, for the American cinema of the age, strikingly original, had never been put into a dramatically coherent and popular form through the trial-and-error process of a stage production. *Baby Doll* was thus undeniably weaker than the films adapted from Williams's Broadway successes, including those that followed it to the screen (such as *Cat on a Hot Tin Roof* and *Sweet Bird of Youth*, both of which attracted a wider audience of filmgoers). Secondly, and ironically, the film's notoriety, in large measure the result of Kazan's carefully calculated marketing campaign, put off many prospective customers and, more importantly, exhibitors, who were pressured by the legion and its allies and hardly encouraged to go against this opposition once *Baby Doll*, as its initial run proceeded, proved to have "no legs," in industry parlance. With its European manner and groundbreaking treatment of the erotic, the film was substantially ahead of its time. Kazan wrote in 1988: "If you were to look at the film right now, you'd see a rather amusing comedy and wonder what the fuss was about."[48] It would be difficult to contest this judgment. *Baby Doll* is aired without editing, comment, or warning on network and cable television today, eliciting no outraged protest from any quarter, including evangelical Christians, who have now taken over the legion's role as the self-appointed guardians of American popular culture. We would find inexplicable today the judgment of *Time*'s reviewer that *Baby Doll* was "just possibly the dirtiest American-made motion picture that has ever been legally exhibited."

Correct Standards of Life

Emotionally cold, *Baby Doll* thematizes lust, not love, pokes fun at marriage, and plays the venality of its grasping, manipulative characters for laughs even as it hints that their predicament reflects some underlying truths of *la condition humaine*. *Baby Doll*'s black comedy, with its darker view of human nature, eschews the festive antics of screwball comedy, Hollywood's conventionally irreverent presentation of the battle of the sexes. In his *Period of Adjustment*, Williams assayed the screwball genre, and that play, despite its focus on sexual maladjustment and frustration, transferred easily and without controversy to the screen.

If *Baby Doll* was the "dirtiest movie" that had yet been made in America, it was not because it featured prohibited themes (no "sex perversion" here), offered the spectacle of the naked female body (Carroll Baker is always more or less fully clothed), or attacked official institutions such as the police, the church, the courts, or the federal government.[49] There is no serious violence (other than that against the inanimate cotton gin), and despite the lewd implications of the film's title and advertising poster, no exploitation of youthful innocence. In a press release that Williams prepared for the premiere of *Baby Doll*, he blasted the condemned rating "from a particular religious organization," stating: "Kazan has always shown a temperate attitude toward the rules of Hollywood's Production Code. When he makes a film, there is always a long and conscientious period of consultation with the code administrators, and so far has never failed to reach a workable agreement with them. On two occasions when we have worked together, on 'A Streetcar Named Desire' and now on 'Baby Doll,' we have always been able to satisfy the demands of the Code and still live up to our own code as theater artists who put honesty first."[50] This is true enough after a fashion, even though Kazan could hardly be said to be someone "who put honesty first" in his dealings with the PCA.

And yet it is clear, as Martin Quigley maintained at the time, that the film violated the general principles of the code in three ways, and its relatively easy passage to certification thus served to chip away at the pillars of the institution itself.[51] First, it creates sympathy for "the side of crime, wrongdoing, [and] sin." Second, "correct standards of life" in the sense of consensus moral values are not upheld. And finally, law, natural and human, is "ridiculed," and "sympathy [is] created for its violation."[52] The formulae of the code made no room for the antiestablishmentarianism of black comedy, not a common genre on the American stage or screen at this time. It is the unexpectedly amoral laughter that *Baby Doll* provokes, not the film's admittedly steamy, though chaste, representation of seduction, that led to both its certification (for there was no objectionable material as such in the final script that could be excised) and condemnation (for the story vigorously opposed the conventional moralism of the code's theory of art). *Baby Doll*, to put it simply, takes sex too seriously and yet not seriously enough. In this respect, Kazan's film is certainly faithful to Williams's original, ambiguous vision of the characters and the plight in which they embroil themselves.

CHAPTER SIX

Tennessee Williams and '50s Family Melodrama

"Possibly the Most Bizarre Film"

In ensuring that *Baby Doll*'s theatrical release was hampered by protest and cancellations, the legion achieved more victory than its leaders, clerical and lay alike, likely thought possible. As Kazan saw exhibition takings dribbling in and the film making only a lukewarm impression on critics and the cognoscenti, he must have realized that his promotion of cultural and artistic modernism had received something of a comeuppance. Monsignor Little and his associates had fought to a draw two of the leading shapers of American culture and an established Hollywood studio. The stand against *Baby Doll*, however, marked the zenith of the legion's power, while the Production Code Administration, in the wake of its being upstaged once again by censors outside the control of Hollywood, rapidly became less and less relevant to the industry's management of its moral relationship with filmgoers. Within the very brief space of three years, in fact, American film culture, and, more surprisingly, the official Catholic Church as well, had moved rapidly toward increasingly liberal positions on what precisely constituted cinematic decency. These positions were rather unimaginable before 1956. Once again, this is a development that can be no more tellingly traced and anatomized than in yet another Tennessee Williams adaptation, the Sam Spiegel production of the playwright's off-Broadway *Suddenly, Last Summer*. This gripping drama had been staged with a one-act play, *Something Unspoken*, under the joint title of *Garden District*. Despite good notices and box office, the production had not moved to a Broadway theatre, its outré themes and minimal dramatic structure apparently considered uncommercial for a more middlebrow, uptown clientele.

Arguably Williams's most formally perfect (and certainly most suspenseful) dramatic work, *Suddenly* consists almost entirely of two delicately counterpointed and dueling female dialogues, a kind of indirect debate between Violet Venable and her niece Catherine Holley that concerns itself with family and psychological issues of the utmost indelicacy. Violet has summoned the psychiatrist Dr. Cukrowicz, or "Dr. Sugar," to her New Orleans Garden District mansion in order to convince him that Catherine is so mentally ill that a prefrontal lobotomy is called for. Catherine, naturally enough, resists both this diagnosis and its projected remedy. Violet is moved to this drastic course of action, she reveals, because Catherine insists on telling what the young girl maintains is the truth about Violet's son, Sebastian, with whom Catherine spent the last summer traveling in the south of Europe as the young man failed for the first time to write his annual poem. The trip ended disastrously, with the frustrated poet's unexpected public death, the exact circumstances of which remain in dispute. Sebastian, Catherine maintains, was murdered, dismembered, and then partly eaten by a horde of young boys Sebastian had apparently paid for sexual favors and who, disappointed and angry, then turned on him. In her monologue, Violet describes Sebastian as witty, cultivated, and "chaste," dismissing Catherine's account as delusional and destructive. However, it soon becomes clear that Sebastian was a homosexual who, necessarily closeted during the year, even in New Orleans, traveled abroad each summer in search of liaisons, and that Violet for years aided Sebastian in making these "connections."[1]

Their unconventional relationship, bordering uneasily on incestuous desire, contributed to the young man's embrace of a Darwinist view of human relations, all red in tooth and claw, enacted in his life at first metaphorically (with Sebastian as the sly seducer) and then literally, as Sebastian brings on the situation that results in his own bizarre death after trading in the aging Violet for the younger Catherine as a cruising partner. This desperate, horrific finale, with its perhaps too-obvious concretization of self-hate (the exploiter conniving at his own poetically just punishment), seems a kind of suicide, as Sebastian realizes that he, too, like his mother, is no longer young. This may be the source of the artistic paralysis that precedes his actual demise. With its antirealist cadre, both mythological (pervasive references to the Orpheus myth) and religious (the invocation of the martyrdom of St. Sebastian), the play departs partially, but not centrally, from the dramatic illusionism of Williams's previous stage successes, such as *Streetcar* and *Menagerie*.

The cannibalism, loveless homosexuality, incest, and procurement themes in the play were meant literally but also metaphorically, as the playwright put it, to make the point that "the human individual is a cannibal in the worst way."[2] Adapted for the screen and the industry's default representational mode, realism, these themes would be shocking, sensational, less poetic—and given the current exhibition climate, probably commercial, or so reasoned the film's producer. Sam Spiegel was a maverick Hollywood insider with an uncanny sense for spotting a profitable property (as he had spectacularly shown when adapting another unlikely work, Pierre Boulle's philosophically dense antiwar war novel, *The Bridge on the River Kwai* [1957]). Seeing *Suddenly* in New York, Spiegel immediately phoned Williams in Miami, where the playwright was vacationing, and a deal was quickly cut without the intervention of an agent. Spiegel hired the best scriptwriting and directorial talent (Williams's friend Gore Vidal and Joseph L. Mankiewicz, respectively) available in the industry at that time to mount a screenplay that would enhance rather than diminish the play's literary value.

A stellar cast was engaged: Katherine Hepburn as Violet; Montgomery Clift as Dr. Cukrowicz; and Hollywood's hottest actress, Elizabeth Taylor, as Catherine. Spiegel quite evidently did not fear that Williams's material was too extreme for an industry and public that only three years before had been scandalized by the merest suggestion of unconventional (though heteronormal) sex in *Baby Doll*. However unusual its source, Hollywood's *Suddenly* (1959) was, without either extraordinary effort or artistic compromise, turned into the kind of serious adult drama that was becoming one of the era's most profitable and acclaimed genres: the family melodrama.

Of more interest at the moment is the property's unusual production and reception history. Quickly completed without the playwright's participation (though Williams did receive screen credit as a courtesy), Vidal's working draft of the screenplay was duly forwarded to PCA chief Geoffrey Shurlock for comment and, it was hoped, preshooting approval. In a conference called to discuss the project with producer Spiegel, Shurlock recalled:

> I told him that the script presented serious Code, and other, problems. The specific Code violation is that fact that your leading char-

Catherine Holly (Elizabeth Taylor) in the scandalous swimsuit scene from
Suddenly, Last Summer. *Photo courtesy of The Historic New Orleans Collection.*

acter is a homosexual. We also felt that the ending—cannibalism
with its sexual overtones—was so revolting, that we did not feel justified in giving the Code seal. We felt that Mr. Spiegel should take
his finished picture before the Appeals Board. We also suggested
that the expressed attitude toward God, on the part of the leading
character and his mother, verges so closely on blasphemy, that the
picture might be condemned by religious groups generally.[3]

Though he turned down the request for approval as such, Shurlock gave the hard-nosed producer an easy out, suggesting, as Breen would never have done, that Spiegel might go before the PCA Appeals Board if he disputed the PCA's final judgment *once the picture was completed*.

In other words, Shurlock's revulsion at the film's themes did not embolden him to reject it either out of hand or until substantial changes were wrought that he would review and approve. Suggesting recourse to the Appeals Board meant relinquishing the power of granting or withholding the certificate. And if the PCA was in no uncertain terms abrogating its responsibility by shifting it to the Appeals Board, where Spiegel, taking the case to his peers, was more likely to get a satisfactory result, it is to some degree because the threat of withholding a certificate was no longer formidable, and in fact was fast becoming irrelevant. All that Shurlock apparently felt empowered to do was to make a thinly veiled reference to the legion and its rating system (the unspecified "religious groups" that might "condemn" the film because of the irreligion of the cinema's most unusual mother and son, perhaps from a traditional moral point of view the least offensive element of their weltanschauung).

Spiegel responded in a disingenuous fashion that would hardly have fooled Breen, arguing that the film's homosexual, only vaguely a character in any case, "pays for his sin with his life." The film's cannibalism could, he said, "be deleted by the elimination of one line." This is a doubtful claim, but it proved to be a bluff in any case, since Spiegel probably never intended to follow up on this promise. Odd couple Violet and Sebastian, he pledged, would offer "no offense on religious grounds," because they are "obviously psychopaths." Breen would never have agreed that chalking up grossly immoral behavior to some kind of mental deviance justified its textual representation, even if "compensating moral value" could be contrived and added. In fact, adding "compensating value" aptly characterizes much of what Vidal did to the play, even if not with the intention of mollifying the PCA. Taking a leaf from Kazan's book, Spiegel refused to submit the final screenplay incorporating the PCA's general and specific recommendations before shooting began. The producer instead expressed his willingness to lodge an appeal against the negative judgment he felt sure of receiving. This appeal would be adjudicated, of course, when the film was already in the can and those in the industry, who would act as Spiegel's judge and jury, would therefore be very unwilling to deny it a certificate or demand a radical recutting, given the financial loss that either decision would likely involve.

Spiegel arranged a viewing for Shurlock, as promised, and the PCA chief put up a bold front, affirming the incompatibility of the sexual material in the story with code restrictions that had always been strictly enforced. He wrote Spiegel: "It is the unanimous opinion of the PCA that this picture violates that section of the Code which states 'sex perversion or any inference of it is forbidden.' In view of the fact that the dead man, Sebastian, is definitely indicated to have been a homo-sexual, we are unable to issue the Association's Certificate of Approval. We regret having to take this action, but in view of the circumstances, it is the only judgment we can render."[4] But this refusal to compromise was, it turned out, just posturing, perhaps *pour encourager les autres* in the industry; it quite evidently did not reflect Shurlock's moral opinion of the project. Spiegel appealed, and was with great rapidity granted an exception, to Shurlock's obvious relief. Strangely, it seems that the PCA chief was as happy as the film's producer to have his judgment set aside, with not even a written explanation or apology forthcoming from the disagreeing board. In fact, in the aftermath of the "controversy," he wrote Spiegel something in the nature of a congratulatory note: "Now that the dust has finally settled, we are in a position to send you the Association's Certificate of Approval for SUDDENLY LAST SUMMER. . . . I don't need to tell you what a treat it is for us to meet you under all circumstances, and even in the melee of an Appeals hearing. And I want to thank you again for getting me in to that magnificent performance of 'Figaro' at the Metropolitan."[5] It would probably be naive to think of those prize opera tickets as some kind of bribe. More likely, the gesture was meant to salve the (only slightly) wounded sensibilities of the PCA chief, whose future cooperation Spiegel needed to be able to count on.

Unlike Breen, Shurlock did not take his position as moral censor with a sense of high seriousness. Revolting material could be allowed, provided his industry peers agreed. The PCA head's relief at the more or less uncontroversial certificating of *Suddenly*, however, is perhaps more appropriately understood as a sign of the fast-changing times than as proof of the young man's unsuitability for the position. The review process was quickly becoming a meaningless (perhaps even slightly fraudulent) exercise, as another document in this case reveals. In the required synopsis that accompanies the certificate of acceptability, to the question "Is illicit sex an element in the picture?" the answer given by the PCA is no, even though the same form goes on to state: "Catherine reveals what she learned in Spain last summer: that Sebastian used his mother to procure for him." Only a Clintonian definition of what actually constitutes "illicit sex" could reconcile the truth claims of these two statements. Later in the report, the starving boys are referred to as "his court of adolescent hangers-on," certainly an interesting characterization of young hustlers turned murderers and cannibals. And so the homosexuality and its uniquely brutal consequences, at one time so obvious and obnoxious to PCA officials, mysteriously disappear from the film's final documentary record.[6]

Lifting the Roof on Hell?

Suddenly took industry reviewers by surprise, even though they perhaps should have known more about the shifting internal politics of Hollywood and film culture more generally. The *Hollywood Reporter* (December 16, 1959) sniffed that "since, baldly stated, [*Suddenly*] deals with homosexuality and the prostitution of one's mother, it is possible some puritans will not agree with that arbiter of industry morals, Eric Johnston, that it is a fit divertissement for little children." But the anonymous reviewer also observes that what Williams, Mankiewicz, and Vidal had confected would not differ, in the emotions aroused, from the standard Hollywood product: "This play has the advantage from an exhibitor's viewpoint of favoring what most members of the public will consider good people and of saving them from the machinations of evil people. This makes possible a strong sense of spectator identification and involvement."[7] *Variety* admitted shock at the unusual subject matter and its treatment, observing that this was "possibly the most bizarre film ever made by any major American company . . . it is like lifting the roof on Hell to see these characters in action."[8]

Writing in *Motion Picture Daily*, James D. Ivers makes the obvious point that the film presents "subject matter never before dwelt upon in a medium of mass entertainment, specifically prohibited by the Production Code and, in fact, not frequently treated so explicitly in a medium of mass entertainment." Nonetheless, he opined, "The Sam Spiegel production of the Tennessee Williams stage play is an extraordinary exercise in the cinematic art." Ivers recognized the problem that any such film, however artistic, posed for the industry under the current system of universal admission: "It raises grave questions as to what is proper matter for ordinary theatrical distribution. The subject is perversion, especially the darker reaches of sexual psychopathy. . . . But the world of Tennessee Williams is not the world of millions of moviegoers and this has been made without even the compromises to popular appeal which brought his previous works to the screen. The esoteric nature of the subject obviously limits both its appeal and its acceptance for general theatrical exhibition."[9]

If such films were going to be endorsed by the PCA and certified for release, then the next logical step would be to rate them "adult" in order to restrict access. Nine years later, the industry would set up the Code and Ratings Administration to do just that, a move that likely owes something to the fact that *Suddenly* and other Williams properties were brought to the screen after the mid-1950s without the long-customary "compromises to popular appeal."

A Sexual Geiger Counter

It was one thing for industry insiders to register surprise, however obliquely, at how the provisions of the code were being set aside in favor of a cinematic art that no longer needed to avoid giving offense to the culturally conservative wing of American Catholicism. It was quite another for conservative Catholics not to find the film shocking or corrupting. With the thunderous assertion of traditional morality upon the release of *Baby Doll* still a recent memory, many in 1959 must have thought it quite extraordinary that the Legion of Decency itself would agree with reviewers like Ivers that *Suddenly*, in spite of its unusual subject matter, was art, not exploitation, and thus worthy of informed adult Catholic viewership.

The legion's judgment on the film reflects nothing so much as the then-current trend evident in the obscenity cases adjudicated by the Warren Court, especially the evolving notion of "redeeming" artistic value. Even to the Legion of Decency, it seems, the obscene was fast becoming a conditional rather than a self-evident and substantial quality of certain materials, including the so-called perversion to be found in *Suddenly*:

This motion picture is judged to be moral in its theme and treatment, but because its subject matter involves perversion, it is intended only for a serious and mature audience. In view of the mass medium nature of the American entertainment motion picture presentation, both distributor and theatre owner are urged to manifest social and moral responsibility to the impressionable and immature in the exhibition of this film.

Like Shurlock, the legion reviewers permitted themselves a face-saving bit of bluster, pointing out that the PCA, in certifying the film, had violated its own standards. Shurlock had pleaded with legion officials not to condemn the film but, if they did, to lay the blame at the door of the Appeals Board and so get him off the hook.[10] Perhaps there was some ressentiment within the legion that it had been forced to make the obvious point about the growing irrelevance of the code, whose pertinent clause is quoted in the review, a move that quite obviously refuses to do the whitewashing Shurlock requested:

> Granted the acceptability of the film for a mature audience, nevertheless the Production Code, in giving its Seal to the film and thereby indicating its approval of it for general patronage, violates a particular application of its general principle, namely that "sex perversion or any inference of it is forbidden."[11]

This particular provision would soon be abrogated entirely as the PCA tried desperately to keep in step with rapidly changing American values. But it was also true, as the decade came to an end, that the legion was no longer resisting that moral transformation with either the same conviction or energy. What had happened?

Historian Frank Walsh explains the changing policies of the legion as a desperate attempt to keep the loyalty of an increasingly mainstream religious community in which liberal opinions on a variety of matters were gaining more traction: "Any effort to return to the more rigid standards of the past would risk losing whatever influence the Legion had over the growing number of independent-minded Catholics."[12] Writing about the contemporary media, two prominent Catholic intellectuals provide some insight into this altered cultural and theological climate. Frank Getlein and Father Harold C. Gardiner's *Movies, Morals, and Art* (1961), a popular guidebook of the era intended for Catholic filmgoers, was invoked in Chapter 4 for its vigorous defense of the traditional view that art should be moral and, in particular, should concern itself with identifying sin as what it is: "an offense against God . . . a violation of the social order . . . a degradation of the value of the individual."[13] Though unshakable proponents of the view that true art (the only "legitimate" kind) differentiates clearly between virtue and vice, Getlein and Gardiner also vigorously advocated for the position that an enlightened laity does not require the kind of intellectually unsophisticated censorship hitherto practiced by both the PCA and the legion: "When Catholics allow the irritations of the industry to make Catholic interest in the motion picture exclusively a matter of holding a sexual Geiger counter against décolletage and *double entendre*, they write off art, demean sex, and betray religion."[14] Such ideological and theological narrow-mindedness, Getlein and Gardiner contend, also makes American Catholics appear "a rather featherbrained pressure group, capable of causing a certain amount of trouble, but also capable of being cajoled, bought off, gulled."[15] In fact, as the "Publisher's Preface" proclaims, the aim of this volume was to contest the impression of Catholic opposition to modern art, a view perhaps fostered by clerical agitation in favor of the code during the 1930s and the interventions organized by the legion in subsequent decades: "*Movies, Morals, and Art* is the third in a series of books designed by the publisher to meet repeated papal injunctions [here the reference is mainly to the encyclical *Miranda Prorsus*] that the motion picture be made *the object of serious positive study by Catholics.*"[16]

Such "positive study" included a more appreciative approach, in particular to Tennessee Williams. Getlein and Gardiner, in fact, discuss *Suddenly, Last Summer* as an illustration of a general aesthetic prescription with which the playwright would certainly have concurred: "True art cannot escape a moral dimension."[17] Moreover, Catholics like Getlein and Gardiner had moved closer to the concept of morality held by Williams, with its emphasis on an unflinching engagement with the discontents of the human condition. Acknowledging that Williams had been "blasted enough in the Catholic press for being an immoral writer," Getlein and Gardiner suggest that the characters and events treated in *Suddenly* are "about as dubious raw material for artistic treatment as one could imagine." And yet, surprisingly and impressively, they conclude, "This somber story is a deeply impressive commentary on the doom (Eternal? Temporal? Williams does not say, nor does he have to) that lies in wait for the transgressor."[18] *Baby Doll*, in contrast, was justly condemned by the legion because of "the total suggestiveness that was the cumulative effect of the whole." In short, Williams as a moralist passing judgment was acceptable in the liberalizing atmosphere of post–*Miranda Prorsus*, but Williams as a sardonic, blackly humorous commentator on human frailty was not. *Suddenly* "takes moral deviation seriously," and as a result, the film is "a real entertainment experience."[19] Getlein and Gardiner may not have known it, but in describing *Suddenly* in this fashion, they were calling attention to how Mankiewicz's film fit neatly into a revamped and revitalized genre that was one of the era's most profitable studio types: the family melodrama.

The Discrepancy of Seeming and Being

The term "melodrama" has too vexed and complicated a history in academic film criticism to rehearse at length here, but some brief definitional work is certainly in order. In the largest sense, there is no contesting the view of Linda Williams that "melodrama is the fundamental mode of popular American moving pictures" and that, in that inflection, it is "a peculiarly democratic and American form that seeks dramatic revelation of moral and irrational truths through a dialectic of pathos and action."[20] But in addition to being a "fundamental mode," melodrama also designates an important genre, whose most interesting sub-types, at least in the 1940s and 1950s, were the woman's picture and the family melodrama.[21] Here the pathos so important to Hollywood filmmaking in general (both the emotions portrayed in the world of the story and the feelings they arouse in viewers) is deployed toward anatomizing what Thomas Elsaesser identifies as "the contradictions of American civilization." The action of such dramas results in characters being "constantly dazzled and amazed." This puzzlement strikes at the heart of individual and social experience: "The discrepancy of seeming and being, of intention and result, registers as a perplexing frustration, and an ever-increasing gap opens between the emotions and the reality they seek to reach. What strikes one as the true pathos is the very mediocrity of the human beings involved, putting such high demands upon themselves trying to live up to an exalted vision of man, but instead living out the impossible contradictions that have turned the American dream into its proverbial nightmare." Because such films are not only "critical social documents but genuine tragedies . . . they record some of the agonies that have accompanied the demise of the 'affirmative culture.'"[22] Rejecting at least in part the social conservatism of the happy ending, in which consensus values are restored and put beyond question, the family melodrama concludes with some sort of restoration, but, in general at least, only after undermining the deep claims of these values on characters and viewers as decisive measures of the social order.

In launching this muted critique against the status quo, the family melodrama, as Thomas Schatz has written, responded to "the dominant intellectual fashions of the postwar era . . . Freudian psychology and existential philosophy." These modes of analyzing the human condition, in Schatz's words, identify "the alienation of the individual due to the inability of familial and societal institutions to fulfill his or her particular needs."[23] But such a deconstruction of the traditional claims of affirmative culture (no more firmly established than in the postwar film industry's enduring Victorian aesthetic) proved extremely popular at a time when Hollywood was struggling to regain an audience lost to the suburbs and television. In that regard, it was the innovative explicitness of these psychodramas, as Barbara Klinger reports, that drew in filmgoers eager for the kind of visual drama they could not find on the small screen:

> Indeed, many of the biggest grossing films during this era . . . were melodramas with social, psychological, and/or sexual problems at their core. For their materials, studios often adapted novels and plays with celebrated adult profiles, enhancing the prestige as well as the notoriety of these films indebted to these prior works. Tennessee Williams's stories . . . were thus adapted. So were a host of novels and other plays. . . . Racy topics in these texts included homosexuality, sexual initiation, prostitution, rape, abortion, sexual frustration and temptation, alcoholism, and murder. It was through this dominant trend in production that melodrama came to be equated with adult subject matter and promises of sensationalism.[24]

Williams's dramatic texts played a key role as source material in this profitable development of adult films in crisis-ridden Hollywood, beginning a trend that would culminate during the late sixties in the institutionalization of the adult film and the ratings system that now defines it. In the remainder of this chapter, we will focus on the screen versions of *Cat on a Hot Tin Roof* (1958) and *Sweet Bird of Youth* (1962), both directed by Richard Brooks, as well as Mankiewicz's *Suddenly, Last Summer*, with a brief glance at Williams's "serious comedy," *Period of Adjustment* (1962).

Along with Elia Kazan, Brooks and Mankiewicz were beyond doubt the most celebrated and successful of the era's "literary" directors, and their involvement in these projects indicated both the growing prominence of the family melodrama and the central role Williams played, as the source of the genre's most artistically successful and sensational material, within its institutional development. These Williams films seize on (with great finesse of social observation) what Elsaesser identifies as one of the chief themes of fifties family melodrama: the discrepancy that opens up between seeming (the societal and gender roles characters are presumed and expected to fulfill) and being (the natures they yearn to inhabit fully, the selves that correspond, so they think or dream, to their deepest desires and needs). If Williams's characters in these films live out in this way their generically resonant "mediocrity," they confront as well a central contradiction of mid-century American culture: its exaltation yet proscription of untrammeled individuality.

Cat on a Hot Tin Roof (1958): Melodrama and Maturation

The stage version of *Cat* offers a more or less uncompromising enactment of rebellion against the social order. The play centers on the Pollitts, a Mississippi Delta family that has been called together to celebrate the birthday of Big Daddy, the patriarch of the clan. Lurking behind the celebration, however, is the horrible news, at first obscured from revelation, that Big Daddy is suffering from inoperable cancer and will soon die. As the older son, Gooper, and his manipulative wife May conspire to secure their inheritance, the younger son, Brick, an alcoholic who is essentially uninterested in the family wealth, progressively distances himself from his wife Maggie by shunning her tenderness and sexual advances. Their relationship is complicated by two estranging factors: Brick's guilty memory of his homosexual friend Skipper, who committed suicide when Brick failed to reciprocate his devotion, and Maggie's convoluted effort to "get through to Brick" by sleeping with Skipper, a dalliance that failed because of Skipper's heterosexual impotence. Maggie desires not only a rapprochement with Brick; she also seeks control of the family estate, and thus fabricates her sudden pregnancy (fecundity being the gold standard for the Pollitt inheritance). The dramatic action thus focuses on the reconciliation of this uneasy past with the present as well as on Big Daddy's determination to reach a father-son understanding with Brick—and vice versa. Brick Pollitt at first chooses the slow death of self-poisoning alcoholism rather than accede to the demands that society and his family make on him: to afford his wife Maggie her conjugal rights; to forgo the homosocial, perhaps even homosexual, pleasures afforded by the company of men's men; to father children and help raise them; to assume the role of patriarch and replace his dying father, Big Daddy, as master of a vast estate; and, perhaps most importantly, to give up his adolescent devotion to athletics for the adult world of less enjoyable labor, acknowledging in the process that his youth is at an end. This is the life toward which Brick is called by the inevitably unfolding span of his own adulthood.

And yet this life seems to Brick hopelessly compromised by bad faith, by the "mendacity" he finds everywhere and in everyone (including and especially himself). Hardly the Camusian rebel, Brick cannot find a place outside this realm of lies. Touched by the revelation of his father's impending death and his wife's devotion, he seems by play's end in fact more drawn (as he endorses Maggie's lie that she is pregnant) toward the assumption of his male responsibilities than toward some kind of hitherto unimaginable independence. Brick never conceives of a life that might include decisively breaking the ties that bind. Acknowledging (even if not unambiguously) the power of family to define individuals according to archetypal roles, *Cat* somewhat irresolutely resolves the conflict between embracing the necessary fictions of social and family life and releasing the authentic self from soul-destroying obligations.

After the Broadway failure of *Camino Real*, undoubtedly his most complexly modernist text, Williams penned *Cat* with more regard for mainstream tastes. Unlike *Camino*, *Cat* is Aristotelian (driven by plot), melodramatic (dominated by a rhetoric of affect and the representation of emotion), realistic (dependent on credible illusion), and socially conservative (supportive, though not unambiguously, of traditional sexual politics). Here was a more accessible drama that would prove immensely successful in both its theatrical and cinematic forms. When *Cat* was produced on stage, director Elia Kazan pushed Williams even further in the direction of middlebrow taste, and the playwright skillfully rewrote act III to his director's specifications. The film version by Richard Brooks takes these modifications several steps further, reshaping the play in ways that caused Williams substantial distress even as the changes made possible a critical and box-office success such as few playwrights have enjoyed on the silver screen.

Williams was determined to include in the printed text of *Cat* his original draft alongside the Broadway version he had written in response to Kazan's criticisms. In a brief introductory essay, the playwright somewhat hesitatingly rejects the director's influence on his writing. Though happy to be successful yet again, Williams resented what he felt was the compromise that had made it possible. He confesses with some reluctance that playwriting involves the transformation of private feelings into public art:

It is sad and embarrassing and unattractive that those emotions that sit in him deeply enough to demand expression . . . are nearly all rooted, however changed in their surface, in the particular and sometimes peculiar concerns of the artist himself.[25]

But if Williams, as an artist, feels driven to communicate personally and intimately, to his chagrin he must take into account the needs and desires of his audience:

Of course, I know that I have sometimes presumed too much upon corresponding sympathies and interest in those to whom I talk boldly, and this has led to rejections that were painful and costly enough to inspire more prudence. But when I weigh one thing against another, an easy liking against a hard respect, the balance always tips the same way, and whatever the risk of being turned a cold shoulder, I still don't want to talk to people only about the surface aspects of their lives.[26]

A Pollitt family tableau from Cat on a Hot Tin Roof, *with Big Daddy (Burl Ives) and Big Mama (Judith Anderson) in the foreground. Brick (Paul Newman) and Maggie (Elizabeth Taylor) are pictured in the back left, and Mae (Madeleine Sherwood) and Gooper (Jack Carson) are to the right. Photo courtesy of The Historic New Orleans Collection.*

On the Side of Seeming

Albert J. Devlin persuasively argues that the fictional cadre of *Cat* is meant to "obscure Williams's skepticism for the theatre of 'de-monstra-tion.'"[27] To put it somewhat differently, the fiction, then, is an Aristote-lian form that enables yet denies the playwright's controlling idea, which paradoxically is anti-Aristotelian. Ostensibly committed to action and change, the drama features a hero who refuses to engage in the conflict that confronts him. Obviously, this is an antidramatic notion that, taken to its conclusion, would shift the work decisively to lyricism. Lyricism and struggle were uneasily balanced in the play's first version. Kazan, and then Brooks, however, would help the playwright shift his conception decisively toward the melodramatic.

Kazan had already worked box-office magic and received critical acclaim for a series of films (including *Pinky* [1949], *A Tree Grows in Brooklyn* [1945], and *Gentleman's Agreement* [1947]) that were all dependent upon an affecting staging of family and cultural problems that are neatly resolved by characters who learn and grow from their dramatic interac-tions. This was not an aesthetic that Kazan in any sense discarded after working so successfully with more "literary" material on Broadway, as his film *On the Waterfront* (1954) clearly demonstrates. Here was yet another critical and popular triumph justly famed for its carefully developed and deeply affecting moments of recognition and reversal. The anguished confession of failure that Terry Malloy (Marlon Brando) makes to his brother (Rod Steiger) prepares the way for his tortured perseverance in the final, penitential struggle with union thugs. Terry's rejection of men-dacity (the easy road to financial security ensured by cooperation with union gangsters) allows him to reclaim his authentic self, now defined by doing the right thing, in the eyes of his girlfriend and his priest, by testi-fying against his erstwhile compatriots.

Like Terry Malloy, Brick is persuaded by the woman who loves him to face the guilty secret that prevents him from doing what would restore his integrity and position in society. Brick, too, finds that he has had enough of those lies that isolate and destroy. In the end, he is moved to take action that is less public and heroic than Malloy's, but equally as effective. His endorsement of Maggie's lie, should he turn it into truth, will save him and his family from a perhaps fatal decline into penury. Through Brick's apparent transformation, *Cat* comes close to celebrating the social importance of heterosexual coupling. With *Cat*, Williams thus moves far from the thematics of *Streetcar*. For there the playwright thoroughly ironizes the heterosexual imperative through the mock triumph of Stanley's reconciliation with Stella.

As first written, the play was self-reflexively melodramatic in its ostentatious denial of melodrama. Maggie's relentless battering and Big Daddy's empathetic interrogation push Brick toward the change of heart that should restore the family to itself. And this is nothing less than the softening of Brick's obdurate refusal to procreate, to mature in the way demanded by an institutionalized heterosexuality with no vested concern for the vagaries of desire (as Big Daddy's proud report of passionless love-making with Big Mama exemplifies). Brick's refusal is the textual reflex of Williams's initial reluctance to provide in act III the dramatic structure that the first two acts build toward. Big Daddy's failure to appear robs the play's conclusion of its most powerful advocate of acceptance and resignation (and the at least conventional success that flows from them), even as it obscures the generational continuity and male common cause implied in the reconciliation of father and son that ends act II. Devlin perceptively suggests that the double, contradictory turning of *Cat* should be traced to Williams's "practice of a deceptive realism that satisfied both the economic law of Broadway and the artistic prompting of Tennessee Williams's endangered career."[28]

Plantation Patriarchy

Merely an undramatized set of allusions in *Streetcar* but the cultural cadre that provides the setting, plot, and characters of *Cat*, the plantation myth shows the imaginative and literary connection between the two plays. In *Streetcar*, the myth explains the social failure whose implications the play dramatizes in a working-class New Orleans, far from the aristocratic refinement of Belle Reve. To account for her penury and rootlessness, Blanche describes the inability of the plantation, because of the family's weak and dissolute males, to sustain itself as an economic unit. What her precipitous arrival in New Orleans signifies is that the plantation has also failed to properly monitor sexual desire. The unattached and unsupervised widow of a homosexual driven to suicide by her rejection, Blanche cannot prevent her own slide into a self-destructive promiscuity. Blanche's demise thus repeats that of the feckless males in her family, whose "epic fornications" also managed to squander everything through a failure of self-control. The desire that the play thematizes cannot be institutionalized; it motivates only predation and exploitation, not the building of society.

As Stanley's sexual bondage to Stella exemplifies, moreover, such a desire imparts a power defined most tellingly by the weakness at its very center.

These terms are reversed in *Cat*. Here it is the damaged and dissolute heir apparent whose rejection of his patrimony is deflected, perhaps forever, by a woman who insists, perhaps triumphantly, on the heterosexual imperative, that is, procreative marriage. During the turbulent course of Brick's regeneration, the justice of that imperative is called into question several times: by Maggie's liaison with Skipper; by Skipper's inability to perform; by the mediocre and obnoxious fertility of Gooper and Mae (cast in the derisive gay-subculture stereotype of "breeders"); by Brick's homosocial, perhaps homosexual, inclinations; and by the aging young man's attachment to an adolescent world of self-satisfaction and arrested boyish pleasure in the transitory acclaim of the admiring crowd.[29] Even so, a fecund heterosexuality, here defined by its essential role within the multigenerational life of the family, is reestablished by the indomitable integrity of Big Daddy, a strong patriarch of the type whose absence from Blanche's family is not even lamented in *Streetcar*. Big Daddy models for his troubled son acceptance of the necessary lies and discontents of family relations.

Because it deals with failure rather than refusal, *Streetcar* satisfies the average playgoer's need for engagement with both sympathetic characters and a narrative that carries them from ignorance, confusion, and conflict to a moving and fulfilling resolution. In contrast, *Cat*'s initial working version, with its structurally weak third act, did not deliver the tight dramatic structure of *Streetcar*. And so Kazan, who was eagerly sought out by Williams to direct again, offered three suggestions for improvement. Each of these was very much in line with his characteristic (and melodramatic) concern for affect, both the feelings that the characters on stage were encouraged to express and the emotions they encouraged in the audience. Big Daddy, so powerfully developed in act II, was to reappear in act III. Maggie, moreover, was to be made more sympathetic. And Brick's unyielding refusal to deviate from his chosen course of self-destruction and to reconcile with his wife was to show some sign of weakening. With Kazan's modifications written into the play script by Williams, *Cat* became the playwright's greatest critical and popular success.

"You Never Growed Up"

Brooks's *Cat*, we could well say, offers more radical versions of the alterations incorporated into the Broadway version. His Maggie (Elizabeth

Taylor) is an even more sympathetic character. She cheerfully and readily accepts not only the authority of Big Daddy (Burl Ives), but also the leadership of her husband once he has made his peace with mendacity. The film's Brick (Paul Newman) not only endorses Maggie's lie; he finds in her trust of his renewed masculinity the strength to reassert his sexual control, summoning her to their bed at film's end (a command to which the relieved Maggie utters "Yes, sir"). Brooks's Big Daddy not only helps Brick fight through to a healing understanding of the disgust that disables him (analyzing it as Brick's anger at himself for failing to mature). Big Daddy also comes to grips with the rejection he felt from his own father, whose failure bequeathed him an irrepressible desire for success and the acquisition of things, impulses that, as Brick painfully instructs him, he thought could substitute for loving his children and acting in full the role of paterfamilias. Brick's unending quest for athletic excellence and the accompanying cheers of the crowd figure, so father and son decide, is just another version of the success ethic that has poisoned Big Daddy's relationship with his sons, including the compliant Gooper (Jack Carson), and his wife, Big Mama (Judith Anderson). As Big Daddy heals Brick's psychic wound, so the son proves able to heal the father's when they meditate on what the paternal role properly requires of men. In the film, a strongly emphasized element of Brick's disgust turns out to be his disappointment in Big Daddy as a father. But because he now learns in extremis of the dying man's similar dissatisfaction, Brick can accept the Abrahamian demand to be fruitful and multiply.

In the original, the transition from act I to act II separates the dialogue between Maggie and Brick from Brick's subsequent dialogue with his father; these two *scènes à deux* dominate the first two-thirds of the play but are not connected very effectively, either dramatically or thematically, to act III. The film version offers a more fluid dramatic structure, which highlights the complex interactions of Brick, Maggie, and Big Daddy with others in the family. The Pollitt mansion, inside and out, becomes a more plastic playing space, with the characters' restless movements through it indexing their turmoil and transformation.

Maggie and Brick's bedroom conversation is first interrupted by Maggie's departure to greet Big Daddy at the airport, who returns to the plantation in her car and chastises Maggie for not yet having three kids and a fourth "in the oven." Upon her return, the couple's quarrel is again interrupted, this time by a parental visit from Big Mama. She upbraids her daughter-in-law for failing to have children and, perhaps, not giving Brick "what he wants." While Maggie attends Big Daddy's birthday party downstairs, Brick learns the truth about his father's cancer from the family doctor. Brick and Maggie then resume their quarrel, which touches a painful nerve when Maggie mentions Brick's feelings of disgust, and this encounter ends with Maggie's resolution to do something about having Brick's baby, even though he can't stand being with her. The birthday party moves up to Brick's room, where, among other revelations, Big Daddy laments upon how dissatisfied he has been with their marriage, and it becomes even clearer that Gooper is terribly henpecked by his wife Mae (Madeleine Sherwood).

The others then leave the bedroom to Brick and Big Daddy, where the father's questions about Brick's coldness toward Maggie soon turn into a discussion of the son's self-destructiveness. The two move downstairs to the study, where Brick's refusal to answer his father's questions about Skipper prompts Big Daddy to summon Maggie. Much of the angry interchange between Brick and Maggie that occurs privately in the play's act I here occurs in Big Daddy's benevolent presence. The father ascertains that nothing happened between Maggie and Brick's best friend. Brick, it turns out, thinks himself to blame for Skipper's death because he did not reassure him of his support and mutual affection. The homosexual implications of Brick's attachment to Skipper (and Skipper's to Brick), handled more directly delicately in the original, are here effectively explained away. Brick, Big Daddy thinks, cannot embrace adult responsibility: "The truth is that you never growed up." Brick runs out into the storm to drive away (in a top-down convertible awash with rain), but gets stuck in the mud, a fitting image of both his immaturity and also his inability to escape from the truth and his responsibilities to wife and family.

Before his abortive flight, Brick refuses to go along with the family lie about his father's health and informs Big Daddy that his condition is in fact terminal. Concerned for his father's pain, Brick slips by the rest of the family members, who are squabbling over who should inherit the family business interests, to join Big Daddy in the mansion's basement—a dollar-book Freudian symbol for what the two men have been repressing as well as a treasure trove of symbolic objects, the things that each man has hitherto mistakenly lived for. The two find themselves uncomfortable among box after box of unpacked statues and objets d'art purchased long ago on a European junket, as well as Brick's athletic memorabilia, trophies, and a life-size photo of his younger self passing a football. The scene Brooks here adds to the play script exemplifies the family melodrama's means of discovering a reflex in action for overwhelming inner feelings, as Thomas Elsaesser suggests: "The social pressures are such, the frame of respectability so sharply defined that the 'strong' action is limited . . . the hysterical outburst replaces any more directly liberating or self-annihilating action, and the cathartic violence of a shoot-out or a chase becomes an inner violence, often one which the characters turn against themselves. . . . Violent feelings are given vent on 'overdetermined' objects . . . and aggressiveness is worked out by proxy."[30] Brick's self-containment, his unwillingness to address for much of the film's initial movement Maggie's complaints with more than a few bitter words, turns into an extended vent of self-loathing and anguished pleading. Brick destroys his trophies and, with a crowbar, rips up his glamour poster, reminding his father that all he has purchased with his time and energy is meaningless, as the basement resting place of the memorabilia and still-packed art objectifies. As Big Daddy, chastened, explores his own painful memories of a father who did not show him love, Brick comes to realize that there are no longer any lies to divide them and that, in fact, his own father does love him deeply.[31] What the two men in pain and crisis share most deeply, in fact, is the unhappiness they have experienced in marriage because of their failings as fathers and husbands.

Less Sound, Less Fury

This storm of emotion is not shared with the rest of the family, and the final reordering of family relationships occurs with the male characters forgoing anything like male hysteria. Tiptoeing over to the basement stairs, Maggie listens in approvingly on their raucous dialogue. Undisturbed because Big Mama, suspecting that a powerful reconciliation is playing itself out, prevents Gooper from going down to investigate, the pair are free to speak as they wish. With nothing more to say, they ascend to the study, there to allay Big Mama's uncertainties about the family's future. Maggie's sudden lie about being pregnant throws into question Gooper's claim to inherit the plantation. Endorsing the truth of this unexpected revelation, Brick thereby agrees to take on the patriarch's responsibilities upon his father's death. He will be helped in this endeavor by his brother, with whom Brick wordlessly reconciles. At Brick's command, he and Maggie together climb the stairs back to their bedroom, there to reestablish their sexual bond and produce the promised heir, with the husband now occupying the domestic high ground.

The melodramatization begun with Kazan's modifications is thus carried through to its logical conclusion. The troubled family is restored to itself. Just as Brick reasserts his control over Maggie, who is happily reduced to approving and obedient silence, so Big Daddy takes leadership of the family back from Big Mama, who has proved unable to decide among or properly discipline the endlessly squabbling females, the unofficial representatives of the competing interests of their respective husbands. Even Gooper's masculinity is restored, though by proxy, as he effectively silences his endlessly carping wife with a very loud "Shut up!" Mae is cowed into sour silence by Gooper's forcefulness and, like her sister-in-law, shows herself obedient at last to spousal command.

In the service of the essentially conservative agenda of family melodrama, the ambiguities of Williams's original stage play are drastically simplified. Ironically, the very quality that made this Williams property appealing to a mainstream film audience—the story's notorious engagement with a problematic, perhaps perverse sexuality expressed by the uncertainty of Brick's real nature—is thereby preserved in the only form that Hollywood would unproblematically accept, as a sensational thematizing of the more acceptable, but still risqué, issue of marital rights. Consider the initial reaction of the PCA to an inquiry about the property from Paramount's Hal Wallis. Geoffrey Shurlock wrote to Wallis's assistant Paul Nathan that: "It would be necessary to remove every inference of implication of sex perversion and to substitute some other problem for the young husband. . . . I also emphasized that the fact that the young wife's problem consisted entirely of trying to get her husband to sleep with her and get her pregnant, seemed to present a very definite Code problem by reason of over-emphasis on this extremely delicate relationship."[32]

These problems, it turned out, could be easily remedied, though Wallis perhaps passed on the project because he thought they were intractable. In the film, Brick's puzzling and disturbing rejection of Maggie's obvious sexual charms (a reflection of his rejection of his patrimony) motors the narrative, but is successfully explained away. For both Brick's "unnatural" connection to Skipper as well as Maggie's adultery are shown to be mirages. These misunderstandings are settled, at the urging of a concerned patriarch, by the Pollitts' loving dialogue with one another. If, in the end, the relationship between Brick and Maggie seems fully as "carnal" as that between Stanley and Stella, their connection lacks the strong sense of interlocking psychopathologies, both violent jealousy and infantile need. It is once again easy enough to see how the Hollywood *Cat* is a

Brick (Paul Newman) stalks his wife, Maggie (Elizabeth Taylor), in this confrontation from Cat on a Hot Tin Roof. *Photo courtesy of The Historic New Orleans Collection.*

more socially conservative dramatic fiction than either the stage or screen version of *Streetcar*.

In giving constant, desperate voice to her frustration with Brick's withdrawal from their physical relationship, perhaps Maggie reflects a general truth of the era: as three prominent feminist historians put it, "the Kinsey reports encouraged women to take a more hardheaded—the critics said 'selfish'—view of sex. . . . Thus sex was not just an extension of love but a separate realm within which a marriage could either falter or succeed."[33] Williams's ingenious plot allowed audiences to understand Maggie's unhappiness traditionally, as both the result of sexual frustration (made worse by the constant presence of her attractive husband in their bedroom) and also as stemming from her (as yet) unfulfilled desire to bear children, which is for her a desperate economic and social imperative. For if Brick fails to remain the heir apparent, the once "dirt poor" Maggie would soon find herself again out in the cold. In unambiguously closing the gap between desire (now shown to be thoroughly heteronormal) and procreation, the film powerfully installs one of the key elements of 1950s ideology—the recuperative power of family solidarity.

Interestingly, to attain this end, the film promotes a view of marriage with which even conservative Catholics at the time would have scarcely disagreed. Procreation becomes the end that the couple's sexual connection, obviously enjoyable *in se* as well as *per se*, to use the language of papal meditation on the subject, has been reestablished to fulfill. Williams's "provocative" drama becomes instead an appealingly "naughty" though morally unobjectionable film. The play hints at another way of life that it cannot fully imagine, a place where homosexual desire could declare itself and where the family, dependent for its continuation on the succession of generations, would lose its claim on individual destiny. In contrast, Brooks's *Cat* mounts only a weak challenge to the regnant power of monogamous heterosexuality, for it is the temporary failure of Brick to grow up that disrupts the ostensibly natural order of things.[34] Unlike the play, the film does not point (even uncertainly or obliquely) toward another form of adult life. It discovers its sensationalism only in giving voice and image to the fact of marital intercourse and its consequences, a form of sexuality sanctioned by law and religion but never hitherto thematized so directly on celluloid.

"Within the Bounds of Good, Adult Taste"

Such was the opinion, at least, of industry reviewers, who quickly recognized that *Cat* would be a box-office winner. The *Hollywood Reporter* observed that "as adapted by screen playwrights Richard Brooks and James Poe, the Tennessee Williams drama acquires more universal appeal than the stage version, more philosophical depth, and leaves the audience with more satisfactory conclusions . . . their interpretation of the high-voltage events is so accurate to human behavior that it will be appreciated in the South as well as the North."[35] *Variety* opined that the filmmakers, though toning down the playwright's sensationalism, had hardly emptied the property of its adult appeal: "Aspects of the celluloid 'Cat' might be mild compared with the way it has clawed the legit boards, but by no means is it an explosive that's been watered down to a fizzle . . . the motivations had been held psychologically sound . . . a powerful, well-seasoned film . . . within the bounds of good, adult taste."[36] *Harrison's Reports* enthused that "as an entertainment . . . it is an emotion-packed, heavily dramatic conversation piece that should find its best reception among sophisticated audiences in large cities. Some slight and necessary changes have been made in the story to clean it up for this screen version

. . . but the considerable talk about sex is as frank and forthright as anything ever heard in a motion picture."[37]

"Frank and forthright," certainly, but Brooks's *Cat*, with its strong neo-Freudian emphasis on the healing powers of the talking cure, might be seen as lacking the critique of bourgeois society that is such a prominent element of the era's family melodrama, especially those directed by Douglas Sirk, Nicholas Ray, and Vincente Minnelli.[38] Elsaesser observes: "The family melodrama . . . more often records the failure of the protagonist to act in a way that could shape the events and influence the emotional environment, let alone change the stifling social milieu. The world is closed, and the characters are acted upon. Melodrama confers on them a negative identity through suffering . . . they emerge as lesser human beings for having become wise and acquiescent to the ways of the world."[39] *Cat*, in contrast, does not seem to indict some "stifling social milieu," a phrase that accurately describes life in the Pollitt mansion only at the beginning of the narrative. Brick and Big Daddy both yearn to break free of the hold that mendacity and hypocrisy have upon them, and manage ultimately to do so.

A Mutineer in His Heart?

If Brick has by film's end "acquiesced" in the ways of the world (heteronormality in particular and adult responsibility in general), he has in no way become the lesser for it, having rejected, through his destruction of the life-sized photograph, what he suggests, and what the film in part argues, is the phantom, insubstantial self of arrested adolescent dreams. "By the 1950s and '60s," Barbara Ehrenreich observes, "psychiatry had developed a massive weight of theory establishing that marriage—and within that, the breadwinner role—was the only normal state for the adult male."[40] We may perhaps appreciate better Williams's perceptive analysis of the era's masculine crisis and, with Kazan and Brooks, the normative way in which the crisis might be resolved, if we recall that, to quote Ehrenreich again, "in psychiatric theory and in popular culture, the image of the irresponsible male blurred into the shadowy figure of the homosexual."[41] In the clinical language of the day, Brick would be classified a "pseudo-homosexual," as a man who suffered from "some 'adaptive failure' to meet the standards of masculine conformity and had begun a subconscious slide toward a homosexual identity."[42]

This slide (an apt characterization indeed for Brick's gradual disengagement) could be cured by an acceptance of the male call to author-ity and an assumption of the necessity to lead and instruct women.[43] The view that Brick's attachment to Skipper is in some sense homo-sexual, an opinion that seems to be held decisively in the film only by Big Daddy, who questions Brick probingly about the relationship, could thus quite plausibly be explained away for filmgoers of the era, as it eventually is for his own father, as a misidentified symptom of Brick's immaturity. Williams and his adaptors encourage this interpretation by making Brick and Skipper not only childhood pals, but also teammates whose appointed path toward adult responsibility is immobilized by a joint, fervent devotion to adolescent games. Brick's final acquiescence in orders both social and sexual thus appears inevitable. It is revealed to be an artificially delayed embrace of normality rather than a painful rejec-tion of the urge toward individuality and the enactment of a desire that might truly and scandalously turn out to be, to use the Freudian term, polymorphous.

And yet the film's working-through of the conflict between seeming and being is perhaps not quite so thoroughly conservative. In the 1950s, the pressure to conform to a narrow definition of masculinity, especially to surrender economic self-sufficiency to corporate collectivity, found itself under sustained attack, part of the more general fearful reaction, particularly among intellectuals, to the evolution of what was then called "mass society." What Brooks had made of the inexorable progress toward normality in *Cat*'s narrative was revealingly contextualized by the con-troversy aroused in the era by William H. Whyte, Jr., whose *The Organi-zation Man* (1956) offered a sardonic analysis of life within big organiza-tions—government, business, and even the university. The organization man firmly commits himself to collectivity. In Whyte's view, he is guided by "a belief in the group as the source of creativity; a belief in 'belonging-ness' as the ultimate need of the individual."[44]

And yet Whyte catalogues the discontents of what he calls the social ethic, concluding that the individual must struggle against those forces that urge conformity upon him: "It is wretched, dispiriting advice to hold before him the dream that ideally there need be no conflict between him and society."[45] Robert Lindner, most famous for authoring a widely read sociological tract on the adolescent male crisis called *Rebel Without a Cause* (the source of the Nicholas Ray film), saw the threat of confor-mity at the time as even more serious, worthy of an extended meditation entitled *Must You Conform?* To this question, Lindner utters a resounding no. Our national culture, he pleads, is infected with the "rot-producing idea that the salvation of the individual and of society depends upon conformity and adjustment." The consequences for the young are especially regrettable: "Our adolescents reflect the slow but ominous advance of a psychic contagion. They are but one step from us along the road to Mass Manhood. . . . In our stead they are expressing the unrelieved rage, the constricting tension and the terrible frustration of the world they were born into. Their revolt, as much as the world they face, is not of their making. They are helpless and hopeless, imprisoned by the blunders and delusions of their predecessors; and like all prisoners, they are mutineers in their hearts."[46]

The lyric idea of that inner mutiny (Brick slowly but steadily committing suicide), with which Tennessee Williams began, becomes by the end of the film version a thoroughgoing endorsement of maturity, with even Big Daddy now resolved, as his penance for decades of selfishness, to pay Big Mama more attention and respect as life drains from him. Many at the time might have looked on this "conversion" as less than positive. According to Lindner, the notion of maturity takes no account of "man's nature and spirit, of his innate rebelliousness, of his intrinsic values, or of his individuality."[47]

The play, of course, can imagine no space in which Brick's perhaps nonconformist sexuality might play itself out. Like many of Williams's homosexual characters, Skipper is conveniently (and unthreateningly) dead before the drama begins, precluding the staging of a too revealing *scène à deux* or, even more confrontationally, one *à trois*, with Maggie and Skipper representing competing objects of desire, contrasting *moyens de vivre*. Despite its thematic emphasis on maturity, the film also represents what it is that Brick must relinquish of his "intrinsic values." Brooks clearly shows us the road that can no longer be taken. In fact, by dramatizing an episode that is only rendered in the play's dialogue, the precredit sequence evokes a sense of deep and abiding loss. It is night at the local high school athletic field, now deserted of student life. Brick pulls up in his convertible, staggers drunkenly out of the car, and sets up the high hurdles. He then attempts to run the course at full speed. Hearing again, and for the last time, the crowd roar in his imagination, he almost succeeds. Though impaired by age and drink, Brick's athleticism still serves him well as he speeds down the track, his form impressive, his sense of accomplishment irreducibly male and individual.

But Brick just misses clearing the final hurdle and, falling, breaks his ankle. It is that disability, the mark of a not inglorious yet sad failure, that confines him to the family home, where the process of his domestication and "adjustment," chronicled in the film proper, inexorably proceeds toward its maturational goal. As Brooks undoubtedly recognized, what makes Brick attractive is precisely his nonconformity, his refusal to surrender, before he must, his hard-won pride of place in the competitive world of sports to an inevitably feminizing domestication.

A Masculinized Space?

Tellingly, in both play and film, the dangers to the male sense of self posed by conformity to the conventional maturational path are exemplified by the henpecked Gooper, the older son whose patrimony has against his will, and despite loyal and constant service to his father, been passed to his younger brother. At film's end, finding his gifts as despised as Cain's, Gooper bitterly complains that he always unquestioningly followed the path Big Daddy dictated for him: pursuing a college education and a career as a lawyer; submitting to marriage with a socially acceptable woman and the attendant siring of an impressive brood of children; and, finally, responsibly managing the family estate when his father's health failed. Yet Big Daddy prefers the unreliable, perpetually adolescent younger son, suggesting that, in some sense, he seems to recognize what Lindner calls the "psychic contagion" of the conformist drive toward maturity that has made Gooper less worthy. Perhaps then, the mendacity against which Brick and Big Daddy both rail is not just the lies others tell (and, more damagingly, the lies one tells oneself), but a larger untruth, that what is thought to be maturity is merely a sham, not the fulfilling and dominant position toward which manliness summons them, but a soul-destroying uxoriousness, a submission by the younger generation to what Lindner so bitterly terms "the blunders and delusions of their predecessors."[48]

The film, we suggest, asks its audience to endorse a contradiction at the heart of melodrama: to believe both that the individual finds himself only within the family, and also that individuality exists only in that space beyond the conventional demands of domestic life. Despite a very conventional ending, Brooks's version follows Williams's closely in presenting Brick as a character who cannot break his attachment to what society defines as the only acceptable set of roles and responsibilities for a mature man, but who also cannot easily abandon his urge toward self-fashioning. Interestingly, the film emphasizes this contradiction by its sudden focus near the end on Gooper, who has hitherto functioned exclusively as a foil. Unexpectedly, the younger brother's mistreatment is at least symbolically rectified by the reassertion of male power effected by Brick and Big Daddy, who triumphantly ascend to the living room from what was hitherto the only masculine space in the house, its cellar. This is a movement in which Gooper is permitted to participate, even if only at secondhand. Neither a dissatisfied rebel nor an alpha male like his father and brother, he does not include himself, and is not included, in their intimate conversation. Brick initiates this encounter by searching out Big Daddy, who has secreted himself downstairs so that he can endure the pain of his cancer in peace. This is a pain the younger son tellingly alleviates by bringing him a syringe of morphine, an offering that corresponds to his own bottle of whiskey.

Gooper, of course, has need of neither crutch, for he is, as the era's pop psychology phrased it, perfectly adjusted to his roles as dutiful husband, provident father, and loyal son. Not enduring that uncertainty of self that torments his father and brother, he is denied membership in their fraternity of suffering. Tellingly, he hardly seems aware that it exists. And yet he, too, is ravaged by a deep sense of dissatisfaction, the sense that his responsible conformity has purchased him nothing but the scorn of his father and brother. At the very end, the film makes space for his ressentiment as well. Once the group reassembles in the living room, Gooper is allowed to ape the gesture of his more masculine brother, as he, too, acts out an archly misogynist stereotype, aggressively silencing a "nagging" woman, who is standing up, ironically enough, for him. If only for a brief moment, even the conformist becomes the rebel protesting the surrender of his individuality, which Brick and Gooper now both prove able to reclaim in some sense by putting their wives in their "proper places." The irony of this sudden moment of male solidarity in the contested space of the family home, however, is that the anger of the two brothers has different sources, surely a significant indication that neither rebellion nor conformity offers lasting satisfaction.

And so the reassertion of male independence from female control seems hollow at the core. Accession to womanly demands for male presence, interest, and devotion, so at least the film struggles to assert, brings about the refiguration of the home, from basement to bedroom, as the space in which the familial enactment of true masculinity as the power to lead and determine finds its appropriate theatre—in contrast to the pursuit, just discredited, of individual accomplishment in the world outside the front door, either in business or on the football field. But, as the satisfied faces of Maggie and Big Mama make clear at film's end, while the home can make a place for real men, it continues to be, even if sub rosa, under female rule.

Can it truly be that Big Daddy now suddenly finds the meaning of life to be this long-stale connection to the mother of his children? Are we to imagine a Brick reinstalled in the conjugal bedroom as happier than the Brick who once ran for touchdowns? It seems instead that Brooks's film critiques affirmative culture in the sense that Thomas Elsaesser suggests all family melodrama of the era does. These films, he says, manifest the truth that "true pathos is the very mediocrity of the human beings involved, putting such high demands upon themselves trying to live up to an exalted vision of man."[49] In this way, their experiences expose the impossible contradiction at the heart of an America that demands conformity in the very act of reprehending it.

Sweet Bird of Youth (1962): Chance as Reformed Playboy

Brooks's *Cat* was a huge financial success, costing only about $3 million to produce but grossing nearly $18 million (perhaps more, since industry figures notoriously underreport earnings).[50] It was also much honored by the film community. *Cat* was put up for best picture and received five other nominations as well: Newman, Taylor, and Ives for their acting; Brooks for his directing; and William Daniels for his beautiful color cinematography. It is not surprising, then, that Brooks and others concerned (especially Paul Newman) were eager to repeat their success with a strikingly similar Williams property, *Sweet Bird of Youth*. Both dramas hinge on the confrontation between a dominating father figure and an aging adolescent hero who has hitherto proved able to cash in on his looks and athleticism (roles ideally suited to Newman's screen persona). But as we shall see, the plays and, especially, the films made from them otherwise offer very different perspectives on the postwar crisis of masculinity, whose dramatization was such an important element in family melodramas of the 1950s.

What gives both the stage and screen versions of *Cat* their deep resonance is that Brick's paralysis generally reflects the broader masculine crisis of the period, in which men had everything to lose (their independence) and nothing very certain to gain (except dependents) by living out the traditional male role. After providing a sensitive and informed queer reading of the play, the kind of analysis simply not possible in a more closeted age, critic Michael Paller concludes: "As drama and as theatre, *Cat on a Hot Tin Roof* is the story of human beings contending with competing emotions and desires, written by another human being engaged in his own struggle for something of unspeakable importance: a resolution in the battle between living an authentic life and keeping the material comfort and fame that may be acquired if one fudges."[51] "Fudging," of course, is what Brick terms *mendacity* and Big Daddy *hypocrisy*. Both play and, to a much more muted extent, film suggest that the "other way" possible for Brick, the unfudged, more authentic path, is the homosocial (perhaps homosexual) coupling with his "best friend" Skipper, a form of living that would allow Brick to avoid the daunting responsibilities of adulthood and domesticity. Such a choice can hardly be acknowledged, only bitterly regretted as eternally unattainable after the rejected man's suicide and Brick's loss of youth. In the film, Brick can choose only between a slow alcoholic death (the executioner passing judgment on himself for failing his friend) and life (the confused adolescent finally understanding the meaning of manhood's obligations).

Sweet Bird of Youth's plot structure is, by his own admission, Williams's most unwieldy, as he tried to meld what are essentially two competing narratives. One "story" features Chance Wayne, a would-be actor who is now a gigolo in the service of Alexandra Del Lago, a fading actress. But Wayne and Del Lago have driven to St. Cloud, a town on the Gulf Coast that is home to Heavenly Finley, Wayne's former lover, and thus the other "story" involves Chance's attempt at reconciling with Heavenly, even as he tries to keep Del Lago sexually satisfied. Any reunion between Chance and Heavenly is complicated by the fact that he had previously infected her with a venereal disease, which required a hysterectomy, and he has therefore become persona non grata in St. Cloud. In the meantime, Heavenly's father, Boss Finley, is a racist demagogue seeking reelection and is bent on keeping Chance away from his daughter by any means necessary. As Chance futilely seeks a return to the promises of his youthful romance, Del Lago rejuvenates her movie career and moves on, leaving Wayne behind to face castration at the hands of Finley's mob.

In the profligate character Chance Wayne, *Sweet Bird* constructs male rebellion in quite different terms, reflecting the development within American society during the 1950s of yet another form for manhood to assume, what Ehrenreich calls that "fraternity of male rebels," whose foundational text became the hyper-heterosexual magazine *Playboy*. Tirelessly preaching a philosophy of sexual Don Juanism and spurning traditional notions of monogamy and commitment, influential *Playboy* editor Hugh Hefner had another idea of what constituted the "good life" for men. It was hardly the traditional triad of job, wife, and family. The *Playboy* ethos did not in the least demean the notion of work, promoting in fact the kind of frantic, income-boosting careerism that made for full participation in the consumer society. But why, Hefner asked (and he was not alone), should men have to spend their hard-earned money on a wife and children? Refusing such economic bondage, Hefner argued, rendered them not less but rather more manly, as they cannily avoided the feminizing pressures of domestication. In fact, because they were bachelors living in a world where contraception was fast becoming an ordinary practice, men could more fully indulge their sexual interests in women without worrying that an unwanted pregnancy might lead to a disastrous lifelong commitment. Thus, as Ehrenreich declares, the playboy approach to grown-up living "was impervious to the ultimate sanction against male rebellion—the charge of homosexuality. The playboy didn't avoid marriage because he was a little bit 'queer,' but, on the contrary, because he was so ebulliently, even compulsively heterosexual."[52]

Brooks opens his *Cat* with a bittersweet image of Brick's failure to be what he once was, but his *Sweet Bird*, in contrast, begins with an image that powerfully communicates the *Playboy* ideal of making it big. At the wheel of a shiny Cadillac convertible, its top down, is where the camera first locates Chance Wayne, his face set in what seems a permanent smirk of self-satisfaction, driving along the Florida coast. An attractive older woman (Del Lago) slumps in the seat beside him, and he stops to purchase a bottle of liquor to keep her happy. Once they arrive at their hotel destination, Chance registers for a room in her name and then effortlessly carries his unconscious companion upstairs, where he readies himself for a day of wheeling and dealing. The elements of the *Playboy* image ostentatiously make themselves present: conspicuous consumption of status-conferring "toys" (the self-indulgent automobile), freedom (Chance's job seems to be self-promotion, not climbing the corporate ladder), and sexual indulgence (the obviously compliant companion hardly seems to be a spouse, the hotel rendezvous promising a bedroom encounter).

But the film shows this playboy image to be a mirage, and in that thematic movement it is quite faithful to the playwright's original conception. If *Sweet Bird*'s Chance Wayne is, as Hefner might have advised and applauded, compulsively heterosexual, the play poignantly but trenchantly (and, one might say, conservatively as well) anatomizes the tragic personal and social consequences of this evolving masculine role, which in the postwar era was more a fantasy, of course (as it turns out to be for Chance), than what we would now term a lifestyle. As sexuality became increasingly conceived, in the age of Kinsey, as a natural urge to which both genders powerfully responded, the oversexualized man could be easily turned into an object of desire for women. Now valued for his physical charms alone, he could even demand money or favors for sexual services. Initially presented as a kind of playboy, Chance is quickly revealed as a hustler, a man eager to partake of the goods a powerful, successful woman has at her command. His hypermasculinity is unmasked to reveal his feminization. Chance's handsome face and muscular torso, featured on the silver screen, might be traded in for more substantial treasure and even fame; should that come to pass, Chance would become the object of a desiring gaze, the role in which the Princess has already cast him.

But if Chance, initially at least, rejects monogamy and willingly surrenders himself to an economy of glamour hitherto in American culture available only to women, he does so anachronistically. For his overall aim is to transform himself into a fit mate for his true love, Heavenly, the daughter of the political boss of his southern hometown, whom he left behind in order to pursue fame and fortune as an actor. Though both characters wind up happily domesticated, Chance is initially the reverse image of Brick, for he seems desperate to escape into marriage. He has returned to the place of his birth with two aims. First, he intends to convince his erstwhile companion, Alexandra (Geraldine Page), a princess because she was once married to royalty, to set him up with a lucrative performance-services contract that would be the start of a movie career. Only then, his status as a fitting claimant for his beloved's hand finally confirmed, would he take Heavenly as his wife, righting the wrong he thinks was committed when sometime before her father, Boss Finley, dismissed him as a loser.

On stage, *Sweet Bird* traces the tragic consequences of this double, contradictory wish. The film, in contrast, works to discredit Chance's absorption in his acting career (for which he has yet to demonstrate any real aptitude) and to provide him with a penitential path toward a socially acceptable marriage to the woman he loves. Born of pain and suffering,

Chance Wayne (Paul Newman) and Heavenly Finley (Shirley Knight) in a publicity still from Sweet Bird of Youth. *Photo courtesy of The Historic New Orleans Collection.*

the film's happy ending proceeds with symbolic appropriateness from the destruction of Chance's good looks and hence the taming of his playboy dedication to self. The film follows, in fact, the same generically sanctioned movement toward maturity that Brooks had already used in *Cat*.

The filming of *Sweet Bird* was to follow the pattern, mutatis mutandis, established by *Cat* as far as possible. In so doing, Brooks was forced to alter his source substantially, most notably by confecting (or, more accurately, acceding to the imposition of) this happy ending. Perhaps because it did not focus on a dysfunctional family whose sympathetic principals (Brick, Maggie, and Big Daddy) could be delivered to a powerful reconciliation, *Sweet Bird* did not meet with the same critical and popular success achieved by *Cat*. *Sweet Bird*'s endorsement of conservative values is in every way more problematic because of the more forceful and compelling presence within it of the woman Chance does not choose (for she is something like his female double, destined to remain forever outside the orbit of family). Unlike any character in *Cat*, the princess embodies the persistence of the urge toward self-fashioning; the film can devise no scenario of domestication to contain her energies and desires.

In other ways, however, *Sweet Bird* was an ideal property for the making of a sequel in the traditional Hollywood sense. Brooks read the two plays as variations on a theme, since they both feature young men enduring a crisis of sexual desire and identity. As the films open, Brick and Chance, who have barely survived an extended adolescence, must reconcile themselves to assuming adult responsibilities, including agreeing to monogamous heterosexuality. According to what we might call their philosophy of adaptation, the two projects are very similar as well. In the writing of both scripts, Brooks tried to follow the spirit of Williams's conception whenever this proved possible. In the case of *Sweet Bird*, Brooks even reports that he tried to retain the essence of the playwright's tragic finale:

> I had a different ending for *Sweet Bird*, but they wouldn't let me use it. What I wanted Chance Wayne to do was this. . . . He goes to the house, calling for the girl. The brother shows up with the boys and they drag him over to the car. They begin to destroy him. You don't have to see the castration, but first they destroy his looks, and then they go to work on him. . . . You dissolve, in my other ending, straight to the ferry. At the beginning of the picture you saw the ferry as they arrive. The Princess and Lucy are leaving in the car and they stop for a moment. Once they're on the ferry boat, they're out of that town. . . . The boat slows down, toots its horn, pulls away a little bit to cross over, because passing is a garbage scow. On that scow is Chance Wayne.[53]

MGM, not surprisingly, nixed this ending, at least for the initial tradeshow version. Few Hollywood films of the period kill off the leading man (and only fully realized, sympathetic character) at the end, leaving the heroine's erotic and domestic expectations forever unfulfilled. Brooks, however, did not shoot the necessary footage during initial production so that he might substitute his preferred ending if the executives had an unpredictable change of heart. The director maintains that the studio "felt it was bad enough they were doing this picture."[54] This hardly seems likely since Williams had been paid the then princely sum of around $500,000 for the screen rights even before the Broadway production had proved successful. Like the director, MGM was banking on another critical and box-office success from a play authored by Broadway's hottest playwright. They were surely not eager to homogenize any more than was absolutely necessary this expensive and potentially lucrative property.[55]

Brooks surely protests too much. The ending that was shot not only fits the prescribed Hollywood formula for the family melodrama, but also the overall pattern of adaptation. Boy gets the girl he comes for only after paying for his many misdeeds and discovering what is truly important, which is loving a good woman rather than achieving success as a performer. And Brooks, occupying the unusual position of writer-director, exercised a great deal of control over that pattern. As Gene Phillips has perceptively remarked, "The upbeat ending of the film does grow out of the foregoing two hours with a logic comparable to that with which the downbeat ending of the play develops its foregoing two hours."[56] The appropriate ending could hardly have been the result of a happy accident resulting from the proverbial studio hacks knowing better than the very talented Mr. Brooks how to resolve the drama of what becomes Chance's quest for Heavenly rather than for self. In any case, Williams found much to like in the film version, the happy finale excepted: "*Sweet Bird of Youth* was a brilliant film until the end."[57] Williams's risqué and tragic story of maladjustment, anomie, and the horror of aging was transformed into a more conventional screen romance that ends with the two young lovers together at last.

In its original form, *Sweet Bird* owed more than a little to the tragic form of nineteenth-century melodrama. Consider the playwright's deployment of venereal disease as the outward sign of Chance's violation of social norms, the flawed hero's inevitable defilement of female purity through its transmission in an unsanctioned act of love, and the castration he suffers as a symbolically appropriate punishment. In contrast, the film more clearly resonates with the preoccupations of postwar American culture. Many acclaimed and serious films of the period, ranging from *On the Waterfront* (1954) to *The Man in the Grey Flannel Suit* (1956), focus on men who, caught in moral dilemmas or failing in their drive to achieve, cannot easily reconcile themselves to the mature demands of career and marriage. Paul Newman, we might even say, specialized in such projects. *From the Terrace* (1960), *The Young Philadelphians* (1959), *Hud* (1963), and *The Hustler* (1961), among other films, showcased Newman as an angry young man searching for direction and authenticity in a world of exploitative females, misleading and antagonistic father figures, and fierce competition for success. In these films, as in Brooks's *Cat*, wayward women, uncertain or ineffective patriarchs, and directionless young men find themselves "properly" situated after all dramatic conflicts have run their course.

In the case of *Cat*, Brooks could travel further down the path of melodramatization already blazed by his theatrical counterpart, Elia Kazan, "straightening" out Brick in every sense. Although he also oversaw the initial Broadway production of *Sweet Bird*, this time Kazan did not ask the playwright to change substantially what he had written (or so the director says). Unlike Kazan, Brooks did not have to consult with Williams about his production and so could be less inhibited about changing the playwright's conception. Brooks had to deal somehow with the way the princess dominates act I but then recedes in importance until close to the finale, when she offers Chance an opportunity (which he declines) to escape from the danger that threatens because he will not abandon the attempt to connect with Heavenly. In Kazan's view at least, *Cat* posed a somewhat similar problem in emphasis, since Big Daddy provides an important presence in the first two acts, but then disappears from act III. This was easy to remedy, however, as Kazan advised Williams, simply by bringing Big Daddy back in the final act (and Brooks in the film version, as we have seen, increased this sense of male presence and drama by staging a long scene between father and son in the mansion's basement).

In the case of *Sweet Bird*, however, such a solution would not work: the princess is too powerful a presence and draws attention away from the frustrated desire of the nominal protagonist. Unlike Maggie's frustration, moreover, the dissatisfaction of the Princess has nothing to do with a disturbance in the established family order. Her drives for creative expression, popular acclaim, and power over others, not to mention her sexual aggressiveness, are rooted in a desire for self-sufficiency, which is traditionally considered a masculine trait. With the important exception of desiring Heavenly and thus the spiritual satisfaction of romantic love,

Chance wants exactly what the Princess has had and is eager to regain. Protagonist and antagonist in the beginning of both play and film are much the same.

Act I stages the conflict between Chance and the Princess, with the latter, despite her dependence on drugs, her hypochondria, and her disorientation (she is brought to Chance's hometown barely conscious), managing to retain her dignity and control in the face of Chance's attempt to transform her into a stepping-stone for his career. Act I thus thematizes the play's structural problem and foregrounds it as a dramatic question that succeeding acts will have to answer in some fashion. Who is the main character? Chance's more dangerous antagonists, Boss Finley and company, do not make an appearance until act II, although the struggle between the father of the violated young woman and the man who has unwittingly betrayed her is introduced in the brief conversation between Chance and George Scudder, a local who also hopes to make Heavenly his wife. Chance certainly does not lay clear claim to the role of protagonist early in the play. In the unforgettable opening sequence of the film, Brooks makes sure he does so. The director's effective reformulation of the relationship between the Princess and her "boy" is thus an important element in the masculinizing (which is also the melodramatizing) of *Sweet Bird*.

If in *Cat* a key cultural theme is the inseparability of sexual pleasure and procreation, with the family furnishing the only structure within which desire can assume proper regulation, in the stage version of *Sweet Bird*, Chance's sexual power destroys rather than creates life, making it impossible for him to be accommodated as easily as Brick is within family life. The venereal disease with which he infects Heavenly results in her hysterectomy—this loss of the ability to bear children being fittingly matched by the castration Chance undergoes at the hands of her rightfully angered family. The disconnection between desire and procreation is also evident in the extended encounter between the Princess and Chance, which ironically mirrors that between Maggie and Brick in *Cat*. Both plays feature a sexually aggressive woman eager to sleep with a reluctant man. Maggie, however, wants Brick's baby as much as she wants Brick. In contrast, the Princess desires only an impersonal sexual release. And Chance finds himself with a woman he does not want (a just consequence of his hustling), hoping that she will somehow transform him into a man whom the woman he does love could want. The woman's role in *Sweet Bird* is split, an index of the division between Chance's sexual identities, between his desire for fame and his desire for an idealized romantic fulfillment.

Though prompted by PCA rules against venereal disease or castration as thematic elements, Brooks's changes restore the inseparability of desire and procreation, or at least make possible such a restoration once the divisive presence of the Princess has been neutralized. For the film's Chance is neither promiscuous nor a hustler in the ordinary sense, only a "man on the make" willing to exploit his good looks and hoping to gain the favor of the princess by making her an endlessly deferred promise of his company in bed. And so the castration Chance suffers in the play for his misdeeds is easily eliminated, and instead, perhaps more appropriately, he suffers a career-ending blow to his handsome face from Boss Finley's men. The end of his sex appeal will, so it is implied, ease the process of domestication with Heavenly.

The film's Heavenly and Chance demonstrate that their love can lead to a pregnancy, aborted only because of the objections of Boss Finley to their marrying. Most importantly, Heavenly and Chance remain "whole" at film's end and thus capable of beginning family life together now that they have evaded the evil father, melodrama's typical blocking character. The thematic logic of these changes means that a happy ending makes better sense. Brooks's Chance Wayne is no longer what his name suggests, a child of fortune whose luck is running out. Brooks's narrative delivers Chance from the calculating self-absorption that in the play provokes a disastrous sexual vengeance. His Chance finds that foolish posturing and the exploitation of women bring him to a failure that paradoxically offers him his main chance, which is to adopt a more humble masculine style.

In this progress toward an endorsement of traditional moral values (family and love as opposed to careerism), the Princess now occupies the position of object lesson; devoted to a career that must shortly end in heartache, she represents the road not taken. At the film's beginning, Chance paradoxically seems both her superior and servant. The opening sequences show him in obvious charge of their southern swing. What this part of the film demonstrates is that Chance has considerable charisma and personal power, but he has put himself in a position of servitude to the fading star in order to further a career for which, it soon becomes evident, he has no aptitude. Like Heavenly, the Princess facilitates Chance's maturation, providing him, with the example of her own experiences, an alternative to life with Heavenly. It is Heavenly who, after Chance has been disfigured, drives her mutilated lover out of town in yet another fancy convertible, the Princess having earlier left alone in hers. This complex rhyme with the initial sequence makes crystal clear what Chance has lost and gained in the course of the dramatic action.

Though *Sweet Bird* required considerably more alteration to achieve something like the melodramatization of Brooks's *Cat*, it is interesting that the director-screenwriter was once again able to bring off such a transformation while preserving the play's basic elements, including the Princess. As two of the most popular and critically successful of the Williams films, *Cat* and *Sweet Bird* likely served for many as their introduction to the playwright's work. They discovered a playwright who could celebrate the difficult passage to independence and reconciliation, who could limn with affecting depth and insight the crisis of masculinity that so pervaded American culture in the 1950s and early 1960s. They could only glimpse, here and there in the lyricism of the dialogue or the occasional, especially resonant detail, the poet of insufferable despair and loneliness familiar to playgoers of the era.

Sweet Bird's reviews reflect this opposition between the melodramatic impulse toward reaffirming consensus values and the more characteristically Williams concern with the sensational, in which the ironies and pain of the human condition more clearly reveal themselves. Richard Gertner, writing in *Motion Picture Daily*, praises Brooks's success in making something more traditional from Williams's text: "A solid piece of adult entertainment. Brooks has taken all the disparate elements of the Williams play, and with only minor changes in detail, woven them into a smooth-flowing and absorbing story that follows one general plot line—the efforts of the hero, a mixed-up character who feels his youth slipping away, to stem the tide and find himself before it is too late. It also has a clarity and narrative drive in the Brooks version that it lacked on stage."[58] On stage, of course, there is no question of Chance finding himself—he discovers instead that his efforts to make something worthy out of his life have all been in vain, for his future promises no film career and no Heavenly.

Variety, in contrast, emphasizes the story's more sensational and taboo themes, commenting that though the market appeal of this kind of adult material was seemingly on the wane, the film might be saved by its production values. The reviewer finds little in the film that could be called "moral": "One has to pry deep to find any source of edification or human enlightenment in what is essentially a provocative slice of raw melodramatic meat calculated to intoxicate the senses and arouse the emotions."[59] Such a condemnation might be more expected from the Legion of Decency than from an industry insider. It could be that *Sweet Bird*'s box office, not mediocre but less than might have been expected after the standard set by *Cat*, was hurt by a perception that the filmmakers' rhetorical intentions were compromised by a bad-faith Aristotelianism: intoxicating the senses and arousing the emotions while abjuring the offer of any edification. Perhaps Brooks and company should have paid better attention to how Joseph L. Mankiewicz, producer Sam Spiegel, and screenwriter Gore Vidal finessed this same problem just a couple of years before.

Suddenly, Last Summer: More Melodramatic Raw Meat?

Suddenly's press materials demand a careful reading. The poster art centers on what has become perhaps the most notorious Elizabeth Taylor glamour shot: the actress, dressed in a skimpy white bathing suit, kneeling on a beach, her hands at her sides, her face turned toward the camera, which, in this way, captures both her beautiful eyes and her voluptuous figure. A deceptively simple slug line asserts: "Suddenly last summer Cathy knew she was being used for something evil." Are we then to see the obviously seductive pose as the reflex of the "evil use" to which Cathy is being put? It seems so, but what is also clear is that the image, reflecting the pinup art of the war years and after, both constructs and responds to the desire of the heterosexual male viewer. If in *Suddenly*, on screen as well as on stage, Williams treats homosexual themes more openly and extensively than he had ever done before, the poster art only hints at what the film will detail, that the "evil use" in which Cathy is caught up has to do with the predatory homosexuality of her cousin Sebastian, who is the story's controlling (though barely glimpsed) presence, but remains entirely absent from the publicity campaign. The dominating image of an attractive woman also hints at the story's resolution: its decisive rejection of Sebastian's "deviance" and its restoration of sexual normality through the romance that develops between Cathy and the psychiatrist Dr. Cukrowicz, a Sebastian stand-in who prevents Cathy from being destroyed by the same kind of animalistic depravity that claimed the life of her cousin.

The key word in the poster is perhaps "evil," an invocation of traditional morality that is picked up in the copy that, most unusually, appears below the poster itself. This self-styled "statement" is signed by producer Sam Spiegel. He asserts:

What interested me thematically in "Suddenly, Last Summer" was delving and prying into the essence of corruption and depravity and bringing out the moral theme that one cannot abuse other beings without paying for it either with one's life or sanity.

And so what seems sensational in the film is not:

The shock values in this picture are used for their dramatic impact to strengthen the moral intent of the picture. At no point is there a hint or suggestion that corruption could be pleasurable or that cruelty and immorality might be rewarded.

A harsh, thoroughly traditional sort of poetic justice sorts out the fates of all concerned: "the user of others is himself symbolically used"; "his mother, who abetted him all his life, pays with her sanity"; but the girl who "tragically exposes the facts of the story" is "restored to sanity and happiness by that truth." The result, Spiegel boasts, is "a highly moral motion picture . . . an extraordinary moral vision."[60] Even Catholic clergy endorsed this view of *Suddenly*, as we have seen.

To achieve this sort of moral clarity, the screenplay takes advantage of the film medium's capacity to "open out" beyond a limited set. If the play is confined to the Venable house (whose exterior garden Sebastian planted with insectivorous plants in a telling expression of his Nietzschean worldview), the film offers an effective counterpoint in staging important scenes in the state mental hospital where Dr. Cukrowicz is the resident surgeon, specializing in lobotomies. These settings do not simplistically contrast: the hospital as the site of healing and regeneration; the home as the very image of Sebastian's devotion to predation, with his mother, in her attempts to save his image from Catherine's revelations, ready to carry on the son's destructive manipulation of others. It is in the Venable garden that Catherine convinces the psychiatrist that she is telling the truth, therefore saving her own brain from the knife. The narration of the hard facts of life, which is what Sebastian devoted himself to facing, ironically enough, thereby dooms his mother to madness, since she retreats into the past and her own distorted version of her son.

And it is in the hospital, interestingly enough, where Sebastian's view of life receives a chilling confirmation, in a pair of similar scenes added by Vidal and Mankiewicz. Both of these sequences begin with Catherine fleeing Dr. Cukrowicz and the hospital staff. In both, Catherine finds herself alone, an "obviously" sane woman among hopeless mental cases, first on the walkway above the men's dayroom, and later on the walkway above the women's dayroom. This second scene is important because it images what Catherine's miserable fate will be if she has to suffer the lobotomy, which will probably necessitate her confinement for life. But it is the first "escape" that significantly enriches the film's moral themes.

She is attacked by the aroused, incoherent inmates in an ironic restaging of the assault that led to her cousin's death. Catherine's successful (though inadvertent) display recalls Sebastian's deliberate use of her glamour to lure men to his side. This wordless, bestial assault also echoes Violet's frightening tale of the baby turtles she and Sebastian saw devoured by savage birds in the Encantadas. An innocent who believes in human virtue and not in Sebastian's theory of a universe whose operative principle is cruelty, Catherine evades her attackers with the help of her psychiatrist. Condemned in a sense by his own amorality, Sebastian is devoured by those who assault him. The hospital sequence thus interestingly rhymes with the film's climactic reenactment of Sebastian's murder.

Catherine Holly (Elizabeth Taylor) and Dr. Cukrowicz (Montgomery Clift) in a garden scene from Suddenly, Last Summer. *Photo courtesy of The Historic New Orleans Collection.*

Catherine's escape to the comforting arms of Dr. Cukrowicz presages her eventual flight to sanity and safety, when, aided by the doctor's careful administration of sodium pentothal, she is able to recall completely the horror of Sebastian's death and thus release herself from the guilt she wrongly feels.

This last sequence is the dramatic center of the film and is handled brilliantly by Mankiewicz, who again uses images, this time to underscore the power of Catherine's involuntary narrative. Onstage, the stories both women tell about their experiences with Sebastian remain just that: narratives that illuminate the present concerns of their narrators as much as they evoke a series of past and unrecoverable moments. Sebastian never appears on stage because the dramatic action remains completely in the present. In film, such reminiscences are usually handled more dramatically: through flashback, with the teller's narration gradually transformed into an objective, enacted representation of the past. The stage method inevitably emphasizes the teller more than the tale, while the cinematic flashback, even when accompanied by sporadic voice-over or brief cuts back to the narrator (another hackneyed Hollywood convention), literally makes the teller largely invisible. Mankiewicz and Vidal correctly thought that Violet's unrelieved narration of the past was all the film could bear, since it was already essentially a talkathon, in which nearly all of Williams's dialogue was retained in the screenplay.

Catherine's drug-authenticated recollections are not only true (for it is mother's version of Sebastian that proves only partially accurate and ultimately delusional); her tale is also dramatically indispensable, for it establishes Catherine's sanity by grounding her fears in true horror. As Mankiewicz recognized, this part of the film could not be all talk. To actualize Catherine's monologue, Vidal and Mankiewicz designed a unique combination of stage and film methods, utilizing strikingly composed and photographed double images. Catherine tells her story from beginning to end, but the images and sounds of her telling are combined in the same frame with silent, fragmentary enactments of the story she relates. In this long sequence, these images intercut effectively with reaction shots of the psychiatrist and Mrs. Venable, thus reminding the spectator that Catherine's story is both exculpatory and condemnatory. Violet must listen to a horror about Sebastian that she cannot deny without retreating into madness, for she is brought to recognize that her son's death recapitulates the attack of the savage birds on the baby turtles in the Encantadas. Interestingly, Mankiewicz shoots the final reaction shots of Violet without the glamorizing techniques employed earlier, so she literally grows older before our very eyes.

To some degree, the film's success with audiences must be traced to its carefully orchestrated publicity campaign, its most important element being the famous glamour shot of Elizabeth Taylor as Catherine (wearing the almost transparent suit that, the film viewer learns, was purchased for her to wear against her will). Though making Catherine the erotic center of the film, Mankiewicz does not deny the story its most compelling and sensational element, which is the Orphic Sebastian. The pairing of Taylor and Clift decisively claims the film for heterosexuality, in a movement that makes the most of the actor's sexually ambiguous persona. As Violet earlier remarks, "Dr. Sugar" reminds her of Sebastian, and so in a sense the relationship that develops between Catherine and the psychiatrist images the sexual conversion of the bitter, unhappy poet manqué. The play ends ambiguously, with the psychiatrist perhaps accepting that Catherine is telling the truth and saving herself from misguided mutilation. But in the manner of the era's family melodrama, the film decisively separates virtue from vice, eliminating the possibility that Sebastian's vision of the world might triumph—but with great irony, of course. For were Catherine to be surgically "corrected" for speaking the truth, the result would be that the inauthentic version of Sebastian's life would prevail; he would be remembered not as he was, but as his mother wished him to be. And so Sebastian's desire to have others see the inherent cruelty of existence would be denied. Yet in a sense, it would also be confirmed, since Violet would extend Sebastian's manipulation of Catherine, leading her to share in his final, horrible mutilation.

If Williams's art as a whole, as Michael Paller has suggested, is structured on opposing aims of revelation and concealment, then the stage version of *Suddenly* is in some sense an exemplary text: a duel between characters, one of whom would tell only the worst and the other who would make sure that the worst is not told about the (dis)honored dead. Like Dr. Cukrowicz, however, the playwright refuses in the end to reveal all, even after all is told. Catherine makes the truth known, but will the truth prevail? The filmmakers eschew such ambiguity. Mankiewicz and Vidal, under Spiegel's watchful eye, turn *Suddenly* into a clear-visioned morality play, its finale both an acknowledgment of horrifying evil in the world and a demonstration that this evil need not destroy the innocent.

Coda: *Period of Adjustment*—A "Harmless Trifle"?

Interestingly, Williams's own work seems to have been influenced by the Hollywood melodramatization of *Cat*, *Sweet Bird*, and *Suddenly*. At least that is one way of explaining why he surprisingly undertook the composition of a mainstream family melodrama—one that would require no writer-director with the talents of Richard Brooks or Joseph L. Mankiewicz to transform it into an acceptable and profitable commercial film. *Period of Adjustment*, written during the late fifties is, so the playwright maintains in order to distinguish it from his earlier plays, a "serious comedy." Williams confessed: "It's an unambitious work. I only wanted to tell the truth about a little occurrence in life, without blowing it up beyond its natural limits."[61] His hope was, he averred, to "cast a kinder shadow . . . on the quieter aspects of existence."[62]

In this he succeeded, although as Gene Phillips comments, it is true that the play deals with a kind of "grotesque comedy which . . . makes one a bit uncomfortable about laughing at other people's pain."[63] *Period*'s fundamental perception about human nature seems to be that men and women prove unsuited for monogamy or even living together peacefully—at any age. But this theme is explored more conventionally than it is in *Streetcar*, *Cat*, *Sweet Bird*, or *Suddenly*. Expressing mock relief when the play came out, Williams's brother, Dakin, observed that "not a single person was raped, castrated, lynched, committed or even eaten."[64] Despite the inevitable perception that he had abandoned his customary themes, Williams was convinced (at least early on) that it would be his most popular play.

And indeed *Period* enjoyed a modicum of Broadway success, running for 132 performances under the direction of George Roy Hill. Critical notices, however, were generally unenthusiastic, and Williams would eventually consider this major foray into mainstream comedy a failure. He would never again attempt something similar.[65] But the playwright and director Hill thought that this domestic comedy would prove more popular with filmgoers, and they were right. Reviewers seemed pleased with Williams's determination to strike out in a new direction. Brendan Gill termed *Period* "a cheerful, harmless trifle,"[66] *Time* called it "Wholesome Williams,"[67] and *Saturday Review* and *Newsweek* judged the film one of the year's best.

In *Period*, Williams treats familiar themes in anatomizing the recalibrating process that tests all newlyweds. George (Jim Hutton) suffers from what is apparently a psychological form of impotence, while Isabel

(Jane Fonda) is paralyzed by sexual inhibitions. On the night of their wedding, George either bungles his attempt to consummate the marriage or Isabel proves frigid, depending on whose story one believes. The examination of this impasse unfolds at the home of George's friend Ralph (Anthony Franciosa), whose five-year marriage to Dorothea (Lois Nettleton) is likewise on the rocks. While the couples' marital troubles remain at the film's center, George's relationship with old army buddy Ralph reveals an intimacy completely missing from the men's marriages, at least until the conclusion of the film.

Derided as "war heroes" by Dorothy's father, the pair remain in a state of arrested development, and their bonhomie and jocular horseplay mask a darker issue—George's ambiguous sexuality. Their friendship lacks the sexual tension found in *Cat* between Brick and his dead friend Skipper; instead of exploring lingering questions about a homosexual past, the film centers on Ralph's steadfast dismissal of George's tales about his manly sexual exploits. George boasts of his amorous conquests with Korean prostitutes, referring to himself as "an Eveready battery." Ralph tries to steer George away from this self-delusion: "When will you stop playing Superman, like the way you act with your wife—maybe that's what's wrong."

Eager to escape his new responsibilities, George hatches an adolescent plan that he thinks should guarantee his friend's continuing company: he and Ralph will move to Texas, there to raise longhorn cattle on a ranch they will purchase. George is essentially a comic version of *Cat*'s Brick, an "irresponsible male blurred into the shadowy figure of the homosexual," as Barbara Ehrenreich maintains in a discussion of the era's cultural politics. George's grotesque, misogynist parody of the American Dream ("We'll live like men! With dignity!" or so the frightened young husband enthuses) never, of course, materializes. Like Brick, George has to settle for a more conventional life, and he retires at film's end to bed in order to pay his bride the marriage debt. No more thoughts of lounging under the stars with Ralph.

By the time George shows up at his house, Ralph's rocky marriage has collapsed. Ralph has quit his job, abrogating his responsibilities as breadwinner. The angry couple battles over money, her father's domineering role in their lives, and how best to raise their young son, who, according to Ralph, is turning into a "sissy." The film thus examines gender adjustment issues in small children as well as adults. Their effeminate little boy, who carries a doll and plays the piano, clearly disgusts the "war

In this scene from Period of Adjustment, *Ralph Bates (Tony Franciosa) and his wife, Dorothea (Lois Nettleton), effect a rapprochement as George Haverstick (Jim Hutton) and his spouse, Isabel (Jane Fonda), look on. Photo courtesy of The Historic New Orleans Collection.*

hero" father, who in turn builds his son a model-rocket launcher and tells his wife that the boy "needs to get what he is firmly fixed in his mind," which is precisely what Ralph tries to tell George. As the couple argues about how best to orient their sexually confused child, Ralph throws his doll into the fireplace, and Dorothea leaves him. Their separation allows Ralph to reflect on the failed union. He muses about how he married Dorothea for the money, even though he found her physically repellent. Her buckteeth, he complains, felt like "kissing a rock pile." Both men, familiar with each other's misery, admit that that they each "married a stranger." In addition, Ralph alludes to his own problems in the bedroom, stating that Dorothea has been frigid, insisting on twin beds.

The film takes a thoroughly masculinized view of domestic crisis: while George and Ralph explore their discontent and sense of unfulfillment, the wives are either absent or find themselves marginalized. George belittles Ralph's conformity by mocking his suburban house, obsession with mindless TV, and self-medicating beer drinking. Complementing this male descent into unhappiness, Ralph's house continues to sink and settle—metaphorically mocking his reluctant, continuing adjustment toward heteronormality. But these real and apparent schisms yield to paired tableaux of blissful rapprochement as at film's end Dottie and Ralph retire behind the door to renew their conjugal vows, while George and Isabelle inch toward consummating their honeymoon on the sleeper sofa.

Williams's "serious comedy" thus concludes with the bed as the site of marital reconciliation. The dark issues raised earlier, including male impotence, homosociality, and female frigidity, are seemingly not only assuaged but also solved by sex. But this finale, like the closing movement of Brooks's *Cat*, remains unconvincing, as Williams and Hill apparently expect the careful viewer to note. There is, in fact, so the film argues, no transitory "period" of adjustment, no time of discord that passes into settled mutual accommodation, for even Dorothea's aging, long-married parents find themselves beset by discontent and wounded feelings as they bicker and viciously denounce each other throughout their brief scenes in the film. *Period* is hardly the "harmless trifle" it seemed to some at the time.

CHAPTER SEVEN

The Williams Films and the Southern Renaissance on Screen

No Longer the Sahara of the Bozart

With its gloomy analysis of the contemporary South, said to be blighted by a resurgent Ku Klux Klan, self-destructive devotion to one-crop agriculture, a pervasive failure to provide humane prisons, and intractable racial injustice, historian Frank L. Tannenbaum's *The Darker Phases of the South* (1924) adduced strong evidence to support the view that the region found itself in need of desperate solutions, both economic and cultural. In fact, the underlying problem with the South, Tannenbaum suggested, could not have been more serious: it was its people. And so he recommended mandating "forced immigration as a tonic to its spiritual and social well-being." New blood would ameliorate an ideological predisposition that was hurting the region's chances for economic recovery and cultural renaissance. What held the region back was that "there is a kind of pride of race in the South that is well-nigh morbid."[1]

Tannenbaum's view reflected that of many intellectuals both north and south of the Mason-Dixon line; his study, inspired by professor Wendell T. Bush of Columbia University, was made possible by cooperation from fellow academics in Georgia and the Carolinas. Many agreed with its northernizing thesis (first advanced by others during Reconstruction) that an influx of immigrants might reinvigorate a decaying semifeudal society that seemed incapable of self-help. Otherwise, the South seemed beyond redemption. For many in America in the early decades of the twentieth century, the persistent backwardness of southern culture, particularly its anti-Enlightenment rejection of modern science, was confirmed by the so-called Scopes "Monkey Trial," which was held in Dayton, Tennessee, in 1925, the year after Tannenbaum's book appeared. In the wake of that trial, one of the signal national events of the era, the famously dim assessment of the region's intellectual and artistic failings published a few years before by America's most noted public intellectual, H. L. Mencken, seemed increasingly relevant and difficult to dispute.

In his oft-reprinted, much discussed, and endlessly controversial essay, "The Sahara of the Bozart" (which first appeared in 1917), Mencken lamented that culturally the South was "so vast a vacuity" as to be "almost as sterile, artistically, intellectually, culturally, as the Sahara Desert." Formerly, with its planter aristocracy supporting the study of humane letters and the pursuit of a refined *moyen de vivre*, the South had been far superior to the way of life of "New England shopkeepers and theologians," who were at best "tawdry and tacky fellows, oafish in manner and devoid of imagination." But the Civil War had "stamped out every last bearer of the torch, and left only a mob of peasants on the field." When he republished the essay in 1949, Mencken recalled how its initial appearance had prompted a "ferocious reaction in the South," where it was violently denounced by the older generation. But what soon followed, he observed, was a "favorable response from the more civilized youngsters." The result, for which Mencken gave himself no little credit, was "that revival of Southern letters which followed in the middle 1920s."[2] This cultural explosion gave the lie to what Tannenbaum and Mencken, among others, had argued. The South turned out to be no cultural Sahara after all, and, amazingly enough, the "beaux arts" could be seen flourishing better there than in any other region of the country.

In roughly three decades (c. 1925–1955), the Southern Renaissance (or Renascence) witnessed an unprecedented outpouring of creative writing from and about the region, not only putting the South squarely back on the American cultural map, but also arguably inaugurating nothing less than a southernization of the national culture.[3] This impressive body of work ranges from novels (penned by William Faulkner and Robert Penn Warren, among others), to poetry (the work of the Nashville Fugitives in particular), to drama (the successful Broadway productions of Tennessee Williams and Lillian Hellman), to history (such as C. Vann Woodward's revisionist accounts of the postbellum era) and what we would now term cultural studies (primarily W. J. Cash's influential meditation on the southern "mind").

For its most popular chronicler, Richard H. King, the Southern

Renaissance was a "cultural awakening" whose leading figures sought a "greater understanding of the relationship between past and present." This relationship was for them "fraught with ambivalence and ambiguity." In the fiction produced by such masters as William Faulkner, Ellen Glasgow, James Agee, and Thomas Wolfe, the past took intellectual and representational shape metonymically, with the family embodying both traditional and emergent values: "The 'object' of their historical consciousness was a tradition whose essential figures were the father and the grandfather and whose essential structure was the literal and symbolic family. In sum, the Renaissance writers sought to come to terms with what I call the 'Southern family romance.'"[4] Such thematic concerns certainly seem, on their face, an understandable retreat from the public to the private sphere in the face of an absence of values and a "usable past" of tradition.

But this is deceptive. As King asserts, the "Southern family romance" embraces the region's political essence, for "there was a strong strain in Southern thought which saw society as the family writ large." In this imagined family could be found the region's structure of feeling, and in these compelling representations of family could be glimpsed "the values, attitudes, and beliefs that white Southerners expressed in their attitudes toward the region itself." Or to put this another way, the writers of the Southern Renaissance were committed to the notion that "the actual family was destiny, and the region was conceived of as a vast metaphorical family, hierarchically organized and organically linked by (pseudo-) ties of blood."[5]

This was by no means a radically innovative mode of cultural belief. At the turn of the century, bestselling novelist Thomas A. Dixon had used family as a framework for analyzing the supposed evils of Reconstruction, his works like *The Clansman* (1905) furnishing filmmaker D. W. Griffith with the white-supremacist politics, cast in riveting melodrama, that take center stage in his *The Birth of a Nation* (1915). More widely seen than any previous film, and applauded by audiences in every section of the country, *Birth* was arguably the era's most potent, and most widely approved, representation of southern culture. These "family problems" are presented by the director, following the novelist's lead, as eminently soluble. What the region needed was the reassertion of traditional values, especially separation of the races; this was shown when a truly intersectional white family came into existence in response to this moral reawakening. Such a straightforward return to the past would produce a "New South." The writers of the Southern Renaissance saw matters differently. Unlike Dixon and Griffith, these writers found themselves caught between honoring regional traditions and accepting, in the spirit of Tannenbaum and Mencken, that this treasured inheritance also posed problems—economic, cultural, and racial—that the present could ill afford to ignore.

Historian James C. Cobb provides a persuasive sociological explanation for why this generation of intellectuals, who were all young men in the 1920s, felt the need to explore the complex senses in which the "actual family" of their region constituted its "destiny." Educated outside the South, their horizons expanded by international travel, their understanding of the arts influenced deeply by modernisms both aesthetic and economic, the writers of the Southern Renaissance recognized the pointlessness of clinging to a discredited or irrelevant past (the Lost Cause, the plantation myth). Yet they still felt "ambivalent about sweeping, externally induced social and economic changes that may destroy some of the best of their society's traditions along with the worst." The result was that these writers developed something of a "love-hate" relationship with their native culture.[6] The novelists and dramatists of the Southern Renaissance clung to the past but were convinced as well that the present—which had undeniably come of that past—was culturally, morally, and economically bankrupt.

Such, at least, is the quality of much of this writing: the fascinating degradation of Caldwell's grotesques, portrayed with furious yet sympathetic indignation (heightened by the novelist's Marxist scorn for the moribund agricultural economy); the evident delight Jack Cash takes in demolishing the moonlight-and-magnolias myth of the antebellum era, exposing what he terms the region's unrepentant "savage ideal" (including the southerner's purported propensity to "break forth in queer, feverish fits of defiance and abandon");[7] C. Vann Woodward's demonstration that segregation disposed of no honored cultural pedigree and was thus not a "folkway" central to the region's conception of itself;[8] and, last but certainly not least, the poignant, demythologizing unpleasantness of Tennessee Williams's heroines, from Amanda to Blanche to Maggie the Cat and Violet Venable, all constitutionally indisposed or unable to reconcile the competing claims of gentility and desire, thus casting a harsher light on those received notions of white, sexually virtuous southern womanhood so unambiguously celebrated by Dixon and others.[9]

A similarly ambivalent intensity characterizes the desperation with which some of Williams's most memorable male protagonists, like Brick and Chance, trapped in a social landscape they find hostile to their desires and talents, pursue something like self-destruction, a condition they prefer to a life lived in defiance of their felt need for family. Even Tom, in *Menagerie*, ostensibly safe in self-imposed exile, finds that memory, fueled by guilt and loneliness, relentlessly draws him back into the hopelessly troubled familial past. Perhaps the "love-hate" mind-set that is typical of the Southern Renaissance writer helps explain how, as critic Michael Paller argues, Williams's work seems to be organized "around the poles of revealing and concealing," as mentioned earlier. Illuminated by the playwright's literary context, this thematic complex asks to be read as powered by a double, conflicted sense of regional shame and pride—overdetermined, of course, as Paller persuasively demonstrates, by Williams's own sexual struggle, his desire to proclaim and yet disavow his homosexual inclinations.[10]

Southern Gothic: Images of Decadence

Where, we might ask, does Hollywood figure in the Southern Renaissance, which is arguably the most important American cultural development of the twentieth century? Like most commentators, King and Cobb surprisingly ignore, or at least minimize, the way in which this fiction finds its way to the silver screen and thus even greater cultural prominence. And yet the Hollywood presentation of Southern Renaissance works and themes is arguably crucial to its movement as a national and international force. Indeed, it would require a special explanation of some kind if a popular and critically acclaimed tradition of fiction and drama did not become grist, at least in part, for Hollywood's production mills, which are always insatiably hungry for presold properties, especially those that mine a broad, well-established vein of middlebrow taste. And it certainly has not escaped the notice of film historians that nineteenth-century plantation culture and the nostalgically remembered Lost Cause, dominant in filmic representations of the South through the end of the 1930s (as bear witness not just *The Birth of a Nation*, but also *Gone with the Wind* [1939], which are doubtless the American cinema's most successful and influential productions ever), gave way in the postwar period to a very different kind of film.

Film historian Edward D. C. Campbell, Jr., offers a bitter comment on this radical change: "The majority of movies presented a postwar South populated by pitifully poor farmers, unrepentent [*sic*] bigots, sadistic red-necks, sex objects, and greedy ambitious members of a corrupt upper class . . . most of the releases were hard-hitting dramas."[11] This trend prompts him to pose the obvious question: "How could the pleasant nostalgia found in even films of postwar settings such as *The Little Colonel* or *In Old Kentucky* be so shattered in *The Intruder*?"[12] Indeed, it is hard to imagine how *The Intruder*, Roger Corman's unsettling film about southern racism, based on the novel by Charles Beaumont and released in the middle of the turbulent civil rights era (1962), could have found either a producer or audience in immediate prewar years. For solid commercial reasons, the industry then seemed to prefer sentimental treatments of Old South culture, such as Lionel Barrymore, replete with a white linen suit and a stagy drawl, posing as a postbellum relic of the planter class in *The Little Colonel*; and Will Rogers playing his "aw shucks" common man with a southern twist in *In Old Kentucky* (both 1935). For Campbell, what had changed was an American society facing the social dislocations caused by global war. A generation of Hollywood's customers had come to "know" a different South, based on what they had gleaned from the headlines and newsreels of the day. By 1950 (and even before), the older, nostalgic view of the region seemed too far removed from a rapidly changing social reality whose contours, because of the media attention paid to the struggle for racial equality, were becoming continually more familiar to Americans everywhere.

Yet the turn toward a different program of representation was more than a "mirroring" of the cultural politics of a rapidly changing era. Campbell makes no reference to the Southern Renaissance, though it is this cultural movement, beginning at least a decade before World War II, that provides much of the intellectual and creative stimulus, not to mention a plethora of source texts to be adapted, for a shockingly new type of film.[13] In any event, Campbell suggests that this emerging trend was hardly to be welcomed: "The films' symbolic Southerners [are]—destitute, depraved, and often ensnared in a once proud but now bankrupt tradition . . . but too often these movies concentrated on the sensational effect . . . such films, though drastically altering the public perception of the South, could do little in developing a better understanding of the region and its problems."[14] And the dominant literary voice behind this celluloid trend was Tennessee Williams, whose influence on the course it took in Hollywood extended considerably beyond the adaptations themselves.

Hollywood, pace Campbell, has never taken on, or been assigned, the considerable social responsibility of promoting the "better understanding" of any region, including the South. Living in an age dominated by the competing agendas of identity politics, we can perhaps understand the historian's frustration. There were some exceptions to the new trend he identified, of course, such as Disney's successful Joel Chandler Harris adaptation, *Song of the South* (1946), which harkened back to an earlier era, as well as mildly deconstructive versions of the plantation myth, especially *Raintree County* and *Band of Angels* (both 1957). These last two films explore, in somewhat provocative (but largely uncommercial) fashion, sexual relations between black and whites and the resultant racial mixing (or a culturally paranoid fear of same). Except for a few films such as these, *Gone with the Wind* would prove an exception to industry wisdom. For it was a spectacularly successful production that neither spawned a series of imitations nor (re)founded a genre, marking instead the imminent end of a representational era, soon as "gone" as its nineteenth-century subject matter.[15] Here was nostalgia of the second degree—a hopeless yearning after an era in which an inspired yearning for the past was still possible.

An Insufficiency of Brain, an Excess of Bottom

As Campbell recognizes, the focus of postwar movies about the South had shifted decisively to naturalist exposés of the "destitute" and "depraved" lower orders, the post-Reconstruction inheritors of a tradition that was now "bankrupt." For proud southerners such as he, such a radical shift in the representations of the region must have seemed profoundly disturbing. And yet this transformation reflected not only negative northern stereotypes about southern culture that had been long held (as witness Mencken's scornful broadsides), but also a more cynical version of the "love-hate" approach of some (an important point—not all or even most) Southern Renaissance writers toward their region.[16] This tradition, eventually called (stigmatized as?) "gothic," reflected the "savage ideal" Cash had discovered in southern culture, and it came to be dominated by such writers as Erskine Caldwell, Carson McCullers, Flannery O'Connor, and, especially, Tennessee Williams.

Campbell (who was curator of the Museum of the Confederacy when he wrote this book) indicts the general failure of postwar Hollywood productions to provide positive images of the region. His disappointment points toward an important truth about the politics of the Southern Renaissance, which since the 1960s has often been promoted by academics for both its purported uplifting message about the region as well as its conspicuous display of the intellectual and artistic talents of its people. Gothic or "savage ideal" fiction, however, did not prove particularly useful for this kind of regional self-promotion, for it seemed instead to confirm the damning judgment implicit in Yankee stereotypes about the South.

We should not be surprised, then, that Richard H. King's thick tome on the Southern Renaissance makes room for only one brief, and very negative, comment about Williams, who is imagined as belonging to a whining community of self-exiled voices living up north and prompted by their Yankee hosts to recycle disagreeable stereotypes: "Some Southern writers who went north in the 1940s and 1950s—McCullers, Truman Capote, and Tennessee Williams in particular—seemed bent on perpetuating the image of decadence that careless readers of Faulkner and Erskine Caldwell in the 1930s had taken to be typical of things south of the Mason-Dixon line."[17] King, who was raised in Tennessee and educated at the University of North Carolina at Chapel Hill, theorizes that by living in some northern "metropolis," these writers became aware that the "North would not let Southerners forget who they were, since the metropolis needs the province explained to it, piquing curiosity here and being assured there that the province is backward, if charmingly so."[18] Williams's writing about the South, presumably, like that of McCullers and Capote, could then be dismissed from consideration as an authentic part of the Southern Renaissance because he was simply telling Yankees racy tales about a region they were already convinced was a cultural backwater, inhabited by genetically challenged religious fanatics and their sexually depraved relations.

In his treatment of Williams's place in the Southern Renaissance, John M. Bradbury follows the line traced by King, though he does think the writer's considerable oeuvre worthy of more extended comment. The creative arc of the playwright's career took him, in Bradbury's view, from "compassion and poetry" to a "harshly dramatic exposure of twisted and perverted lives." In this artistic development, Bradbury finds manifest both Williams's "deeply ingrained moral sense" and poetic gifts. Yet he concludes that Williams's "concern with misplaced, frustrated, and distorted love cannot be exorcised." Why, we might ask in any event, would an artistic concern with such forms of love need to be exorcised? Presumably because this thematic does not reflect well on a South trying to escape being stigmatized as intellectually stunted and pathological. In any case, this failure to present his native land in a better light apparently accounts for Bradbury's view that Williams's "promise still awaits fulfillment." Such a patronizing judgment about a man whom many considered the nation's greatest living playwright seems mean-spirited and strikingly perverse, for Bradbury's book was published in 1963, close to the height of Williams's popularity.[19]

Even literary historians more sympathetic to the gothic tradition mined by Caldwell, Williams, McCullers, and others tend toward a dim view of such representations of the South. Sylvia Jenkins Cook, for example, observes of Faulkner and Caldwell that while these two were often "bracketed together as primitivists, decadents, or naturalists," it was Faulkner who "used the same material in a conservative and finally quite optimistic vein." Conservativeness and optimism, it seems, meant not raising uncomfortable questions about the social and economic changes of the post-Reconstruction era. It meant, in effect, not revoicing the criticisms of Tannenbaum, Mencken, and Cash: "Faulkner established . . . a sense of community with traditions of independence and personal generosity worthy of perpetuation, while Caldwell used the same material in recording the breakdown of rural community and family life and the enforced exodus of country people to the cotton mills."[20] Jenkins Cook opines that Caldwell failed to be taken seriously because "prurient shock" was the reaction his work provoked, along with "revulsion and shame." Faulkner, in contrast, is judged to have celebrated "the poor white paradox," since his "poor whites are never divorced from the worldly conditions of their existence . . . but these conditions are not . . . the substance nor even the most influential shaper of their lives."[21] In Faulkner's fictional version of the South, therefore, heroic transcendence of social conditions is always possible, Jenkins Cook observes, citing as an example "the individual efforts of people like Ruby [in *Sanctuary*] to survive with their own kind of integrity."[22]

If King, Bradbury, and most in the literary establishment prefer Faulkner and Agee to Caldwell and Williams, at least of those classed as "southern writers," their judgment has been confirmed by a broad vein of middlebrow taste as it has developed in the last fifty years. The past half century has witnessed in particular an amazing upsurge in the popularity of Faulkner's fiction and the imaginary Mississippi created therein, transforming the writer's hometown of Oxford, Mississippi, into one of the nation's very few literary tourist attractions. This preference for what we might call "positive image" writing can also be glimpsed in middlebrow tastes for southern fiction that engages with the issue of racism. Eager for reassurance about the essential virtue of southern society, perhaps, American readers have overwhelmingly preferred the status quo politics of Harper Lee's *To Kill a Mockingbird* (1961), in which the region's racial injustice is projected onto a family of redneck trash right out of *Tobacco Road*, to the more threatening, but consensual, miscegenation and the resultant horrific, because socially sanctioned, lynching dramatized in Lillian Smith's *Strange Fruit* (1944). Unlike *Mockingbird*, which celebrates the inherent moral sensibility of the region's patrician class, *Strange Fruit* issues a strident call for radical social and political change, limning what Tannenbaum identifies as one of the "darker phases" of the South.

For those of highbrow sensibilities, Caldwell and Williams, like McCullers, Capote, and O'Connor, often proved too vulgar and direct in their presentation of sexual unconventionality, too pessimistic about the region's decaying culture and seemingly intractable economic problems, too given to the black humor that Faulkner deploys more sparingly and dialogically, too interested in exploring darker and more difficult religious questions, and too unwilling to abandon a muckraking naturalism for a modernism that glorified a desperately perverse mundanity, discovering in the process uplifting truths about *la condition humaine*.

Caldwell, Williams, and the other southern-gothic writers could, of course, be accused of one-dimensionality as well, even if they were simply following a cultural trend begun by Jack Cash, whose *Mind of the South* had effected, according to historian David Joseph Singal, "a complete reversal of the region's history once offered by New South writers [of the late nineteenth and early twentieth centuries]." Like King and Bradbury, Singal finds little to admire in this emerging tradition: "From Erskine Caldwell to Tennessee Williams . . . southern authors carried the critical spirit to its logical extreme, until Americans living outside the region formed a picture of southern society as one immense *Tobacco Road*."[23] James C. Cobb offers a mild correction to this view, suggesting that the negative stereotype of the poor white had attained cultural prominence long before Cash wrote his book and Tennessee Williams dramatized it for the Broadway stage and the international screen. And that stereotype, as he points out, was always more sexual than social. In Cobb's memorable phrase, southern culture celebrated "an insufficiency of brain and an excess of bottom."[24]

An Exoticised South

Whatever its origins, here certainly was a theme with a strong appeal for both literary primitivists like Williams and also for the general public, whose tastes the Hollywood film industry was determined to satisfy. If the world of polite literary fiction, concerned about the South's image in the popular mind, bestowed respectability only on the version of the region produced by its particular lions, the more demotic institutions of American commercial filmmaking preferred, in Allison Graham's formulation, "an exoticised South of finely tuned eccentricities," a fictional realm for whose resurgence in the 1950s, she concludes, "Tennessee Williams was largely responsible."[25] And though the effect on American culture of his immensely successful Broadway productions of the period should not be ignored, it was undoubtedly the Williams films that were largely responsible for popularizing this version of southern culture.

Faulkner, James Agee, Thomas Wolfe, and Robert Penn Warren— the leading lights among the fiction writers of the Southern Renaissance who did not pursue, at least consistently, the gothic style—were for the most part indifferently or haphazardly adapted by Hollywood.[26] It seems that the film industry, like popular culture more generally, had come to prefer sensationalism to gentility. The savage ideal of the post-Reconstruction South, anatomized in Cash's *The Mind of the South*, first took fictional shape almost a decade earlier in the works of Erskine Caldwell, especially *Tobacco Road* (1932) and Faulkner's admitted "potboiler" *Sanctuary*, published the year before. As is well known, writing *Sanctuary* had been a conscious attempt on the novelist's part to exploit what he saw as an emerging popular trend.

Faulkner was right about what people wanted to read about the South, of course. But largely because of his commitment as a modernist to stylistic and narrative experimentation, not to mention what we might now term his embrace of positive-image identity politics, Faulkner remained uninterested in exploiting this kind of commercial success. He would continue to envy the substantial royalties earned by the likes of Caldwell and James M. Cain (the purveyor of what we might call urban savage-ideal fiction set in a transient California culture, more anomic than Caldwell's rural Georgia or Faulkner's Mississippi). But he set himself thereafter a quite different writerly task. Caldwell would persist, of course, down the literary road he had set out upon, even if by the early postwar epoch his popularity had begun a precipitous decline, along with his gifts as a writer. With a few exceptions, the fiction of Carson McCullers, Truman

Capote, and Flannery O'Connor, for various reasons, proved generally unattractive to Hollywood.[27]

In the postwar era, Williams, whose popularity with the general public had been well established, became the dominant figure in this transition. It might seem that, as Jack Temple Kirby writes, "by the late fifties the typical southern film was a Hollywood version of stories or plays by Faulkner, Caldwell, or Tennessee Williams."[28] In fact, however, the popularity of these savage-ideal films was due largely to the amazingly successful experience Hollywood had with adapting just the various Williams properties. Perhaps the most notable and successful of Caldwell's novels, *God's Little Acre* (1933), was finally brought to the screen in 1958, but it was undoubtedly because the road had been paved two years earlier by Tennessee Williams (and Elia Kazan). *Baby Doll* had demonstrated the acceptability of a Caldwellian treatment of poor-white-trash sexual antics and pathetic scheming, with an emphasis on high-tension drama in which a sudden outbreak of terrifying violence always seems possible.

Though Caldwell, as we have suggested in Chapter 5, proved an important source for the complicated confection of *Baby Doll*, Williams and Kazan returned the compliment by inadvertently showing the film industry that a Hollywood version of *God's Little Acre* (in the mid-1950s, the bestselling American novel of all time, with more than 7 million copies in print) might at last be a commercial possibility. That the Caldwell novel bore a striking resemblance to *Baby Doll* certainly did not hurt the project's chances with the industry. And it is hard to imagine *God's Little Acre* achieving the swift and easy passage it did through PCA and legion review had not *Baby Doll* first to some degree blunted the ardor of social conservatives who were advocating "decency in motion pictures."[29]

In the case of Faulkner, *Sanctuary* had been adapted for the pre–PCA screen as *The Story of Temple Drake* (1933), and it became one of that brief era's taboo-breaking dramatizations of lust, while his postwar novel *Intruder in the Dust*, a somewhat confused attempt to lobby for a regional, gradualist solution to the South's radical problem, proved attractive to Hollywood, where it was adapted by Clarence Brown in 1949 as part of what proved to be a brief series of "liberal" films dealing with race.[30] Faulkner's minor novel *Pylon* was brought to the screen in 1957 by Douglas Sirk as *The Tarnished Angels*; Hollywood was interested in the property because it offered a powerful romantic triangle that could serve as the framework for a remake of Sirk's *Written on the Wind*, which had been a smash success two years before. *Angels* recycled the dynamic casting of Rock Hudson, Robert Stack, and Dorothy Malone from *Wind*, but to no avail; *Angels* became one of the least profitable films that Sirk, otherwise a studio darling, directed in the decade. And this failure certainly did not help Faulkner's stock in Hollywood.

In any event, the bulk of Faulkner's oeuvre, especially novels such as *Light in August* (1932) and *Absalom! Absalom!* (1936), upon which his ever-growing literary reputation had come to rest, proved of no interest to Hollywood, despite his receiving the Nobel Prize in 1949 and becoming by common consent the nation's most significant social chronicler. If a desire to adapt Faulkner for the screen revived the year after *Tarnished Angels* had hit the nation's screens with a resounding thud, it had little to do with the film industry's estimate of the novelist's bankability. It had more to do, or so we will argue, with the phenomenal success Williams had achieved on Broadway with dramas about the contemporary South and the obvious commerciality of the first screen versions (especially *Streetcar*, *Tattoo*, and *Baby Doll*), which had demonstrated the appeal of the savage-ideal version of the region.

If a Faulkner property could be transformed into an effective vehicle for the presentation of the themes and character types Williams had popularized, then so much the better. Such a film would be doubly presold, drawing in effect on the talents of two authors, both of whom had shown a deep and abiding interest in what King identifies as the "Southern family romance." This seems to have been the impulse behind the project developed from one of Faulkner's least admired novels, which, ironically perhaps, became one of the most profitable southern films of the 1950s.[31] Though not "based" on one of the playwright's works, this film, paradoxically enough, is also one of the most successful Williams adaptations.

The Long, Hot Summer (1958): Mississippi Williams

The year 1958 proved to be an *annus mirabilis* for Hollywood's increasingly popular savage-ideal films, as all the following examples of the genre achieved substantial box-office popularity: *Cat on a Hot Tin Roof*; Daniel Mann's *Hot Spell* (adapted from Lonnie Coleman's novel and play); Stanley Kramer's morality play about a white man and a black man chained together by destiny (or perhaps mischance), *The Defiant Ones*; Anthony Mann's *God's Little Acre*; and perhaps most significant of all, Martin Ritt's *The Long, Hot Summer*, ostensibly adapted from Faulkner's novel *The Hamlet* and his stories "Barn Burning" and "Spotted Horses." These works all belonged to what became the so-called Snopes saga, a trilogy that also includes the novels *The Town* and *The Mansion*, published after the film began production. Here was a film that, Bosley Crowther correctly predicted, "will do for the screen what Tennessee Williams did for the stage with 'Cat on a Hot Tin Roof.'"[32] In fact, *Summer* brought to the film medium much of what Williams had introduced on the Broadway stage, not only with *Cat*, but also with *Sweet Bird* (first produced in Miami in 1956), *Summer and Smoke*, and *Orpheus Descending*, of whose themes the film is a virtual repertoire.

If with *Cat* Williams had transformed the outmoded plantation myth into a framework ideal for probing the social and sexual discontents of the southern family romance, then screenwriters Harriet Frank, Jr., and Irving Ravetch (working under the careful supervision of producer Jerry Wald, a screen melodrama specialist) proved able to confect an even more commercially appealing version for a mass film audience. Williams's various dramas with southern settings served the writers and director as a handy quarry of themes and character types. Here was a film, it was expected, that would capture the essence of the savage ideal. Contrary to the usual industry wisdom about the adaptation of notable literary properties, the producers rejected using the novel's title, choosing instead to evoke, unmistakably but delicately, something of the languor and super-heated sexual themes associated stereotypically with the South since the Broadway opening of *A Streetcar Named Desire* (compare the transparent double entendre in the titling of Lonnie Coleman's novel *Hot Spell*). Though Faulkner's connection with *Summer* was not ignored, it was the film's purportedly sensational version of the southern family romance that the marketing campaign identified as the main selling point, as the ad copy suggests: "Not since 'Peyton Place' has a story been told so boldly . . . The red-hot lowdown on a southern family . . . that people talked about in whispers."[33]

Hollywood's scandalously profitable *Peyton Place* (1957), based on Grace Metalious's purportedly "journalistic" bestseller, had shown that the savage ideal could be found beneath the deceptively prim ordinariness of a New England town still in thrall to its Puritan heritage. Interestingly, the publication of a book in this vein with a northern subject was scandalous in a way that Williams's plays never were (Metalious became something of a pariah as a result of her success). *Summer* offers the more expected kind of fiction, something "red hot" and focusing on the sensational doings of a "southern family" that the socially respectable could mention only in whispers.

This was Williams rather than Faulkner country. However, as with many a Hollywood knockoff before and since, the film easily avoided the pitfalls of copyright infringement because its borrowings from Williams were too general to prove actionable.[34] But *Summer* did repay the favor in another unexpected and unintended fashion by furthering the popularity of the savage-ideal series and thus making it possible in part for three older Williams properties (and a newer one with similar themes), previously thought rather uncommercial, to be mined for screen treatment. These were *Summer and Smoke* (first produced on Broadway in the late 1940s); *The Fugitive Kind* (the film version of *Orpheus Descending*); *This Property Is Condemned* (a much-expanded rewriting of an early one-act that had been considered for "consolidation" during early stages of the *Baby Doll* project); and *The Last of the Mobile Hot-Shots* (based on a Williams play produced and written in the 1960s, *Kingdom of Earth*, also called *The Seven Descents of Myrtle*). Of course, this development was also aided by the playwright's post-*Summer* screen success with both *Cat* (produced and released just a few months after *Summer*) and then *Sweet Bird* four years later.

An interesting triptych, *Summer*, *Cat*, and *Sweet Bird* were immensely profitable entrants into this new series, which would also include a much less successful, substantially Williams-ized version of *The Sound and the Fury* (1959) as well as late productions such as *The Chase* (1966) and *Hurry Sundown* (1967), which met with mixed box-office and critical success despite the novel and screenwriting talents of Lillian Hellman and Horton Foote. *Fury*, interestingly enough, is another ostensibly Faulkner film that, like *Summer*, bears little resemblance to its acknowledged literary source.[35]

The three popular productions, in contrast, all star Paul Newman in a role that he had played before and was to play again and again throughout his early career: the handsome, athletic, sexually passionate young man on the make, rootless to some degree (belonging to what Williams called the "fugitive kind"), but looking to make a place for himself in a world dominated by powerful, censorious fathers whose disapproval must be overcome (Big Daddy, Boss Finley, and Will Varner in these films).[36] Such roles take full advantage of Newman's Method training, since each production gives him scenes (so-called performance moments) in which his hard-edged exterior falls away to reveal a more vulnerable and confused soul beneath, a callow youth struggling to transform himself into a fully adult male. These three films share another important quality: they each end conservatively, with the Newman character about to be either married to his true love (*Sweet Bird*, *Summer*) or reconciled with his wife (*Cat*), whom, it is revealed, he cares for deeply.

Summer begins with the expulsion of Ben Quick (Newman), a hard-edged but enterprising roughneck, from his small-town Mississippi home because he is suspected of burning down a neighbor's barn. The sheriff cannot prosecute the insolent young man, but his reputation as a disruptive and difficult loner seems to have already convicted him in the eyes of his fellow citizens. But then the town itself and the good opinion of his neighbors seem to matter little to Ben, who quickly and almost lightheartedly packs up and departs. He is at once picked up by two beautiful women in a shiny Cadillac convertible: Clara Varner (Joanne Woodward), daughter of the local grandee, Will Varner (Orson Welles); and Eula Varner (Lee Remick), who is married to Clara's brother Jody (Anthony Franciosa), the heir apparent to the Varner estate and fortune. They drive him as far as their hometown, Frenchman's Bend, where Ben soon makes the acquaintance of the elder Varner, a coarse-mannered parvenu who tells Ben he started life dirt poor and admits to being impressed by Quick's alpha-male self-possession and evident drive for self-improvement. Varner apparently sees something of himself in the young man. For his part, Quick knows a good opportunity when he sees one, and signs on at once as a Varner sharecropper, settling down to life in town. This development is carefully watched by Clara, who is obviously attracted to Ben, yet resents his arrogance (for he is too much like her father, with whom she has a stormy, though mutually respectful, relationship).

It soon becomes clear why Varner takes such an interest in the stranger. Anticipating the passing down of his estate to the next generation, the old man is concerned that neither his son nor his daughter has produced an heir. Jody is lazy and feckless, not a useful partner for his father (he seems completely lacking in business sense), and he is interested only in constant, but apparently unproductive, lovemaking with Eula. Sensing Jody's weakness, the local high school boys haunt the Varner place, calling out for Eula, who is flattered by the attention and refuses to send them away (Jody's attempts to do so prove laughably inept). A schoolmarm whose prim and proper surface conceals a passionate interior, Clara has found herself mired for years in a relationship with a member of the local gentry, Alan Stewart (Richard Anderson). Alan is a polite but spineless mama's boy, and Will despises him for his weakness, while Clara finds his gentle nature appealing. Thinking his son a lost cause and despairing of his daughter's ever finding a suitable husband, Will tries to force Clara to marry Ben, a prospect she both resists (resenting her father's attempt to direct her life) and welcomes (finding herself increasingly drawn to the young man).

In the fashion typical of the 1950s Hollywood melodrama, these initiatives are frustrated (for the son cannot be denied and the daughter cannot be compelled), but in such a way that the underlying problems from which the Varner family suffers are dramatically resolved, delivering one and all to a happy end. Hoping to eliminate a powerful rival, Jody attempts to murder Ben, but is persuaded by the quick-witted intended victim to join with him instead in a search for buried Confederate treasure. Jody, of course, winds up deceived and humiliated.

Jody's anger and frustration soon turn once again to violence. The relationship between father and son comes to a spectacular crisis as Jody locks Will in the barn and sets fire to it. The men in town spy the smoke and immediately conclude that Ben Quick has shown his true colors as an arsonist. A lynch mob forms. Meanwhile, Jody relents and releases the old man, who is implausibly overjoyed to learn that Jody truly loves him. Will explains to the would-be lynchers that the barn catching fire was simply an accident, and they head back to town, disappointed at their failure to hang someone.

His heart apparently softened by Clara's selfless effort to rescue him, Ben decides he will not take advantage of the Varners' troubles. He tells Clara that the marriage deal brokered by her father is now off, but this selfless act brings Clara to admit that she loves him, and the couple soon agree to marry—but now for their own reasons. No longer oppressed by his father's ill opinion, Jody reconciles with Eula. And to complete the scene of romantic fulfillment (however improbably), Will even agrees to marry his longtime mistress, Minnie (Angela Lansbury).

The Vermouth in a Very Dry Martini

Readers of Faulkner's *The Hamlet* and the other two Snopes stories officially identified as the film's source will find little that is familiar here. The main character in the Snopes trilogy is Flem Snopes, the most villainous figure in a degenerate family of white-trash social climbers, and he makes no appearance in the film. Even stranger, there is no reference to other members of the Snopes family. While the theme of *The Hamlet* is the Snopeses' success in taking over their society (a movement completed in the final two novels of the series), the theme of *Summer* is the reconciliation and renewal brought by the new blood of Ben Quick to the Varners, who may be arrivistes (like his prospective father-in-law), but also seem deeply committed to the community's core values. A very minor presence in the novel, Ben becomes the film's main character. Like Flem, Ben is a Horatio Alger figure, and he is even given some of Flem's more admirable qualities (especially animal cunning and relentless energy in self-promotion).

But Flem (as his humorous name suggests) is more villain than hero, a disagreeable presence from a lower order of existence. Ben, in contrast, is only apparently an unprincipled and ruthless outsider, charged with but never convicted of barn burning, that most destructive and cowardly crime against property. Though at first a loner who is out strictly for number one, in the film Ben finds his inner virtue coming to the surface when he falls in love with Clara Varner—a romantic theme for which the novel offers no equivalent (there is no Clara Varner in the novel in fact)—bettering his social condition by agreeing to marry her. Yet in the process he resolves the family's difficulties by forcing Jody to confront his father's low opinion and Clara her dissatisfaction with sexually challenged Alan. Above all else, the finale, with its triple coupling, reverses the meaning of the Snopes trilogy, which is that the most precious heritage of southern society (a "better" class of people who provide the values everyone in the culture should both respect and live by) has been decisively replaced by amoral upstarts devoted only to acquisition and profit. If only in this respect, the film is more Faulknerian than its supposed Faulkner source (the writer's pessimism in the trilogy about the future of the region is uncharacteristic), showing as it does that the land will not pass to the morally corrupt Snopes but to the Varners, who are savage in manner perhaps but devoted to core southern values: love of the land, respect for community, and fierce protection of family integrity.

Faulkner's bitter evocation in *The Hamlet* of the self-made man who rises by dint of his own efforts, only to become the curse of the land that gave him birth, thus differs absolutely from the American Dream scenario concocted by the Ravetches, Martin Ritt, and Jerry Wald. In fact, beyond a few incidents (all drastically altered), some character names, and the broad outlines of a setting (a Mississippi small town), not much in the film can be traced back to the Snopes stories and novel. After attempting heroically to discuss *Summer* as a Faulkner adaptation, critic Bruce Kawin is forced to conclude that the screenwriters "deliberately reversed the value structure of [*The Hamlet*] . . . turning Faulkner's anti-capitalist black comedy into a Horatio Alger bedtime story . . . *The Long, Hot Summer* is just the kind of success story *The Hamlet* parodies." This transformation, Kawin suggests, came about not "through misreading but through grafting." And, as he sees it, these textual "cuttings" are "stock Hollywood figures."[37]

In a global sense, of course, Kawin is correct. The Faulkner material has been subjected to the same kind of "melodramatization" so evident in the Hollywood versions of *Cat*, *Sweet Bird*, and *Suddenly*. Here, too, the characters are softened, the seeming irreconcilability of their conflicts erased by scenes in which authentic emotions surge to the surface, prompting the speaking of truths that dispel misunderstandings and, often implausibly, alter harsh but accurate judgments: most startlingly, Will Varner with bewildering suddenness abandons his view of Jody as a wastrel, a character flaw hardly eliminated by the feckless young man's inability to follow through with his plan to make his father suffer a miserable death.

Like both *Cat* and *Sweet Bird*, *Summer* thus falls into two distinct parts, as Bosley Crowther recounts in his review. Replete with obsessions, deep-seated flaws, and morally ambiguous energies, the characters are all at first, he says, "clicking nicely . . . when suddenly the script takes a plunge from its level of hard, ruthless logic into sheer story-telling make-believe." For Crowther, *Summer* slides irrevocably thereafter into bathos: "The writers, who have kept their characters ice-cold in the midst of the summer heat, turn around in the flutter of an eyelash and make them melodramatic, magnanimous, and warm."[38]

To put this somewhat differently, the film is a typical family melodrama of the period. Yet *The Hamlet* was transformed for the screen by far more than the imposition of improbable character "arcs" and a happy ending that defies credibility. Eager to demonstrate his distaste for standard Hollywood fare (he was a strong supporter of the international art film, then an increasingly important presence on American screens), Crowther misses a more important point. What is unusual, and largely unprecedented, about *Summer* is that the central material of Faulkner's novel (the chronicle of the Snopes) has been decisively eliminated, making it possible to install new characters (such as Clara), new themes (a young man growing to maturity, a woman accepting her need for sex), and new plot motifs (the triumph of desire and love, the necessity of personal authenticity, the importance of loyalty to the family, the sanctity of marriage).

In short, the Faulkner novel and stories serve the filmmakers as disposable pretexts; they are the vermouth in a very dry martini. A reader of the book, seeing the film, could only with difficulty identify anything therein as Faulknerian except for the odd motif or minor character (e.g., barn burning, Will Varner). In contrast, anyone familiar with the Williams plays and films of the period would be struck by the scope and depth of the film's shameless borrowings from the era's most successful Broadway playwright.

Consider only the most obvious:

1. A southern patriarch, father to two children he loves but does not respect, worries whether his considerable legacy (property and a business he has come to own through his own energies and cunning) will be bestowed on an heir who will prove its good steward. (*Cat, Sweet Bird*)

2. The patriarch has risen from nothing (fitting, by the way, Cash's explanation of the origin of the planter class in general; cf. the O'Haras in *Gone with the Wind*), and he is overbearing, devoted to a mistress he has refused to marry, as well as manipulative, rough-edged, and unashamedly vulgar (and as played by both Burl Ives, who inaugurated the role of Big Daddy on Broadway, and Orson Welles, the patriarch is also a man, shall we say, of considerable presence and hearty appetites). (*Cat, Sweet Bird*)

3. The patriarch is desperate for his children to show their fitness to succeed him by producing children of their own. (*Cat*)

4. The son is handsome and appealing, but he finds himself unable to produce heirs despite a sexually eager, even demanding wife. (*Cat*)

5. Father and son, who have never enjoyed a satisfying relationship, manage a dramatic rapprochement, admitting that they love each other, in archetypal melodramatic scenes that feature the destruction of symbolic objects. (*Cat*)

6. After this rapprochement, the son accepts the responsibilities of being an adult male fit to receive his inheritance, and then reconciles with his wife, over whom he reasserts his sexual control. (*Cat*)

7. Desperate to remain virtuous and genteel, but unable to deny her

desire, a young woman is initiated into sexual maturity after breaking with a man who will not sleep with her. (*Summer and Smoke*
and, in an ironic form, *Streetcar*)

8. The social order is threatened by a promiscuous woman. (*Streetcar*,
   Orpheus Descending, *Baby Doll*, *Sweet Bird*)
9. An exotic stranger appears on the scene to relieve the sexual frustration of a woman or women (*Orpheus Descending*, *Baby Doll*, *Tattoo*, *Sweet Bird*)
10. A charismatic young man discovers that family and marriage mean
    more than self-realization. (*Sweet Bird*, *Cat*—a motif developed
    ambivalently or tragically in the stage and more conventionally in
    the film versions)

Faulkner is a chronicler of social change, unmatched in his perceptive
re-creation of postbellum cultural politics, which are explored through
the detailed evocation of an imagined region and the histories of several
local families. Williams, in contrast, lacks the chronicler's sense of history, but he is unparalleled as a dramatist of the workings of love and
desire, whose eccentricities he traces with finesse and power. It is easy,
therefore, to see to whom this film more decisively belongs. The source
novel (*The Hamlet*), which outlines the beginnings of a degrading transformation of a place, is transformed by Jerry Wald and company, who
use a template provided by the stage and screen works of Tennessee Williams, into a brief period in the life of a family, a season that is hot and
long enough to dramatize desire, romance, and passions of every kind in
audience-pleasing depth.

With its sympathetic characters and a happy ending that confirms the
sacredness of family, marriage, and rootedness in community life, *Summer* borrows not only from Williams but from Hollywood films more
generally. Along with director Ritt, the screenwriters accommodated the
playwright's themes and characters more thoroughly to the family melodrama of the period than either Richard Brooks or Joseph L. Mankiewicz were able to manage. Here was a version of Williams that was truly
for the masses, its mildly ironic handling of regional stereotypes and its
thoroughgoing avoidance of destinal impasse yielding something perilously close to the schmaltz of *The Waltons*, for most of a decade (1972–1981)
America's most beloved family of poor, plain white folks (southern, naturally). In fact, speaking of that most demotic of media, *Summer* achieved

a popularity enduring and wide enough to prompt its transformation some seven years after its theatrical release into a "continuing drama" for television. Though it garnered a loyal and enthusiastic audience, the network version of *Summer* was canceled after one season (1965–1966). But the concept had "more legs," as the show biz cliché has it. *Summer* was remade one more time for the small screen as a TV feature film in 1985. The somewhat old-fashioned material was given a sprightly updating by Rita Mae Brown, and it proved entertaining and witty enough to garner several Emmy nominations. The acting was memorable, with Don Johnson as Ben, Jason Robards as Will, and Ava Gardner as Minnie, all delivering crowd-pleasing, over-the-top performances in roles that, by 1985, had become even more recognizable as two-dimensional cultural stereotypes (a process completed nearly two decades earlier, with Otto Preminger's nearly risible *Hurry Sundown*).

The most Hollywood-ized version of Williams's southern drama evidently had substantial, continuing appeal to a mass public. Carefully constructed as a kind of bowdlerized bricolage of sensational characters, themes, and narrative motifs borrowed from two of the South's most famous writers, the production achieved an easy success by drawing on resources, human and artistic, that the industry readily disposed of, very much reflecting its own particular tradition of quality. If, as we have argued, it is chiefly a Williams film, *Summer* was, in the final analysis, no more representative of the full range of the playwright's mature vision of his homeland than it was authentically Faulknerian in its entirely untragic evocation of postbellum history.

The irony, however, is that *Summer*'s success helped revive industry interest in adapting less easily assimilated Williams properties (most pre-*Cat*; the exception is *The Seven Descents of Myrtle*) that had been bypassed earlier in the fifties, when Hollywood did its best to extract everything of commercial value from the playwright's oeuvre. Interesting, challenging, disturbing riffs on the savage ideal, these southern films were no *Summer* (or *Cat* or *Sweet Bird* for that matter). As with Ritt's version of *The Sound and the Fury*, also scripted by the Ravetches (here was a text that also decisively resisted melodramatization), none of these other Williams southern films enjoyed the popular and critical success achieved by that notable Paul Newman triptych. However, as we will see in the remainder of this chapter, each did succeed in transferring something of the playwright's vision of southern life to the popular screen.

A Different Kind of Savage Ideal

Bosley Crowther observed about the original film version of *Summer* that what had seemed at first a "pack of little foxes" soon becomes "as romantic as doves." The finale, he correctly points out, is strictly Hollywood fantasy because "it all ends with them all settling down to raise babies and love their homes." As we have maintained, such cloying sentimentality may be read as an oversimplified version of Faulkner's celebration of (or sometimes thwarted utopian hope for) communalism and generational continuity. Of course, something close to this theme is almost endorsed by Williams in the Broadway version of *Cat*, the chief model for *Summer*, but we should not forget that this working-through of the *Cat* material made the playwright more than a little uneasy. Williams, we repeat, was more characteristically drawn to the dark side of the southern condition, as he was never loath to admit.

As we recall from Chapter 5, Williams wrote Kazan a basic outline for *Baby Doll*, declaring, "There should be something grotesque and gothic about the whole thing, the half comic, half disgusting absurdity of human relations and behavior and existence."[39] The South he would portray in many of his plays was repulsive and yet compelling, a heritage that he was ashamed of but found impossible to shake. The South seemed to Williams a microcosm of life's absurdities, forcing the artist on occasion, for its portrayal, to abandon the sober modality of traditional realism for less conventional aesthetics that Hollywood could only with difficulty accommodate: the teasing ironies of kitsch (*The Last of the Mobile Hot-Shots* [1968]) and the antirealist invocation of mythology (*The Fugitive Kind* [1959]). Here were films that, in both form and content, could hardly contrast more strongly with the ultra-melodramatized version of Williams found in *Summer*. To this group, we should add *This Property Is Condemned* (1966), which, while more conventionally realist, could most accurately be termed an antimelodrama, a dramatization of the failure of desire to effect an enduring moral reformation.

In his preface to Carson McCullers's *The Member of the Wedding*, Williams gives in to an archly Jack Cash moment. He argues that the South itself is responsible for the kind of representation it has received: "There is something in the region, something in the blood and culture, of the Southern state that has somehow made them the center of this Gothic school of writers." And yet this writing, he goes on to say, transcends regionality and the engaging limitations of local-color observation, for it resonates with the thematizing of alienation and spiritual terror so prominent in European fiction of the period. Like the existentialists, especially Sartre and Camus, the southern gothicists, Williams suggests, have a "sense, an intuition, of an underlying dreadfulness in modern experience."[40] In exploring these themes, the playwright implies, he and his fellow writers (such as McCullers and Flannery O'Connor) not only connect to their cultural roots but also embrace something of a modernist, European approach to the portrayal of experience, based less on essence (a part of which is surely a sense of regional affiliation) and more on existence, the sense of self that emerges from the individual, solitary encounter with reality.

The Last of the Mobile Hot-Shots: More Caldwell than Camus

The Seven Descents of Myrtle, also known as *Kingdom of Earth*, opened in March 1968 at the Barrymore Theatre, but closed after a very brief run of only twenty-nine performances and, at best, indifferent critical notices. *Myrtle* has since enjoyed only limited revivals, especially in the United Kingdom, where Williams's less conventional properties have characteristically been better received. *Myrtle*'s setting is familiar Williams and Caldwell country: a run-down plantation in the Mississippi Delta, now dilapidated but once a rich and prosperous property, during a flood in early spring. The property seems to belong to Chicken, a muscular young man with an obvious animal magnetism that recalls Stanley Kowalski, but the arrival of his half brother, Lot, and his new wife, Myrtle, threatens to dispossess him. The brothers could hardly be more different. Lot is a homosexual suffering the terminal stages of tuberculosis, which seems only one sign of his weakness; he is also a transvestite who, as the drama unfolds, becomes increasingly obsessed with taking on the identity of his dead mother. Though younger, Lot has been willed the family home, for Chicken cannot be its legitimate heir, being a bastard son with black blood. Nevertheless, he has continued to work the property in hopes of inheriting it after the death of Lot, which all agree is imminent.

And yet his brother's marriage has changed everything, for Myrtle, an ignorant but energetic low-rent city dweller of dubious morals, would (no small irony, this) become the owner of a property that once housed a proud and genteel family. Seeing his chance for a secure life slipping away, Chicken does his best to seduce Myrtle, managing the trick just as Lot, having completely assumed his mother's identity, succumbs. The play ends with Chicken and Myrtle scrambling to the roof to avoid rising floodwaters. With its oftimes campy recycling of elements made famous in Williams's earlier plays and the films made from them (especially *Baby Doll*, likewise staged in a once impressive but now decaying residence), its seemingly tongue-in-cheek historical allegory (which reenacts the passing of the genteel South to its white-trash inheritors), its evocation of the Jacob and Esau story from the Old Testament (but replayed as a struggle between sexual "orientations"), *Myrtle* struck most critics as self-parody.[41] They appreciated the playwright's witty dialogue, especially the extended encounters between Chicken and Myrtle, but were hardly convinced that the play had anything new, or indeed anything serious, to say.

Theatergoers were perhaps amused at seeing the only person of color to play a major role in a full-length Williams drama. Little notice was paid to the play's underlying metaphysical theme (already developed in its short-story source), that Lot's desire for a kingdom of heaven (to be realized by an impossible return to the vanished antebellum past and, perhaps, a rejection of the burden of sexual identity) must give way to the kingdom of earth, the realm of those who, like Chicken and Myrtle, live in the present with energy and gusto—and, it must be said, with no feeling of uncertainty about who they are. Because of his interesting ruminations on the meaning of life, Chicken is the play's intellectual center, however unlikely.

As far as Hollywood was concerned, Williams properties, even at the end of the 1960s, were still desirable, and thus it is not surprising that the playwright proved able to sell the film rights to *Myrtle* before the Broadway production opened. Despite the play's very poor showing in New York, the film production went ahead, giving Williams another chance to see his vision realized in a form that might please audiences and critics alike. Late in the winter of 1967, Williams sold the rights to Warner Bros./Seven Arts for a down payment of $400,000 and a share of the box-office gross. One of America's finest novelists and screenwriters, Gore Vidal, who had done marvels with the script for *Suddenly, Last Summer*, was hired to do the same for this new play. Sidney Lumet, also familiar with Williams, having done *The Fugitive Kind*, was hired as director, and James Wong Howe, who won an Academy Award for cinematography for *The Rose Tattoo*, was brought in to shoot the picture. Quincy Jones agreed to compose the music. The leads were given to established actors: James Coburn plays Jeb Stuart Thornington, a bizarre version of Lot (impotent but no longer a homosexual or transvestite); Lynn Redgrave is

Myrtle; and Robert Hooks is Chicken. Judging by the impressive assembly of talent, one might think that the picture should have been an artistic and commercial success. The film's utter failure proves that even if a highway is laid with gold bricks, it still has to lead somewhere. It was a bad omen that the Broadway title became something no less mysterious and confusing, *The Last of the Mobile Hot-Shots* (a reference to Myrtle's "once promising career" in an all-girl band, whose other members have subsequently met unfortunate fates).

Gore Vidal made a valiant but ultimately failed attempt to open out a three-hander heavy on talk and almost devoid of action. Perhaps to satisfy a lowbrow audience, he cut out most of Chicken's philosophizing, thus turning the play's vital center into a much more subdued (and simpleminded) presence. The film opens with Jeb Stuart, dressed in a white linen suit that could use a good dry cleaning, being thrown out of a bar; he immediately purchases a six-pack at the liquor store next door and lurches into the audience line for Rube Benedict's game show, in which the contestants, all of whom must be "happy couples," play mud volleyball to win prizes. Eager to win the stage full of modern kitchen appliances, Myrtle pairs up with a vaguely willing Jeb to compete. Winners because of her enthusiastic play, the pair agree to be married on the show in order to claim the prizes and a cash award. Jeb takes Myrtle and her truck full of electronic "aids" to Waverly (the setting having been shifted from Mississippi to Louisiana), where he proclaims his desire to restore the house "to the way we used to live in the 1840s." Part of this restoration project, now that he is serendipitously married, is to sire a son and heir, but this becomes impossible, since Jeb proves unable to consummate the marriage.

Once settled in the family home, they encounter a very suspicious Chicken, who worries that Jeb is trying to do him out of his inheritance. But Jeb himself is unsure of the legal situation and dispatches Myrtle to get the property deed somehow from Chicken. What unfolds is a seduction sequence obviously modeled on the similar scene in *Baby Doll*; it ends with Chicken convincing the young woman to perform oral sex, which she is not unwilling to do (the scene is subtly handled, but the film otherwise does not shy away from some soft-core female nudity). Meanwhile, Jeb has receded ever more deeply into his desire to relive and reinstate the past, donning a Confederate uniform as he becomes weaker and more feverish, even fantasizing about a woman dressed in period clothes (his mother perhaps?). The floodwaters continue to climb, threat-

Myrtle (Lynn Redgrave) tries to engage an uninterested Chicken (Robert Hooks) as his half-brother, Jeb (James Coburn), slips toward death in Last of the Mobile Hot-Shots. *Photo courtesy of The Historic New Orleans Collection.*

ening both the property and its otherwise preoccupied residents. After their "lovemaking," Chicken tells a surprised Myrtle and Jeb his deepest secret—that he was conceived upon the roof during a similar flood many years before, when his mother was left alone with a family servant, George, who still lives on the property. Everyone thinks that Chicken is the bastard son of Jeb's father, but they in fact share the same mother, who, with some foresight, put into her will that the next of blood kin would inherit the plantation. This revelation so disturbs Jeb that he suffers a fatal hemorrhage, dying in the living room with blood seeping from his nose. As the film ends, a flood engulfs the property, forcing Chicken and Myrtle to ascend to the roof. Survivors both, the implication is that the ill-assorted pair will live to share Jeb's erstwhile inheritance and perhaps produce the heir that Jeb's physical weakness and obsession with re-creating a vanished past have denied him.

Its middle extremely short on dramatic action and long on talk, its characters (except for Myrtle) barely two-dimensional and hardly sympathetic, its raucous music wildly inappropriate for what might be better presented as a slower-paced drama, its attempts to probe Jeb's fixation on his and Chicken's youthful sexual escapades strikingly amateurish (a clumsy reuse of the Resnais-style flashbacks Lumet deployed so effectively in *The Pawnbroker* [1965]), *Hot-Shots* was deservedly savaged by the critics. Vincent Canby faulted the "frantic, farcical pacing" of the film and summed it up as a "slapstick tragicomedy that looks and sounds and plays very much like cruel parody—of Tennessee Williams."[42] *Newsweek*'s S. K. Oberbeck sniffed that "Gore Vidal's script sounds like French-fried Pinter, with loads of catsup" and lamented Lumet's "long descent" from his more celebrated earlier films such as *Twelve Angry Men* (1957) and *Long Day's Journey Into Night* (1962).[43]

Kitsch and Commerce

What could be the explanation for a film that deploys considerable and canny talent and recycles, even if in an exaggerated fashion, the most characteristic elements of Williams's take on the "savage ideal" tradition? As in *Baby Doll*, *Cat*, *Sweet Bird*, and their many imitators, especially *The Long, Hot Summer*, here is yet another family squabble over inheritance, with the antebellum genteel South of the lamented past once again casting a dark shadow on the white-trash present. Here again, sexual antics and disabilities take center stage, with the interracial pairing in the present figuring as a dramatically scandalous moment that recalls a similar event from the more distant past. And once again, the myth of virtuous white womanhood is exploded, scandalously enough, with the coupling of Chicken and Myrtle earning the film, in the post-Code era, an "X" certificate, which did little to facilitate its distribution.

Connecting closely with both Williams's most noted works and also to the postwar tradition of films about the South, *Hot-Shots* might have expected a better fate, especially given the participation of Williams, Lumet, Vidal, Howe, and the rest of a heavily talented company. Screenwriter Vidal found the original play both "very bad" and also, if only in part, "marvelous."[44] He and Williams hoped that the picture could be made quickly and profitably, a knowing exploitation of the tried and true, a film in which the well-known Williams version of the modern South would be on self-conscious display. Perhaps that was the foundational error. But it was, perhaps, this kind of half-committed exploitation of earlier material that had led to the original stage failure.

According to critic Matei Calinescu, the most celebrated form of contemporary art—modernism, with its cult of the unique artifact and the singular voice—is the least characteristic form in what Walter Benjamin has famously termed "the age of mechanical reproduction." Modernism's other is kitsch: art that is "expendable," repetitive, banal, and trite. It is produced by those who desire "quick and predictable effects" and "are more interested in immediate financial rewards" than in creating what might be of lasting value.[45] In fact, kitsch, whether in paintings, sculpture, music, television, or cinema, is "a specifically aesthetic form of lying" and is "subject to the essential market law of supply and demand."[46] Kitsch finds its essence in the already used, the overfamiliar, the clichéd; as Calinescu puts it: "predictable audience, predictable effects, predictable rewards."[47] *Hot-Shots* was made mostly for money, but how did Vidal, Lumet, and others hope to make it a profitable enterprise?

The simple answer is that they created a "predictable" Tennessee Williams facsimile, a form of Williams kitsch, played more than a little for laughs. By the time the picture was made, Williams's name carried such box-office weight that some in Hollywood thought that any product with his signature might be profitable. Kitsch, Calinescu suggests, exploits the uniqueness and aura of the modernist text by responding to "the demand for spurious replicas or reproductions of objects whose original aesthetic meaning consisted . . . in being unique and therefore inimitable."[48] One has to look only at the advertisement on the VHS box to see how marketing plays a vital role in creating an illusion of authenticity: "Brutes and faded belles. Mint juleps and chicory coffee. Sexual propriety and kinky behavior. Old eras shoved aside kicking and flailing by the inevitable new. They're signposts of a distinctive territory, one visited in *A Streetcar Named Desire*, *Baby Doll*, *Cat on a Hot Tin Roof*, and more movies. It's Tennessee Williams territory."

This marketing cynically (though correctly) assumes a passiveness on the part of the consumer, who accepts the product as "genuine Williams." With the marketing (and of course the film itself), "the aesthetic charm of kitsch is transparently commercial." Additionally, as Calinescu points out, "the deceptive character of kitsch does not lie in whatever it may have in common with actual forgery but in its claim to supply its consumers with essentially the same kinds and qualities of beauty as those embodied in unique or rare and inaccessible originals."[49] Of course, the original in this case was neither "rare" nor "inaccessible." A confection of familiar Williams elements itself, *Myrtle* was seen by few and read by even fewer. Therefore it could be easily (and loosely) adapted to the screen for consumption by a general public that would not find troubling its substantial unfaithfulness to the original play.

Calinescu maintains that although "the kitsch-artist may have no conscious intention of producing kitsch . . . he should realize that he is doing so," and Vidal's screenplay (as well as Lumet's direction) seems to have been molded toward this counterfeit art form. With the frenzied flashbacks to Lot and Jeb's sexual escapades, Jeb's pot-induced haze, and the surreal fade-outs during Jeb's prolonged lapses of consciousness in his wheelchair, the film seems eager to invoke kitsch's "'hallucinatory' power, [its] spurious dreaminess."[50] But, while hallucinatory, these scenes are hardly mesmerizing. Stacking these "rich" images one upon the other creates tedium rather than interest. Perhaps even more importantly, earlier Williams southern films had limned the region's savage ideal at a time when this potent set of stereotypes could still be credited as authentic. By the late 1960s, however, what Allison Graham calls the "exoticised South" had become little more than cultural fantasy, to be evoked in hothouse, audience-pleasing confections such as *In the Heat of the Night* (1967), in which New Yorker Rod Steiger hams it up as a gum-snapping, small-town sheriff unable to plumb the depths of the sexual iniquities of his neighbors without the assistance of a better-educated detective from up North, who just happens to be black.

That filmgoers at the end of the sixties could not take such representations of the South *au grand sérieux* reflects a changed social climate. As James C. Cobb points out, for twenty-five years after its publication in 1941, Cash's *The Mind of the South* promoted, to universal acclaim, "the seemingly indelible image of an intellectually stunted, emotionally dysfunctional South too obsessed with the past to cope with the present, much less comprehend the future." In *Hot-Shots*, Jeb Stuart's dream of reinstating the South of the 1840s (while in fact he inhabits its ruins) gives indelible dramatic shape to Cash's view. But, particularly with C. Vann Woodward's critique of Cash's sociopolitical conclusions, "*The Mind of the South*'s reputation as the last word on Dixie began to crumble at the end of the 1960s." What gave the lie to what the previous decade had established as "Tennessee Williams country" was not the methodological shortcomings of Cash's methods, but, Cobb observes, "events in the real world."[51] By 1968, Williams, Vidal, and Lumet could resurrect the Williams savage-ideal South only through the distorting lens of kitsch, but even what was intended to be a pleasure-invigorating rhetoric could not make these fictional representations interesting to an audience that was now no longer persuaded of either their cultural relevance or their value.

This Property Is Condemned: Ersatz Williams

In a 1966 piece intriguingly titled "Instant Tennessee Williams," which was devoted to the newly released *This Property Is Condemned*, the *Saturday Review* decried another result of the playwright's immense popularity with theatre and film audiences in the two decades that had passed since the end of World War II: "Movies have been adapted so frequently from the works of Tennessee Williams that Hollywood is now able to whip up the familiar Southern mixture with very little help from the master himself." *The Long, Hot Summer*, we have seen, resulted from such a process, providing an appealing (though hardly contradiction-free) confection of Williams savagery and Faulknerian optimism. In contrast, *This Property* demonstrates the pitfalls of such an approach to "adaptation," broadly considered. Much in the tradition of *Summer*, this film, the *Saturday Review* proclaims, is "Tennessee Williams turned out to order": from "the wistful, sleazy Southern girl" to the dilapidated boardinghouse, the attractive stranger, the steamy atmosphere, and the "drawling dialogue." Yet if "the resemblance is astonishing," it does not prevent the final product from being "ersatz."[52]

This Property, it turns out, did not start out as an "adaptation" as such; producer Ray Stark's idea was to create a vehicle for Natalie Wood that would exploit her success playing sexually troubled characters in such films as *Splendor in the Grass* (1961), *Love with the Proper Stranger* (1963), and *Inside Daisy Clover* (1965).[53] The difficulty lay in unifying what soon became a witches' brew of scripts that had been hashed out by a number of different writers. In addition, directorial responsibilities, first assigned to John Huston, eventually passed on to Sydney Pollack (in the final credits, the screenplay is attributed to Francis Ford Coppola, Fred Coe, and Edith Sommer).[54] Producer John Houseman recalls that as many as five writers were employed at different times, "each trying to strengthen the film's contrived and dubious love story."[55] In the end, Pollack, faced with more than a dozen drafts, simply, as he says, "laid out each draft on the floor and cut out the scenes in each I thought best."[56]

For *Baby Doll*, Williams and Kazan were able to design the script around two one-acts, but with *This Property*, the writers were able to draw on only one short play that, more lyrical than dramatic, treated loneli-

Alva Starr (Natalie Wood) falls in love with outsider Owen Legate (Robert Redford) in a scene from This Property Is Condemned. *Photo courtesy of The Historic New Orleans Collection.*

ness and the healing power of memory. Once the decision was made to use the play's material and dramatized characters only as a narrative frame (young Willie tells the story of her family to Tom), the writers were placed in the position of actually "ventriloquizing" something that convincingly represented a Tennessee Williams property. Because of the playwright's reputation, the fact that Williams had little or nothing to do with making the film was not considered important. What was deemed crucial was to attach his name to the property; this association, so those involved thought, would guarantee a substantial box-office draw. This marketing strategy persists. The DVD box cover for *This Property Is Condemned* enthuses: "Repressed desires, sultry women, sweltering weather, and a handsome new stranger in town . . . this is playwright Tennessee Williams at his best." The problem with this alluring promotional material is that while it might be fairly descriptive of another Williams film (*The Fugitive Kind*), *This Property* is not really Tennessee Williams *at all*. The credits very cannily note that the film is "Suggested by a one act play of Tennessee Williams."

Even if the playwright's involvement was minimal, his artistic fingerprints, however counterfeited, remain on the celluloid. Like *Hot-Shots*, *This Property* is a virtual collage of scenes and moments from more-familiar Williams properties. In short, so many aspects of the picture—mood, character, plot, even dialogue—are redolent of Williams's work that one can almost hear Pollack telling the writers, "Pretend you're Tennessee Williams. Give me a Williams script." In any case, the result was less than satisfactory. As Gene D. Phillips remarks, "The story has been stretched to feature length by piling incident upon incident in a way that does not really help the viewer to get to know the central characters much better, but serves only to delay the inevitable outcome of the story for too long."[57]

The film develops along familiar Williams lines of confinement and escape, as Alva (Natalie Wood), who is Willie's sister, runs off to New Orleans to try to get away from what seems her inevitable destiny: a life of prostitution. What prompts this flight is the appearance in town of Owen Legate (a character, played by Robert Redford, who does not figure in the original). Owen convinces Alva that she is doomed if she remains in her mother's boardinghouse, which is little more than a bordello. But then her mother, Hazel (Kate Reid), a domineering character obviously modeled on *Menagerie*'s Amanda Wingfield, makes her way to the city to rob Alva (whose loving nature and sexual proclivities recall those of Blanche DuBois) of her dreams for a better life. As in *Streetcar* (with Mitch's finding out about Blanche's sordid past), Alva's attempted sexual reformation comes to nothing, as Owen leaves her once he learns that, after his impulsive departure for New Orleans, she drunkenly accepted the proposal of one of the older men in town who had taken a fancy to her.

We learn in an epilogue that Alva, her heart irremediably broken, later dies alone from lung cancer. The brief romantic idyll she enjoys with Owen thus comes to nothing. Like Chance Wayne in the stage version of *Sweet Bird*, she proves incapable of moral reformation. The film ends with a painful return to the after-scene of romance. As with Tom at the end of *Menagerie*, all that Willie has to cling to is the memory of a past filled with loss and failure, a story that, pathetically enough, is not even her own. Though *This Property* invokes such familiar Williams motifs as the salvific power of the imagination, the double-edged (insupportable yet comforting) burden of the past, and the characters' need to adjust to a changing South, these fixtures cannot provide an adequate spine for the script. Not surprisingly, the counterfeit nature of the film did not convince reviewers that this was actually a Williams property. Typically, *Newsweek* faulted the "committee of writers," which had no grasp of Williams's "intuition."[58] What *This Property* lacks, as unimpressed cinemagoers and critics alike readily recognized, is poetry of poignant beauty, sharp-eyed insight into the dark recesses of the human condition, and characters who, because they speak to the hopes and fears shared by one and all, live on in the imagination. In short, the film lacks the remarkable, unmatched contributions that Tennessee Williams made to the Broadway stage and the Hollywood cinema. These were qualities that could not be confected, even by a talented scriptwriting team with the master's motifs in mind.

The Fugitive Kind: A Savage Apocalypse

The world that emerged from the senseless fury of World War I, Jack Cash suggests, was marked by an uncertainty described by its most pessimistic analyst in a work tellingly entitled *The Decline of the West*: "Nobody might be sure that tomorrow the dark prophecies of a Spengler might come dreadfully true—that civilization might not completely collapse into the chaos of recrudescent and blood-drinking barbarism."[59] Intimations of collective disaster, of course, are arguably the most common theme of a modernity dismayed by the shattering of its belief in progress, but these feelings, Cash argues, were incredibly powerful in a South that had been founded on "an assertion of a passionate desire to keep on believing, willy-nilly, in the great master narrative faith of the nineteenth-century . . . continual advance through always more signal achievements to always more splendid goals."[60]

But by the end of the 1920s, many southerners could no longer sustain this narrative faith, focused particularly on the dream, now seemingly unattainable, of an economically reconstituted "New South," or so

Cash thought. In a region still emerging from its deep ressentiment of humiliating military defeat and the imposed political transformation of Reconstruction, this combination of, in Cash's terms, "fear and wills," led to the worst kind of nativist excess, a "hate for whatever differed from themselves and their ancient pattern." These southerners of the first decades of the twentieth century, Cash concludes, were "superlatively ripe for hating."[61]

In *Orpheus Descending* (1957), Williams returned to the play that had failed him some seventeen years earlier (*Battle of Angels*), but that, reworked, offered Broadway playgoers a deeply affecting, perhaps even terrifying meditation on the ripe hatred that, as the stereotype evoked by Cash has it, was endemic in the small-town South of Williams's youth. The discontent of such an insulated, isolated life, Williams demonstrates, is not only xenophobic fear (of the Negro, of the white ethnic, of the charismatic stranger from the big city), but a widespread sexual malaise that calls out for renewal.[62] *Orpheus*, in fact, offers the same narrative and thematic patterns of the era's most successful southern film, *The Long, Hot Summer*, with the Orphic Val Xavier, an attractive singer expelled from New Orleans because of his frequent attendance at "parties," playing the role, like Ben Quick, of sexual healer. Instead of a finale that incorporates the charismatic outsider's energies into a collective process of renewal, the play concludes with a series of violent deaths, including the execution by blowtorch of its protagonist (a horrifying evocation of lynching), as the townspeople make sure that their stolid world will not change. No dramatist had ever evoked the "darker phases" of the South, especially the blight of extrajudicial murder, with such emotional impact. *Orpheus* was for many reasons an ill-starred production (plagued especially by casting problems), but its frank treatment of unmitigated savagery (a variation on one of the playwright's central themes, the destruction of innocence) certainly did not do much to increase business. Lacking anything like the melodramatic uplift (or, perhaps better, the possibility of such uplift) that had made productions like *Suddenly* and *Cat* more palatable to theatergoers, *Orpheus* closed, disappointingly, after only sixty-eight performances.

A further problem may have been Williams's abandonment of traditional realism for something approaching religious or philosophical abstractionism. Indeed, for many at the time the play's cultural references were blunted by what at times was a somewhat confusing symbolism. Bosley Crowther was one of the few to recognize that the film version, like the play, deals with "a broad scan of moral corruption and degeneracy in the South."[63] Thoroughly European in both its evocation of a mythological cadre and self-conscious deployment of symbolist elements, Williams's *Orpheus Descending* invites comparison with a number of similar French works, written in the 1930s, that had a significant impact on the postwar American theatre: chief among them Albert Camus's *Caligula* (1938), and three plays by Jean Giraudoux, *The Trojan War Will Not Take Place* (1935), *Amphitryon 38* (1929), and *Electra* (1937). In confecting *Orpheus Descending* from his earlier failure, *Battle of Angels*, Williams scaled down a complex, often contradictory program of Christian symbolism to emphasize instead a cadre based on the classical legend of Orpheus, most influentially retold by the Roman poet Ovid in the *Metamorphoses*. Williams evokes the most notable elements of the Orpheus myth: the rescue, successful at first, then failed, of the poet's beloved Eurydice from Hades, as well as the handsome man's dismemberment, after forswearing the love of women for that of attractive boys, at the hands of furious female devotees of Dionysus. But Williams makes something so different from them that the mythological references confuse more than enrich the meaning of the dramatic action.

Williams's bankability in Hollywood, however, was so great in the late fifties that it proved sufficient enough to convince two would-be producers, Martin Jurow and Richard Shephard (who were former agents), that the play's treatment of southern themes would be sufficient to guarantee box-office success. For a property that was hardly presold (having failed not once but twice to garner the approval of playgoers), Jurow and Shephard assembled an impressive crew and cast, raising a substantial amount of money to finance the production. Sidney Lumet, a leading figure at the time, fresh from the astounding success of his first film, *Twelve Angry Men* (1957), would direct, while Meade Roberts would partner with Williams himself to write the script. Marlon Brando agreed (for, at the time, the amazing figure of $1 million) to play Val, while Anna Magnani (for whom the part had been written) would play Lady Torrance (an imprisoned Eurydice married to Jabe, a Hades struck with a fatal illness). The supporting cast was also impressive, featuring Maureen Stapleton as Vee, the unhappy wife of the town sheriff, and Joanne Woodward as Carol Cutrere, a would-be reformer of the town's regressive racial politics who, frustrated in her inability to effect change, becomes sexually self-destructive.

Despite Lumet's heroic attempts to focus audience interest on visual style and performance, *Orpheus* (now retitled *The Fugitive Kind*) failed on screen for much the same reason it had done so on stage: it was weighed down with a structure that emphasized speechmaking rather than dramatic action (making for a middle that is agonizingly slow, a fatal script fault). Brando and Magnani, it is true, did not strike sparks as a romantic couple (the actors experienced terrible problems working with each other), but a better property might have easily masked this problem. Because it was arty, slow, emotionally detached, and confusingly plotted, *Fugitive* never found an audience.[64] Bosley Crowther was almost alone in insisting on the effectiveness of the film's more conventional elements: "a surprisingly decent account of two lonely and sad, but normal, persons trying hard to get a little out of life against the adversities compounded by the meanness and weaknesses of man."[65] Perhaps, but such a reading ignores the confusing symbolic burden these characters are meant to bear. For that reason, not many among the film's viewers and critics would have counted it a success.

But artistic and popular failures may nonetheless hold considerable interest of a different kind, and this is the case with *Fugitive*. At the beginning of this chapter, we emphasized that the Southern Renaissance was a complex movement, characterized not only by nostalgic self-defensiveness about southern culture (the Nashville Fugitives, William Faulkner) but also by a desire to limn, however much in an "exoticized" fashion, the region's "darker phases" (in the various works of Caldwell, McCullers, O'Connor, and preeminently Williams). If, as Crowther maintains, *Fugitive* deals with the "meanness and weaknesses of man," it does so within a cultural and social setting drawn with much specificity. The "savage ideal" to which *Fugitive* gives voice is itself a mythic structure (as artificial, perhaps, as the film's convoluted references to Orpheus). And yet it nonetheless says much that is true about Hollywood's postwar version of the South, an imaginary landscape, the authenticity of whose contours were endorsed by many filmgoers until the mid-1960s.

The Mississippi Delta town where the action unfolds is a locus of discontent, and an unfortunate destination for Val after he is expelled from New Orleans for what, it seems, is his participation in something like male prostitution. Tired of the way he has been used by women (his principal Orphic quality), Val flees in search of a different kind of life, but instead finds himself trapped by the hamlet of Marigold, which both desperately needs the kind of renewal he might bring and at the same time fears the possibility of regenerating change. Helped by the sheriff's wife,

Vee, when his car breaks down, Val is offered shelter in the city jail, from which, we learn, another stranger, previously imprisoned, escaped, only to be hunted down by dogs and then killed by the sheriff's gun. Wary of needy women, Val shuns the proffered affections of Carol (like Blanche DuBois, a daughter from a well-to-do family who has become an out-of-control tramp), and he remains cold to the advances of Lady Torrance, who gives him a job in her store, until she finally confesses her desperate need for his affection (connecting her to *Tattoo*'s Serafina). These women are both associated with death and destruction: Carol takes Val to the local "bone orchard" to explain her deep spiritual malaise, while Lady points out to him the ruins of her immigrant father's store, burned down some years back by town bigots, including, as it later turns out, her own husband, who was resentful of foreigners. Val helps Lady resurrect her father's ideal of a beautiful "confectionary" that might bring something sweet and pleasant to a collective existence that is uniformly glum, but her jealous husband shoots and kills her when it is completed, unable to bear her connection with the life-giving Val. The confectionary catches fire, and Val is prevented from escaping the flames by the aroused towns-

Val Xavier (Marlon Brando) serenades Lady Torrance (Anna Magnani) in a scene from The Fugitive Kind. *Photo courtesy of The Historic New Orleans Collection.*

people, including, most prominently, the sheriff, who mans a fire hose that propels Val back into the blaze, where he perishes. At the end, all that is left of Val is his snakeskin jacket (an emblem of his difference and potency), which a distressed Carol collects. In the film's final scene, she drives furiously out of town, whose presiding genius is now a lone crow sitting on a naked tree limb, an image of the death and destruction to which almost everything there has been delivered in one way or another. *Fugitive*, as Gene D. Phillips declares, is filled "with doomed creatures struggling to regain their footing in a hostile world which offers them no support or encouragement to be better than they are."[66]

The film, to put this another way, gives fascinating, perhaps even definitive, dramatic shape to what Cash identifies as the vices of southern culture: "Violence, intolerance, aversion and suspicion toward new ideas . . . an inclination to act from feeling rather from thought, an exaggerated individualism and a too narrow concept of social responsibility, attachments to fictions and false values, above all too great attachment to racial values and a tendency to justify cruelty and injustice in the name of these values."[67] Hollywood and its audience, as we have seen, were more interested in the imaginative landscape of decadence and deliverance so cunningly contrived in *The Long, Hot Summer*. Like Frank Tannenbaum, Williams tended to see his countrymen more bleakly, and as unwelcoming to those who, like Val Xavier, might demonstrate the self-destructiveness of their "attachments to fictions and false values."

CHAPTER EIGHT

Tennessee Williams and the End of an Era

Fading Fortunes

If the Williams films from the 1950s were on the whole hugely successful with American and international audiences, those made during the next decade largely failed either to turn a profit or meet with critical approval. In part, this trend reflected the playwright's diminishing success in the commercial theatre. While revivals of his early plays continued to sell tickets, New York audiences in the 1960s did not generally find Williams's new work appealing—largely, it seems, because it was less dependent on the sympathetic, realistic dramatization of complex characters that had made productions like *Menagerie* and *Streetcar* such spectacular successes. The closing of the second production of *The Milk Train Doesn't Stop Here Anymore* after only five performances in 1964 marked a low point from which Williams, as a commercially viable playwright, never fully recovered. That Williams's reputation as a dramatist went into a precipitous decline during the decade, relieved only by the success of *Iguana* in 1961–1962, certainly contributed to the relative indifference of filmgoers to the 1960s films. *Sweet Bird* and *Iguana* excepted, none could be described as either a box-office smash or an "event" release that, like *Baby Doll*, made critics and public alike take notice. Several of the sixties films, in contrast, were spectacular, even embarrassing failures that deeply harmed Williams's reputation, suggesting that his talent and originality might have been overrated in the flush of popular success a decade earlier.

The plays written by Williams after *Iguana* were not generally considered by Hollywood for adaptation, and this neglect was probably a sign of his changing reputation (and, of course, his radically evolving artistic interests). Failing to receive a Broadway production, they were, for the most part at least, aesthetically experimental, short (many were one-acts), and preoccupied, in the European manner, with philosophical and cultural themes that only the literati were likely to appreciate. But even this narrow coterie was not universally impressed. Williams had perhaps too solidly established himself as a poetic realist (an impression substantially reinforced by *Iguana*) to suddenly metamorphose into an absurdist (like Samuel Beckett) or a surrealist (like Jean Anouilh or Antonin Artaud). Though intellectually sophisticated and generally appreciative of highbrow dramatic imports from Europe, the New York critical establishment was generally puzzled or even put off by Williams's artistic transformation. Hollywood correctly judged that the film-going public was hardly likely to find much of interest in these rather inaccessible properties. Before the decade ended, the soundness of that commercial judgment was evidenced by the utter failure of the two post-*Iguana* productions that were filmed: *Myrtle* (as *Hot-Shots*) and *The Milk Train Doesn't Stop Here Anymore* (as *Boom!*). These movies failed to find an audience despite the participation of considerable directorial talent (Sidney Lumet and Joseph Losey) and actors of unquestioned popularity and talent (an honor roll that includes James Coburn, Lynn Redgrave, Elizabeth Taylor, Richard Burton, and Noel Coward).

Though clearly conditioned by Williams's New York miseries, the slip in his popularity with filmgoers had industry-specific sources as well. We must remember that Hollywood continued, for the most part, to screen properties he had written a decade or more earlier. The expectation was that these films would mine a well-established vein of popular taste and connect with audiences as effectively as had *Cat*, *Tattoo*, *Streetcar*, and *Suddenly*. But they did not. Sometimes these later films did not fit well with production trends (*The Fugitive Kind*, for example, does not evoke the "exoticised South" made popular by *Cat* and *Sweet Bird*). Sometimes they were fatally flawed by the kitschy or ersatz fashion in which the filmmakers sought to recycle characteristic Williams themes (this was especially true of *This Property* and *Hot-Shots*). But in a decade that saw America undergo rapid social change and often violent cultural conflict, Williams and his adaptors faced a more general and, unfortunately, intractable problem. With the exception of *Iguana* and *Boom!* (which were accommodated with contrasting success to the art cinema, outside the industry mainstream), the sixties adaptations found themselves hopelessly out of step with a central development within Hollywood filmmaking: the decisive turn away from a cinema of sentiment toward a cinema of sensation.

The Advent of a Cinema of Sensation

This transformation was already in progress when, in the late 1940s, Williams was exploring with producer Charles K. Feldman the adaptation of *The Glass Menagerie*. That Hollywood took up with growing enthusiasm and to its profit the cinematizing of a body of work both notorious and highbrow was a symptom that the industry was in deep crisis. This crisis was the result of the confluence of a number of factors that we outlined in Chapter 1. Undoubtedly, the most significant of these for long-term developments was that in 1948 the U.S. Supreme Court determined that Paramount Pictures, being in violation of antitrust regulations, would have to divest itself of its theatrical holdings. Within a few years, the remaining four major studios (Warner Brothers, Fox, MGM, and RKO) were forced to follow suit, thus ending the practice of vertical integration, which had allowed the organization, under one corporate structure, of the three areas of the film business: production, distribution, and first-run theatre exhibition. The legal dismantling of this corporate structure meant that the industry was forced in some important ways to reinvent itself at a time when, because of profound demographic changes in American society, it had already begun to lose its traditional audience. During the next two decades, as studio soundstages and back lots were sold off, Hollywood, in fact, was transformed into a metonymy, a way of speaking about a tradition of film production that no longer had a geographical center, as the industry became more and more enamored of the "runaway" production. When the few surviving major studios were absorbed into corporate conglomerates during the 1970s, the studio era appeared to have definitively ended.

Surprisingly, perhaps, this transition raises a central question for historians of the American cinema. If the "national" film business can now be termed New Hollywood, then the question is raised of how it differs from the industry that preceded it. Perhaps no final answer is possible—or even desirable. Murray Smith, for example, usefully cautions that although many would argue that postwar Hollywood was on the "brink of crossing a threshold into a new epoch," others emphasize that "superficial changes are likely to obscure our view of underlying continuities."[1] But whatever perspective scholars adopt on the advent of the New Hollywood, most agree that the end of vertical integration had a major impact on film production and exhibition, inaugurating a period of transition filled with uncertainty about what kind of films to offer a public whose tastes and preferences were also rapidly shifting. Because his properties pointed toward a different direction that Hollywood production might take, Tennessee Williams became for a decade or so a central figure in that era.

The business model of the studio era depended on a continuing filling and refilling of seats in local theatres around the country and around the world. By generating massive, reasonably predictable attendance at studio-owned first-run venues, admission prices could be kept relatively low while production values remained relatively high. What made such a strategy profitable was encouraging the mass habit of going to the movies, through a constant flow of first-rate films whose most significant (but never only) attractions were the exciting dramas and compelling narratives that the sound cinema quickly became well equipped to offer. Since the early 1930s, the industry had done its best to provide itself with the services of the country's most acclaimed and popular writers, acknowledging that successful films, as experience seemed to show, required the snappy dialogue, intriguing plotting, and affectingly dramatic character relationships that only such talented authors could provide.

That model would change in the wake of the Paramount decision. Deprived by the early 1950s of dependable markets for their product by the forced "divorce" from their first-run theatres, the studios quickly divested themselves of contract personnel, thereby making inevitable the flourishing of the so-called package system, in which each film was designed and produced on a "one-off" basis. The case histories traced in earlier chapters (especially those of *Menagerie*, *Streetcar*, *Tattoo*, and *Baby Doll*) neatly exemplify this emerging practice. The package system meant that films were not only produced, but also marketed individually, with the result that uniqueness and difference (always important in an industry devoted to the constant provision of the new) became ever more desirable, perhaps even necessary qualities. With its dramatic and narrative emphases and heavy investment in the profitable repetitiousness of genre and star-driven formulae, the older approach to filmmaking was embraced wholeheartedly by the television industry in the 1950s. While not abandoning completely this time-honored approach to crafting appealing visual narrative, Hollywood, eager to outdo its small-screen rival, found increasing success by exploring two quite different alternatives that went beyond the institutionally and technologically imposed limitations of televisual drama: blockbuster productions that emphasized the outsized deployment of cinematic resources (wide-screen color photography, multistar casts, lavish production values, and eye-popping action set pieces or special effects); and the blockbuster's stylistic and thematic other—the small-scale adult film, generally in black-and-white, which pushed the boundaries of the representation of sexual and related themes, riding the rapidly cresting wave of a thoroughgoing transformation of traditional mores while adopting, if only in part, the aesthetic richness of the increasingly popular international art film.

Despite obvious contrasts, these two film types share one crucial quality: their investment in what theorist Joan Hawkins calls "the ability of a film to thrill, frighten, gross out, arouse, or otherwise directly engage the spectator's body."[2] In the period of transition during the early 1950s that saw producers reluctant to abandon the writerly form of the classic studio film, there is no doubt that Williams was initially sought after by film producers because of his popularly endorsed dramatic skills and talent for confecting stylish, engaging dialogue—qualities that were thought important enough to have a significant presence in marketing campaigns. It mattered, in short (or so industry insiders agreed), that Williams was a Pulitzer Prize winner, a much-celebrated public intellectual, and the toast of Broadway, whose elite tastes and educated sensibility were certainly no secret. But it is also true that Williams became a central figure for Hollywood production in the 1950s and early 1960s because his properties were sensational as well as literary. Had he kept penning poignantly poetic, quietly despairing domestic dramas along the lines of *Menagerie* rather than departing, with *Streetcar*, for a very different thematic destination, Williams, there seems no doubt, would have remained a marginal figure in Hollywood. He would have been less widely celebrated outside intellectual circles and probably would have enjoyed no more profitable notoriety in American cultural life of the period than did his contemporaries, the greatly talented Arthur Miller and William Inge, both of whom also wrote their share of Broadway hits and won prestigious literary awards. Not sharing Williams's interest in the sensational, Miller and Inge exerted only negligible influence on the new directions Hollywood filmmaking was then taking. The early Williams films, as Hawkins would surely admit (concurring with the censors at the PCA and legion), directly engaged the spectator's body, and that made all the difference.

Historian Paul Monaco agrees with Hawkins that central to the gradual development of the characteristic forms of New Hollywood filmmaking was the "emergence of a cinema of sensation." This new film type, he suggests, was inaugurated by Alfred Hitchcock's *Psycho* (1960). The studio-era film, in contrast, exemplified a "cinema of sentiment," differentiated by its focus on sympathetic characters whose fates are energetically put into play by an expertly crafted, suspenseful narrative. Monaco states that the cinema of sensation eventually came to be defined essentially by "speeded-up pacing," "the sweep of color production," and "an increased reliance on graphic visual and sound effects," features all too familiar to cinemagoers in the early twenty-first century. But the sensational film is innovative, he allows, in more than its abandonment of classic visual style and embrace of medium-specific wizardry: "*Psycho* breaks entirely from the demands of classical Hollywood film that placed a primacy on the narrative. It also bypassed the conventions of scripting characters as opposing forces that guided the viewer toward clearly empathizing with one of them." What the sensational film offers instead is carefully orchestrated affect, groundbreaking in its depth and complexity. Monaco quotes with approval reviewer Vincent Canby's enthusiasm for the originality of Hitchcock's film: "*Psycho* is probably the best scare film ever made and one in which there is not a single character to engage our sympathies."[3] With its archly Aristotelian design on the viewer's emotions (mostly fear, of course, rather than pity), *Psycho* is a perfect transitional text, a potent combination of art-film antimelodrama and home-grown show biz, with all the transgressive energy of its pulp-fiction source cunningly preserved. But, pace Monaco, we could say much the same about *Streetcar*, *Tattoo*, and *Baby Doll*, except that these much earlier films titillated rather than terrified and featured a highbrow approach to character and theme. The cinema of sensation, we would suggest, clearly predated Hitchcock's low-budget masterpiece, and Tennessee Williams was recruited as (or did he volunteer to be?) a central figure in its development.

Cotton Mather Out-Mathered?

The postwar move toward a cinema of sensation looks forward to a blockbuster style of filmmaking displayed since the 1980s, in which, as Geoff King suggests, "the spectacular qualities of the audio-visual experience have become increasingly important," not the least because there is a "growing demand for product that can be further exploited in multimedia forms such as computer games and theme-park rides," uses for which a transferable affect is perhaps essential.[4] More to our purpose in this chapter, however, the cinema of sensation can also be seen as an eclectic response to a shift in audience taste. As Paul Monaco reports, "Throughout the 1960s, the demographics of movie theater attendance in the United States shifted toward younger, unmarried people . . . [who were] increasingly male." Bored by Hollywood's traditional genre offerings such as romances and bio-epics, Monaco concludes, "the young male audience for movies appeared to be most interested in stories and characters that challenged their adolescent boredom and their parents' conventional values." Perhaps surprisingly, "these elements also appealed to the tastes of educated sophisticates living in metropolitan areas."[5] Occupying the extreme end of this vein of taste was what Jeffrey Sconce identifies as a cinephilic elite who "explicitly situate[d] themselves in opposition to Hollywood cinema" by preferring that on-the-margin form of filmmaking he terms "paracinema."[6]

Speaking of audiences that favored something other than the standard commercial product, as it took definitive shape in the 1950s, Joan Hawkins observes that the "most frequently expressed patron desire [was] to see something 'different,' something unlike contemporary Hollywood cinema."[7] The approved cinematic object, then, might be a Roger Corman "B" movie, a soft-core skin flick, a cheaply made horror film, or a picture such as Godard's *Breathless* (1959). Because they have become venerated objects of study in film courses, it is now easy to forget that much of the European art cinema (like literary modernism) first disposed of a profitably scandalous reputation before enjoying highbrow critical approval. Alongside what are now acknowledged as masterworks by Truffaut and Godard, the key New Wave film, at least from the viewpoint of U.S. exhibitors, was Roger Vadim's *And God Created Woman* (1956), essentially a showcase for star Brigitte Bardot, who became the latest in a series of "sex goddesses" emerging from the international art film in the postwar era. "Art film," in fact, quickly became the 1950s euphemism for more or less pure exploitation, a trend to which even self-confessedly highbrow auteurs like Godard, who liked to feature the scantily clad female body, were not reluctant to further.[8] Like *Baby Doll*, Godard's *Breathless*, for example, is structured around an unconventional romance, one of whose most acclaimed sequences is a seduction scene teased out to a tantalizingly ambiguous conclusion.

One reason—perhaps the most crucial reason—that the Williams films became popular and critical successes in the postwar era is that they, as Hawkins says of paracinema in general, promised "both affect and 'something different' . . . films that seem to have a stake in both high and low art."[9] Elia Kazan, the self-styled Greek Barnum but also one of the American cinema's most talented directors, could not have put it better himself. His Times Square billboard for *Baby Doll*, in fact, extended a promise so sensational (because so outrageously provocative) that those intrigued by the image of Carroll Baker must surely have realized that a film could not have made good on it. Here was an art form that could be represented by a "high concept" that recalled nothing more than the lurid covers of cheap drugstore novels, even as the film itself, with its deglamorized visual style and emphasis on enigmatic, unusual characters, flaunted its obviously European inspiration in a blatant bid for critical approval.

Naturally, paracinema depends on a "something different" that is startlingly innovative. And what constitutes this kind of difference, of course, depends on aesthetic and cultural trends that (especially in the postwar era) proved to be in a state of rapid transition. Providing an audience with pleasurable difference, then, meant hitting a cultural target always on the move. What was sensational one year might well be cornball the next. By temperament, talent, and happy coincidence, Williams (abetted particularly by Kazan) proved well equipped to cater to the early stages of the emerging cinema of sensation in Hollywood. His focus on sexual desire and the difficulties of its accommodation, rather than on romance *tout court* (as Hollywood had been doing for decades), offered the film industry something intriguingly new, as Americans, while clinging perhaps in desperation to traditional mores, found themselves ever more inclined toward a liberal embrace of sexual freedom.

Williams's heroines (from Blanche to Serafina and Karen Stone) could be shown exploring long-forbidden, but then just barely accessible cultural territory, illustrating the playwright's conviction that women not only liked but needed sex, even without love, a perception for whose popularization, among other "dangerous ideas," Alfred Kinsey was mercilessly pilloried in the 1950s.[10] What made Blanche acceptable to industry censors, as we have seen, is that having forfeited the status of "nice girl," she is terribly punished for her transgressions by Stanley, who only takes what Mitch, an average Joe, also thinks she has lost the right to refuse. It was because of this conception of dramatic character that Kazan taunted Williams with the derisive title of "moralist," and the playwright agreed that his deep sense of right and wrong might even show up that most noted of early American divines, Cotton Mather, who was positively a reprobate by comparison, or so the playwright, only half in jest, suggested.[11]

Conservative Catholics were not perverse to see the film version of *Suddenly* as deeply critical of Darwinian predatoriness, with Sebastian's *moyen de vivre* decisively rejected by all who survive him, including his mother, who seemingly goes mad rather than live with the truth. Even Mann's *Tattoo* was easily fitted out with an ending that safely incorporates the passion of Serafina and Rosa within the bonds of matrimony. *Sweet Bird* and *Cat*, we have suggested, were readily accommodated to one of Hollywood's most socially mainstream genres, the family melodrama, their transgressive, tragic energies easily diverted into support for the social status quo. *Period of Adjustment*, requiring little alteration for screen transfer, seemed conceived by Williams from the beginning as an entrant in this genre, which was thoroughly invested, like *Cat* and *Sweet Bird*, in the social accommodation of the sexual impulse, though, no doubt, the story is wittier, darker, and more subversive perhaps than most of the family melodramas Hollywood produced.

Naughty as a Corn-Silk Cigarette: *The Roman Spring of Mrs. Stone* (1961)

During the sixties, however, the cultural ante was continually being upped. Prodded by international releases that had been made and distributed without PCA oversight, such as Michelangelo Antonioni's controversial *Blow Up* (1966), American filmmakers increasingly turned to forms of the sensational that, like the terror aroused by *Psycho*, were quite different from anything that Tennessee Williams was prepared or inclined to provide. This emerging form of affect, as Hitchcock's film decisively showed, was based on representation, on the forms of pleasure that could be made available through spectacle. Captivating visuals, particularly sexy ones, were not a new idea for Hollywood, but this strategy, successful when tried in the early 1930s, had been decisively thwarted by the Code, whose strictures on such points were easily enforced because it was the unarguable content of images that was at stake.[12] *Blow-Up* rapidly became notorious as the first mainstream film exhibited in the United States since 1934 to feature full frontal female nudity. Just a few years later, films made by prestigious auteurs, like Stanley Kubrick's *A Clockwork Orange* (1971), would be able to present simulated intercourse, even of the nonconsensual variety. Even more startling, it seemed for a time, before commercial considerations and a suddenly more conservative judicial environment eliminated the possibility, that Hollywood might turn to making hard-core sex films. Three self-styled XXX-rated independent releases, *Deep Throat*, *Behind the Green Door*, and *The Devil in Miss Jones* (all 1972), did excellent business in selected legitimate outlets, mainly on the east and west coasts, and classy pornography seemed for a year or two to be in the industry's future. One wonders what Joseph Breen would have thought about theatres around the country screening films that detailed in living color unsimulated sexual acts that many Americans would have considered disgustingly immoral or, at best, amazingly exotic.

Williams wasn't the only one left behind as audiences' tastes toward the acceptably sensational rapidly changed. The playwright's former collaborator, Charles K. Feldman, for example, thought in the early sixties that he could work the same kind of magic as he had done with *Streetcar* by producing a screen version of Nelson Algren's *Walk on the Wild Side*, a novel whose sexual explicitness had made it quite notorious upon initial publication in 1956. But six years (an immense interval during that era of rapid cultural change) intervened between the novel's appearance and the exhibition of its screen version, which, true to the book, traces the journey of a morally loose vagabond (Laurence Harvey) to New Orleans to find the woman he loves, the beautiful, exotic Hallie (Capucine). Readers of the novel, like Hallie's chagrined lover, were shocked to discover the beautiful young woman enjoying a career in the French Quarter as the madam of a prominent bordello, where an older woman (Barbara Stanwyck) in the same business lusts insanely after her. These features of the book were retained in the film version with little complaint from the PCA, since the producers took advantage of a recent change in the code that permitted direct representations of the world's oldest profession. But what Americans found shocking about sex in the midfifties had changed radically by the early sixties. Because *Walk on the Wild Side* did not show anything sensational (no nudity, no sexual situations), its flirtation with previously forbidden subject matter left filmgoers generally unimpressed. Finding that *Walk on the Wild Side* smacks of "sentimentalism and social naiveté," Bosley Crowther sniffed: "It is incredible that anything as foolish would be made in this day and age. And the suggestions in advertisements and awesome press releases that there is something 'adult' about it, that is, a little too strong for the kids, are sheer, unadulterated eyewash. It's as naughty as a cornsilk cigarette."[13]

Much the same might be said about two Williams films from this

The Contessa (Lotte Lenya) has some confidential words for Karen Stone (Vivien Leigh) as Paolo di Leo (Warren Beatty) looks on in a scene from The Roman Spring of Mrs. Stone. *Photo courtesy of The Historic New Orleans Collection.*

period. Audience taste had moved decisively beyond an interest in a moralism that did not disengage from the destructive energies of desire and narcissism (essential elements of Williams's theatre), as was demonstrated by the nearly complete indifference of critics and audience alike to the release of *The Roman Spring of Mrs. Stone.* The film was based on a novella Williams had penned during the same visit to Italy in 1948 when he also wrote *Tattoo.* Published in 1950, the book had met with a largely hostile reception from critics. Orville Prescott, writing in the *New York Times*, suggested that the tale had none of the dramatic power evident in Williams's stage work and was "only an erotic and depressing study of the crack-up of a brittle and shallow character." *Roman Spring*, moreover, was offensive: "Its subject is distasteful; its atmosphere is drenched from beginning to end in sexual decadence." Though "a specialist in the unhappiness of psychopathic ladies," Williams had in this prose work failed to achieve much more than a portrait of "decadence lacking significance." Was it "a healthy thing for the art of literature," Prescott wondered rhetorically, for the young playwright to "write with such relish about vicious and psychopathic characters?"[14]

Roman Spring would give American filmgoers a Blanche who did not endure a saving madness. Karen Stone is permitted no escape from the grisly, shameful consequences of a sexual desire that violates both convention and reason. A film version of the novella would surely have proved sensational in the early 1950s, but, for various reasons, Williams turned down several offers from producers eager to purchase the screen rights at that time. Finally, he agreed to sell them to Louis de Rochemont on the condition that Broadway director José Quintero (who did not share Kazan's interest in and talent for emphasizing the sensational) should make screening the novel his initial film project. It is difficult to imagine a more unlikely producer for a Williams property than de Rochemont, the inventor of the *March of Time* newsreel series in the 1930s and a pioneer of the noir semidocumentary genre during the following decade, with hits like *The House on 92nd Street* (1946) and *Boomerang* (1947). During the 1950s, however, de Rochemont was by no means a major Hollywood player, involving himself mostly in various wide-screen ventures. Without a doubt, by the time that *Roman Spring* was to be brought to the screen, he was a figure from Hollywood's past who retained little connection to the ways in which the industry was rapidly changing during the early 1960s. Gene Phillips reports that the producer "wondered if Williams's story, with its assortment of aging homosexuals, aristocratic procuresses, and other decadent types, was too hot to handle for the cinema of the Sixties."[15] Actually, it seems that this material, especially when developed, as it was, with the playwright's characteristic moralism, proved too tame for the era. The surprising critical and popular reception of *Suddenly*, not to mention that film's easy passage through PCA and legion review, had recently demonstrated how quickly popular taste and conventional morality had changed.

Quintero's version of *Roman Spring* follows the novella closely, treating the slow slide into decadence of an aging actress, Karen Stone (played superbly by Vivien Leigh). Fearful that her stage career is now at an end as a result of her disastrous decision to play Juliet in early middle age, Stone also suffers the death of a loving husband and the onset of menopause (the novel's early working title was "Moon of Pause," and Williams wrote the novel hoping to bring Greta Garbo out of retirement to star in the screen version). Clearly, the Desire streetcar she is riding is headed straight for Cemeteries. In full crisis, she flees to Rome, where she makes contact with, among others, the contessa (Lotte Lenya), who indulges in a lucrative sideline: finding young male companions for older women. Resisting at first, Karen eventually allows herself to make contact with one of the contessa's most popular and attractive "associates," Paolo (Warren Beatty). Karen finds much pleasure in this new relationship, which seems to be developing as a May-September romance, but soon becomes a prisoner of Paolo's childish whims and tantrums. All this time, moreover, Karen finds herself shadowed by a more desperate hustler, dirty and unkempt but eager to earn her favor or perhaps slit her throat for her money and jewels. When Paolo deserts her for a more attractive rival, Karen loses all self-respect and, eager for more of the sexual pleasure she had been receiving, invites Paolo's desperate double up to her hotel room, paying no attention (or perhaps eager to expose herself) to the evident danger.

Though it deals with, to use some phrases familiar from the PCA lexicon of the 1950s, "carnality" and "matters of gross sex," the screenplay was approved without a murmur—surely an ominous sign that the producers might have heeded. When the final print was reviewed, only a few problems were noted by Jack Vizzard, most notably, that "there is a love scene between Warren Beatty and Vivien Leigh in which he kisses her breasts and other parts of her body, and then forces her down on a couch where he ends the scene with an outrageous open-mouth kiss."[16] Williams agreed to the deletion of this and two other short scenes, but the film's depiction of sexual trafficking remained essentially intact, its meaning clear enough even to adolescent filmgoers. Nervous about such a bold treatment of degradation, Vizzard suggested that more could have been done to make the film conform more precisely to the code, but he confessed that at this late stage, it would not have been practical to make any further recommendations for changes. Vizzard's remark may be little more than a face-saving gesture, a preemptive strike in case the film's release proved controversial.[17] Such caution proved unnecessary. In yet another surprise decision, the legion assigned *Roman Spring* an A-3 rating, which was roughly similar to the former "B" category, which *Suddenly* had been assigned two years earlier; there would be no condemnation to boost ticket sales.

But, like *Psycho*, released a year previously, *Roman Spring* violates one of the cardinal rules of classic Hollywood filmmaking: it fails to provide sympathetic characters. *Variety* correctly predicted: "The Warner Bros release seems in for some tough sledding, principally because of the unhappy, unsavory characters dealt with . . . characters with whom an audience will have enormous difficulties establishing compassion, let alone identification."[18] Bosley Crowther agreed: "All in all, there is very little substance of likelihood or feeling in this film, which bumps along from quarrel to quarrel between the lovers until it flops into a quite preposterous end."[19] A cold depiction of Karen's descent into the self-destructiveness of a sexual underworld hitherto barely glimpsed on the screen (a description that, mutatis mutandis, might fit *Psycho*'s first half as well), the film nonetheless offers no compensatory and earth-shattering surprises in the manner of Hitchcock's film. There is no sudden stabbing death in the shower at the hands of a barely glimpsed monstrous presence, no meditation on the horrifyingly still finality of a violent death, no creepy anatomizing of the discontents of voyeurism, no insoluble enigmas of gender and sexual desire, no failure of the therapeutic and legal establishments to explain away psychopathic motive and energy.

No doubt, the film version of *Roman Spring* suffered from considerable difficulties, its thin, perhaps implausible plot hardly energized by what are, in the end, two-dimensional characters. Played by the same actress who had been such a success in the screen *Streetcar*, Karen Stone suffers something of the fate of Blanche DuBois, with whom, as yet another one of the playwright's "psychopathic ladies," she obviously shares much in common besides a bad end. But what is remarkable about popular reaction to the film is that, unlike the novel, it was not met with outrage at its undisguised dramatization of, in Orville Prescott's phrase, "sexual decadence." In 1961, critics and filmgoers (who mostly stayed away, as the film quickly sank out of sight) were not shocked at the story of an older respectable woman who purchases the services of a gigolo, with a member of Rome's upper class serving as a procuress, and who then, desperate for further sexual attention when the fickle young man deserts her, surrenders dignity and possibly life itself by luring a more disreputable and disagreeable substitute literally in off the streets.

As innovative as its portrait of female sexual discontent, which motors a rapid fall from respectability, may have been in 1950, this Tennessee Williams property no longer struck the American public in 1961 as provocative in the least. Warner Bros., which handled distribution, can hardly be faulted for its attempt to sell the film with the same kind of marketing campaign that had worked so well for *Streetcar* a decade earlier. The film's pressbook suggests the following slug lines for poster copy:

> In Rome there is a countess who "arranges" things. If you are wealthy and no longer young, like Karen Stone, you cover your shame with perfume and you call the countess.
>
> His name is Paolo. He has no job. He waits, handsome, sleek,

charming, for the American widows to come to Rome. Of this boy and one American widow named Karen Stone, of the glittering decadence of modern Rome, TENNESSEE WILLIAMS wrote his only novel. It is now a powerful and provocative motion picture.

If you are wealthy and no longer young, like Karen Stone, you cover your shame with perfume and call the countess who "arranges" for Paolo . . . Young enough to be her son. Old enough to be her sin. The sensational new role for WARREN BEATTY, the screen's sensational new star.[20]

Filmgoers, however, were unimpressed. *Roman Spring* was considered outrageous in only one quarter—by the Italian government, which thought that the film's portrait of Rome as rife with prostitution and decadent aristocrats might hurt the city's tourist business. The Italians were smarting in the wake of the release of Federico Fellini's *La Dolce Vita* (1959), which achieved a worldwide notoriety, but they had nothing to fear from the Williams film, which never caused a ripple. Quintero's film was thoroughly Anglo-Saxon in its deadly serious handling of morality and sexual misconduct; it lacks the wit of Fellini's multilevel anatomizing of a self-destructive, self-indulgent modernity not yet cut entirely loose from traditional values. *Roman Spring* offers nothing along the lines of Fellini's provocative, even insolent amoralism (a famous shot in *Vita* captures a helicopter hauling a statue of Christ over the city). The pairing of Leigh and Beatty might have been intellectually interesting in its exploration of the persistence of erotic urges past middle age, but the May-September romance simply did not play well on the screen, especially after director and playwright agreed to cut their only steamy love scene. The intrigue in which these characters became embroiled was simply too unengaging and old-fashioned, little more than a sketch of moods, as Bosley Crowther opined, that were "based upon a supposition of weak confusions and trashy desires."[21]

No Clothes Torn or Participants Spent:
Summer and Smoke (1961)

Much the same can be said of another early Williams property, sensational enough in its own time, that probably came too late to the screen, where it also failed to win an audience. Written while *Menagerie* was beginning its run, *Summer and Smoke* opened on Broadway after *Streetcar*,

Alma Winemiller (Geraldine Page) and John Buchanan (Laurence Harvey) in a scene from Summer and Smoke. *Photo courtesy of The Historic New Orleans Collection.*

in 1948. *Streetcar* was then continuing to shock and amaze theatergoers, and this new Williams production suffered by comparison with both the playwright's maiden effort and his groundbreaking success. Overly allegorical in a schematic way, loosely structured with not much of a plot, with only one memorable, sympathetic character (Alma), the production closed after only a hundred or so performances, a result, as Gene Phillips suggests, of the play being "too baffling for the taste of the critics and the playgoers of the commercial Broadway theatre of the day."[22] A chronicle of the ultimately disastrous relationship between a sexually promiscuous young man, Dr. John Buchanan, and his childhood sweetheart, the more spiritually inclined Alma, *Summer and Smoke* demonstrates the irony at work in human character, since, in the end, Buchanan abandons self-indulgence and dedicates himself to humanitarian work, while Alma becomes something like the town prostitute. Thinking that her sexual explorations have finally made her a fit partner for John, Alma proposes marriage, but John tells her he is engaged to a "nice" girl. What each had found both repellent and attractive in the other animates a relationship that can never find the accommodation to succeed. Divided between the rectory presided over by Alma and the medical office, with its anatomy chart, where John dominates, the set design of the play somewhat heavy-handedly suggests the characters' irreconcilability.

Revived off-Broadway in 1952 in a more intimate venue, *Summer and Smoke* found a more sympathetic audience and turned out to be one of the season's substantial hits. But by the time that a film production got under way in 1960, the play's popularity had dissipated. Paramount's Hal Wallis, who had earlier succeeded with *Tattoo*, purchased the film rights, convinced, perhaps, that the property could be turned into yet another big-budget Williams southern film, along the lines of *Cat* and *Sweet Bird*. It would be provocative enough to entice paying customers, but conventional enough to exert a broad appeal. Fresh from his success as a sexy leading man in the British New Wave drama *Room at the Top* (1959), Laurence Harvey was signed to play John Buchanan, while Geraldine Page reprised her stage role as Alma, even though nearly a decade had passed since she had starred in the off-Broadway production. Well-known for his London theatre work, Peter Glenville would direct, making one of his only occasional forays (which were mostly unsuccessful) into filmmaking.

Paramount attempted to turn Williams's fragile, intimate drama (the play closely resembles *Menagerie*) into a wide-screen color spectacle. It was a substantial miscalculation, as Bosley Crowther remarks, to visualize this drama of "two psychologically clouded people" in such a fashion: "There was surely no reason for making 'Summer and Smoke' into one of these big pictorial pictures, and there plainly was no artistic point in loading it with scenery and color that are clearly contrary to its mood."[23] But a larger problem was that Williams's tender story of Alma's decline into a sexual purgatory (after strangely effecting John's rehabilitation) seemed out of date in a post-*Psycho* Hollywood more interested in Freudian than moral explanations for human psychopathology.

Nothing makes this point clearer than another, more sensational dramatization of the ruinous effects of sexual repression, which hit American screens in the same season. Working with former Williams collaborator Elia Kazan (who also produced), William Inge seemed for once more in touch than Williams with the times, penning the original screenplay for one of the year's most acclaimed and notorious films, *Splendor in the Grass*. Like Williams's Alma and Blanche, Deanie (Natalie Wood) is a nice girl who runs afoul of the double standard of twentieth-century America's dating culture, which encouraged high school girls to indulge in "petting" in order to keep their boyfriends, but required them to refuse "going all the way." Bud (Warren Beatty) is desperately in love with Deanie, but his businessman father (Pat Hingle) refuses to allow his son to marry early. Following his father's advice, Bud takes up with a more pliant classmate so that he can continue to respect Deanie's virginity. Miserable at this desertion and plagued as well by sexual frustration, Deanie suffers a nervous breakdown (the scene in which she is overwhelmed by hysteria provides the film's most dramatic and affecting moment). Released from the hospital some time later, Deanie, though now involved with a former patient, seeks out Bud, but finds that he is married.

The marketing campaign devised by Kazan for *Splendor in the Grass* was as effective as the one he designed for *Baby Doll*. Aware that a new generation now constituted the bulk of filmgoers, Kazan argued for the current relevance of this portrayal of the tragedies of young love (which had been explored in the teenpic *Blue Denim* a few years before in 1959): "Whether you live in a small town the way they do, or in a city, maybe this is happening to you right now . . . maybe (if you're older) you remember . . . when suddenly the kissing isn't a kid's game any more, suddenly it's wide-eyed and dangerous."[24] Kazan and Inge provide a sensational dramatization of how "dangerous" a game American dating had become, whereas Williams and Glenville in *Summer and Smoke* emphasize the continuing dialogue between the contrasting allegorical (or moral) positions supported by John and Alma, with nothing in the way of affecting spectacle. *Splendor*, Bosley Crowther enthuses, abjures the comforting pieties of the previous decade's family melodrama (in which "sex and parental domineering" had become a common theme) for an innovative anatomizing of the disturbing reality of young romance: "Petting is not simply petting in this embarrassingly intimate film. It is wrestling and chewing and punching that end with clothes torn and participants spent. And boozing is not simply boozing with adults, and also with kids. It is swilling and reeling and hollering and getting disgustingly sick."[25]

Embracing a realism that successfully challenged Hollywood's increasingly old-fashioned approach to representing experience, the European art cinema of the era had already redefined the ways in which romance could be depicted. This was particularly true of the literary adaptations then issuing from independent British studios, a movement soon to be termed the British New Wave. Films like *Room at the Top* (1959) and *Saturday Night, Sunday Morning* (1961) featured steamy, but deliberately deglamorized, treatments of the sexual life. With *Splendor*, Kazan managed to do more of the same, even though, as he acknowledged, he was working with an author who "wrote what seemed like *Ladies' Home Journal* litera-ture," conceding that Inge did work through this banal material in a man-ner "just a little deeper than you expected."[26] Crowther considered that Kazan had made something special from a story and themes that might have been ruined by the kind of studio-era, self-consciously stagy "picto-rialness" Glenville had deployed in screening *Summer and Smoke. Splen-dor*, instead, offered filmgoers a persuasively authentic slice of life: "The torment of two late-adolescents, yearning yet not daring to love, is played against the harsh backdrop of cheapness, obtuseness and hypocrisy."[27]

The directness of Kazan's approach contrasts with Glenville's perhaps excessive reliance on symbolic detail. John's desire to initiate Alma into physicality, for example, is displaced onto the invitation he extends her to attend a cockfight (pun obviously intended). Dressed in an immacu-late, though overly sedate outfit, her restraint and embarrassment defin-ing her as different from the sweaty, excited crowd, Alma is at one point spattered with the blood of a mortally wounded avian combatant. Hor-rified, she flees. This might have been an effective scene in the cinema of sentiment for which classic Hollywood, unable to offer much in the way of sexual display, had been justly famous for decades. But times had changed. Viewers were no longer interested in the kind of allegorized eroticism in which the industry had, since the adoption of the code, been forced to specialize (e.g., the broken-mirror shot in *Streetcar*'s rape scene). Not constrained by the code from frankly representing sexuality, Euro-pean art films, wildly successful in U.S. distribution, had made such dis-placements obsolete, starting a trend that resulted by 1968 in the aban-donment of the code altogether and the institution of the ratings systems overseen by a new body, the Code and Ratings Administration (CARA).

Even producer Wallis's valiant attempt to turn *Summer and Smoke* into a star production with the hiring of one of the era's most desirable leading men misfired. Although just two years earlier he had created an inter-national sensation as the sexy Joe Lampton, who sleeps his way into the upper class in *Room at the Top*, Laurence Harvey proves unable to breathe life into the one-dimensional John Buchanan, a problem for which the writers (James Poe and Meade Roberts, along with Williams) seem more responsible than the actor. In *Room*, director Jack Clayton stages effective bedroom scenes for Harvey to play with international sex kitten Simone Signoret. *Summer and Smoke* provides Harvey with little opportunity of this kind to ply his considerable masculine charms on a much-older Ger-aldine Page, providing an unfortunate contrast between the innovativeness of the British New Wave treatment of the sexual life and the more traditional forms of the sensational to be found in much of early postwar Hollywood cinema, always with more suggestion than display (consider the notorious "swing scene" in *Baby Doll*).

Producer Hal B. Wallis was aware of the romantic mismatch. Earlier in preproduction, he had pushed for a younger, sexier actress. Audrey Hepburn, Eva Marie Saint, and Jean Simmons, all of whom would have been good choices, were considered. Williams, however, was given a voice in the casting, and persuaded the producer to hire Page. It was a fatal miscalculation, even though the talented actress managed to transfer much of her Broadway magic to the screen. An ever-younger cinema audience was more intrigued by the sparks-flying pairing of youngsters Warren Beatty and Natalie Wood in *Splendor*, which was released at more or less the same time and made the Williams film seem even more the relic of a bygone era than it perhaps was.

Williams and the Beginnings of an American Art Cinema

Roman Spring and *Summer and Smoke*, it cannot be denied, are well-crafted, eminently literate productions (directed, tellingly, by theatre hands Peter Glenville and José Quintero, neither of whom was in any sense a Hollywood professional or a European auteur). These films feature bravura performances from two of the period's leading stage actresses (Vivien Leigh and Geraldine Page), and they explore the questions of female sexual desire that had seemed so insistent in an earlier era, when Americans could be genuinely shocked by the revelations about women contained in Kinsey's second, more controversial volume, which was devoted to the habits and proclivities of the gentler sex. Like the fifties Williams films that had done well at the box office and with the industry's critics, *Summer and Smoke* and *Roman Spring* examine issues that remained controversial into the following decade (promiscuity and prostitution chief among them, themes interestingly taken up in *Midnight Cowboy*, the X-rated Best Picture of 1969). But the Williams films were uncritically conventional in ways that did not appeal to the era's filmgoers. Perhaps most importantly, though directed by Europeans, these two films were by no means au courant with the cinematic trends coming from across the Atlantic.

From *And God Created Woman* to *Room at the Top* and *Blow Up*, European films were showing Hollywood one profitable way how to reconnect with its changing audience. Building on its considerable success during the fifties, the European art cinema continued to turn out films that made money and won critical respect in the following decade. At the end of the decade, as historian Peter Lev suggests, "a second path taken by the art film was a move toward American auteurs and American art films," a trend best exemplified by spectacular successes such as Arthur Penn's *Bonnie and Clyde* (1967—from a script originally written with Truffaut and Godard in mind) and *Midnight Cowboy* (1969), directed by British émigré John Schlesinger. John Huston's version of *The Night of the Iguana* is an American art film of this kind. A third development, Lev argues, was "a move toward European-American hybrids, combinations of American and European approaches to filmmaking," an important trend to which Joseph Losey's *Boom!* connected in interesting, though unprofitable, ways.

What Lev calls the "Euro-American" cinema of the period consists of films made in English and featuring both more substantial production values than were generally possible in Europe and also a crew and cast drawn from at least two countries. Such films conform in general to the art cinema model, in that they focus more on character than plot, rely on ambiguous rather than straightforwardly "happy" endings, and emphasize a realistic treatment of milieu and theme, disregarding the simple formulae characteristic of Hollywood production at its most mediocre. But Euro-American films resemble the standard Hollywood product in featuring stars and, at least to some degree, recognizably generic elements; they also tend toward the dramatic rather than the spectacular, but do not entirely eschew the fast-paced action and other forms of visual pleasure and spectacle common to all varieties of the cinema of sentiment. The Euro-American cinema is also, to a large extent, an auteurist cinema; these films are usually "signed," and ask to be read and consumed as expressions of the directors' well-known personal styles and thematic obsessions. Widely distributed and marketed in the manner of the Hollywood product, but aimed at the tastes of more elite viewers, Roman Polanski's *Repulsion* (1965), Michelangelo Antonioni's *Zabriskie Point* (1970), and Bernardo Bertolucci's *Last Tango in Paris* (1972) usefully exemplify the Euro-American film. Stanley Kubrick's *2001: A Space Odyssey* (1969) shows that an American director, albeit self-exiled in England, could also produce a film of thematic ambiguity and complexity. *2001* is a work of Euro-American sensibility that appealed to audiences on a visceral level even as it proved endlessly provocative to the critical establishment, which was only just getting accustomed to films that connected to a traditional genre (science fiction) while also commenting obliquely and perhaps mystically on metaphysics.[28]

A Fuzzy, Unconsummated Work: *Boom!* (1968)

The Euro-American cinema attempted to pull together attractive elements from two separate traditions—indeed from one tradition that took shape in opposition to the other, for the art cinema is largely the "unHollywood," as Steve Neale describes, resulting from "attempts made by a number of European countries both to counter American dominance of their indigenous markets in film and also to foster a film industry of their own."[29] The art cinema, in effect, was the material result of an unconsciously collective drive on the part of several national cinemas at product differentiation as they sought to carve out a niche in domestic and international markets. Such hybrids are notoriously unstable. Joseph Losey's *Boom!* exemplifies the dangers and the difficulties involved, particularly when it came to adapting an eminently theatrical and only minimally realistic property to a tradition in which realism is important. David Bordwell suggests that the deployment of "psychologically complex characters" is of paramount importance in the art cinema, but this was something that Williams's *Milk Train*, with its strange mixture of Christian symbolism and Greek mythology (reminiscent of *Orpheus*), could not supply.[30]

It may be, as Gene Phillips suggests, that *Milk Train* is one of the playwright's "least accessible" works as a result of its often confusingly invoked intellectual frames.[31] And so the play, reviewer Vincent Canby accurately noted, is even in its final dramatic form (the result of myriad revisions) "a fuzzy unconsummated work caught like so many of the playwright's heros [*sic*], midway between a real world and a symbolic one."[32] As a result, the major problem the property posed to its adaptors (a typically Euro-American production consortium including John Heyman Productions, Moon Lake, Universal Pictures, and World Film Services) was its rejection of realism. Early in the production, Losey wrote to Williams, suggesting that it might be filmed in Lipari, Italy: "I do feel strongly that the picture ought to have an unreal quality and [that it ought] to be shot in a place not immediately identifiable, and quite eerie, unfamiliar and vaguely frightening."[33] Though *Milk Train* failed miserably in a Broadway production in 1963, Williams still had enough mus-

Flora Goforth (Elizabeth Taylor) beckons Chris Flanders (Richard Burton) on the striking set of Boom! *Photo courtesy of The Historic New Orleans Collection.*

cle in the commercial theatre to have a revised production mounted the following year, based on a substantially revised play text. It seems true enough, as critic Howard Taubman observed at the time, that Williams intended the play as "an allegory on man's need for someone to mean God to him." But, in giving prominence to this symbolic level (enhanced by director Tony Richardson's extremely stylized production), Williams, to quote Taubman again, "abandoned the realism and literalism" of the original version in an attempt, mostly unsuccessful, to "evoke the mood and implications of parable."[34]

Milk Train is correspondingly thin on plot, even for a Williams play, consisting of little more than a continuing dialogue, at times contentious, at times interestingly filled with theological and psychological speculation, between a rich, older woman, Flora Goforth, who inhabits a magnificent hilltop villa on the Italian Mediterranean, and a young interloper, Christopher Flanders, who has mysteriously made his way to her. Dying from some unnamed condition, Flora is obsessed with writing her memoirs, apparently in a self-deluded attempt to postpone her imminent demise, until this unusual houseguest appears. Though he is a handsome, vital young man, Flanders bears the nickname "Angel of Death" because, as he later reveals, he characteristically seeks out dying, older women (always rich) who have lived immorally. Part confessor, part tempter, part bearer of the message that salvation or deliverance of some kind awaits those who confront the sinfulness of their lives, Christ(opher) preaches the obliquely theistic admonition that one and all should be resigned to the inevitable. As death comes closer, Flora reluctantly accepts the vague consolation he has to offer.

Confusingly, Christopher also appears to be a two-dimensional character in the mold of *Roman Spring*'s Paolo, a hustler and parasite who lives off the hospitality and good graces of the rich women he seeks out. As in *Summer and Smoke*, this character, representing the contradictory impulses of the flesh and the spirit, is more allegory than substance, and he simply fails to come alive on stage. Loud-mouthed, coarse, and yet filled sympathetically with existential angst, Flora, in contrast, is perhaps one of Williams's most interesting creations, and the few encounters with other characters that round out the drama are dominated by the sheer force of her personality. Yet an ebullient and complex Flora was not enough to sustain a full-length drama that, as Howard Taubman conceded, may have been "lightfingered and imaginative," but not enough to compensate for what he called the play's "disappointing substance."[35] The interesting May-December pairing of old Broadway hand Tallulah Bankhead and juvenile heartthrob Tab Hunter could not save a doomed play. *Milk Train* closed after an embarrassingly swift five performances, not making it into a second week.

Such was Williams's bankability in Hollywood, however, that he still managed to sell the film rights to Universal Pictures, with associate producer Lester Persky acting as the impresario for what the playwright hoped would be the cinematic redemption of a play in which he still had confidence. Joseph Losey was signed early to direct, and he seemed enthusiastic about the property, largely because of the opportunity to adapt the work of a famous playwright (much of his success earlier in the decade had come through a series of extraordinary collaborations with Harold Pinter).[36] Persky, Williams wrote his agent at the time, wants "an art-film that will also be commercial . . . the vital thing is to have no studio interference."[37] And the contract indeed provided him and Losey with a free hand that would have been unthinkable only a decade earlier. Williams would do the script, consulting with the director, while much else would be left to their discretion and professional judgment: "All decisions and approvals regarding stars, feature players, sets, etc. shall be made jointly by Losey and Williams."[38] Persky, Losey, and Williams put together what was indeed an impressive package, signing two of the era's hottest stars to play the leads: Elizabeth Taylor as Flora and Richard Burton as Christopher. Though such casting obviously vitiated the play's central contrast between an older, dying Flora and a young and vital Christopher (at the time of the film's release, Burton was in his early forties and Taylor was just a few years his junior), in the absence of a presold property, such stars were deemed necessary to secure financing. In fact, even with Losey directing a Williams property, and the promised participation of world cinema's most notorious battling couple, raising production funds took more than two years. With location shooting, star salaries, and large amounts to be paid to the director and screenwriter, *Boom!* was an expensive production, finally costing more than $10 million.[39]

The result was a strangely incongruous mixture of styles and modes, a star vehicle that offered little more than an intellectual and a spiritual confrontation between Flora and Christopher, neither of whom was very knowable or sympathetic. In the initial treatment he provided Losey, Williams recognized this problem, but thought it could be overcome: "The film is more verbal than has been the fashion with films lately, but I feel that the dialogue of the duel between Flora Goforth and Chris Flanders with strong casting of the roles would catch and hold an audience with its continual and increasing tension."[40] Few successful films, however, can be sustained by a 120-minute verbal battle, and *Boom!* proved no exception to the general rule, despite Losey's frantic blocking on a capacious and intriguingly designed interior set. The problem with the representational mode, however, was even more serious. Especially in its last Broadway form, which Williams used as the basis for his screenplay, *Boom!* is an eminently theatrical piece, best rendered, as Tony Richardson had done on Broadway,[41] with antirealistic stylizations in acting, costuming, and staging. Transferred to an intractably realistic medium (the film's beautiful Sardinia locations are lovingly evoked in Douglas Slocombe's color cinematography), much of its visual program makes no sense or is simply risible. Richard Burton at one point dons what Flora identifies as an "authentic Samurai costume," replete with sword, looking the perfect fool as he tries to make a series of philosophical points. Elizabeth Taylor manages very well to be a petulant bitch goddess, ordering servants around with a voice like fingernails scratching a blackboard, but she seems unable to bear up under the film's allegorical program, hardly fulfilling Williams's expectations that the play is meant to evoke the universal human condition in the manner of the medieval *Everyman*.

But Williams was pleased. He had finally had a chance, after years of what he saw retrospectively as disastrous compromises, to make a film using his own script. He was working with a world-renowned, intellectually minded director sympathetic to his talent and eminence, and he had been able to make, or at least strongly influence, all important production decisions. The campy casting of Noel Coward as the "Witch of Capri," one of Flora's decadently rich neighbors, certainly seems like a Williams touch; no other Losey film features anything similar. *Boom!* was as personal a big-budget film as Williams, or any other writer, would ever have the chance to participate in during the era. A first viewing left him close to ecstatic. Williams wired Losey to express his deep satisfaction: "Have just seen the film and am totally delighted with it / Each shot is like a fabulous painting / There was quite enough dialogue . . . I am very grateful to you Joe / This is the best film ever made of my work and if God is provident we will work together again."[42] Such a judgment shows how much Williams at this point was out of touch with what filmgoers at the time might have found appealing.

In the late sixties, Euro-American and homegrown auteurist films did excellent box office when they satisfied the tastes of the youthful, educated segment of the declining moviegoing audience. These viewers were eager for the sensational and the engagingly countercultural, and they were not averse to a well-developed intellectual theme. Two of the top grossing films of 1968 were Roman Polanski's *Rosemary's Baby* (a complex homage to Hitchcock's *Psycho*, Clouzot's *Diabolique*, and the low-budget supernatural thriller that had been made popular in the era by such directors as Roger Corman and Mario Bava) and Mike Nichols's *The Graduate*, which popularized for American audiences the ebullient stylizations of the French New Wave. *Boom!* in contrast, as Losey pointed out years later, is "slightly necrophilic," while "everything that went into it is very old." Moreover, if audiences found the film confusing, so did its director: "I would be hard put to it to say what it's about."[43]

Critical reaction was negative. Vincent Canby found little good to say about the production, and he spoke for the majority: "The fey, black fairy tale, which still has no real confrontations or dramatic progression, is overwhelmed by the sheer physical presences of everything from the locale . . . to the shadowy awareness of a bunch of monolithic stone heads, apparently borrowed from Easter Island, which litter an adjoining hillside . . . the movie is essentially the sort that Baby Doll would have hitched a ride into Blue Mountain to see—a tale of the very-very rich that tells the miserable critters in Dogpatch that money can't buy happiness."[44] Williams was correct when he told Losey that the audience he was envisioning was "craving for something else," but at the dawn of the youth-film breakthrough in the late sixties, that something else was not a grim, confusing tale of an older, unsympathetic woman preparing for her imminent demise.[45] Why did one of the international art cinema's leading figures involve himself in a project he should have known was bound for box-office disaster? Losey offered Michel Ciment a clue: "There was a certain amount of opportunism involved in making it. It comes into that category of films of which there are not very many, that have been brought to me. I didn't go looking for it."[46]

No Betrayal of Despair: *The Night of the Iguana* (1964)

Boom! demonstrated beyond any reasonable doubt that the kind of theatre to which Williams became increasingly attracted during the sixties was not likely to find much success on the screen, even if adapted in the Euro-American fashion and under the close supervision of the playwright. But Williams did see produced earlier in the decade a play that suited perfectly the requirements of the international art cinema as it was being accommodated to American audiences by homegrown directors. *The Night of the Iguana* anticipates the spiritual, vaguely religious themes that dominate *Milk Train*; here, too, Williams concerns himself with the need to meet death bravely, to draw comfort from others, to push beyond simple understandings of the conflict between flesh and spirit. But *Iguana* was no simple philosophical-mystical tract. With its quartet of finely drawn characters, audiences could, as Gene Phillips suggests, overlook the play's religious implications, since there were "enough melodramatic elements . . . to hold their attention."[47] Upon its Broadway opening late in 1961, *Iguana* struck New York critics as a welcome, new direction for Williams's theatre, working, according to Howard Taubman, a deep change in the "tone of the Broadway season," which thereby "gain[ed] greatly in quality." Here was a play that abandoned the "explosive and shocking gestures" of the playwright's earlier successes and turned the stage into a place "where the sources of man's nature may be explored with boldness and wonder."[48] Williams concurred with such judgments. He commented to an interviewer at the time: "I didn't feel like writing a 'black play.'"[49]

The setting is simple: a broken-down, off-the-beaten-path Mexican seaside hotel, where, having come to the ends of their lines in various ways, are a defrocked Episcopal minister, T. Lawrence Shannon, who is in the process of failing at his job of last resort, conducting guided tours for American Baptist ladies; an aged poet, Nonno, working on his final poem, accompanied by his granddaughter Hannah, a forty-year-old spinster who supports the pair by selling caricatures and drawings to tourists; Maxine, a blowsy, middle-aged widow lady, who owns the establishment and entertains herself with a pair of local beach boys.[50] Two of Shannon's erstwhile clients complicate his attempts to escape from the existential trap to which his sexual weakness has brought him: Charlotte, the young girl whom he, offering but an ineffective protest, allows to seduce him; and Miss Fellowes, a tightly wound lesbian school-marm, who is officiously obsessed with protecting Charlotte from a man she sees as a ruthless predator.

Brought together by accident, these characters provide one another with spiritual companionship and understanding, leading to a series of more or less happily resolved endings. Nonno finishes his magnum opus (which, in part, celebrates a nature that countenances "no betrayal of despair"), and dies, to be buried by the sea he had always loved. Hannah determines to carry on, reaffirmed in her knowledge that the future, however uncertain and apparently unpromising, must be faced with equanimity. Learning from Hannah to be tolerant of his own weakness and accept the fleshly part (the "spook") of his nature, Shannon emerges from a deep psychological crisis (at one point he is tied up by Hannah and Maxine so he can do himself no harm) to accept the possibility of a new life with Maxine. As Taubman puts it, in *Iguana* Williams declares "his respect for those who have to fight for their bit of decency."[51] Like Shannon, the iguana of the play's title is also bound so that it can be fattened up before being slaughtered for a tasty meal. After Hannah releases the ropes than bind him to the hammock, Shannon cuts loose the lizard in a gesture that provides a fitting correlative for the play's commitment to freedom and deliverance.

If lacking the energetic, forward-moving plot and focus on romance that was thought necessary in the standard Hollywood product, *Iguana* lent itself to being reworked with relative ease into a profitable and artistically successful art film. Crucial was the play's focus on an anguished

In this scene from The Night of the Iguana, *Maxine Faulk (Ava Gardner) and Lawrence Shannon (Richard Burton) accept a compromised version of happiness. Photo courtesy of The Historic New Orleans Collection.*

male, the Reverend Shannon, who could readily be transformed into the main character—and was. Typically male (consider the major films of Truffaut, Godard, Bergman, Fellini, and Antonioni), the art-film protagonist provides the structural frame for the narrative, especially if, as in the case of *Iguana*, it is devoted principally to tracing his biography, which means that, to quote David Bordwell, "events become pared down toward a picaresque successivity." This is fitting because, as Bordwell goes on to suggest, "characters of the classical narrative have clear-cut traits and objectives, [while] the characters of the art cinema lack defined desires and goals." Such formlessness gives them the representational space in which to "express and explain their psychological states," which Hannah (Deborah Kerr), Lawrence (Richard Burton), and Maxine (Ava Gardner) do at affecting length, spending a long night of the soul together in which they separately and together confront the largest of questions: how to live beyond despair. At the end, the ethereal Hannah is bravely confirmed in her self-containment, while Maxine and Shannon agree to the exploration of a life together (in a rewritten, somewhat "happy" ending confected by director and screenwriter).

If Bordwell is correct that in the art cinema, "characters and their effects on one another remain central," then *Iguana* nicely exemplifies the type.[52] The adaptation did not attempt to confect plot elements to stretch out what on stage was essentially an extended talkfest, but, instead, added episodes to deepen the portrayal of Shannon's fall from grace and inability to resist the advances of lustful young women.[53] Almost the first third of the film was added by experienced screenwriter Anthony Veiller, with the close collaboration of Huston, but the narrative of how Shannon manages to wind up in Maxine's hotel with a passel of angry tourists simply expands on the backstory presented in the original stage dialogue, remaining faithful to Williams's conception. Bosley Crowther, however, complained that the film, like its source, fails to explain its characters adequately: "But who are these dislocated wanderers? From what Freudian cell have they been sprung, and why are they so aggressive in punching their loneliness home to the world? These are the basic revelations that are not communicated by the film, which follows fairly closely the dialogic substance of the play."[54]

Though an avid fan of the international art cinema, Crowther here judges *Iguana* as if it were a standard Hollywood product, committed to characters who, as Bordwell puts it, possess "clear-cut traits and objectives." However anatomized at length and provided with episodic narratives that require them constantly to adjust to changing circumstances, characters in the art cinema always "lack defined desires and goals." We never discover "who they are." Bordwell sees this vagueness or unknowability as essential to what art films of the period, made under the spell of existentialism, always have to say about human experience, which is nothing less than to "pronounce judgments on 'modern life' as a whole": "During the film's survey of its world, the hero often shudders on the edge of breakdown. There recurs the realization of the anguish of ordinary living, the discovery of unrelieved misery."[55] Under Huston's skillful direction, and working with a fine script that remains true to the spirit of Williams's conception, the film provides what Howard Taubman terms "the tender, futile gropings of its characters" and the struggle of Hannah, Maxine, and Shannon to "slash the rope that tethers them to their grim, lonely destinies."[56] Arguably, no other Williams property lent itself so readily to the art cinema's commitment to explore (but never explain or explain away) the experience of those shuddering "on the edge of breakdown."

I'll Get You Back Up, Baby

It was a happy accident that Williams wrote a play that perfectly fit the qualities of the art film precisely at the moment when what we might call the first wave of an emergent American art cinema was gathering commercial momentum. Ray Stark played a central role in packaging the project, and that proved crucial to the film's success. Stark represented Seven Arts Productions, which he had formed in 1957 with fellow producer Eliot Hyman, and Seven Arts was particularly interested in turning Broadway hits and other literary properties into films that were a cut above ordinary Hollywood entertainment. In July 1962, Seven Arts announced an unusual agreement with MGM to coproduce and cofinance as many as twenty feature films over the next five or six years. Several of these were, interestingly enough, to be produced first by the noted David Merrick on stage, and only then, having earned their presold bona fides, to be made into films. To acquire properties with proven appeal to the educated and sophisticated, Seven Arts thus connected the theatre and the Hollywood cinema in a fashion never attempted before or since, at least on this scale.[57] Part of this deal was the signing of John Huston in July of the following year to a three-film agreement. Huston would direct the adaptation of an honored (even if not well-known property), Rudyard Kipling's fable of the discontents of British colonialism, "The Man Who Would Be King," a project that the director had been planning for nearly a decade. The resulting film, released many years later in 1975, is acknowledged as one of Huston's finest. For Seven Arts, he would mount another literary adaptation, bringing to the screen Brian Moore's novel about the drab existence of a middle-aged piano teacher, *The Lonely Passion of Judith Hearne* (Huston was later replaced on this project by Jack Clayton).

The Night of the Iguana was the third film in the deal and the only one to be realized quickly and without difficulty. It proved an immense success both with filmgoers and, Bosley Crowther's misguided caviling aside, with the critical establishment as well. If Williams really felt that *Boom!* was "the best film made of my work," *Iguana* is arguably the most artistically successful film made from his works (more critically acclaimed and of more significance to Hollywood history, *Streetcar* nevertheless is essentially a filmed play). As a sophisticated exploration of American modernity and its discontents, it anticipates the more celebrated works of that second wave of auteurs, the directors of the Hollywood Renaissance in the late sixties and early seventies. Probably too ambitious, the overall aim of Seven Arts to form an intimate, enduring connection between the theatre and Hollywood was not to be realized except for the remarkably profitable eleven films that Stark made from various Neil Simon properties, including the celebrated *The Goodbye Girl* (1977), *The Sunshine Boys* (1975), *California Suite* (1978), and other plays such as *Funny Girl* (1968). But Stark showed wisdom and sound judgment in assigning the project of making *Iguana* to the finest literary adaptor of the era. Who else can claim to have filmed, often with great success, works by Stephen Crane, Herman Melville, James Joyce, Rudyard Kipling, Carson McCullers, and Flannery O'Connor?

Stark may have sensed more than a commercial opportunity in pairing Huston with Williams. The main themes of the stage *Iguana*, Lesley Brill suggests, "are among Huston's lifelong preoccupations": "people who have reached the end of their emotional endurance, the necessity to confront one's own weakness, the equivocal connections between love and sex, people's desperate need to make a place for themselves in the world and among other people."[58] Many of Huston's films, like many of Williams's plays, end with images of failure: the meticulously planned robbery in *The Asphalt Jungle* (1950), which results in the death or imprisonment of all the highly skilled criminals involved; the loss of the gold gained at such terrible cost in *The Treasure of the Sierra Madre* (1947); Sam Spade's decision to turn over his untrustworthy beloved to the police at the end of *The Maltese Falcon* (1941); the realization by the boxers in *Fat City* (1972) that they will never be more than third-rate; the failure of the two adventurers to hold onto their conquest in *The Man Who Would Be King* (1975); and the destruction of the entire whaling crew, except one, in *Moby-Dick* (1956). And yet Huston, like Williams, never underemphasized that, in confronting their own weaknesses and the seemingly insuperable vagaries of existence, his protagonists might find a triumph of sorts.

In fact, in all of the films just named, there are characters who in failure somehow manage to find something of what they are looking for, who beat the odds despite a deck stacked against them. Much the same may be said of the sad, alienated, rootless malcontents who populate the theatre of Tennessee Williams. For all the images of terrible decline and destruction that they offer (the erstwhile deliverer Val burned alive, Blanche victimized by her own delusions and a hard-hearted reality, Chance suffering a well-deserved castration, Alma losing dignity and self-respect), Williams, like Huston, held out the possibility of transcendence, the bare shred of hope that all might be put right. We have only to think of Laura's hard-won self-knowledge, Catherine's serum-induced narration of Sebastian's dark night of the soul, Big Daddy's coming to terms with his mortality, and Nonno's perseverance, rewarded with the beauty of that final poem, which, like much of what Williams wrote, is a prayer for courage in a darkening world. As we saw in the case of *Cat* and *Sweet Bird*, if Hollywood chose to emphasize the positive aspects of Williams's theatre, these transformations were often subtle changes in tone more than explicit statements of the playwright's ultimate optimism about human experience. In the films, "the long delayed but always expected something we live for" undoubtedly takes more concrete and unambiguous shape in order to please audiences used to happy endings or, in the art cinema, a meaningful resolution. Nonetheless, the expectation of deliverance belongs to Williams; the hope for a better, brighter world that suffuses his early theatre is his own.

Speaking of the adaptation of *Iguana*, Maurice Yacowar expresses the contrary view, observing that: "John Huston has always expressed a more robust spirit than Williams has, a vision less bleakly in line with defeat and destruction and one where the joys of life and the quest make up for loss and defeat."[59] In response, we would point to the ending of Huston's *Iguana*, which alters the original only slightly in order to provide the sense that the characters, while not delivered to what would in the 1940s have been termed a happy ending, are now able to glimpse clearly a future in which their isolation and emotional poverty might end. The play ends with Shannon's agreement to make himself the object of the desire Maxine has always felt for him—and with Hannah, left alone with Nonno's corpse, momentarily bewildered about what path to take. In the film, these two sequences are reversed and their sense of irresolution removed: Hannah's courageous departure for parts unknown (after a gracious refusal to accept Shannon as a traveling partner) is followed by a scene in which Shannon accepts Maxine's offer to stay and help run the hotel. She suggests that they share a swim before embarking on this new life together (a connection that may, but need not, be romantic; in any case, the water is archetypically life affirming, whereas earlier in the play and film, the ocean is the site of Shannon's would-be suicide). Shannon admits that he could descend the hill to the beach, but would be unable to climb back up to the hotel. The film ends with Maxine's response: "I'll get you back up, baby. I'll always get you back up." If this double entendre of comradeship is thoroughly Hustonian, it also fulfills the commitment of Williams in this play, as Howard Taubman puts it, to "transcend the raging pessimism that has permeated so much of his work."[60] In the postwar era, Hollywood did much to further that project, which was, in the playwright's own words, to dramatize the lives of characters "who are learning to reach the point of utter despair and still go past it with courage."[61]

Appendix A
Filmography with Principal Cast Members

The Glass Menagerie, 1950
United States
PRODUCTION: Charles K. Feldman Group
PRODUCERS: Charles K. Feldman and Jerry Wald
DISTRIBUTION: Warner Bros., Twentieth-Century Fox Film Corp.
DIRECTION: Irving Rapper
SCREENPLAY: Peter Berneis, Tennessee Williams
PHOTOGRAPHY: Robert Burks
EDITING: Dave Weisbart
MUSIC: Max Steiner
ASSISTANT DIRECTION: Joseph Don Page
COSTUME DESIGN: Milo Anderson
SOUND EDITING: Oliver S. Garretson
CAST: Amanda Wingfield (Gertrude Lawrence), Tom Wingfield (Arthur Kennedy), Laura Wingfield (Jane Wyman), Jim O'Connor (Kirk Douglas)
B/W
107 Minutes
AVAILABILITY: (VHS—very limited availability)

A Streetcar Named Desire, 1951
United States
PRODUCTION: Charles K. Feldman Group, Warner Bros.
PRODUCERS: Charles K. Feldman
DISTRIBUTION: Warner Bros.
DIRECTION: Elia Kazan
SCREENPLAY: Tennessee Williams, Oscar Saul (adaptation)

PHOTOGRAPHY: Harry Stradling
EDITING: David Weisbart
MUSIC: Alex North
ASSISTANT DIRECTION: Joseph Don Page
COSTUME DESIGN: Lucinda Ballard
SOUND EDITING: C. A. Riggs
CAST: Blanche DuBois (Vivien Leigh), Stanley Kowalski (Marlon Brando), Stella Kowalski (Kim Hunter), Mitch (Karl Malden), Steve (Rudy Bond), Pablo (Nick Dennis), Eunice (Peg Hillias)
B/W
122 minutes (125 minutes, rerelease)
AVAILABILITY: Warner Home Video (DVD)

The Rose Tattoo, 1955
United States
PRODUCTION: Paramount Pictures
PRODUCERS: Hal B. Wallis
DISTRIBUTION: Paramount Pictures
DIRECTION: Daniel Mann
SCREENPLAY: Tennessee Williams, Hal Kanter (adaptation)
PHOTOGRAPHY: James Wong Howe
EDITING: Warren Low
MUSIC: Jack Brooks, Alex North, Harry Warren
ASSISTANT DIRECTION: Richard McWhorter
COSTUME DESIGN: Edith Head
SOUND EDITING: Bill Wistrom
CAST: Serafina Delle Rose (Anna Magnani), Alvaro Mangiacavallo (Burt Lancaster), Rosa (Marisa Pavan), Jack Hunter (Ben Cooper), Estelle Hohengarten (Virginia Grey), Bessie (Jo Van Fleet), Father De Leo (Sandro Giglio), Assunta (Mimi Aguglia), Flora (Florence Sundstrom)
B/W
117 minutes
AVAILABILITY: DVD

Baby Doll, 1956
United States
PRODUCTION: Newtown Productions
PRODUCERS: Elia Kazan and Tennessee Williams
DISTRIBUTION: Warner Bros. Pictures
DIRECTION: Elia Kazan
SCREENPLAY: Tennessee Williams

PHOTOGRAPHY: Boris Kauffman
EDITING: Gene Milford
MUSIC: Kenyon Hopkins
ASSISTANT DIRECTION: Jack Garfein, Charles H. Maguire
COSTUME DESIGN: Anna Hill Johnstone
SOUND EDITING: Edward J. Johnstone
CAST: Baby Doll Meighan (Carroll Baker), Archie Lee Meighan (Karl Malden), Silva Vacarro (Eli Wallach), Aunt Rose Comfort (Mildred Dunnock), Rock (Lonny Chapman)
B/W
114 minutes
AVAILABILITY: Warner Home Video (DVD)

Cat on a Hot Tin Roof, 1958
United States
PRODUCTION: MGM
PRODUCER: Lawrence Weingarten
DISTRIBUTION: MGM
DIRECTION: Richard Brooks
SCREENPLAY: Richard Brooks and James Poe
PHOTOGRAPHY: William H. Daniels
EDITING: Ferris Webster
MUSIC: Charles Wolcott
ASSISTANT DIRECTION: William Shanks
COSTUME DESIGN: Helen Rose
SOUND EDITING: Van Allen James
CAST: Margaret Pollitt (Elizabeth Taylor), Brick Pollitt (Paul Newman), Big Daddy Pollitt (Burl Ives), Big Mama Pollitt (Judith Anderson), Mae Pollitt (Madeline Sherwood), Gooper Pollitt (Jack Carson), Dr. Baugh (Larry Gates)
Color
108 minutes
AVAILABILITY: Warner Home Video (DVD)

The Fugitive Kind, 1959
United States
PRODUCTION: Pennebaker Productions, United Artists
PRODUCERS: Martin Jurow and Richard Shepherd
DISTRIBUTION: United Artists
DIRECTION: Sidney Lumet
SCREENPLAY: Tennessee Williams and Meade Roberts

PHOTOGRAPHY: Boris Kauffman
EDITING: Carl Lerner
MUSIC: Kenyon Hopkins
ASSISTANT DIRECTION: Charles H. Maguire
COSTUME DESIGN: Frank L. Thompson
SOUND EDITING: James Gleason
CAST: Valentine Xavier (Marlon Brando), Lady Torrance (Anna Magnani), Carol Cutrere (Joanne Woodward), Vee Talbot (Maureen Stapleton), Jabe Torrance (Victor Jory), Sheriff Talbot (R. G. Armstrong)
B/W
119 minutes
AVAILABILITY: DVD

Suddenly, Last Summer, 1959
United States
PRODUCTION: Academy Productions, Camp Productions, Columbia Pictures Corp., Horizon Films
PRODUCER: Sam Spiegel
DISTRIBUTION: Columbia Pictures
DIRECTION: Joseph L. Mankiewicz
SCREENPLAY: Gore Vidal and Tennessee Williams
PHOTOGRAPHY: Jack Hildyard
PRODUCTION DESIGN: Oliver Messel
EDITING: William Hornbeck and Thomas Stanford
MUSIC: Malcom Arnold and Buxton Orr
ASSISTANT DIRECTION: Bluey Hill
COSTUME DESIGN: Norman Hartnell, Jean Louis, and Oliver Messel
SOUND EDITING: Peter Thornton
CAST: Catherine Holly (Elizabeth Taylor), Violet Venable (Katharine Hepburn), Dr. Cukrowicz (Montgomery Clift), Grace Holly (Mercedes McCambridge), George Holly (Gary Raymond), Miss Foxhill (Mavis Villiers), Sister Felicity (Joan Young)
B/W
114 minutes
AVAILABILITY: Columbia TriStar Home Video (VHS, DVD)

Summer and Smoke, 1961
United States
PRODUCTION: Hal Wallis Productions
PRODUCER: Hal B. Wallis
DISTRIBUTION: Paramount Pictures

DIRECTION: Peter Glenville
SCREENPLAY: James Poe and Mead Roberts
PHOTOGRAPHY: Charles Lang Jr.
EDITING: Warren Low
MUSIC: Elmer Bernstein
ASSISTANT DIRECTION: Michael Moore and James Rosenberger
COSTUME DESIGN: Edith Head
SOUND EDITING: Charles Grenzbach
CAST: Alma Winemiller (Geraldine Page), John Buchanan, Jr. (Laurence
    Harvey), Rosa Zacharias (Rita Moreno), Mrs. Winemiller (Una Merkel),
    Dr. Buchanan (John McIntire), Papa Zacharias (Thomas Gomez), Rev.
    Winemiller (Malcom Atterbury), Nellie Ewell (Pamela Tiffin)
Color
118 minutes
AVAILABILITY: Paramount Home Video (VHS)

The Roman Spring of Mrs. Stone, 1961
UK
PRODUCTION: A. A. Productions, Seven Arts Pictures,
    Warner Bros. Pictures
PRODUCER: Louis De Rochemont
DISTRIBUTION: Warner Bros. Pictures
DIRECTION: José Quintero
SCREENPLAY: Gavin Lambert
PHOTOGRAPHY: Harry Waxman
PRODUCTION DESIGN: Roger K. Furse
EDITING: Ralph Kemplen
MUSIC: Richard Addinsell
ASSISTANT DIRECTION: Peter Yates
COSTUME DESIGN: Pierre Balmain and Beatrice Dawson
SOUND EDITING: Keith Batten, Leslie Hodgson, and Cecil Mason
CAST: Karen Stone (Vivien Leigh), Paolo di Leo (Warren Beatty), Contessa
    (Lotte Lenya), Meg (Coral Browne), Barbara Bingham (Jill St. John)
Color
103 minutes
AVAILABILITY: Warner Home Video (DVD)

Sweet Bird of Youth, 1962
United States
PRODUCTION: Roxbury Productions Inc.
PRODUCER: Pandro S. Berman

DISTRIBUTION: MGM
DIRECTION: Richard Brooks
SCREENPLAY: Richard Books
PHOTOGRAPHY: Milton Krasner
PRODUCTION DESIGN: Kathryn Hereford
EDITING: Henry Berman
MUSIC: James Rox
ASSISTANT DIRECTION: Hank Moonjean
COSTUME DESIGN: Orry-Kelly
SOUND EDITING: Franklin Milton
CAST: Chance Wayne (Paul Newman), Alexandra Del Lago (Geraldine Page), Heavenly Finley (Shirley Knight), Boss Finley (Ed Begley), Tom Finley, Jr. (Rip Torn), Aunt Nonnie (Mildred Dunnock), Dr. George Scudder (Philip Abbott)
Color
120 minutes
AVAILABILITY: Warner Home Video (DVD)

Period of Adjustment, 1962
United States
PRODUCTION: MGM
PRODUCER: Lawrence Weingarten
DISTRIBUTION: MGM
DIRECTION: George Roy Hill
SCREENPLAY: Isobel Lennart
PHOTOGRAPHY: Paul Vogel
EDITING: Frederic Steinkamp
MUSIC: Lyn Murray
ASSISTANT DIRECTION: Al Jennings
SOUND EDITING: Franklin Milton
CAST: Ralph Baitz (Tony Franciosa), Isabel Haverstick (Jane Fonda), George Haverstick (Jim Hutton), Dorothea Baitz (Lois Nettleton), Stewart McGill (John McGiver) Mrs. Alice McGill (Mabel Albertson)
B/W
112 minutes
AVAILABILITY: VHS

The Night of the Iguana, 1964
United States
PRODUCTION: MGM, Seven Arts Productions
PRODUCERS: John Huston and Ray Stark

DISTRIBUTION: MGM
DIRECTION: John Huston
SCREENPLAY: John Huston and Anthony Veiller
PHOTOGRAPHY: Gabriel Figueroa
PRODUCTION DESIGN: Clarence Eurist (production manager)
EDITING: Ralph Kemplen
MUSIC: Benjamin Frankel
ASSISTANT DIRECTION: Tom Shaw
COSTUME DESIGN: Dorothy Jeakins
SOUND EDITING: Van Allen James
CAST: Rev. T. Lawrence Shannon (Richard Burton), Maxine Faulk (Ava
    Gardner), Hannah Jelkes (Deborah Kerr), Charlotte Goodall (Sue Lyon),
    Judith Fellowes (Grayson Hall), Nonno (Cyril Delevanti), Hank (Skip Ward)
B/W
125 minutes
AVAILABILITY: Warner Home Video (DVD)

This Property Is Condemned, 1966
United States
PRODUCTION: Paramount Pictures, Seven Arts Productions
PRODUCERS: John Houseman and Ray Stark
DISTRIBUTION: Paramount Pictures
DIRECTION: Sydney Pollack
SCREENPLAY: Francis Ford Coppola, Fred Coe, David Rayfiel, and Edith R.
    Sommer
PHOTOGRAPHY: James Wong Howe
PRODUCTION DESIGNER: Stephen Grimes
EDITING: Adrienne Fazan
MUSIC: Kenyon Hopkins
ASSISTANT DIRECTION: Eddie Saeta
SOUND EDITING: Charles Grenzbach and Paul K. Lerpae
CAST: Alva Starr (Natalie Wood), Owen Legate (Robert Redford), J. J. Nichols
    (Charles Bronson), Hazel Starr (Kate Reid), Willie Starr (Mary Badham)
Color
110 minutes
AVAILABILITY: Paramount Pictures (DVD)

Boom! 1968
UK
PRODUCTION: John Heyman Productions, Moon Lake,
    Universal Pictures, World Film Services

PRODUCER: John Heyman
DISTRIBUTION: Rank Film Distributors Ltd., Universal Pictures
DIRECTION: Joseph Losey
SCREENPLAY: Tennessee Williams
PHOTOGRAPHY: Douglas Slocombe
PRODUCTION DESIGN: Richard MacDonald
EDITING: Reginald Beck
MUSIC: John Barry
ASSISTANT DIRECTION: Carlo Lastricati
COSTUME DESIGN: Valentino
SOUND EDITING: Gerry Humphreys
CAST: Flora Goforth (Elizabeth Taylor), Chris Flanders (Richard Burton), Witch of Capri (Noel Coward), Miss Black (Joanna Shimkus), Rudi (Michael Dunn)
Color
113 minutes
AVAILABILITY: VHS

The Last of the Mobile Hot-Shots, 1970
United States
PRODUCTION: Warner Bros.
PRODUCER: Sidney Lumet
DISTRIBUTION: Warner Bros.
DIRECTION: Sidney Lumet
SCREENPLAY: Gore Vidal
PHOTOGRAPHY: James Wong Howe
PRODUCTION DESIGN: Gene Callahan
EDITING: Alan Heim
MUSIC: Quincy Jones
ASSISTANT DIRECTION: Burtt Harris
COSTUME DESIGN: Patricia Zippprodt
CAST: Jeb (James Coburn), Myrtle (Lynn Redgrave), Chicken (Robert Hooks)
Color
100 minutes
AVAILABILITY: VHS

Appendix B
Select Small-Screen and Television Productions, with Principal Cast Members

Note: For more complete (and constantly changing) listings, as well as full casts, consult the Internet Movie Database (imdb.com).

Television (U.S. and UK)

The Roman Spring of Mrs. Stone (2003). Dir.: Robert Allan Ackerman
   Helen Mirren (Karen Stone), Oliver Martinez (Paolo), Anne Bancroft (Contessa), Brian Dennehy (Tom Stone)

A Streetcar Named Desire (1998). Opera. Dir.: Kirk Browning
   Renée Fleming (Blanche), Rodney Gilfry (Stanley)

A Streetcar Named Desire (1995). Dir.: Glenn Jordan
   Alec Baldwin (Stanley), Jessica Lange (Blanche), John Goodman (Mitch)

Suddenly, Last Summer (1993). Dir.: Richard Eyre
   Maggie Smith (Violet), Natasha Richardson (Catharine), Rob Lowe (Dr. Cukrowicz) (UK)

Orpheus Descending (1990). Dir.: Peter Hall
   Kevin Anderson (Val), Vanessa Redgrave (Lady)

Sweet Bird of Youth (1989). Dir.: Nicholas Roeg
   Elizabeth Taylor (Princess), Mark Harmon (Chance)

Cat on a Hot Tin Roof (1985). Dir.: Jack Hofsiss
   Tommy Lee Jones (Brick), Jessica Lange (Maggie), Rip Torn (Big Daddy)

A Streetcar Named Desire (1984). Dir.: John Erman
   Ann-Margaret (Blanche), Treat Williams (Stanley)

Cat on a Hot Tin Roof (1976). Dir.: Robert Moore
   Natalie Wood (Maggie), Robert Wagner (Brick), Sir Laurence Olivier (Big Daddy) (UK)

Eccentricities of a Nightingale (1976). Dir.: Glenn Jordan
  Blythe Danner (Alma), Frank Langella (John Buchanan)
The Migrants (1974). Dir.: Tom Gries
  Written by Tennessee Williams and Lanford Wilson
  Cloris Leachman, Ron Howard, Sissy Spacek
The Glass Menagerie (1973). Dir.: Anthony Harvey
  Katharine Hepburn (Amanda), Sam Waterston (Tom), Joanna Miles
  (Laura), Michael Moriarty (Jim)
Summer and Smoke (1972). Dir.: Peter Wood
  Lee Remick (Alma), David Hedison (Dr. John Buchanan)
Dragon Country (1970). Dir.: Glenn Jordan; combines the one-acts *Talk to Me*
  Like the Rain and Let Me Listen and *I Can't Imagine Tomorrow*
The Glass Menagerie (1966). Dir.: Michael Elliott
  Shirley Booth (Amanda), Hal Holbrook (Tom), Barbara Loden (Laura),
  Pat Hingle (Jim)
Ten Blocks on the Camino Real (1966). Dir.: Jack Landau
  Carrie Nye (Marguerite), Martin Sheen (Kilroy)
Portrait of a Madonna (1965). Dir.: Geoffrey Nethercott
  Irene Worth (Mrs. Collins)
Three Plays by Tennessee Williams (Kraft Television Theatre, 1947). *This Property*
  Is Condemned, The Last of My Solid Gold Watches, Mooney's Kids Don't Cry

Limited Release and Small-Screen Versions (U.S. and UK)

The Yellow Bird (2001). Dir.: Faye Dunaway
  Faye Dunaway, James Coburn
27 Wagons Full of Cotton (1990). Dir.: Don Scordino
  Leslie Ann Warren (Flora), Ray Sharkey (Silva), Peter Boyle (Jake)
The Glass Menagerie (1987). Dir.: Paul Newman
  Joanne Woodward (Amanda), John Malkovich (Tom)
  Karen Allen (Laura), James Naughton (Jim)

**Foreign Adaptations for Television, Theatrical Release,
and the Small Screen**

Akale (2004, Indian, *The Glass Menagerie*). Dir.: Shyamaprasad
Poko u trati (1994, Czech Republic, *The Strangest Kind of Romance*).
  Dir.: Ivan Zacharias
Vreemde liefde, Ein (Dutch, *The Strangest Kind of Romance*) (1990).
  Dir.: Edwin de Vries

Noir et Blanc (1986, French, based upon an uncredited Williams short story).
  Dir.: Claire Devers
Linje lusta (1981, Swedish, *A Streetcar Named Desire*). Dir.: Bo Widerberg
Sırça Kümes (1977, Turkish, *The Glass Menagerie*)
Sprich zur mir wie der Regen (1975, German, *Talk to Me Like the Rain and Let
  Me Listen*). Dir.: Douglas Sirk
Lasinen eläintarha (1973, Finnish, *The Glass Menagerie*). Dir.: Mirjam Himberg
Glassmenasjeriet (1969, Norwegian, *The Glass Menagerie*). Dir.: Sverre Udnaes
Hilsen fra Bertha (1968, Norwegian, *Hello from Bertha*). Dir.: Gunnel Bruström
Zoo di vetro, Lo (1963, Italian, *The Glass Menagerie*). Dir.: Vittorio Cottafavi
Tranvia llamado Deseo, Un (1956, Argentinian, *A Streetcar Named Desire*)
Senso (1954, Italian). Dir.: Luchino Visconti
  Tennessee Williams, writing credit

Published Screenplays by Williams

All Gaul Is Divided
Stopped Rocking
The Loss of a Teardrop Diamond
One Arm

Unpublished Screenplays

For a complete listing of all of Williams's unpublished screenplays, scholars should consult the online finding aids at the Harry Ransom Humanities Research Center (University of Texas at Austin), the Columbia Rare Books and Manuscript Collection, the Pusey Library (Harvard University), the University of Delaware, and the Todd Collection of the Historic New Orleans Collection. Some unpublished screenplays may also be located in smaller repositories as well as in private collections.

Appendix C
Some Notes on Produced and Unproduced Works

Unproduced Works

Throughout his career Tennessee Williams wrote numerous screenplays that were never published or produced, but in 1984 his collection *Stopped Rocking and Other Screenplays* came out under New Directions. Perhaps the longest evolving of these unrealized screenplays is *One Arm* (published in *Stopped Rocking*), a project that remained on Williams's mind for decades, first taking form as a short story in the early 1940s. In 1963, during a production of *Milk Train* at the Barter Theatre in Abingdon, Virginia, Williams wrote to Elia Kazan, expressing his opinion that "*One Arm* could make a strong film; I've thought about it before. But [because of the sexual content] I think it would have to be filmed and released in Europe."[1] Once the screenplay was completed, Williams began exploring production possibilities. In a November 1967 letter to Williams, British director Ronald Platt mentioned several possible choices to direct the film, including Michelangelo Antonioni, François Truffaut, and Franco Zeffirelli, Richard Brooks, Sidney Lumet, John Schlesinger, and Stanley Kubrick. Three years later, Williams still had thoughts about the adaptation, and wrote that he was going to Hollywood "to peddle my film-script of my story One Arm."[2] At one point Marlon Brando became seriously interested in producing a film version, but the project was never realized.

All Gaul Is Divided, which is also published in the collection *Stopped Rocking*, is an unproduced teleplay based on the late play *A Lovely Sunday for Creve Coeur*. According to Williams, "This work has had quite a remarkable history. I would guess that the 'teleplay' was written almost twenty years before I wrote the play which appeared last season [1978] at the Hudson Guild Theatre. The most remarkable thing about it is that I had *totally* forgotten its existence when I wrote the play Creve Coeur in San Francisco about three years ago."[3]

The title play in the collection, *Stopped Rocking*, began as a starring vehicle for Maureen Stapleton and was initially entitled "A Second Epiphany for My Friend Maureen." In 1975, Universal Television brought Williams to Hollywood to announce that the playwright was composing a television movie for NBC entitled *Stopped Rocking*. Shortly afterward, Williams completed the script and sent it in to Hollywood filmmakers. According to one unidentified NBC spokesperson, the material was considered "too potent for commercial TV" and was never produced. *Stopped Rocking* takes place in a mental ward, and in a letter to Elia Kazan written shortly after his 1969 stay in Barnes Hospital, Williams indicated that he would like to write a screenplay based on his experience there. It is not known whether this is the screenplay Williams had in mind. For further information on unproduced/unpublished screenplays, please see Appendix B.

Produced Works

Several of Williams's major plays as well as lesser-known short plays and even short stories have been adapted for television over the years. One of the most obscure and interesting bits of film is the Actors Studio production of *Portrait of a Madonna* (1948), starring Jessica Tandy. The teleplay was produced by Tandy's husband, Hume Cronyn, and directed by Ralph Warren. It aired on ABC, and the "scripter" is listed as Williams, who apparently was not terribly satisfied with the production.[4] After Jessica Tandy called Audrey Wood to discuss a proposed television production of *The Lady of Larkspur Lotion*, Wood immediately wrote to Williams, "I told her that you had only had one broadcast of the one-acts and that it hadn't been too happy an experience. My personal feeling is that I would rather not have any television broadcasts at all of this one act material until television has gotten a little further ahead."[5] Whether or not television had progressed to Wood's satisfaction, in 1958 a Kraft Theatre production featured "Three Plays by Tennessee Williams," which included *Mooney's Kids Don't Cry*, *The Last of My Solid Gold Watches*, and *This Property Is Condemned*. Sidney Lumet directed the production, and Williams himself made a special appearance on the show.

In February 1974, Playhouse 90 (CBS) featured a production entitled *The Migrants*, a tale vaguely reminiscent of the Joads in *The Grapes of Wrath*. The story focused on the lives of migrant farm workers, and in particular upon the Barlow family, played by Cloris Leachman, Sissy Spacek, and Ron Howard. Playwright Lanford Wilson based his script on an unpublished short story by Williams.

On October 7, 1966, the National Educational Television (NET) Playhouse showcased *Ten Blocks on the Camino Real*, starring Martin Sheen and Carrie Nye. The teleplay was based on a one-act version of the full-length *Camino Real* that had been produced about ten years earlier. In 1970, the NET Playhouse also produced the ninety-minute *Dragon Country*, which featured the two one-act plays: *I Can't Imagine Tomorrow* and *Talk to Me Like the Rain and Let Me Listen*. In 2001, Faye Dunaway directed and acted in *The Yellow Bird*, based on Williams's short story. The film enjoyed its world premiere at Cannes, and Williams narrated part of the script from an earlier recorded reading of the story. For more on the minor adaptations, please see the filmography in Appendix B.

Williams's major plays have also enjoyed several television adaptations, including two versions each of *The Glass Menagerie* (1966 and 1973), *Cat on a Hot Tin Roof* (1976 and 1985), and *A Streetcar Named Desire* (1984 and 1995, as well as André Previn's operatic version in 1998). Productions also include *The Eccentricities of a Nightingale* (1976), *Sweet Bird of Youth* (1989), *Orpheus Descending* (1990), *Suddenly Last Summer* (1993), and *The Roman Spring of Mrs. Stone* (2003). The 1976 *Cat*, which launched NBC's "A Tribute to American Theatre," starred Laurence Olivier (Big Daddy), Natalie Wood (Maggie), Robert Wagner (Brick), and Maureen Stapleton (Big Mamma).

In 1985, Showtime aired *Cat* with Jessica Lange (Maggie), Tommy Lee Jones (Brick), Rip Torn (Big Daddy), and Kim Stanley (Big Mama). The production was later rebroadcast on PBS as part of the "American Playhouse" series. The production, which had been planned as a starring vehicle for Elizabeth Ashley (who had to bow out because of her very ill mother), was eagerly anticipated by Williams. There was also a plan to do a documentary about the filming of the play, which would have shown Williams on the set working with the director and the cast, but Williams died before the documentary could be filmed. Most reviewers found the actors successful in their roles except for the miscast Rip Torn.

In 1966, *The Glass Menagerie* moved to London for the CBS production with Shirley Booth (Amanda), Hal Holbrook (Tom), Barbara Loden (Laura), and Pat Hingle (Jim). The adaptation was credited to Williams. Seven years later, Katharine Hepburn made her television drama debut as Amanda in an ABC production of *The Glass Menagerie*, along with performances by Sam Waterston (Tom), Joanna Miles (Laura), and Michael Moriarty (Jim). This teleplay had a lengthy period of incubation. In 1968, Hepburn and English director Anthony Harvey were working on *The Lion in Winter*. Harvey mentioned that *The Glass Menagerie* was the first American play that he had ever seen, and he liked it so well that he was thinking about turning it into a movie. Hepburn told Harvey she would play Amanda if he directed and David Susskind produced it in London.

In June 1976, PBS offered a new production of *Eccentricities of a Nightingale*, starring Blythe Danner as Alma and Frank Langella as Dr. John Buchanan. The teleplay was rebroadcast concurrently with a Broadway run in December of the same year (featuring a different cast), and the television production fared much better, at least according to the critics. Danner won exceptional praise for her role.

The ABC Theatre adaptation of *A Streetcar Named Desire* in 1984 was billed as a major television event. Starring Ann-Margaret as Blanche, Treat Williams as Stanley, and Beverly D'Angelo as Stella, the production, which had been "blessed" by Williams before he died the previous year, featured a Blanche unlike any previous incarnation. To the apparent surprise of many critics, Ann-Margaret helped redefine the role that had long been laboring under the shadow of Vivien Leigh. Because of production code issues detailed earlier in this book, several reviewers found the television version more faithful to the play than the 1951 movie.

The television adaptation of *Streetcar* in 1995, with Jessica Lange as Blanche, Alec Baldwin as Stanley, and Diane Lane as Stella, won Lange a Golden Globe award for best television actress and received generally positive notices from reviewers. The made-for-television film, which was based on the 1992 Broadway production, resisted creative impulses to open up the set, and instead found the claustrophobia of the Kowalski apartment essential to the themes of confinement and escape.

The television version of *Orpheus Descending* in 1990 starred Vanessa Redgrave in the role of Lady. The play, which had recently been revived by Sir Peter Hall in London, was soon brought to Broadway, and it was this production that served as the model for the 1990 teleplay, which aired on TNT.

The movie version of *The Glass Menagerie* released in 1987 is something of an anomaly in the canon of Williams adaptations. It was not filmed for television; nor was it a Hollywood production. The film enjoyed only a limited release (by Cineplex Odeon Films, which financed and distributed the film in its theatres), but was directed by one of Hollywood's major stars of the century (Paul Newman) and starred well-known, established actors Joanne Woodward as Amanda and John Malkovich as Tom. James Naughton (Jim) and Karen Allen (Laura) completed the cast. The stage production originated in Williamstown (with the same cast except for Malkovich), then moved to New Haven before Newman signed on to direct the picture. According to Newman, one of his most compelling reasons for filming the picture was to record the stage performances, especially his wife's extraordinary interpretation of Amanda. One of the challenges, Newman recalls, was "to see if pure Tennessee Williams works: to see if the play can really survive translation in its purest state to the screen, with no 'opening up,' no following Tom to the movies or Laura to typing school, which is my memory of what other versions tried to do, but simply to stay within the confines of Tennessee's characters and make cinematic virtue of claustrophobia."[6] The exterior shots were filmed in a New Jersey tenement, and Tony Walton fashioned the set to accentuate the play's sense of confinement. Newman shot the film in sepia tones, cinematically complementing the structure of the memory play, but the director's attempt to adapt a production that had worked so well in Williamstown earned mixed reviews. Most notices focused on Newman's faithfulness to the spirit of the play script, but faulted his "plodding" direction. According to most records, the film grossed less than a million dollars.

In September 1989, NBC aired *Sweet Bird of Youth*, with Elizabeth Taylor as the Princess, Mark Harmon as Chance, and Rip Torn as Boss Finley. Williams's longtime friend Gavin Lambert wrote the teleplay, and it was filmed outside of Pasadena, California. Lambert made some alterations to the script, including downplaying the subplot with Boss Finley. In trimming the material, Lambert cited Williams's own admission that he attempted to pack too much into one play, and he consequently made cuts and alterations to help keep the focus on Chance and the Princess.

A teleplay of *Suddenly, Last Summer* starring Maggie Smith (Violet Venable), Natasha Richardson (Catharine), and Rob Lowe (Dr. Cukrowicz) was filmed in 1993 at Shepperton Studios, London, by the BBC in association with WNET. The teleplay followed the script carefully and avoided the flashbacks and background scenes featured in the 1959 Mankiewicz film version starring Elizabeth Taylor, Katharine Hepburn, and Montgomery Clift. According to most reviewers, the teleplay cast held its own in comparisons with the previous film.

In May 2003, Showtime produced *The Roman Spring of Mrs. Stone*, with Helen Mirren starring as Karen Stone. The adaptation, directed by Robert Allan Ackerman, was immediately—and unfavorably—compared with the 1961 version starring Vivien Leigh. The script was faulted for its insertion of a Tennessee Williams character whose presence serves as a distraction rather than as a convincing persona. Finally, as this book goes to press, another screenplay, *The Loss of a Teardrop Diamond* (published in *Stopped Rocking*), has just wrapped production, with Ann-Margaret, Ellen Burstyn, and Bryce Dallas in starring roles.

Appendix D
Key to Collections

AFI	American Film Institute
CKF	Charles K. Feldman Collection
COLUMBIA	Rare Book and Manuscript Library, Columbia University
HERRICK	Margaret Herrick Library, Center for Motion Picture Study, Academy of Motion Picture Arts and Sciences, Beverly Hills, California
HRC	Harry Ransom Humanities Research Center, University of Texas at Austin
JLA/BFI	Joseph Losey Archives, British Film Institute
PCA	Production Code Administration Files
TODD COLLECTION	Todd Collection, Historic New Orleans Collection
U OF DELAWARE	Special Collections, University of Delaware Library, University of Delaware
WB/USC	Warner Bros. Archives, University of Southern California
WUCA	Wesleyan University Cinema Archives, Middletown, Connecticut

Notes

Preface

1. For thorough overviews of Williams's work and career, see Philip C. Kolin, *Tennessee Williams: A Guide to Research and Performance*, as well as his *Tennessee Williams Encyclopedia*.

2. We refer to the studies by Maurice Yacowar, *Tennessee Williams and Film*, and Gene D. Phillips, *The Films of Tennessee Williams*.

3. Sam Staggs, *When Blanche Met Brando: The Scandalous Story of "A Streetcar Named Desire."*

4. An important point, but one seldom remarked upon in theoretical accounts of adaptation. An interesting recent exception is Linda Hutcheon, *A Theory of Adaptation*, 6–7, 79–105.

5. Dudley J. Andrew, "Adaptation," in James Naremore, ed., *Film Adaptation*, 35.

6. Robert Stam, "Introduction," in Robert Stam and Alessandra Raengo, eds., *Literature and Film: A Guide to the Theory and Practice of Film Adaptation* (Oxford: Blackwell, 2004), 9–10.

Chapter 1

1. For example, Williams scholar Allean Hale has counted at least 130 plays that have never been published or produced.

2. Annette Saddik, *The Politics of Reputation: The Critical Reception of Tennessee Williams' Later Plays*, 74.

3. Ibid., 150.

4. The Boston City Council responded to the outrage felt by many influential citizens, and discussed censoring the production; the police commissioner adamantly demanded changes in the dialogue if an obscenity charge were to be avoided. With such adverse publicity, and with a dramatic structure and themes reminiscent of the contemporary European stage and thus far in advance of what the American theatre had witnessed, *Battle* could not find an appreciative audience, and closed in less than two weeks.

5. Quoted in Lyle Leverich, *Tom: The Unknown Tennessee Williams*, 393. The only other (and not as reliable) biography of Williams, *The Kindness of Strangers: The Life of Tennessee Williams*, by Donald Spoto, may be consulted for the post-*Menagerie* years, since Leverich's volume covers Williams's life only up to this play. John Lahr is working on a biography of Williams, but the publication date was unknown as the present volume went to press.

6. While he kept working on new projects, Williams struggled in artistic doubt and penury before winning some more minor literary prizes and an important but short-lived contract as a screenwriter for MGM in 1943, which provided him with his first experience of the peculiar world of studio filmmaking in Hollywood.

7. Leverich, *Tom*, 544.

8. Lucy Freeman and Edwina Dakin Williams, *Remember Me to Tom*, 128.

9. C. W. E. Bigsby, *Modern American Drama, 1945–1990*, 33.

10. Bron, review of *Summer and Smoke*, *Variety*, October 13, 1948.

11. Magnani reportedly turned down the role because of her poor command of English. She was eventually persuaded to star in the film version.

12. George Jean Nathan, "The Tattoo on Tennessee Williams' Brain," *New York Journal-American*, February 12, 1951.

13. Brooks Atkinson, "At the Theatre," *New York Times*, February 5, 1951.

14. Walter Kerr, review of *The Rose Tattoo*, *Commonweal*, February 23, 1951, 492–494.

15. Walter Kerr, "*Camino Real*," *New York Herald Tribune*, March 20, 1953.

16. Quoted in Albert J. Devlin, ed., *Conversations with Tennessee Williams*, 36.

17. Brooks Atkinson, "Williams' Tin Roof," *New York Times*, April 3, 1955.

18. Arthur Miller, *Timebends: A Life*, 181.

19. Ibid., 180.

20. Devlin, *Conversations*, 51.

21. Ibid.

22. Wolcott Gibbs, "Oddities, Domestic and Imported," *New Yorker* January 18, 1958, 66.

23. Walter Kerr, "Williams' 'Garden District' Presented at York Theater," *New York Herald Tribune*, January 8, 1958.

24. Devlin, *Conversations*, 56.

25. Robert Brustein, "Sweet Bird of Success," *Encounter*, June 1959, 59–60.

26. Harold Clurman, review of *Sweet Bird of Youth*, *Nation* 188 (March 1959): 281.

27. Brooks Atkinson, review of *Sweet Bird of Youth*, *New York Times*, March 11, 1959.

28. Phillips, *Films of Williams*, 267. See also David Goff's brief discussion, "Tennessee Williams's Films," in *Tennessee Williams: A Guide to Research and Performance*, ed. Philip Kolin, 232–241.

29. Phillips, *Films of Williams*, 267.

30. Ted Kalem, "The Angel of the Odd," *Time*, June 9, 1962.

31. Richard Gilman, "Mistuh Williams, He Dead," *Commonweal*, February 8, 1963, 515–517.

32. John S. McCann, *The Critical Reputation of Tennessee Williams: A Reference Guide*, xxviii.

33. Devlin, *Conversations*, 157–158.

34. Saddik, *Politics of Reputation*, 150.

35. Devlin, *Conversations*, 284–285.

36. *USA Today*, October 21, 2003.

37. Inducted into the Broadway elite as a young man, Williams was less concerned with maintaining his membership than with having his plays produced without financial constraints. As he told an interviewer in 1975, "I find that my great happiness in the theatre now is not on Broadway, but off-Broadway and off-off-Broadway. There's not the financial responsibility hanging over your head. You don't feel there's three hundred sixty thousand dollars riding on something that you've written" (Devlin, *Conversations*, 291).

38. The experience of going to a picture palace like the Tivoli in the 1920s differed greatly from its contemporary equivalent in the suburban mall multiplex. Customers, as Robert Sklar describes, encountered a fantastic world from the moment they entered the lobby: "You passed from usher to usher as you moved through ornate lobby corridors, hushed by the atmosphere of an Egyptian temple or a baroque palace that had provided the inspiration for architectural imitation . . . Eventually you came to the auditorium itself, or one of its serried balconies, where additional ushers stood, poised beside automatic seating boards that indicated which seats, if any, were empty. One, holding a flashlight to direct your steps, personally escorted you to your seat. There, after live stage

performances, musical interludes played by an orchestra numbering up to thirty pieces, a newsreel and a travelogue, you saw what you can come for—a feature film, accompanied by its own especially arranged musical score" (*Movie-Made America: A Cultural History of American Movies*, 86).

39. Ibid., 3.

40. Victor Campbell, who was Williams's secretary during the 1970s, was interviewed by the authors of this study (June 15, 2005). He described a passage from one of Williams's private diaries, indicating that Williams said he often "envisioned the action of his plays taking place like scenes reeling off of a movie."

41. George Brandt, "Cinematic Structure in the Work of Tennessee Williams," in *American Theatre*, ed. John Russell Brown and Bernard Harris, 166–172.

42. Quoted in Sklar, *Movie-Made America*, 137.

43. Albert J. Devlin and Nancy M. Tischler, eds., *The Selected Letters of Tennessee Williams: Volume I, 1920–1945*, 168.

44. For more on this subject, see Philip Kolin, "Tennessee Williams's 'Interval': MGM and Beyond," 21–27.

45. Leverich, *Tom*, 491.

46. Ibid.

47. Ibid., 495–496.

48. Devlin and Tischler, *Selected Letters* I, 451.

49. Ibid., 495.

50. Donald Windham, ed., *Tennessee Williams' Letters to Donald Windham, 1940–1965*, 114.

51. Leonard J. Leff and Jerold L. Simmons, *The Dame in the Kimono: Hollywood, Censorship, and the Production Code*, 145.

52. Albert J. Devlin and Nancy M. Tischler, eds., *The Selected Letters of Tennessee Williams: Volume II, 1945–1957*, 538.

53. Devlin, *Conversations*, 70–71.

54. Williams, interview by Dick Leavitt, *Showbill: The Program Magazine for Particular Moviegoers*, 3.

55. Devlin, *Conversations*, 67.

56. For an interesting exploration of this question, see Robert Ray, *A Certain Tendency in the Hollywood Cinema, 1930–1980*, 138–141.

57. The account of postwar Hollywood in this chapter is heavily indebted to two excellent volumes in the *History of the American Cinema* series: Tino Balio, *Grand Design: Hollywood as a Modern Business Enterprise*, and Thomas Schatz, *Boom and Bust: American Cinema in the 1940s*.

58. All earnings figures are from Schatz, *Boom and Bust*, 353–394.

59. Ibid., 285.

60. "The Package-Unit System: Unit Management after 1955," in David Bordwell, Janet Staiger, and Kristin Thompson, *The Classical Hollywood Cinema*, 330, 332.

61. Schatz, *Boom and Bust*, 378.

62. Ibid.

63. Quoted in Robert Sklar, "'The Lost Audience': 1950s Spectatorship and Historical Reception Studies," 89.

64. See Gilbert Seldes, *The Great Audience*. On the issue of juvenilization, see Thomas Doherty, *Teenagers and Teenpics: The Juvenilization of American Movies in the 1950s*.

65. Leo A. Handel, *Hollywood Looks at its Audience*.

66. Bosley Crowther, "'Boomerang!': A Factual-Style Film of a Connecticut Slaying," *New York Times*, March 6, 1947.

Chapter 2

1. Mary Ann Doane, "The 'Woman's Film': Possession and Address," 68.

2. Warner Bros. pressbook for *The Glass Menagerie*, Todd Collection.

3. Wald to Feldman, September 29, 1949 (WB/USC).

4. Leff and Simmons, *Dame*, 142.

5. Ibid.

6. Quoted in Yacowar, *Williams and Film*, 14.

7. *New York Times*, September 29, 1950.

8. *Newsweek*, October 9, 1950.

9. For Williams's cinematic considerations in composing this play, see George Crandell, "The Cinematic Eye in Tennessee Williams's *The Glass Menagerie*," and Brandt, "Cinematic Structure." Another informative article is Albert E. Kalson, "Tennessee Williams at the Delta Brilliant."

10. This draft is in the Todd Collection.

11. Audrey Wood to Sidney Fleisher, March 3, 1945 (HRC).

12. Feldman to Williams, May 1, 1950 (CKF/AFI).

13. Wald to Trilling, May 10, 1948 (WB/USC).

14. Wald's list for Amanda included Bette Davis, Miriam Hopkins, Mildred Dunnock, Judith Anderson, and Ethel Barrymore, but none could be signed for the production. For Jim, Wald considered Karl Malden, Glenn Ford, Edmund O'Brien, John Garfield, Montgomery Clift, Joseph Cotten, Marlon Brando, and Cary Grant, who indicated his preference for a happy ending.

15. German-born Berneis had broken into writing for film with William

Dieterle's *Portrait of Jennie* (1948), a moody and unconventional romance, for which he received coscreenwriting credit. After *The Glass Menagerie*, he did the screenplay for one more Hollywood film, the eminently forgettable *Chicago Calling* (1952), a rather drab melodrama, for which he again received coscreenwriting credit, this time with director John Reinhardt. Berneis subsequently departed for Germany, where he spent the balance of his career.

16. Memo entitled "Principal Points Covered and Agreed Upon at Italian Conference," June 27, 1949 (U of Delaware).

17. Devlin and Tischler, *Selected Letters II*, 249.

18. In a letter to Irene Selznick, (June 14, 1949), Williams complains that he was "terribly shocked by the ending": "Unfortunately the only true ending was the one in the play, and the one I have now worked out, to satisfy their demand for 'an up-beat,' is the lesser of various evils—at best" (Tennessee Williams, *Notebooks*, 502).

19. Devlin and Tischler, *Selected Letters II*, 250.

20. Williams to Rapper, August 5, 1949 (CKF/AFI).

21. Ibid.

22. Wald to Feldman, May 29, 1949 (CKF/AFI).

23. Berneis to Wald, August 8, 1949 (U of Delaware).

24. Devlin and Tischler, *Selected Letters II*, 314–317.

25. Warner to Williams, telegram, May 10, 1950 (U of Delaware).

26. Breen to Warner, December 2, 1949: "As we have advised you before, it will be important that there be no flavor, in the finished picture, of a questionable relationship between Tom and his sister. We assume, of course, that it is not your intention to indicate any such relationship" (PCA/Herrick). See Williams's comments about this episode: "Irving [Rapper] tells me that Breen made the disgustingly prurient charges that these lines (!!!!) contained a suggestion of *INCEST*! I cannot understand acquiescence to this sort of foul-minded and utterly stupid tyranny, especially in the case of a film as totally clean and pure, as remarkably devoid of anything sexual or even sensual, as the 'Menagerie,' both as a play and a picture. The charge is insulting to me, to my family, and an effrontery to the entire motion-picture industry! And I think you owe it to motion-pictures to defend yourselves against such prurience and tyranny by fighting it out with them" (Devlin and Tischler, *Selected Letters* II, 317).

27. Feldman to Wood, May 17, 1950 (CKF/AFI).

28. *Hollywood Reporter*, September 19, 1950 (from Herrick clip file).

29. *Variety*, September 19, 1950 (from Herrick clip file).

30. *Motion Picture Daily*, September 19, 1950 (from Herrick clip file).

31. Berneis to Wald, August 3, 1949 (U of Delaware).

32. Williams to Warner, Wald, and Feldman, May 6, 1950 (WB/USC).

33. Warner to Blumenstock, telegram, April 29, 1950 (WB/USC).

34. Feldman to Wood, May 26, 1950 (CKF/AFI).

35. Feldman to Wood, August 2, 1950 (CKF/AFI).

36. Blumenstock to Feldman, telegram, September 19, 1950 (CKF/AFI).

37. CKF/AFI, n.d.

Chapter 3

1. Film historian Lary May observes, "In America the production site was surrounded by a community where the stars really lived the happy endings, in full view of the nation . . . At a time when the birth of a modern family and consumption ideas might have remained just a cinematic fantasy, Hollywood showed how it could be achieved in real life. Out in California, stars participated in an exciting existence, free from the former confinements of work and Victorianism" (*Screening Out the Past: The Birth of Mass Culture and the Motion Picture Industry*, 167).

2. Daniel A. Lord, S.J., was one of the twentieth-century's most prolific producers of popular Catholic devotional literature, specializing in works devoted to the Virgin Mary. In 1926, he became the national director of the Sodality of Our Lady and the editor of *Queen's Work* magazine. By the time of his death in 1955, he had penned a huge quantity of booklets, pamphlets, books, and songs, including an autobiography. A strong advocate of church involvement in obtaining social justice during a period of economic hardship and political turmoil, Lord developed a deep interest in the popular media as a means of social reform. He went to Hollywood to work as a script consultant for Cecil B. DeMille's *The King of Kings*, and not long after was engaged to write the Production Code, which in many ways reflects his optimism about the medium's capacity for moral education.

3. Leonard J. Leff, "The Breening of America," 443.

4. Ibid., 444.

5. James M. Skinner, *The Cross and the Cinema: The Legion of Decency and the National Catholic Office for Motion Pictures, 1933–1970*, 126.

6. David Savran, *Communists, Cowboys and Queers: The Politics of Masculinity in the Work of Arthur Miller and Tennessee Williams*, 98.

7. Quoted in Murray Schumach, *The Face on the Cutting Room Floor: The Story of Movie and Television Censorship*, 72.

8. Savran, *Communists, Cowboys, and Queers*, 98.

9. Bordwell, Staiger, and Thompson, *Classical Hollywood Cinema*, 172.

10. Harold C. Gardiner, S.J., *Norms for the Novel*, 57.

11. Ibid., 120.

12. Quoted in Richard F. Hixson, *Pornography and the Justices: The Supreme Court and the Intractable Obscenity Problem*, ix.

13. Martin Quigley, *Decency in Motion Pictures*, 3.

14. Ibid., 7.

15. Ibid., 9.

16. Ibid.

17. Harold C. Gardiner, S.J., *The Catholic Viewpoint on Censorship*, 27–28.

18. Ibid., 32. This is not to say, however, that the two institutions, and the people who wielded power within them, did not sometimes disagree, even with bitterness and resentment. For details, see the following standard treatments: Gregory D. Black, *The Catholic Crusade against the Movies, 1940–1975*; Frank Walsh, *Sin and Censorship: The Catholic Church and the Motion Picture Industry*; and, especially, Skinner, *Cross and Cinema*.

Similar in intent to the legion, but never as successful or prominent because of the more restricted nature of the commercial stage, was the Catholic Theater Movement, a society founded in 1912 by John Cardinal Farley, whose aim, as the *New Catholic Dictionary* reports, was "to conduct an organized effort against irreligious and immoral tendencies in public amusements . . . The principal activity of the organization was to produce a 'White List' of plays, published as a suggested, not an imposed guide. In addition, critical 'Bulletins' were issued and given generous space in the Catholic press, correspondence was carried on with pastors, parents, and teachers throughout the country, and fortnightly radio talks were given over station WLWL" (www.catholic-forum.com/saints/ncd01775.htm [accessed August 13, 2005]).

19. Richard McKeon et al., *The Freedom to Read: Perspective and Program*, 11.

20. In *Miranda Prorsus* (promulgated September 8, 1957), Pius XII observes that "these new means of communication . . . exercise a powerful influence over men's minds. They can enlighten, ennoble, and adorn men's minds," and the "primary aim of motion pictures, radio, and television . . . [is] to serve truth and virtue" (article 43). See www.papalencyclicals.net/Pius 12/P12MIRAB.HTM (accessed January 12, 2005). Quotations from the Motion Picture Production Code are from the version printed as an appendix in Leff and Simmons, *Dame*, 290–291. The traditionalist aesthetic promoted by Quigley and the code has not gone without its modern secular defenders. Novelist John Gardner similarly observes that "true art is moral; it seeks to improve life, not debase it . . . Art asserts and reasserts those values which hold off dissolution . . . Art rediscovers, generation by generation, what is necessary to humanness" (*On Moral Fiction*, 5–6).

21. While space precludes listing all the articles and chapters devoted to this subject that are not included in the notes of our text, especially helpful materials include Nancy M. Tischler, "Sanitizing the Streetcar"; Brenda Murphy, *Tennessee Williams and Elia Kazan: A Collaboration in the Theatre*, and "Seeking Direction"; Ellen Dowling, "The Derailment of A Streetcar Named Desire"; Linda Cahir, "The Artful Rerouting of *A Streetcar Named Desire*"; Gene D. Phillips, "*A Streetcar Named Desire*: Play and Film"; Vivienne Dickson, "*A Streetcar Named Desire*: Its Development through the Manuscripts"; and Nancy M. Tischler, "Tiger—Tiger! Blanche's Rape on Screen."

22. Russell Holman, memo to William Wyler and Paramount executives Luigi Luraschi and Sam Briskin, December 13, 1949 (PCA/Herrick).

23. Independently, Kazan formed much the same opinion. As he wrote in his notebook for the film production: "CENTRAL SOURCE . . . THE REJECTION BY ALAN GRAY [sic] . . . and the anxiety within her that this aroused. The result, a year later, is that every man she meets is a challenge. He must like her, he must desire her, or she's a failure . . . The more he dislikes her, the greater the challenge, the harder she works, the more she needs to attract him. In effect, therefore, she appears to be trying to 'make' every man she meets. And, especially, and most anxiously, if he does not like her" (WUCA).

24. When Kazan initially decided to produce the film independently, the arrangement would have stipulated that John Garfield, Kazan's friend who aligned with the independent sources and who had originally been considered for the Broadway role, would play Stanley on screen. Garfield, an older man who would have been considered licentious in the role, would have changed the sexual dynamics entirely. Once this idea was abandoned, Kazan and others decided that the most prudent move was to keep the Broadway cast intact with the exception of Jessica Tandy. At first it was difficult to persuade Brando to take the part. Trained as a stage actor, he approached the possibility of being a film star somewhat reluctantly. He had played Stanley for some eighteen months on Broadway, and at times had felt stagnant in the role. Brando was also distrustful of the Hollywood studio system and was especially wary of becoming the "property" of a major studio. Ironically, from Kazan's point of view, Brando's overwhelming talent was actually problematical from the beginning because the actor's performance completely dominated those of the other cast members. During the Broadway run, Kazan thought that the play was in danger of becoming "the Marlon Brando show" (*A Life*, 345), because audiences were increasingly favoring Stanley in this battle of the sexes. The problem of Brando's dominating presence when paired with Tandy, combined with Warner Bros.' insistence on booking star power for the film part of Blanche, led parties to consider Vivien

Leigh as Tandy's replacement. Leigh had, of course, played a southern belle some ten years earlier in her role as Scarlett O'Hara. She had also played Blanche in the Laurence Olivier production of *Streetcar* in London a few years earlier. Her husband's stage direction had left some problematical marks on the way she began playing Blanche, complicated by Leigh's going home with Olivier after each day's shooting and working out the scenes for the next day's shooting with him. At Kazan's demand she dropped this practice and acquiesced in most of Kazan's direction, but from his perspective "it took several weeks to break her down." Consequently, Kazan felt that "the first two or three reels of the picture are not too good" (*Kazan on Kazan* 70). She went on to win the Academy Award for Best Actress, but did not attend the ceremony to accept.

25. Holman, memo to Wyler, Luraschi, and Briskin (PCA/Herrick).

26. For more on this point, see Robert Bray, "*A Streetcar Named Desire*: The Political and Historical Subtext."

27. It is at the end of scene two that Blanche confesses to Stanley that "our improvident grandfathers and father and uncles and brothers exchanged the land for their epic fornications—to put it plainly" (Tennessee Williams, *A Streetcar Named Desire*, 43).

28. Quoted in Elia Kazan, *A Life*, 329–330.

29. Ibid., 300.

30. Quoted in ibid., 330.

31. Quoted in ibid., 300.

32. Devlin and Tischler, *Selected Letters II*, 229.

33. Ibid., 235.

34. Breen to Luraschi, June 27, 1949; Breen to Irene Selznick, July 19, 1949 (PCA/Herrick).

35. Quoted in Phillips, *Films of Tennessee Williams*, 81.

36. Kazan, *A Life*, 330. As the project developed, there was a significant false start. Kazan began a shooting continuity that would have opened up the play. The start of the film would dramatize Blanche's backstory, using as a location the family plantation of Belle Reve, which figures so prominently in her memories. Kazan resolved to find the perfect house in the Mississippi Delta for the house so that those scenes could be shot at an authentic location instead of a studio soundstage. Scenes would be added to include not only her dying relatives but also the drunken soldiers and her disgraceful departure from Laurel. To establish Stanley's milieu as a contrast, Kazan would set scenes in such places as the bowling alley and local bars that Stanley frequented in order to "create a veritable redneck Kowalski world." But after Oscar Saul had completed the first draft of the screenplay, Kazan decided that the plan to open up the play "was a

fizzle." In the tradition of intimate family dramas staged on missing-fourth-wall sets, the Broadway production had exploited the claustrophobic dimensions of the Kowalski flat. As in *Death of a Salesman* and many other Broadway plays of the period, spatial confinement proved to be a powerful metaphor that materialized how the characters were confined by their limited circumstances. Kazan recognized this: "The force of the play had come precisely from its compression, from the fact that Blanche was trapped in those two small rooms, where she'd be constantly aware that she was dangerously irritating Stanley and couldn't escape if she needed to" (*A Life*, 384).

37. Devlin and Tischler, *Selected Letters II*, 260.

38. Breen wrote screenwriter Moss Hart that "it is regrettable that the sympathetic lead in your story should be a divorced woman . . . [we] have endeavored to approve divorce in motion pictures only when it was obtained against the wishes and generally over the objection of the sympathetic lead"; quoted in Gerald C. Gardner, *The Censorship Papers: Movie Censorship Letters from the Hays Office, 1934 to 1968*, 179. The legion's view, expressed by Father Patrick Masterson, was that Catholic opinion was "nearly unanimous that these [subjects] were grossly immoral"; quoted in Black, *Catholic Crusade*, 61.

39. Kazan to Williams, n.d. (HRC).

40. Devlin and Tischler, *Selected Letters* II, 355.

41. Williams to Kazan, January 27, 1950 (WUCA).

42. Kazan to Williams, February 24, 1950 (WUCA).

43. Michel Ciment, *Kazan on Kazan*, 67.

44. Feldman to Kazan, March 30, 1950 (WB/USC). All subsequent quotations from Feldman in this section are from this letter.

45. The term was made famous by social critic Philip Wylie, who, in his controversial *Generation of Vipers* (originally published in 1942), observes that "megaloid momworship has got completely out of hand . . . Mom is everywhere and everything and damned near everybody, and on her depends all the rest of the U.S. . . . Men live for her and die for her, dote upon her and whisper her name as they pass away" (187–188).

46. Williams draws heavily on current social concerns in his formulation of the drama's illusory melodramatic turn. See Elaine Tyler May, *Homeward Bound: American Families in the Cold War Era*, who observes that in the postwar era, the social ideal became a family home "that would fulfill virtually all its members' personal needs through an energized and expressive personal life" (11). See also Sklar, *Movie-Made America*.

47. Memo from Breen Office to Warner Bros., April 28, 1950 (PCA/Herrick). Subsequent quotations in this section from the memo are to this source.

48. Kazan to Jack Warner, n.d., but follows in the files a memo dated February 15, 1951, and provides clear evidence that Kazan thought very little of Charles Feldman's intellect and sophistication: "Once he [Feldman] really got under my skin and I almost told him the truth, which, as I see it, is 'You fucked up the Menagerie. Why don't you leave this one to a couple of guys who know their business?' . . . By the way on the Menagerie he did do exactly what he's trying to do here; bring the thing down to the taste HE THINKS the audience has (as if any but a small percentage of the movie going populace was made up of bobby soxers, autograph waterheads and preview-minded water brains!)" (WB/USC).

49. Jack Vizzard, memo for the file, May 2, 1950 (PCA/Herrick).

50. Minutes of meeting between Kazan, Williams, and Vizzard, April 27, 1950 (PCA/Herrick).

51. On this point, see Leff and Simmons, *Dame*, 141–184.

52. Ibid., 179.

53. Kazan to Jack Warner, October 29, 1950 (WB/USC).

54. Memo for the file, probably written by Vizzard, August 7, 1950 (PCA/Herrick).

55. Memo for the file, October 3, 1950 (PCA/Herrick).

56. Devlin and Tischler, *Selected Letters* II, 355–356.

57. Ibid.

58. Williams to Kazan, December 23, 1958 (WUCA).

59. Kazan to Jack Warner, n.d., but follows in the file a memo dated February 15, 1951 (WB/USC).

60. Kazan's notes, n.d. (WUCA).

61. Notes from meeting between Vizzard and Kazan (WUCA).

62. Williams to Kazan, telegram, November 2, 1950 (PCA/Herrick).

63. Leff, "Breening of America," 432. The following account is much indebted to Black, *Catholic Crusade*, 113–116.

64. Vizzard to Breen, July 12, 1951 (PCA/Herrick).

65. Ibid.

66. Elia Kazan, in his public thrashing on the legion, published in the *New York Times* (October 21, 1951), "Pressure Problem: Director Discusses Cuts Compelled in 'A Streetcar Named Desire.'"

67. Ibid.

68. Vizzard to Breen, July 22, 1951 (WB/USC).

69. Kazan, "Pressure Problem."

70. Ibid.

71. Quoted in Schumach, *Cutting Room Floor*, 78.

72. For further discussion, see Leonard J. Leff, "And Transfer to Cemetery: The Streetcars Named Desire."

73. Quoted in Schumach, *Cutting Room Floor*, 78.

74. Kazan to Quigley, August 16, 1951 (WUCA).

75. Quigley to Kazan, August 20, 1951 (WUCA).

Chapter 4

1. John D'Emilio and Estelle B. Freedman, *Intimate Matters: A History of Sexuality in America*, 284.

2. Ibid., 285, 287.

3. Ibid., 288. For a full discussion of the importance of the *Roth* case, see Harry M. Clor, *Obscenity and Public Morality: Censorship in a Liberal Society*, 14–87.

4. See particularly, from among a wealth of sources from the period, Herbert Marcuse, *Eros and Civilization*, which argues for a nonrepressive culture in which sexuality would be transformed into eros.

5. Eberhard and Phyllis Kronhausen, *Pornography and the Law: The Psychology of Erotic Realism and Pornography*, 18.

6. Ibid.

7. Ibid., 23.

8. Ibid.

9. Phillips, *Films of Tennessee Williams*, 104.

10. Ibid., 104–105.

11. Williams originally contemplated setting the play in Sicily, but eventually decided on the Gulf Coast. The playwright thought of Ocean Springs, Mississippi; Wallis's assistant, Paul Nathan, suggested New Orleans; and other production-site possibilities included the towns of Hammond and Ponchatoula, Louisiana, as well as a seaside hamlet near Hollywood. Mann decided to shoot the film in Florida. After driving around Key West while searching for an appropriately simple frame house, the crew found the perfect wooden bungalow—which turned out to be right next to Williams's own house on Duncan Street. Williams was not enchanted by the coincidence and became increasingly agitated over the hubbub during the filming. In November 1954, he wrote to Kazan, "We arrived back to find our whole property transformed into the Strega's house (next door to Serafina's) trees planted to hide our house and a dilapidated false front with tin roof built over my studio in the back yard. I hit the ceiling, that is, I would have hit it had there been a ceiling to hit (Devlin

and Tischler, *Selected Letters II*, 550). With the set in place and shooting about to begin, Williams found the situation very disruptive of his work on *Cat on a Hot Tin Roof*: "I've never been this close to a movie production before and I must say that it's just too massive, too huge and implacable a machine, to be interesting. It no longer seems to have any relation to me or my own world, it's like some great Frankenstein that suddenly came clomping up to the door and took everything over" (551).

12. Moira Walsh, "*The Rose Tattoo*," *America*, December 24, 1955, 362.

13. Williams to Wood, September 19, 1953 (in Devlin and Tischler, *Selected Letters II*, 498–499).

14. Hal B. Wallis and Charles Higham, *The Autobiography of Hal Wallis, Starmaker*, 134.

15. This is not to say, of course, that Italian neorealist films always avoid erotic sensationalism. One of the most enduring images of that cinema is the shot of a very busty Silvana Mangano, dressed in skin-tight shorts, soaked to the skin as she works the paddies in *Bitter Rice* (Giuseppe de Santis, 1949).

16. Devlin and Tischler, *Selected Letters* II, 342.

17. Wallis and Higham, *Autobiography*, 139.

18. Ibid., 140.

19. Quoted in Brian Parker, "Multiple Endings for *The Rose Tattoo* (1951)," 53.

20. Williams to Wallis, June 14, 1954 (HRC).

21. All above quotations from Breen to Wallis, May 12, 1952 (PCA/Herrick).

22. Nathan to Vizzard, forwarded memo, May 15, 1952 (PCA/Herrick). After he left the PCA, Vizzard wrote a somewhat sensational account of his experiences, *See No Evil: Life inside a Hollywood Censor*, in which he makes clear that he did not share the cultural conservatism of Breen and his other colleagues. Vizzard observes: "In a climate of permissiveness, like the present, there is no body of respected opinion that forms a consensus on the side of controls. Instead, one hears slogans on all sides that are very popular with the electorate, but which are the fruit of a kind of anti-intellectualism that is against the hard think, and the honest think." At the same time, he admits, "We are steeped in self-gratifications almost beyond belief," which makes "the maintenance of a middle ground . . . as difficult as trying to pick up a puddle of mercury between the tips of the fingers" (294). To put it simply, Breen did not see any reason to stake out "a middle ground" of this kind.

23. Williams's arguments over the script cited here and below are from his "Notes on the Filming of *Rose Tattoo*" (PCA/Herrick).

24. In fact, those within the industry were well apprised of the potential difficulties involved in "sex comedies" even before the contentious filming of *The*

Moon is Blue, which was eventually released without a certificate because Preminger refused to modify to the censors' satisfaction the essential feature of the property: its so very genteel spoofing of middle-class mores, including the somewhat hypocritical fixation on official virginity in an age that condoned unchaperoned dating and what was then known as "petting." Even though Herbert's play has a moral theme (the brassy heroine, who keeps her virtue, receives a marriage proposal from her erstwhile seducer, while the "wolf" figure, played largely for comic relief, is brought to see the error of his ways), Hollywood producers were at first reluctant to bid on the property. Warner Bros. and Paramount both passed on the offer from Preminger and Herbert, who then were forced to form their own production company in order to make the film. For further details of the resulting controversy, which shook the PCA badly because the film did very well despite the absence of a certificate, see Skinner, *Cross and Cinema*, 112–116. The legion, perhaps expressing solidarity with the PCA, gave *The Moon is Blue* a "C" rating, despite the raters of the Catholic Theatre Movement (a soon-to-pass-into-history Broadway version of the legion) having awarded it a "B."

25. Breen to Wallis, May 6, 1952 (PCA/Herrick).

26. Ibid.

27. All above quotations are from Breen to Wallis, May 5, 1953 (PCA/Herrick).

28. Breen to Wallis et al., April 13, 1954 (PCA/Herrick).

29. Breen to Kanter et al., April 20, 1954 (PCA/Herrick).

30. This important document was provided to the authors by Mr. Richard Taylor, who received it from Stell Adams, one of Williams's cousins. It is printed in an online issue of the *Tennessee Williams Annual Review* (2003) (www.tennesseewilliamsstudies.org).

31. Many letters from Williams to Kazan explore the boundaries that exist and must sometimes be crossed between collaborators. For example, on November 23, 1954, he wrote Kazan, addressing "a clash . . . between our views," and insisting, "that's what makes us probably the best working combo in the theatre! We have to give a little, both ways, and arrive at the golden mean. I am usually for something less explicit. You are usually for something more explicit. The reason may be that nobody knows quite as well as the writer the things that are buried in his script. On the other hand, the writer is often unable to tell when these things do not communicate to anyone but himself" (WUCA).

32. Devlin and Tischler, *Selected Letters* II, 517–518.

33. Ibid., 538.

34. Wallis and Higham, *Autobiography*, 144.

35. Devlin and Tischler, *Selected Letters* II, 590.

36. Walsh, "*The Rose Tattoo*," 362.

37. Derek Rouse, "*The Rose Tattoo* and *Picnic*," *Sight and Sound*, Spring 1955, 195.

38. Philip T. Hartung, "Mourning Becomes Magnani," *Commonweal*, December 23, 1955, 306.

Chapter 5

1. Kazan, *A Life*, 562.
2. Williams to Kazan, December 21, 1953 (WUCA).
3. Devlin and Tischler, *Selected Letters* II, 415.
4. Ibid., 419.
5. Ibid., 421.
6. Williams to Kazan, n.d. (WB/USC).
7. Kazan to Williams, August 2, 1952 (WB/USC).
8. Jack Warner, memo, August 13, 1952 (WB/USC).
9. Kazan to Williams, n.d. (Todd Collection).
10. Kazan, *A Life*, 562.
11. Ibid., 563.
12. *Baby Doll* pressbook (HNOC).
13. Kazan to Warner, July 25, 1956 (WB/USC).
14. Leff and Simmons, *Dame*, 136.
15. Kazan, *A Life*, 563.
16. Significantly, in his autobiography Kazan makes no mention of his role in designing the billboard, something of which he was proud at the time.
17. Richard Schickel, *Elia Kazan: A Biography*, 384.
18. Interestingly, this collocation of highbrow (though sensationalist) art with very low, even degraded cultural forms is characteristic of a more general trend in film consumption beginning in the sixties and lasting to the present day—what Joan Hawkins has termed "paracinema." In this area of taste, the so-called body genres (pornography, horror, and exploitation films principally) predominate, with a postmodern blurring of the boundaries hitherto separating low from high culture. Hawkins suggests: "Paracinema consumption can be understood . . . as American art cinema consumption has often been understood, as a reaction against the hegemonic and normatizing practice of mainstream, dominant Hollywood production" (*Cutting Edge: Art Cinema and the Horrific Avant-garde*, 7).
19. Bosley Crowther, "Screen: Streetcar on Tobacco Road," *New York Times* December 19, 1956.
20. William L. Howard observes that "whereas Caldwell's style was hardboiled and unflinching in its depiction of the unpleasant realities of a region in

distress, Kirkland's was cliché-ridden, sentimental and sensational" ("Caldwell on Stage on Screen," 60).

21. See, for example, the comment by PCA official Jack Vizzard that the film is a "sly exposure of the Tobacco Road mentality of the South" (*See No Evil*, 170).

22. James E. Devlin, *Erskine Caldwell*, unpaged preface (1).

23. Ibid., 25.

24. Sylvia Jenkins Cook, *From Tobacco Road to Route 66: The Southern Poor White in Fiction*, 83.

25. Arthur Knight, "The Williams-Kazan Axis," *Saturday Review*, December 29, 1956, 23.

26. Williams got this name (but with a different spelling) from his good friend, Marion Black Vaccaro.

27. Ciment, *Kazan on Kazan*, 75.

28. For more on the "subversive" black characters in *Baby Doll*, see Philip Kolin, "Civil Rights and the Black Presence in *Baby Doll*."

29. Philip Lopate, "The Method South," *Oxford American* 42 (Winter 2002), 109.

30. Kazan, notebook, n.d. (probably around 1952; WUCA).

31. Ciment, *Kazan on Kazan*, 74.

32. Breen to Jack Warner, August 1, 1952 (PCA/Herrick). All above quotations are from this source.

33. Devlin and Tischler, *Selected Letters* II, 507.

34. Ibid., 576.

35. Kazan to Jack Warner (who copied Breen and Shurlock), from Mississippi, November 15, 1955 (WB/USC).

36. Shurlock, memo for the PCA files, November 22, 1955 (PCA/Herrick).

37. Vizzard, memo for the PCA files, July 25, 1956 (PCA/Herrick).

38. Vizzard to Kazan, July 25, 1956 (PCA/Herrick).

39. Vizzard, *See No Evil*, 171, 174.

40. Contra Kazan, it was apparently Baker's idea to teasingly lick the vanilla ice-cream cone. See her biography, *Baby Doll: An Autobiography*, for more on the filming.

41. Quotations from the legion review are drawn from Black, *Catholic Crusade*, 168.

42. Quoted in Skinner, *Cross and Cinema*, 128.

43. Ibid.

44. Kazan, *A Life*, 564.

45. Ibid.

46. Quoted in Black, *Catholic Crusade*, 169.

47. Figures from Skinner, *Cross and Cinema*.

48. Kazan, *A Life*, 564.

49. Quoted in Walsh, *Sin and Censorship*, 257.

50. Untitled article originally written for the *Herald Tribune*, December 16, 1956 (typescript copy at HRC).

51. For further discussion, see Walsh, *Sin and Censorship*, 275.

52. Leff and Simmons, *Dame*, 284.

Chapter 6

1. For an interesting discussion of the sexual politics in *Suddenly*, see Stephen Bruhm, "Blackmailed by Sex: Tennessee Williams and the Economics of Desire."

2. Quoted in Phillips, *Films of Williams*, 183.

3. Shurlock, memo for the files, meeting held on May 25, 1959 (PCA/Herrick). All references to this meeting drawn from this memo.

4. Shurlock to Spiegel, October 30, 1959 (PCA/Herrick).

5. Shurlock to Spiegel, November 16, 1959 (PCA/Herrick).

6. Certificate of acceptability synopsis, n.d. (PCA/Herrick).

7. *Hollywood Reporter*, December 16, 1959 (Herrick clip file).

8. *Variety*, December 16, 1959 (Herrick clip file).

9. James D. Ivers, *Motion Picture Daily*, December 16, 1959 (Herrick clip file).

10. For details of this development, see Walsh, *Sin and Censorship*, 293.

11. Legion of Decency review statement (PCA/Herrick).

12. Walsh, *Sin and Censorship*, 294.

13. Frank Getlein and Harold Gardiner, *Movies, Morals, and Art*, 132.

14. Ibid., 99.

15. Ibid.

16. Ibid., v; emphasis added. The other two books in the series are William Lynch, S.J., *The Image Industries: A Constructive Analysis of Film and Television*; and Edward Fischer, *The Screen Arts: A Guide to Film and Television Appreciation*. According to Lynch: "The work of the moralist and the censor may be occasionally necessary, but it is limited. Precisely like the art that it worries about, it can at times get out of hand . . . My own limited function, partly as a theologian and partly as a literary critic interested in these matters, will be to talk about the pluralism of elements that can be introduced, *in a positive fashion*, within our popular imaginative environment, not those elements which must stay outside our image industries as guardians, waiting for a mistake to be made before action" (12; emphasis added). As Fischer similarly observes: "The Church real-

izes that the best thing to do about the aesthetically squalid is not to keep complaining about it . . . the artist deals with evil because it is a part of life, but he shows evil as evil; the pornographer deals with evil because he finds it saleable, and he makes evil seem good." And he draws attention to the division within the Church between those committed to a narrow-minded moralism and those who, following the injunctions of Pius XII, find something positive in challenging modern art: "The best thing is to implant some attitudes that will help the public see the aesthetically squalid for what it is. Some Catholics will not approve of this system . . . They get their satisfaction from legislation, not education. They are more attracted to the don'ts of life than to the do's. They enjoy a bunch of rules and regulations with which they can club others over the head" (164–165). The reference to "some Catholics" here seems a clear swipe at the code, the PCA, and the Legion of Decency.

17. Getlein and Gardiner, *Movies, Morals, and Art*, 140.

18. Ibid., 141.

19. Ibid., 128, 141.

20. Linda Williams, "Melodrama Revisited," 42. For a very useful and updated survey of critical work on American film melodrama since the early 1970s, see John Mercer and Martin Shingler, *Melodrama: Genre, Style, Sensibility*. The more important critical works on melodrama are published and excerpted in Christine Gledhill, ed., *Home Is Where the Heart Is: Studies in Melodrama and the Woman's Film*.

21. Thomas Schatz, *Hollywood Genres: Formulas, Filmmaking, and the Studio System*, observes that "because of a variety of industry-based factors, as well as external cultural phenomena, the melodrama reached its equilibrium at the same time that certain filmmakers were beginning to subvert and counter the superficial prosocial thematics and clichéd romantic narratives that had previously defined the genre" (223). This was in the mid-1950s, precisely the time in which Williams film adaptations attained their greatest popularity and critical success.

22. Thomas Elsaesser, "Tales of Sound and Fury: Observations on the Family Melodrama," 67–68.

23. Schatz, *Hollywood Genres*, 226.

24. Barbara Klinger, *Melodrama and Meaning: History, Culture, and the Films of Douglas Sirk*, 40.

25. Tennessee Williams, *Cat on a Hot Tin Roof*, 3.

26. Ibid., 6.

27. Albert J. Devlin, "Writing in 'A Place of Stone': *Cat on a Hot Tin Roof*," 190.

28. Ibid., 195.

29. Williams's pronouncements on Brick's sexuality have been numerous and contradictory. In perhaps his fullest statement on the subject, he wrote Kazan (November 31, 1954), stating, "Brick did love Skipper . . . to reverse my original (somewhat tentative) premise, I now believe that, in the deeper sense, not in the literal sense, Brick *is* homosexual with a heterosexual adjustment: a thing I've suspected of several others, such as Brando, for instance. He's the nearest thing to Brick we know. Their innocence, their blindness, makes them very touching, very beautiful and sad" (WUCA).

30. Elsaesser, "Tales of Sound and Fury," 66.

31. This "masculinist" emphasis on solving the related problems of desire and emotional well-being, only hinted at in the original play script and Kazan-influenced Broadway version, was not the brainchild of Richard Brooks, but appeared earlier in the film's production history, in the treatment submitted to the PCA by producer Dore Schary, who also eventually passed on the project: "Mr. Schary sketched a new outline he has in mind for this property. This outline would stress the father-son relationship as the central theme. It would omit any inference of homo-sexuality. The son's problem would be that he had idealized the older football player, and looked up to him as a father—and this has always rankled with the father. The situation between the young husband and wife will be as follows: before the story begins, while the husband is recovering from an injury, the wife had traveled with the football team. The older football player had seduced the wife on the occasion of the victory celebration. The young husband has refused to believe that the older man was the guilty party and has blamed his wife for seducing his friend. The climax comes when the father convinces the son that the friend he has idolized is a rotter. This will bring the husband and wife together . . . Mr. Schary indicated that he has no definite plans yet of purchasing this property, but was interested in exploring whether the outline he had developed would meet the Code requirements" (Shurlock, PCA memo for the files regarding a conference with Schary, June 23, 1955 [PCA/Herrick]).

32. Shurlock to Paul Nathan (Hal Wallis Productions), memo, June 6, 1955 (PCA/Herrick).

33. Barbara Ehrenreich, Elizabeth Hess, and Gloria Jacobs, *Remaking Love: The Feminization of Sex*, 45.

34. In his remarkable, autobiographically rich essay, *The Homosexual in America*, Donald Webster Cory argues that at the time the "homosexual life," like Brick's withdrawal from the family and his various appointed roles within it, did not yet exist, for the homosexual had not yet been able "to offer the world at large a pattern for a better social organization in which he could be integrated"

(207). For more discussion of Brick's problems, see Jeffrey Loomis, "Four Characters in Search of a Company: Williams, Pirandello, and the *Cat on a Hot Tin Roof* Manuscripts"; Dean Shackleford, "The Truth That Must Be Told: Gay Subjectivity, Homophobia, and Social History in *Cat on a Hot Tin Roof*"; Mark Royden Winchell, "Come Back to the Locker Room Ag'n, Brick Honey!"; John Clum, *Acting Gay*; Dennis W. Allen, "Homosexuality and Artifice in *Cat on a Hot Tin Roof*"; C. W. E. Bigsby, *A Critical Introduction to Twentieth-Century American Drama*, vol. 2: *Williams, Miller, Albee*, 85–87; John S. Bak, "sneakin' and spyin' from Broadway to the Beltway: Cold War Masculinity, Brick, and Homosexual Existentialism"; Robert F. Gross, "The Pleasures of Brick: Eros and the Gay Spectator in *Cat on a Hot Tin Roof*"; Brenda Murphy, *Congressional Theatre: Dramatizing McCarthyism on Stage, Film, and Television*. For general observations on the subject of masculinity in American culture, see also Robert Vorlicky, *Act like a Man: Challenging Masculinities in American Drama*; Robert Corber, *Homosexuality in Cold War America: Resistance and the Crisis of Masculinity*; Suzanne Clark, *Cold Warriors: Manliness on Trial in the Rhetoric of the West*; Peter Filene, *Him/Her/Self: Sex Roles in Modern America*; Michael Kimmel, *Manhood in America: A Cultural History*.

35. *Hollywood Reporter*, August 13, 1958 (Herrick clip file).

36. *Variety*, August 13, 1958 (Herrick clip file).

37. *Harrison's Reports*, August 13, 1958 (Herrick clip file).

38. For further discussion, see Geoffrey Nowell-Smith, "Minnelli and Melodrama," and Laura Mulvey, "Notes on Sirk and Melodrama." Nowell-Smith observes that in melodrama, "a 'happy end' which takes the form of an acceptance of castration is achieved only at the cost of repression. The laying out of the problems 'realistically' always allows for the generating of an excess which cannot be accommodated" (73), a more accurate description of the stage than the film version of *Cat*. Mulvey similarly observes: "If the melodrama offers a fantasy escape for the identifying women in the audience, the illusion is so strongly marked by recognizable, real and familiar traps that the escape is closer to a daydream than a fairy story" (79).

39. Elsaesser, "Tales of Sound and Fury," 55.

40. Barbara Ehrenreich, *Hearts of Men: American Dreams and the Flight from Commitment*, 15.

41. Ibid., 24.

42. Ibid., 25.

43. Ibid. See also Lionel Ovesey, *Homosexuality and Pseudohomosexuality*.

44. William H. Whyte, *The Organization Man*, 448.

45. Ibid., 7.

46. Robert Lindner, *Must You Conform?* 28. The psychological establishment, of course, influenced by the irrepressible social optimism of neo-Freudianism, largely supported the opposing view at the time. See especially H. A. Overstreet, *The Mature Mind*, the popular encouragement to Americans to "grow up," which concludes with this strident admonition: "Where there is no vision, we are told, the people perish. Where there is no maturity, there is no vision. We now begin to know this. We realize that the evils of our life come not from deep evil within us but from ungrown-up responses to life. Our obligation, then, is to grow up. This is what our time requires of us. This is what may yet be the saving of us" (292).

47. Lindner, *Must You Conform?* 184.

48. Ibid., 28.

49. Elsaesser, "Tales of Sound and Fury," 68.

50. Figures from the Internet Movie Database, http://www.imdb.com/ (accessed December 18, 2006).

51. Michael Paller, *Gentleman Callers: Tennessee Williams, Homosexuality, and Mid-Twentieth-Century Drama*, 112.

52. Ehrenreich, *Hearts of Men*, 50.

53. Richard Brooks, "Richard Brooks," *Movie* 12 (1965): 8.

54. Brooks, "Richard Brooks," 8.

55. The PCA, however weakened by the early 1960s, did make some demands for script changes. Dougherty and Shurlock of the PCA wrote this memo for the files after meeting with Mr. and Mrs. Pandro S. Berman, who would be the producers, on October 19, 1960: "It was understood by all concerned that the story, as presented in the play script, contained a number of specific elements, together with an over-all flavor unacceptable from the standpoint of the Production Code. The following agreements were made: 1. the element of nymphomania on the part of the Princess will be eliminated 2. the direct and blunt portrayal of the relationship between Chance and the Princess would be eliminated 3. the element of venereal disease would be eliminated; and in its place would be substituted an illegal operation (an inference of abortion) which took place *before the picture opens*, and against the will of Heavenly. 4. the various treatments of the subject of castration will be eliminated. In the case of the Negro who was castrated by the lynch mob, some other form of mutilation will be indicated— possibly cutting off his hand 'for having laid his hands on a white woman.' 5. as to the illicit relationship in the past between Chance and Heavenly, it will be indicated that this was not a promiscuous thing, but rather a result of Heavenly's father refusing the young people to be married" (PCA/Herrick). These suggestions were all taken up by the screenwriters in one way or another. In the film,

the Princess still is interested enough in illicit sex to hire a male prostitute, even if she is no longer a nymphomaniac. The relationship between the Princess and Chance is still blunt enough, even if no longer as titillating. Chance's venereal disease, the reflex of his poisonous promiscuity, is changed to an abortion, a violation urged on her by her father, who becomes the villain of the piece. There is no reference to castration in the field—Chance needs to be thoroughly intact if the melodramatic ending is to have the same kind of potentially procreative force it has in *Cat*.

56. Phillips, *Films of Tennessee Williams*, 165.

57. Quoted in ibid.

58. *Motion Picture Daily*, February 28, 1962 (Herrick clip file).

59. *Variety*, February 28, 1962 (Herrick clip file).

60. All preceding quotations from the *Suddenly, Last Summer* pressbook (Todd Collection).

61. Devlin, *Conversations*, 67.

62. Quoted in Phillips, *Films of Williams*, 267.

63. Ibid.

64. Dakin Williams and Shepherd Mead, *Tennessee Williams: An Intimate Biography*, 22. Dakin Williams, in a conversation with one of the authors of this study, said, "*Period of Adjustment* is the only play that has me in it" (June 6, 2006). As with virtually all of Williams's work, there are parallels between his art and his life. One of Edwina Williams's houses in Clayton, Missouri, had foundation problems and was thought to have been built over a cavern. Big Spring, Texas, where Dakin met his future wife Joyce, is mentioned in the film. Dakin was in the air force when he met Joyce, and the masculine world of the air force figures as a backdrop of the past in both the play and film, as does heterosexual impotence. Tennessee Williams once described Dakin's wife as being "psychologically frigid" (*Five O'Clock Angel: Letters of Tennessee Williams to Maria St. Just, 1948–1982*, 169).

65. Williams, *Five O'Clock Angel*, 169, and Devlin, *Conversations*, 285.

66. Brendan Gill, "Family Matters," *New Yorker*, November 10, 1962, 234–235.

67. *Time*, November 16, 1962, 97.

Chapter 7

1. Frank Tannenbaum, *The Darker Phases of the South*, 174.

2. H. L. Mencken, "Sahara of the Bozart," 157–158. For a very useful discussion of the controversy, see James C. Cobb, *Away Down South: A History of Southern Identity* (New York: Oxford Univ. Press, 2005), 109–112.

3. For further discussion of this point, see Cobb, *Away Down South*, esp. 212–329, and his *Redefining Southern Culture: Mind and Identity in the Modern South*, 78–211. See further Peter Applebome, *Dixie Rising: How the South Is Shaping American Values, Politics, and Culture*. Howard Zinn has convincingly argued that what for decades were identified as the unpleasant pathologies of southern culture were in truth always shared by other regions of the country: "For the South . . . far from being utterly different, is really the *essence* of the nation." Thus the South "contains, in a concentrated and dangerous form, a set of characteristics which mark the country as a whole" ("The South as Mirror," in *The Southern Mystique*, 218).

4. Richard H. King, *A Southern Renaissance: The Cultural Awakening of the American South, 1930–1955*, 7.

5. Ibid., 27. The dating of the Southern Renaissance argued for by King differs from that advanced by the movement's other best-known commentator, John M. Bradbury, who in *Renaissance in the South: A Critical History of the Literature, 1920–1960* offers compelling evidence for providing it with another fifteen years of activity.

6. Cobb, *Away Down South*, 139.

7. W. J. Cash, *The Mind of the South*, 137.

8. C. Vann Woodward, *The Strange Career of Jim Crow*, argued in the preface to the book's first edition (1955) that "the twilight zone that lies between living memory and written history is one of the favorite breeding places of mythology." It is that zone his book illuminates, correcting the "distortions and perversions that have taken place in Jim Crow history" (xvi).

9. In regard to his dismantling of the myth of the southern belle (and of the sexual purity of white southern women more generally), Williams can be seen as part of a larger trend. For an interesting discussion of the sexual politics of representations of southern women in the 1950s, see Allison Graham, *Framing the South: Hollywood, Television, and Race during the Civil Rights Struggle*. She observes: "In the aftermath of the *Brown* [the Supreme Court decision], the southern white woman became a pivotal figure not just in the propaganda strategies of segregationists but in the narrative strategies of the movies themselves" (16). See further Pete Daniel, *Lost Revolutions: The South in the 1950s*; Fred Chappell, "The Image of the South in Film"; and, Karl Heider, ed., *Images of the South: Constructing a Regional Culture on Film and Video*.

10. Paller, *Gentleman Callers*, 13.

11. Edward D. C. Campbell, Jr., *The Celluloid South: Hollywood and the Southern Myth*, 143.

12. Ibid., 144.

13. Notably, the essays in Warren French, ed., *The South and Film*, likewise ignore the influence of literary developments on Hollywood's treatment of the South.

14. Campbell, *Celluloid South*, 159–160.

15. Though it features Clark Gable in a role that in some ways resembles that of Rhett Butler, and Yvonne De Carlo as a southern belle (albeit of mixed blood) who is modeled somewhat on Scarlett O'Hara, *Band of Angels* (1957) is more an examination of the bankrupt tradition of the plantation myth than a nostalgic lament for its passing. See also note 19, below.

16. For an excellent account of Mencken's criticisms and the southern reaction, see Fred C. Hobson, Jr., *Serpent in Eden: H. L. Mencken and the South*.

17. King, *Southern Renaissance*, 195.

18. Ibid.

19. Bradbury, *Renaissance in the South*, 192–195.

20. Cook, *Tobacco Road to Route 66*, 82.

21. Ibid., 40.

22. Ibid.

23. David Joseph Singal, *The War Within: From Victorian to Modernist Thought in the South, 1919–1945*, 373–374.

24. Cobb, *Redefining Southern Culture*, 67.

25. Graham, *Framing the South*, 25.

26. Although it is an important American novel, Wolfe's *Look Homeward, Angel* was never adapted by Hollywood. Agee's *A Death in the Family* was indifferently adapted by Hollywood in 1963 and never found an audience (it too has found another life in the format of the made-for-TV movie, having been thus adapted three times for the small screen). Warren's *Band of Angels* (1957) was turned into a Hollywood "A" production that proved to have little popular appeal. The same novelist's *All the King's Men* was successfully adapted in 1949 as part of the social-problem film genre then popular.

27. It was the drastically sentimentalized Broadway version of McCullers's *The Member of the Wedding* that was filmed in 1952, and her *Reflections in a Golden Eye* came to the screen only much later, in 1967. O'Connor's challenging fiction has proved resistant to the Hollywood treatment, with the slight exception of John Huston's *Wise Blood* (1979), an independent production that did not receive wide exhibition. The most notable adaptation of a Capote work is the justly famous *In Cold Blood* (1966), but it is not a "savage ideal" work with a southern theme.

28. Jack Temple Kirby, *Media-Made Dixie: The South in the American Imagination*, 106.

29. Anthony Mann, the film's director, is reported to have said: "We didn't

care if we got a Code Seal or a Legion of Decency rating or not. . . . Any changes I made—except for the lifting of a few bosom lines—were made strictly for theatrical reasons" (quoted in Richard W. Nason, "Bit Stake in 'God's Little Acre,'" *New York Times*, May 4, 1958).

30. The most famous of these was Elia Kazan's *Pinky* (also released in 1949).

31. In 1955, producer Jerry Wald purchased the film rights to Faulkner's *The Hamlet* and *The Sound and the Fury*, both of which were turned over to the husband-and-wife screenwriting duo of Harriet Frank, Jr., and Irving Ravetch, and to director Martin Ritt. Ritt trained at the Actors Studio and, like several other directors of the period, later made a reputation on TV, directing the likes of John Cassavetes and Sidney Poitier, before moving to Hollywood to direct, at first, small adult films (*Edge of the City* and the suburban melodrama *No Down Payment*, a very successful production for Wald).

32. Bosley Crowther, "The Long, Hot Summer," *New York Times*, April 4, 1958.

33. Marketing copy for *The Long, Hot Summer* from imdb.com (accessed January 18, 2007).

34. Even though the film version of *Cat* opened the same year as *The Long, Hot Summer*, its Broadway run began in March 1955 and ended in November 1956.

35. Bruce Kawin says this about Ritt's version of *The Sound and the Fury*: "The sound and the fury are recast as sexual tension and domestic anger," a transformation in which the film's Caddy (Margaret Leighton) "pathetically echoes in her lines and demeanor, Blanche DuBois . . . as if Blanche were the only image of a promiscuous Southern ex-lady the adaptors could conjure up of . . . Caddy's 'doom'" (*Faulkner and Film*, 22). The film is structured around the romance that develops between Caddy's brother Jason (Yul Brynner) and Caddy's daughter, Quentin (Joanne Woodward), with its eventual point being "a conventional demonstration of the value of convention." The film's battle, unlike Faulkner's more complicated points about family and the succession of generations, is "the battle for respectability," (25), which, as we noted in the last chapter, is a key element in Hollywood family melodrama.

36. Especially for director Ritt; see *Paris Blues* (1962), *Hud* (1964), and *Hombre* (1968).

37. Kawin, *Faulkner and Film*, 53.

38. Crowther, "Long, Hot Summer."

39. Williams to Kazan, n.d. (probably 1952; WUCA).

40. Tennessee Williams, *Where I Live: Selected Essays*, 41–42.

41. For more on the politics of the play, see Philip Kolin, "Sleeping with Caliban: The Politics of Race in Tennessee Williams's *Kingdom of Earth*."

42. Vincent Canby, "The Screen: 'Last of the Mobile Hot-Shots.'" *New York Times*, January 15, 1970.

43. S. K. Oberbeck, "Southern Discomfort," *Newsweek*, January 26, 1970, 75.

44. Fred Kaplan, *Gore Vidal: A Biography*, 632.

45. Matei Calinescu, *Five Faces of Modernity: Modernism, Avant-Garde, Decadence, Kitsch, Postmodernism*, 226, 238.

46. Ibid., 229.

47. Ibid., 253.

48. Ibid., 226.

49. Ibid., 252.

50. Ibid., 229.

51. Cobb, *Redefining Southern Culture*, 44, 45, 76.

52. Hollis Alpert, "Instant Tennessee Williams," *Saturday Review*, June 25, 1966, 40.

53. For more on Natalie Wood and the filming of *This Property Is Condemned*, see Rex Reed's feature article in the *New York Times*, January 16, 1966.

54. Gavin Lambert cites James Bridges and David Rayfiel as contributing to the script, and Maurice Yacowar contends that as many as sixteen writers worked on it, but never identifies them. Horton Foote also worked on the project.

55. Houseman, *Final Dress*, 292.

56. Gavin Lambert, *Natalie Wood: A Life*, 227.

57. Phillips, *Films of Tennessee Williams*, 127–128.

58. "Boardinghouse Reach," *Newsweek*, August 1, 1966, 84.

59. Cash, *Mind of the South*, 301.

60. Ibid.

61. Ibid.

62. See Donald Costello, "Tennessee Williams's 'Conjure Man' in Script and Screen."

63. "Screen: 'Fugitive Kind,'" *New York Times*, April 15, 1960.

64. For a detailed discussion on Boris Kaufman's creative black-and-white photography, see Frederick Foster, "Filming 'The Fugitive Kind.'"

65. "Williams' Fugitives," *New York Times*, April 24, 1960.

66. Phillips, *Films of Tennessee Williams*, 213.

67. Cash, *Mind of the South*, 440.

Chapter 8

1. Murray Smith, "Theses on the Philosophy of Hollywood History," 14. The other essays in *Contemporary Hollywood Cinema* (edited by Steven Neale and

Murray Smith [New York: Routledge, 1998]), offer a series of instructive discussions of the various postwar transitions (in aesthetics, exhibition, production, and so on) that have come to distinguish the contemporary Hollywood cinema from its studio-era predecessor. Interestingly, by refusing the term "new" to describe the Hollywood it discusses, this anthology neatly avoids a determinate position on this central issue.

2. Hawkins, *Cutting Edge*, 4.

3. Paul Monaco, *The Sixties: 1960–1969*, 2, 190. In discussing the "high concept" film that has become a staple of Hollywood production during the past two decades, Justin Wyatt makes the similar point that "perhaps the most striking result of the high concept style is a weakening of identification with character and narrative. . . . In place of this identification with narrative, the viewer becomes sewn into the 'surface' of the film, contemplating the style of the narrative and the production" (*High Concept: Movies and Marketing in Hollywood*, 60). For a well-argued contrary view, see Kristin Thompson, *Storytelling in the New Hollywood: Understanding Classical Narrative Technique*.

4. Geoff King, *Spectacular Narratives: Hollywood in the Age of the Blockbuster*, 2.

5. Monaco, *Sixties*, 45.

6. Jeffrey Sconce, "'Trashing' the Academy: Taste, Excess, and an Emerging Politics of Cinematic Style," 381.

7. Hawkins, *Cutting Edge*, 7.

8. An example: One of the most successful independent theatres during the 1970s in Atlanta's posh Northside suburbs was the Buckhead Art Cinema, which promised "XXX action" and extended an interesting invitation to prospective patrons ("couples welcome"). Historian Peter Lev comments interestingly on this development: "*And God Created Woman*'s impact on the film industry was significant. New Bardot films were eagerly snapped up by distributors, and old Bardot films were released or re-released . . . Explicit sexuality became expected in foreign films, to such an extent that 'foreign film,' 'art film,' 'adult film,' and 'sex film' were for several years almost synonyms" (*The Euro-American Cinema*, 13).

9. Hawkins, *Cutting Edge*, 23.

10. See, for example, Reinhold Niebuhr, "Kinsey and the Moral Problems of Man's Sexual Development."

11. See Chapter 3, note 58.

12. For further commentary on this development, see Linda Williams, *Hard Core: Power, Pleasure, and the "Frenzy of the Visible*," and Jon Lewis, *Hollywood vs. Hard Core: How the Struggle over Censorship Saved the Modern Film Industry*. In *Sin in Soft Focus: Pre-Code Hollywood*, Mark A. Vieira offers a very useful dis-

cussion of this body of films, and includes some often-startling production stills and risqué shots rejected because of concerns over public reaction.

13. "Laurence Harvey and Capucine Head Cast," *New York Times*, February 12, 1962.

14. "Books of the Times," *New York Times*, September 29, 1950.

15. Phillips, *Films of Tennessee Williams*, 254.

16. Vizzard, memo for the files, October 2, 1961 (PCA).

17. Vizzard's comments in the above memo reveal a certain weariness with the difficulties of enforcing the code, further evidence of its growing irrelevance to the conduct of the industry: "There are some other items which we would have like to have removed from the picture, such as a quite legitimate use of the word 'pimp,' but we felt we were not in a position to enforce any further requests beyond the three outlined above, since Mr. Jack Warner personally pleaded that it would put him in an impossible position to make further changes. His difficulty is complicated by the fact that Tennessee Williams has a contractual [*sic*] right to approve or disapprove any changes. He has approved the three outlined above, but it would be grossly embarrassing to go to him regarding further alterations, which he would probably refuse to permit. Furthermore, the film would have to be sent back to England for further changes, which would be costly and complicated. In view of these circumstances we abandoned any further efforts to get changes." Ibid.

18. *Variety*, November 3, 1961 (PCA clip file).

19. *New York Times*, December 29, 1961.

20. *The Roman Spring of Mrs. Stone* pressbook (Todd Collection).

21. Crowther, "Roman Spring."

22. Phillips, *Films of Tennessee Williams*, 232.

23. Bosley Crowther, "Hollywood Pictorial," *New York Times*, November 18, 1961.

24. From a film poster reproduced in Jeff Young, *Elia Kazan: The Master Director Discusses his Films*, 262.

25. Bosley Crowther, "Splendor in the Grass," *New York Times*, October 11, 1961.

26. From the interview published in Young, *Elia Kazan*, 265.

27. Crowther, "Splendor in the Grass."

28. For further discussion, see R. Barton Palmer, "*2001*: The Film as Cultural Event."

29. Steve Neale, "Art Cinema as Institution," 103.

30. See David Bordwell, "Art Cinema as Mode of Practice," 96.

31. Phillips, *Films of Tennessee Williams*, 298.

32. Vincent Canby, "Screen: 'Boom!' Goes the Milk Train," *New York Times*, May 27, 1968.

33. Losey to Williams, n.d. (Columbia).

34. Howard Taubman, "Theater: A Play Returns," *New York Times*, Jan. 2, 1964.

35. Ibid.

36. This was not Losey's only motive for agreeing to adapt a property that, he admitted, he had never read or seen on the stage. As he later confessed, "It was an important film for me because, in the first place, it changed my salary level which is economically important!" (quoted in Michel Ciment, *Conversations with Losey*, 276).

37. Williams to Audrey Wood, October 5, 1966 (JLA/BFI).

38. *Boom!* contract (JLA/BFI).

39. Figures from the IMDB (accessed July 14, 2007).

40. Williams, *Boom!* treatment, dated March 8, 1967 (JLA/BFI).

41. The Broadway production had feared a Japanese-style set designed by Rouben Ter-Arutunian. As Howard Taubman remarks, "The fact of the theater is emphasized rather than concealed and the stylized devices—the metal disk of a sun, the flag of a flying griffin on its flagpole, the sliding Japanese walls—tell us to forget realism" ("A Play Returns").

42. Williams to Losey, telegram, May 21, 1967 (JLA/BFI).

43. Ciment, *Conversations with Losey*, 281.

44. Canby, "'Boom!' Goes the Milk Train."

45. Williams, *Boom!* treatment (JLA/BFI).

46. Ciment, *Conversations with Losey*, 281. Losey's dismissive attitude toward the film probably reflects not only his disappointment at its utter failure, but also his own disappointment regarding the contract to direct the film version of *Myrtle* (he turned down the project initially, then changed his mind). Losey wrote to Robert Goldstein at Warner Bros./Seven Arts (July 12, 1968) that *Myrtle* "is a marvelous piece of work with very few faults . . . less expository [than *Milk Train*], more dramatized, less verbose, and with more fully-drawn characters" (Joseph Losey archive, BFI). He declined because "it would be bad for all concerned if the combination of *Boom!* were repeated so soon, particularly as the highly personalized American reviews seemed to indicate they are out to get at Williams and the Burtons." *Boom!* did moderately good box office in France, however, and this encouraged Losey to attempt to put together a package, including the Burtons in the two principal roles, for *Myrtle*. The deal, however, was nixed, despite Williams's agreement and, if Losey can be credited, that of the Burtons as well.

Yet Losey revealed his ambivalence about the film in a September 1968 interview. He cited his fondness for *Boom!* but acknowledged that it would not be favorably received: "I predicted in advance that the Burtons would be criticized for going arty by working with me and that I would be criticized for going arty by working with them. Well, I liked *Boom!* for what it was, and so did the Burtons, who were very pleased with their performances and with the look of the film, as well they might have been" (interview reprinted in Foster Hirsch, *Joseph Losey*, 167).

47. Phillips, *Films of Tennessee Williams*, 301.

48. Howard Taubman, "Changing Course," *New York Times*, Jan. 7, 1962.

49. Quoted in ibid.

50. Although the movie was shot in Puerto Vallarta, the original setting as Williams envisioned it was the Hotel Costa Verde, just outside Acapulco. Williams first traveled there in 1940, and while at the hotel wrote a short story called "The Night of the Iguana" as well as the poem that becomes the centerpiece of the play. The remote shooting location provided logistical problems for transportation, since no roads led to the set. Ava Gardner reportedly got to work on water skis. The publicity surrounding the production was the subject of magazines and tabloids for several weeks during the filming.

51. Taubman, "Changing Course."

52. Quotations in this paragraph are from Bordwell, "Art Cinema," 96.

53. The steamy carnality of the play resulted in very few objections by studio executives. One memo (dated July 29, 1963) expressed concerns about the "skimpy bathing suits" and suggested that Charlotte and Maxine should be "decently garbed." It also stipulated that the number of "hells" in the dialogue be cut (Herrick).

54. Bosley Crowther, "'Night of the Iguana' Has World Premiere," *New York Times*, July 1, 1964.

55. Bordwell, "Art Cinema," 96.

56. Taubman, "Changing Course."

57. Some of these projects were Paul Osborn's adaptation of Max Druon's Paris hit *La Contessa*, retitled *Film of Memory*; *French Street*, noted playwright Norman Krasna's translation of Jacques Deval's *Romancero*; and *Mrs. 'Arris Goes to Paris*, a musical adaptation of Paul Gallico's book. See Sam Zolotow, "Seven Arts Plans to Offer Shows," *New York Times*, May 31, 1962.

58. Lesley Brill, *John Huston's Filmmaking*, 94.

59. Yacowar, *Williams and Film*, 94.

60. Taubman, "Changing Course."

61. Quoted in ibid.

Appendix C

1. Williams to Kazan, 1963 (WUCA). The Todd Collection has a screenplay of *One Arm* that is dated 1969 and credited to Williams, Milton Katselas, and Lanford Wilson. For further listing of unproduced and unpublished screenplays, see Appendices B and C.

2. Both Platt's and Williams's letters are at the Todd Collection. There is a sketch for a TV film-play and a typescript of the unproduced teleplay at the Billy Rose Theatre in New York City.

3. June 1979 (Todd Collection). The Todd Collection also has a 116-page teleplay based on the short story "Grand," adapted by Trace Johnston in 1979, as well as a screenplay based on Williams's story "The Field of Blue Children," adapted for the screen by Richard Pollard, Kathy Billings, and Alfred Ryder.

4. The film may be seen at the Museum of Television and Radio in Manhattan.

5. Wood to Williams, March 1, 1948 (HRC).

6. Quoted in Stewart Sterne, *No Tricks in My Pocket: Paul Newman Directs*, 9.

Bibliography

Allen, Dennis W. "Homosexuality and Artifice in *Cat on a Hot Tin Roof.*" *Coup de Théâtre* 5 (1985): 71–78.

Alpert, Hollis. "Instant Tennessee Williams." *Saturday Review*, June 25, 1966, 40.

Andrew, Dudley J. "Adaptation." In *Film Adaptation*, ed. James Naremore. New Brunswick, N.J.: Rutgers Univ. Press, 2000.

Applebome, Peter. *Dixie Rising: How the South Is Shaping American Values, Politics, and Culture.* New York: Random House, 1996.

Atkinson, Brooks. "At the Theatre." *New York Times*, February 5, 1951.

———. Review of *Sweet Bird of Youth. New York Times*, March 11, 1959.

———. "Williams' Tin Roof." *New York Times*, April 3, 1955.

Bak, John S. "'sneakin' and spyin' from Broadway to the Beltway: Cold War Masculinity, Brick, and Homosexual Existentialism." *Theatre Journal* 56, no. 2 (2004): 225–249.

Baker, Carroll. *Baby Doll: An Autobiography.* New York: Arbor House, 1983.

Balio, Tino. *Grand Design: Hollywood as a Modern Business Enterprise.* Berkeley and Los Angeles: Univ. of California Press, 1993.

Bigsby, C. W. E. *A Critical Introduction to Twentieth-Century American Drama.* Vol. 2: *Williams, Miller, Albee.* Cambridge: Cambridge Univ. Press, 1984.

———. *Modern American Drama, 1945–1990.* Cambridge: Cambridge Univ. Press, 1992.

Black, Gregory D. *The Catholic Crusade against the Movies, 1940–1975.* Cambridge: Cambridge Univ. Press, 1997.

Bordwell, David. "Art Cinema as Mode of Practice." In *The European Cinema Reader*, ed. Catherine Fowler, 94–102. New York: Routledge, 2002.

Bordwell, David, Janet Staiger, and Kristin Thompson. *The Classical Hollywood*

Cinema: Film Style and Mode of Production to 1960. New York: Columbia Univ. Press, 1985.

Bradbury, John M. *Renaissance in the South: A Critical History of the Literature, 1920–1960.* Chapel Hill: Univ. of North Carolina Press, 1963.

Brandt, George. "Cinematic Structure in the Work of Tennessee Williams." In *American Theatre*, ed. John Russell Brown and Bernard Harris, 166–172. New York: St. Martin's, 1967.

Bray, Robert. "*A Streetcar Named Desire*: The Political and Historical Subtext." In *Confronting Tennessee Williams's "A Streetcar Named Desire": Essays in Critical Pluralism*, ed. Philip C. Kolin, 183–198. Westport, Conn.: Greenwood, 1993.

Brill, Lesley. *John Huston's Filmmaking.* Cambridge: Cambridge Univ. Press, 1997.

Brooks, Richard. "Richard Brooks." *Movie* 12 (1965): 2–9, 15–16.

Bruhm, Stephen. "Blackmailed by Sex: Tennessee Williams and the Economics of Desire." *Modern Drama* 34 (1991): 528–537.

Brustein, Robert. "Sweet Bird of Success." *Encounter*, June 1959, 59–60.

Cahir, Linda. "The Artful Rerouting of *A Streetcar Named Desire*." *Literature/Film Quarterly* 22 (1994): 72–77.

Calinescu, Matei. *Five Faces of Modernity: Modernism, Avant-Garde, Decadence, Kitsch, Postmodernism.* Durham, N.C.: Duke Univ. Press, 1987.

Campbell, Edward D. C., Jr. *The Celluloid South: Hollywood and the Southern Myth*: Knoxville: Univ. of Tennessee Press, 1981.

Canby, Vincent. "Screen: 'Boom!' Goes the Milk Train." *New York Times*, May 27, 1968.

———. "The Screen: Last of the Mobile Hot-Shots." *New York Times*, January 15, 1970.

Cash, W. J. *The Mind of the South.* New York: Random House, 1941.

Chappell, Fred. "The Image of the South in Film." *Southern Humanities Review* 12 (1978): 303–311.

Ciment, Michel. *Conversations with Losey.* London: Methuen, 1985.

———. *Kazan on Kazan.* New York: Viking, 1974.

Clark, Suzanne. *Cold Warriors: Manliness on Trial in the Rhetoric of the West.* Carbondale: Southern Illinois Univ. Press, 2000.

Clor, Harry M. *Obscenity and Public Morality: Censorship in a Liberal Society.* Chicago: Univ. of Chicago Press, 1969.

Clum, John. *Acting Gay.* New York: Columbia Univ. Press, 1992.

Clurman, Harold. Review of *Sweet Bird of Youth*. *Nation*, March 1959, 281–283.

Cobb, James C. *Away Down South: A History of Southern Identity.* New York: Oxford Univ. Press, 2005.

————. *Redefining Southern Culture: Mind and Identity in the Modern South.* Athens: Univ. of Georgia Press, 1999.

Cook, Sylvia Jenkins. *From Tobacco Road to Route 66: The Southern Poor White in Fiction.* Chapel Hill: Univ. of North Carolina Press, 1976.

Corber, Robert. *Homosexuality in Cold War America: Resistance and the Crisis of Masculinity.* Durham, N.C.: Duke Univ. Press, 1997.

Cory, Donald Webster. *The Homosexual in America.* New York: Greenberg, 1951.

Costello, Donald. "Tennessee Williams's 'Conjure Man' in Script and Screen." *Literature/Film Quarterly* 27, no. 4 (1999): 263–270.

Crandell, George. "The Cinematic Eye in Tennessee Williams's *The Glass Menagerie.*" *Tennessee Williams Annual Review* 1 (1998): 1–12.

Crowther, Bosley. "'Boomerang'!: A Factual-Style Film of a Connecticut Slaying." *New York Times*, March 6, 1947.

————. "Hollywood Pictorial." *New York Times*, November 18, 1961.

————. "Laurence Harvey and Capucine Head Cast." *New York Times*, February 12, 1962.

————. "The Long, Hot Summer." *New York Times*, April 4, 1958: 16.

————. "'Night of the Iguana' Has World Premiere." *New York Times*, July 1, 1964.

————. "Screen: 'Fugitive Kind." *New York Times*, April 15, 1960.

————. "The Screen in Review: *The Glass Menagerie*, Adapted from the Tennessee Williams Play, Bows at Music Hall." *New York Times*, September 29, 1950.

————. "Screen: *Roman Spring*; Vivien Leigh Stars in Film at the Capitol." *New York Times*, December 29, 1961.

————. "Screen: Streetcar on Tobacco Road." *New York Times*, December 19, 1956.

————. "Splendor in the Grass." *New York Times*, October 11, 1961.

————. "Williams' Fugitives." *New York Times*, April 24, 1960.

Daniel, Pete. *Lost Revolutions: The South in the 1950s.* Chapel Hill: Univ. of North Carolina Press, 2000.

D'Emilio, John, and Estelle B. Freedman. *Intimate Matters: A History of Sexuality in America.* New York: Harper & Row, 1988.

Devlin, Albert J., ed. *Conversations with Tennessee Williams.* Jackson: Univ. Press of Mississippi, 1986.

————. "Writing in 'A Place of Stone': *Cat on a Hot Tin Roof.*" *The Cambridge Companion to Tennessee Williams*, ed. Matthew C. Roudané, 190. Cambridge: Cambridge Univ. Press, 1997.

Devlin, Albert J., and Nancy M. Tischler, eds. *The Selected Letters of Tennessee Williams, Volume I.* New York: New Directions, 2000.

———. *The Selected Letters of Tennessee Williams, Volume II.* New York: New Directions, 2004.

Devlin, James E. *Erskine Caldwell.* New York: Twayne, 1984.

Dickson, Vivienne. "*A Streetcar Named Desire*: Its Development through the Manuscripts." In *Tennessee Williams: A Tribute,* ed. Jac Tharpe, 154–171. Jackson: Univ. Press of Mississippi, 1973.

Doane, Mary Ann Doane. "The 'Woman's Film': Possession and Address." In *Revisions: Essays in Feminist Film Criticism,* ed. Mary Ann Doane, Patricia Mellencamp, and Linda Williams. Frederick, Md.: Univ. Publications of America, 1984.

Doane, Mary Ann, Patricia Mellencamp, and Linda Williams, eds. *Revisions: Essays in Feminist Film Criticism.* Frederick, Md.: Univ. Publications of America, 1984.

Doherty, Thomas. *Teenagers and Teenpics: The Juvenilization of American Movies in the 1950s.* Boston: Unwin Hyman, 1988.

Dowling, Ellen. "The Derailment of A Streetcar Named Desire." *Literature/Film Quarterly* 4, no. 9 (1981): 233–240.

Ehrenreich, Barbara. *Hearts of Men: American Dreams and the Flight from Commitment.* New York: Doubleday, 1984.

Ehrenreich, Barbara, Elizabeth Hess, and Gloria Jacobs. *Remaking Love: The Feminization of Sex.* New York: Anchor, 1987.

Elsaesser, Thomas. "Tales of Sound and Fury: Observations on the Family Melodrama." In Gledhill, *Home Is Where the Heart Is,* 43–69.

Filene, Peter. *Him/Her/Self: Sex Roles in Modern America.* Baltimore: Johns Hopkins Univ. Press, 1996.

Fischer, Edward. *The Screen Arts: A Guide to Film and Television Appreciation.* New York: Sheed and Ward, 1960.

Foster, Frederick. "Filming 'The Fugitive Kind.'" *American Cinematographer,* June 1960, 354–355, 379–382.

Freeman, Lucy, and Edwina Dakin Williams. *Remember Me to Tom.* New York: G. P. Putman's Sons, 1963.

French, Warren, ed. *The South and Film*: Jackson: Univ. Press of Mississippi, 1981.

Gardiner, Harold C. *The Catholic Viewpoint on Censorship.* Garden City, N.Y.: Doubleday, 1961.

———. *Norms for the Novel* New York: The America Press, 1953.

Gardner, Gerald C. *The Censorship Papers: Movie Censorship Letters from the Hays Office, 1934 to 1968.* New York: Dodd, Mead, 1988.

Gardner, John. *On Moral Fiction.* New York: Basic Books, 1978.

Gertner, Richard. *Motion Picture Daily*, February 28, 1962.

Getlein, Frank, and Harold Gardiner. *Movies, Morals, and Art*. New York: Sheed and Ward, 1961.

Gibbs, Wolcott. "Oddities, Domestic and Imported." *New Yorker*, January 18, 1958, 66.

Gill, Brendan. "Family Matters." *New Yorker*, November 10, 1962, 234–235.

Gilman, Richard. "Mistuh Williams, He Dead." *Commonweal*, February 8, 1963, 515–517.

Gledhill, Christine, ed. *Home Is Where the Heart Is: Studies in Melodrama and the Woman's Film*. London: BFI, 1987.

Goff, David. "Tennessee Williams's Films." *Tennessee Williams: A Guide to Research and Performance*, ed. Philip Kolin, 232–241. Westport, Conn.: Greenwood, 1998.

Graham, Allison. *Framing the South: Hollywood, Television, and Race during the Civil Rights Struggle*. Baltimore: Johns Hopkins Univ. Press, 2001.

Gross, Robert F. "The Pleasures of Brick: Eros and the Gay Spectator in *Cat on a Hot Tin Roof*." *Journal of American Drama and Theatre* 9, no. 1 (Winter 1997): 1–25.

Halliwell, Martin. *American Culture in the 1950s* (Edinburgh: Edinburgh Univ. Press, 2003).

Handel, Leo A. *Hollywood Looks at its Audience*. Urbana: Univ. of Illinois Press, 1950.

Harrison's Reports, August 13, 1958.

Hartung, Philip T. "Mourning Becomes Magnani." *Commonweal*, December 23, 1955, 306.

Hawkins, Joan. *Cutting Edge: Art Cinema and the Horrific Avant-garde*. Minneapolis: Univ. of Minnesota Press, 2000.

Heider, Karl G. *Images of the South: Constructing a Regional Culture on Film and Video*. Athens: Univ. of Georgia Press, 1993.

Hirsch, Foster. *Joseph Losey*. Boston: Twayne, 1980.

Hixson, Richard F. *Pornography and the Justices: The Supreme Court and the Intractable Obscenity Problem*. Carbondale: Southern Illinois Univ. Press, 1996.

Hobson, Fred C., Jr. *Serpent in Eden: H. L. Mencken and the South*. Chapel Hill: Univ. of North Carolina Press, 1974.

The Hollywood Reporter, September 19, 1950; August 13, 1958; December 16, 1959.

Houseman, John. *Final Dress*. New York: Simon and Schuster, 1983.

Howard, William L. "Caldwell on Stage on Screen." In *Erskine Caldwell Reconsidered*, ed. Edwin T. Arnold. Jackson: Univ. Press of Mississippi, 1990.

Hutcheon, Linda. *A Theory of Adaptation*. New York: Routledge, 2006.

Ivers, James D. *Motion Picture Daily*, December 16, 1959.

Kalem, Ted. "The Angel of the Odd." *Time*, June 9, 1962.

Kalson, Albert E. "Tennessee Williams at the Delta Brilliant." In *Tennessee Williams: A Tribute*, ed. Jack Tharpe, 774–794. Jackson: Univ. Press of Mississippi, 1973.

Kaplan, Fred. *Gore Vidal: A Biography*. Norwell, Mass.: Anchor, 2000.

Kawin, Bruce. *Faulkner and Film*. New York: Ungar, 1977.

Kazan, Elia. *Elia Kazan: A Life*. New York: Da Capo, 1977.

———. "Pressure Problem: Director Discusses Cuts Compelled in 'A Streetcar Named Desire.'" *New York Times*, October 21, 1951.

Kerr, Walter. Review of *The Rose Tattoo*. *Commonweal*, February 23, 1951, 492–494.

———. "*Camino Real*." *New York Herald Tribune*, March 20, 1953.

———. "Williams' 'Garden District' Presented at York Theater." *New York Herald Tribune*, January 8, 1958.

Kimmel, Michael. *Manhood in America: A Cultural History*. New York: Free Press, 1996.

King, Geoff. *Spectacular Narratives: Hollywood in the Age of the Blockbuster*. London: Tauris, 2000.

King, Richard H. *A Southern Renaissance: The Cultural Awakening of the American South, 1930–1955*. New York: Oxford Univ. Press, 1980.

Kirby, Jack Temple. *Media-Made Dixie: The South in the American Imagination*. Baton Rouge: Louisiana State Univ. Press, 1978.

Klinger, Barbara. *Melodrama and Meaning: History, Culture, and the Films of Douglas Sirk*. Bloomington: Indiana Univ. Press, 1994.

Knight, Arthur. "The Williams-Kazan Axis." *Saturday Review*, December 29, 1956, 22–23.

Kolin, Philip. "Civil Rights and the Black Presence in *Baby Doll*." *Literature/Film Quarterly* 24, no. 1 (1996): 2–11.

———. "Sleeping with Caliban: The Politics of Race in Tennessee Williams's *Kingdom of Earth*." *Studies in American Drama, 1945–Present* 8, no. 2 (Spring 1993): 140–162.

———. *Tennessee Williams: A Guide to Research and Performance*. Westport, Conn.: Greenwood, 1998.

———. *Tennessee Williams Encyclopedia*. Westport, Conn.: Greenwood, 2004.

———. "Tennessee Williams's 'Interval': MGM and Beyond." *Southern Quarterly* 38, no. 1 (Fall 1999): 21–27.

Kronhausen, Eberhard, and Phyllis Kronhausen. *Pornography and the Law: The Psychology of Erotic Realism and Pornography*. New York: Ballantine, 1959.

Lambert, Gavin. *Natalie Wood: A Life*. New York: Knopf, 2005.

Leff, Leonard J. "And Transfer to Cemetery: The Streetcars Named Desire." *Film Quarterly* 55 (Spring 2002): 29–38.

———. "The Breening of America." *PMLA* 106, no. 3 (1991): 432–445.

Leff, Leonard J., and Jerold L. Simmons. *The Dame in the Kimono: Hollywood, Censorship, and the Production Code*. Lexington: Univ. Press of Kentucky, 2001.

Lev, Peter. *The Euro-American Cinema*. Austin: Univ. of Texas Press, 1993.

Leverich, Lyle. *Tom: The Unknown Tennessee Williams*. New York: Crown, 1995.

Lewis, Jon. *Hollywood vs. Hard Core: How the Struggle over Censorship Saved the Modern Film Industry*. New York: New York Univ. Press, 2002.

Lindner, Robert. *Must You Conform?* New York: Holt, Rinehart, and Winston, 1956.

Loomis, Jeffrey. "Four Characters in Search of a Company: Williams, Pirandello, and the *Cat on a Hot Tin Roof* Manuscripts." In *Magical Muse: Millennial Essays on Tennessee Williams*, ed. Ralph Voss, 91–110. Tuscaloosa: Univ. of Alabama Press.

Lopate, Philip. "The Method South." *Oxford American* 42 (Winter 2002).

Lynch, William. *The Image Industries: A Constructive Analysis to Film and Television*. New York: Sheed and Ward, 1959.

Marcuse, Herbert. *Eros and Civilization*. Boston: Beacon, 1955.

May, Elaine Tyler. *Homeward Bound: American Families in the Cold War Era*. New York: Basic Books, 1988.

May, Lary. *Screening Out the Past: The Birth of Mass Culture and the Motion Picture Industry*. Chicago: Univ. of Chicago Press, 1980.

McCann, John S. *The Critical Reputation of Tennessee Williams: A Reference Guide*. Boston: Hall, 1983.

McKeon, Richard, et al. *The Freedom to Read: Perspective and Program*. New York: Bowker, 1957.

Mencken, H. L. "Sahara of the Bozart." In *A Mencken Chrestomathy*, 157–158. New York: Knopf, 1949.

Mercer, John, and Martin Shingler. *Melodrama: Genre, Style, Sensibility*. London: Wallflower, 2004.

Miller, Arthur. *Timebends: A Life*. New York: Penguin, 1995.

Monaco, Paul. *The Sixties: 1960–1969*. Berkeley and Los Angeles: Univ. of California Press, 2001.

Mulvey, Laura. "Notes on Sirk and Melodrama." In Gledhill, *Home Is Where the Heart Is*, 75–79.

Murphy, Brenda. *Congressional Theatre: Dramatizing McCarthyism on Stage, Film, and Television*. Cambridge: Cambridge Univ. Press, 1999.

———. "Seeking Direction." In *The Cambridge Companion to Tennessee Williams*, ed. Matthew C. Roudané, 189–203. Cambridge: Cambridge Univ. Press, 1997.

———. *Tennessee Williams and Elia Kazan: A Collaboration in the Theatre*. Cambridge: Cambridge Univ. Press, 1992.

Naremore, James, ed. *Film Adaptation* (New Brunswick, New Jersey: Rutgers Univ. Press, 2000).

Nason, Richard W. "Bit Stake in *God's Little Acre*." *New York Times*, May 4, 1958.

Nathan, George Jean. "The Tattoo on Tennessee Williams' Brain." *New York Journal-American*, February 12, 1951.

Neale, Steve. "Art Cinema as Institution." *The European Cinema Reader*, ed. Catherine Fowler. New York: Routledge, 2002.

The New Catholic Dictionary. The Catholic Theatre Movement. www.catholic forum.com/saints/ncd01775.htm (accessed August 13, 2005).

Newsweek. October 9, 1950, 90.

———. "Boardinghouse Reach." August 1, 1966, 84.

Niebuhr, Reinhold. "Kinsey and the Moral Problems of Man's Sexual Development" In *An Analysis of the Kinsey Reports on the Human Male and Female*, ed. Donald Porter Geddes, 62–70. New York: New American Library, 1954.

Nowell-Smith, Geoffrey. "Minnelli and Melodrama." In Gledhill, *Home Is Where the Heart Is*, 70–74.

Oberbeck, S. K. "Southern Discomfort." *Newsweek*, January 26, 1970, 75.

Overstreet, H. A. *The Mature Mind*. New York: Norton, 1949.

Ovesey, Lionel. *Homosexuality and Pseudohomosexuality*. New York: Science House, 1969.

Paller, Michael. *Gentleman Callers: Tennessee Williams, Homosexuality, and Mid-Twentieth-Century Drama*. New York: Palgrave, 2005.

Palmer, R. Barton. "*2001*: The Film as Cultural Event." In *Kubrick's 2001: A Casebook*, ed. Robert Kolker, 13–27. Oxford: Oxford Univ. Press, 2006.

Parker, Brian. "Multiple Endings for *The Rose Tattoo* (1951)." *Tennessee Williams Annual Review* 2 (1999): 53–68.

Phillips, Gene D. *The Films of Tennessee Williams*. Philadelphia: Art Alliance, 1980.

———. "*A Streetcar Named Desire*: Play and Film." In *Confronting "A Streetcar Named Desire": Essays in Critical Pluralism*, ed. Philip Kolin, 223–235. Westport, Conn.: Greenwood, 1993.

Pius XII. *Miranda Prorsus*. September 8, 1957. Papal Encyclicals Online. www .papalencyclicals.net/Pius 12/P12MIRAB.HTM (accessed January 12, 2005).

Prescott, Orville. "Books of the Times." *New York Times*, September 29, 1950.

Quigley, Martin. *Decency in Motion Pictures.* New York: Macmillan, 1937.

Ray, Robert. *A Certain Tendency in the Hollywood Cinema, 1930–1980.* Princeton, N.J.: Princeton Univ. Press, 1980.

Rouse, Derek. "*The Rose Tattoo* and *Picnic.*" *Sight and Sound,* Spring 1955, 195.

Saddik, Annette. *The Politics of Reputation: The Critical Reception of Tennessee Williams' Later Plays.* London: Associated Univ. Press, 1999.

Savran, David. *Communists, Cowboys and Queers: The Politics of Masculinity in the Work of Arthur Miller and Tennessee Williams.* Minneapolis: Univ. of Minnesota Press, 1992.

Schatz, Thomas. *Boom and Bust: American Cinema in the 1940s.* Berkeley and Los Angeles: Univ. of California Press, 1997.

———. *Hollywood Genres: Formulas, Filmmaking, and the Studio System.* New York: McGraw-Hill, 1981.

Schickel, Richard. *Elia Kazan: A Biography.* New York: HarperCollins, 2005.

Schumach, Murray. *The Face on the Cutting Room Floor: The Story of Movie and Television Censorship.* New York: Morrow, 1964.

Sconce, Jeffrey. "'Trashing' the Academy: Taste, Excess, and an Emerging Politics of Cinematic Style." *Screen* 36, no. 4 (1995): 371–393.

Seldes, Gilbert. *The Great Audience.* New York: Viking, 1950.

Shackleford, Dean. "The Truth That Must Be Told: Gay Subjectivity, Homophobia, and the Social History in *Cat on a Hot Tin Roof.*" *Tennessee Williams Annual Review* 1 (1998): 103–118.

Singal, David Joseph. *The War Within: From Victorian to Modernist Thought in the South, 1919–1945.* Chapel Hill: Univ. of North Carolina Press, 1982.

Skinner, James M. *The Cross and the Cinema: The Legion of Decency and the National Catholic Office for Motion Pictures, 1933–1970.* Westport, Conn.: Praeger, 1993.

Sklar, Robert. "'The Lost Audience': 1950s Spectatorship and Historical Reception Studies." In *Identifying Hollywood's Audiences: Cultural Identity and the Movies,* ed. Melvyn Stokes and Richard Maltby, 81–92. London: BFI, 1999.

———. *Movie-Made America: A Cultural History of American Movies.* New York: Random House, 1994.

Smith, Murray. "Theses on the Philosophy of Hollywood History." In *Contemporary Hollywood Cinema,* ed. Murray Smith and Steven Neale, 3–20. New York: Routledge, 1998.

Spoto, Donald. *The Kindness of Strangers: The Life of Tennessee Williams.* Boston: Little, Brown, 1985.

Staggs, Sam. *When Blanche Met Brando: The Scandalous Story of "A Streetcar Named Desire."* New York: St. Martin's, 2005.

Stam, Robert. Introduction to *Literature and Film: A Guide to the Theory and Practice of Film Adaptation*, ed. Robert Stam and Alessandra Raengo. Oxford: Blackwell, 2004.

Sterne, Stewart. *No Tricks in My Pocket: Paul Newman Directs*. New York: Grove, 1989.

Tannenbaum, Frank. *The Darker Phases of the South*. New York: Putnam, 1924.

Taubman, Howard. "Changing Course." *New York Times*, January 7, 1962.

———. "Theater: A Play Returns." *New York Times*, January 2, 1964.

Thompson, Kristin. *Storytelling in the New Hollywood: Understanding Classical Narrative Technique*. Cambridge, Mass.: Harvard Univ. Press, 1999.

Time. "Wholesome Williams." November 16, 1962, 97.

Tischler, Nancy M. "Sanitizing the Streetcar." *Louisiana Literature* 14, no. 2 (1997): 48–56.

———. "Tiger—Tiger! Blanche's Rape on Screen." In *Magical Muse: Millennial Essays on Tennessee Williams*, ed. Ralph Voss, 50–69. Tuscaloosa: Univ. of Alabama Press, 2002.

USA Today. "Tennessee Williams Is Hotter Than Ever." October 21, 2003, cover spread.

Variety. Review of *Summer and Smoke*. October 13, 1948, 50.

Vieira, Mark A. *Sin in Soft Focus: Pre-Code Hollywood*. New York: Abrams, 1999.

Vizzard, Jack. *See No Evil: Life inside a Hollywood Censor*. New York: Simon and Schuster, 1970.

Vorlicky, Robert. *Act Like a Man: Challenging Masculinities in American Drama*. Ann Arbor: Univ. of Michigan Press, 1995.

Wallis, Hal B., and Charles Higham. *The Autobiography of Hal Wallis, Starmaker*. New York: Macmillan, 1980.

Walsh, Frank. *Sin and Censorship: The Catholic Church and the Motion Picture Industry*. New Haven, Conn.: Yale Univ. Press, 1996.

Walsh, Moira. "*The Rose Tattoo*." *America*, December 24, 1955, 362.

Weaver, William. *Motion Picture Daily*, September 19, 1950.

Whyte, William H. *The Organization Man*. New York: Doubleday, 1956.

Williams, Dakin, and Shepherd Mead. *Tennessee Williams: An Intimate Biography*. New York: Arbor, 1983.

Williams, Linda. *Hard Core: Power, Pleasure, and the "Frenzy of the Visible"*. Berkeley and Los Angeles: Univ. of California Press, 1989.

———. "Melodrama Revisited." In *Refiguring American Film Genres: History and Theory*, ed. Nick Browne, 42–88. Berkeley and Los Angeles: Univ. of California Press, 1998.

Williams, Tennessee. Introductory essay. *Cat on a Hot Tin Roof*. Rev. ed. New York: New Directions, 1975.

———. *Five O'Clock Angel: Letters of Tennessee Williams to Maria St. Just, 1948–1982*. New York: Knopf, 1990.

———. Interview by Dick Leavitt. *Showbill: The Program Magazine for Particular Moviegoers*. New York: Newcastle, 1960: 3.

———. *Notebooks*. Edited by Margaret Bradham Thornton. New Haven, Conn.: Yale Univ. Press, 2006.

———. "Notes on the Filming of the Rose Tattoo." 1952.

———. "A Playwright's Prayer." *Tennessee Williams Annual Review*, 2003. www.tennesseewilliamsstudies.org (accessed May 10, 2008).

———. *Where I Live: Selected Essays*. New York: New Directions, 1978.

Winchell, Mark Royden. "Come Back to the Locker Room Ag'n, Brick Honey!" *Mississippi Quarterly* 48, no. 4 (1995): 701–712.

Windham, Donald, ed. *Tennessee Williams' Letters to Donald Windham, 1940–1965*. Athens: Univ. of Georgia Press, 1996.

Woodward, C. Vann. *The Strange Career of Jim Crow*. 3rd ed. New York: Oxford Univ. Press, 1974.

Wyatt, Justin. *High Concept: Movies and Marketing in Hollywood*. Austin: Univ. of Texas Press, 1994.

Wylie, Philip. *Generation of Vipers*. New York: Rinehart, 1955. First published 1942.

Yacowar, Maurice. *Tennessee Williams and Film*. New York: Ungar, 1977.

Young, Jeff. *Elia Kazan: The Master Director Discusses His Films*. New York: Newmarket, 1999.

Zinn, Howard. *The Southern Mystique* Cambridge, Mass.: South End, 1959.

Zolotow, Sam. "Seven Arts Plans to Offer Shows." *New York Times*, May 31, 1962.

Index

Baker, Carroll, 124, 129, 131, 139, 141, 145, 147, 149, 248, 311
Baldwin, Alec, 290
Balio, Tino, 298
Band of Angels, 207, 319
Bankhead, Tallulah, 46, 264
Bardot, Brigitte, 247
Barefoot in the Park, 11
Barn Burning, 214
Barrymore, Ethel, 299
Barrymore, Lionel, 206
Barrymore Theater, 224
Barter Theatre, 287
Battle of Angels, 4, 9, 22, 101, 235, 236, 296
Bava, Mario, 266
BBC (British Broadcasting Corporation), 291
Beatty, Warren, 251, 253, 255, 258, 260
Beaumont, Charles, 206
Beckett, Samuel, 242
Behind the Green Door, 250
Bells of St. Mary's, 29
Ben-Hur, 34
Benjamin, Walter, 229
Bergman, Ingmar, 269
Berman, Pandro S., 316
Berneis, Peter, 26, 41, 45, 48, 49, 50–54, 57, 58, 299, 300
Berri, Claude, 129
Bertolucci, Bernardo, 261
Best Years of Our Lives, The, 29, 46
Bicycle Thief, The, 35
Bigelow, Paul, 126
Bigsby, C. W. E., 6, 296, 315
Billings, Kathy, 326
Billy Rose Theatre, 326
Billy the Kid, 20
Birth of a Nation, The, 203, 205

Bitter Rice, 308
Black, Gregory D., 302
Blow Up, 249, 260
Blue Denim, 258
Blumenstock, Mort, 58, 301
Bonnie and Clyde, 261
Boom!, xii, 26, 27, 242, 261, 262, 263, 265, 266, 267, 271, 324, 325
Boomerang!, 34, 252
Booth, Shirley, 104, 105, 106, 108, 289
Bordwell, David, 66, 262, 269, 270, 299, 301, 323, 325
Borzage, Frank, 21
Boulle, Pierre, 152
Bradbury, John M., 208, 209, 210, 318, 319
Brando, Marlon, 6, 9, 58, 65, 75, 141, 166, 236, 237, 238, 287, 299, 303, 314
Brandt, George, 17, 298
Bray, Robert, 304
Breathless, 247
Breen, Joseph, 16, 22, 29, 35, 55, 62, 64, 68, 70, 71, 76, 77, 82–90, 91, 92, 109–118, 119, 131, 141, 142, 143, 155, 156, 250, 300, 304, 309, 311
Bridge on the River Kwai, The, 34, 153
Bridges, James, 321
Brill, Lesley, 272, 325
Briskin, Sam, 303, 304
British New Wave, 257, 258
Brooks, Richard, 63, 162, 164, 166, 170, 174, 175, 178, 180–187, 190, 191, 196, 199, 221, 287, 314, 316
Brown, Clarence, 212
Brown, John Russell, 298
Brown, Rita Mae, 222
Brown v. Board of Education, 318
Bruhm, Stephen, 312
Brustein, Robert, 11, 297

Costello, Donald, 321

Coward, Noel, 242, 266

Crandell, George, 299

Crawford, Cheryl, 126

Critics Prize, 39

Cronyn, Hume, 288

Crowther, Bosley, 33, 34, 42, 43, 134, 135, 147, 214, 219, 223, 235, 237, 250, 253, 255, 257, 258, 259, 270, 271, 299, 310, 320, 323, 325

Crucible, The, 15

Curtiz, Michael, 38

Dallas, Bryce, 291

D'Angelo, Beverly, 290

Daniel, Pete, 318

Daniels, William, 180

Danner, Blythe, 289

Davis, Bette, 57, 299

Dayton, Tennessee, 202

Death in the Family, A, 319

Death of a Salesman, 12, 15, 305

De Carlo, Yvonne, 319

Decline of the West, The, 234

Deep Throat, 250

Defiant Ones, The, 213

Demetrius and the Gladiators, 32

D'Emilio, John, 99, 307

De Mille, Cecil B., 146, 301

Deval, Jacques, 352

Devil in Miss Jones, The, 250

Devlin, Albert J., 166, 167, 209, 296, 297, 298, 300, 304, 305, 306, 307, 309, 310, 313, 317

Devlin, James E., 135, 311

Diabolique, 266

Dickson, Vivienne, 303

Dieterle, William, 299–300

Dixon, Thomas A., 203, 204

Doane, Mary Anne, 37, 299

Doherty, Thomas, 299

Donaldson and Sidney Howard Memorial Awards, 6

Double Indemnity, 33

Douglas, Kirk, 39, 47

Dowling, Eddie, 45, 54

Dowling, Ellen, 303

Dragon Country, 289

Drama Critics' Circle Awards, 2, 8

Druon, Max, 352

Druten, John Van, 38, 112

Duel in the Sun, 29

Dunaway, Faye, 289

Dunnock, Mildred, 147, 299

Eccentricities of a Nightingale, The, 289

Edge of the City, 320

Ehrenreich, Barbara, 175, 182, 197, 314, 315, 316

Electra, 236

Elsaesser, Thomas, 161, 162, 171, 175, 180, 313, 314, 315, 316

Encounter, 297

Everyman, 266

Face in the Crowd, A, 126, 140

Farber, Manny, 33

Farley, John Cardinal, 302

Fat City, 272

Faulkner, William, xii, 20, 70, 97, 136, 202, 203, 208, 209, 210, 211, 212, 213, 214, 215, 217, 218, 219, 220, 223, 237, 320

Federal Communications Commission (FCC), 32

Feldman, Charles K., 27, 36, 40, 41, 43, 46, 47, 48, 50, 52, 53, 55, 58, 59,

Written on the Wind, 212, 213

Wyatt, Justin, 322

Wyler, William, 40, 46, 72, 75, 303, 304

Wylie, Philip, 305

Wyman, Jane, 37, 46, 47, 48

Yacowar, Maurice, 273, 299, 295, 321, 325

Yellow Bird, The, 289

York Theatre, 10

Young, Jeff, 323

Young Philadelphians, The, 187

Zabriskie Point, 261

Zanuck, Darryl F., 77

Zeffirelli, Franco, 7, 287

Zinn, Howard, 318

Zinnemann, Fred, 106

Zolotow, Sam, 325